The Content-Based Classroom

SECOND EDITION

The Content-Based Classroom

New Perspectives
on Integrating
Language and
Content

SECOND EDITION

Marguerite Ann Snow
and **Donna M. Brinton**
EDITORS

UNIVERSITY OF MICHIGAN PRESS • ANN ARBOR

ISBN-13: 978-0-472-03645-5

2020   2019   2018   2017   4   3   2   1

Preface to the Second Edition ||||||||||||||||||||||||||

In 1997, we co-edited *The Content-Based Classroom: Perspectives on Integrating Language and Content*, which consisted of contributions by many of the first cadre of researchers and practitioners working in content-based instruction (CBI). As the book aged, we intended for many years to undertake a second edition, but other projects always seemed to take priority. When we finally developed a blueprint for this book, we realized that a simple update of the original text was no longer feasible—that new perspectives on CBI were needed. Our vision for the volume was to extend the focus to international settings where CBI has seen significant growth and to expand the reach to varieties of models not yet contemplated in our earlier work, such as content and language integrated learning (CLIL) and English-medium instruction (EMI). We also invited key authors from the 1997 edition to update their work. As such, Chapter 2 provides an update of research support for CBI by original authors Bill Grabe and Fredricka Stoller, along with their colleague Shannon Fitzsimmons-Doolan. In addition, Stoller and Grabe update their well-known Six Ts model in Chapter 4. The third original author to contribute was Lynn Goldstein, who provides an updated perspective on the possibilities and pressures of the adjunct model in Chapter 25.

With the exception of the two opening chapters, each chapter of *The Content-Based Classroom: New Perspectives on Integrating Language and Content* begins with a glimpse into the CBI classroom through a scenario that brings to life the particular focus of the chapter, helping readers to envision actual CBI settings. Following each scenario, the author(s) provide a definition of their topic and a brief literature review, discussing key issues and challenges related to the focus. Each chapter also features a detailed table in which the author(s) provide observations/activities and principles that underlie their CBI topic. In more than three decades of CBI activity, classroom implementation has generally been emphasized over research. Because we wanted to take advantage of the scholarly expertise of our authors, we asked them to suggest a research agenda for their particular topic, hoping that their ideas and suggestions will help to forge a CBI research agenda for the coming decades. Finally, readers can reflect in-depth on the topics by completing the discussion questions and tasks that appear at the end of each chapter. We would like to add a final note: While the scenarios presented mainly exemplify English as a Second Language (ESL) or English as a Foreign Language (EFL) applications, there are certainly implications for the teaching of modern and heritage languages using content- and language-integrated approaches, and we hope the content of the chapters will inspire those working in these areas of language education as well.

The volume is divided into six parts. In Part I, *Overview of Content-Based Instruction*, the authors, Donna Brinton and Ann Snow, trace the history of CBI, propose a classification of models and varieties, and discuss ongoing implementation challenges (Chapter 1). Shannon Fitzsimmons-Doolan, Bill Grabe, and Fredricka Stoller next provide research support for CBI from areas such as second language acquisition, cognitive and educational psychology, and CBI program outcomes (Chapter 2).

Part II of the volume focuses on *Program, Curriculum, and Lesson Design in Content-Based Instruction*. In Chapter 3, Tetsuo Harada details the comprehensive development of a new CBI program at the university level in Japan; Fredricka Stoller and Bill Grabe revisit the Six Ts approach to curriculum development (Chapter 4); Kate Mastruserio Reynolds takes on strategic planning of standards and objectives (Chapter 5); Laura Baecher, Anne Ediger, and Tim Farnsworth present supports for teacher planning in CBI (Chapter 6); and Pauline Gibbons illustrates scaffolding strategies for language and content instruction (Chapter 7). Also included in this section is Roy Lyster's argument for a greater focus on language in CBI and a description of a four-phase instructional sequence for language-focused instruction with examples from French immersion classrooms (Chapter 8) and David Nunan's integrated approach to content, tasks, and projects (Chapter 9).

Part III, *Innovative Applications of Content-Based Instruction*, contains examples of a variety of models in diverse CBI settings: Mary Lou McCloskey describes the curriculum of a summer camp held for middle school English teachers and students from European and Balkan countries that was organized around the themes of peace, tolerance, and conflict resolution (Chapter 10); in Chapter 11, Christiane Dalton-Puffer synthesizes the work on CLIL, illustrating application of the model with examples from Spain and Austria. The focus of Chapter 12 is Dudley Reynolds' work with a professional development program in Qatar in which teachers implemented translanguaging strategies in Arabic and English with their students as they learned science. Chapter 13, by Arlys van Wyk, details an adjunct program in South Africa for underprepared university students that focuses on critical academic language skills. Using both onsite and online approaches, Lisa Chou and Sherise Lee, in Chapter 14, highlight features of theme-based and adjunct models to teach art to university ESL students at the Academy of Art University in San Francisco, California. In Chapter 15, Anne Burns and Sue Ollerhead describe adult continuing education programs in the United States and Australia where content that is both meaningful to the lives of immigrants and to vocationally oriented students is integrated with language teaching aims. Joyce Kling, in Chapter 16, looks at applications of English-Medium Instruction (EMI) at the postgraduate level in Denmark that seek to meet the goals of internationalization of students/staff and the curriculum. In Chapter 17, Chris Stillwell focuses on the EMI setting as well, but with a view toward ways to support lecturers with professional development and learners with needed language skill instruction.

Part IV, *Content-Based Instruction and Related Approaches: Shared Connections*, seeks to elaborate on the connections between CBI and other related approaches that often overlap in terms of audiences and goals. In Chapter 18, Donna Brinton presents scenarios from New Zealand and Hong Kong to explore the relationship between English for Special Purposes

(ESP) and CBI. Jan Frodesen, in Chapter 19, provides examples of theme-based and adjunct courses implemented in English for Academic Purposes (EAP) college preparatory programs for matriculated multilingual and ESL students. In Chapter 20, Ann Snow, Jennifer McCormick, and Anna Osipova discuss difficult conceptualizations of academic language and examine its features and progressions across educational levels. The last chapter in Part IV presents Viviana Cortes' treatment of corpora and corpus tools and their applications to content-based teaching.

Part V, *Focus on Assessment and Research in Content-Based Instruction*, contains chapters by Maureen Snow Andrade and Brent Green, who delineate the principles and challenges of assessing language and content in CBI courses (Chapter 22), and Sandra Zappa-Hollman and Patsy Duff who provide a comprehensive treatment of research needs in CBI (Chapter 23).

Finally, Part VI deals with *Ongoing Challenges in Content-Based Instruction*. In Chapter 24, Faridah Pawan and Michelle Greene tackle the challenging issues of collaboration between language and content instructors and present cases of successful outcomes. In Chapter 25, Lynn Goldstein returns to the adjunct model experience she and her writing instructor colleagues described in 1997 in *The Content-Based Classroom*. In an updated look, Goldstein reexamines the lack of collaboration that they experienced with content faculty (dubbed the "flight attendant syndrome"); she also reports on the results of a current survey of adjunct model instructors, discussing ongoing challenges with collaboration and status, including power issues and the implications for workload equity in CBI programs.

An edited volume is only as good as the efforts of its contributors and the support provided by the publisher. So while we as editors have worked hard behind the scenes to compile a volume that illustrates our vision of CBI today, the volume itself would not have been possible without the quality contributions that we received from our wonderful colleagues around the world and the non-flagging enthusiasm and support of our editor, Kelly Sippell, from the University of Michigan Press. It is therefore with a great deal of gratitude and admiration that we acknowledge their collective expertise, time, and energy in helping us realize our vision and carry through to fruition the project begun back in March of 2014, when we first met with Kelly at the international TESOL conference in Portland (Oregon) to discuss the feasibility of this volume. We sincerely hope that you, our readers, benefit from this truly collaborative venture and are inspired to try CBI and implement many of the ideas discussed in the volume.

Finally, we would like to honor our fathers: Philip Snow, Harry Daubert, and Robert Kenneth Brinton.

Marguerite Ann Snow
California State University, Los Angeles

Donna M. Brinton
University of California, Los Angeles (retired)

Common Acronyms Used Throughout the Book

Content-Based Instruction – CBI

Content and Language Integrated Learning – CLIL

English-Medium Instruction – EMI

English as a Foreign Language – EFL

English as a Second Language – ESL

English for Academic Purposes – EAP

English for Specific Purposes – ESP

First Language – L1

Second Language – L2

Second Language Acquisition – SLA

Test of English as a Foreign Language – TOEFL®

Contents ||||||||||||||||||||||||||||||||||||||||||||

Part I

Overview of Content-Based Instruction

Chapter 1

The Evolving Architecture of Content-Based Instruction

Donna M. Brinton & Marguerite Ann Snow

Introduction |||

In 1989, together with our colleague Marjorie Wesche from the University of Ottawa, we published a volume on content-based instruction (CBI)—then an emerging trend on the second/foreign language (SFL) scene (Brinton, Snow, & Wesche, 1989). At the time, it was impossible to envision the scope of CBI's influence today. The volume provided a rationale for CBI and its historical antecedents. We also proposed three "prototype" models of CBI at the university level, noting that a benefit of viewing them as prototypes was that it would allow "consideration of other content-based variations which combine features of the three prototype models" (p. 23). Eight years later, we co-edited *The Content-Based Classroom* (Snow & Brinton, 1997), which dealt with CBI in a more comprehensive fashion, expanding our focus from the post-secondary level to include CBI programs for younger learners and treating such topics as syllabus, materials, and course design; teacher preparation; assessment; research; and alternative models such as peer tutors and the training of discipline faculty. We also discussed practical issues such as language and content teacher collaboration and the challenges of administering CBI programs. Finally, we sought experts to make connections between CBI and related areas such as task-based instruction, English for Specific Purposes (ESP), and English for Academic Purposes (EAP).

Over the past three-and-a-half decades since the original publication of *Content-Based Second Language Instruction* (Brinton, Snow, & Wesche, 1989), CBI has emerged as one of the primary approaches used in teaching SFLs. Geographically, it has spread to virtually all parts of the world; it has also been implemented at all educational levels, from elementary school instruction to adult continuing education and from college preparatory courses to post-graduate educational contexts. As we indicate in our chapter title, CBI is a continually evolving model, with multiple alternative or "hybrid" models that have branched off from the original three prototype models we focused on in our original publication. In this chapter, we will provide a definition and underlying rationale for CBI, describe the original prototype models and some more recent modifications of the model, and examine some of the most frequently encountered issues in implementation.

A Definition and Rationale |||

At the heart of CBI is the integration of language and content. As defined by Snow (2014), CBI:

> . . . is an umbrella term for a multifaceted approach to SFL teaching that differs in terms of factors such as educational setting, program objectives, and target population but shares a common point of departure—the integration of language teaching aims with content instruction. (p. 439)

This definition echoes that of Davison and Williams (2001), who describe integrated language and content teaching as ". . . a heuristic label for a diverse group of curriculum approaches which share a concern for facilitating language learning broadly defined, through varied but systematic linking of subject matter and language in the context of learning activities" (p. 57).

We can trace the impetus for CBI to the advent of communicative language teaching (CLT) in the 1970s, which was profoundly influenced by Hymes (1971) and others who proposed a more socially oriented approach to linguistics. The notion of "communicative competence" proposed by Hymes and his colleagues refers to the ability to use language effectively and appropriately in a variety of contexts. CLT formed a suitable backdrop to approaches such as immersion education in Canada (Genesee, 1987; Tedick, Christian, & Fortune, 2011); other curricular approaches compatible with CLT such as CBI, ESP, EAP, and task-based language teaching (Duff, 2014); and the language across the curriculum movement in the U.K. and U.S. (A Language for Life, 1975; Parker, 1985)—all of which advocate, to some extent, for the integration of language and content teaching aims.

A Brief History of CBI |||

CBI first appeared on the scene in North America in the early 1960s with French immersion programs in Canada being the earliest precursor of other types of CBI (Lambert & Tucker, 1972). At the post-secondary level, centers of activity included the University of California, Los Angeles, and the Monterey Institute of International Studies in California along with the University of British Columbia and the University of Ottawa in Canada. The first published volume on CBI appeared in 1986, with Bernard Mohan's aptly named volume *Language and Content*. In the introduction to the volume, Mohan exposed the following paradox when he noted, "In subject learning we overlook the role of language as a medium of instruction. In language learning we overlook the fact that content is being communicated" (p. 1). CBI seeks to eliminate this compartmentalization through its emphasis on the need to integrate the teaching of language *and* content. Further, Mohan laid the ground work for CBI pedagogy:

> Recent research on language and learning in the content class suggests that we need more than a laissez-faire approach to help students with the language demands of the content class. A central concern of research conducted on second language acquisition is the extent to which second language learners are able to learn the second language in the content classroom, and this research contradicts the older laissez-faire arguments. (p. 7)

As we shall see in this chapter and elsewhere throughout this volume, this quote remains as timely today as it was when his book was first published.

By the late 1980s, the modern language teaching community in the U.S. also began to apply CBI principles to "disciplined-based" approaches. Foreign languages across the curriculum programs sprang up at such places as St. Olaf College (Minnesota), the University of Minnesota, Eastern Michigan University, Earlham College (Indiana), and the University of Rhode Island (Krueger & Ryan, 1993).

Since these beginnings, CBI has spread literally throughout the world, with the movement taking hold in both the ESL and EFL contexts. Increasingly today, it is being used in contexts where English functions as an international language of communication, or *lingua franca*. (See also the respective chapters by Dalton-Puffer, Kling, and Stillwell, this volume.)

Genesee and Lindholm-Leary (2013) offer the following rationales for CBI:

1. It allows L2 learners to develop their language skills in tandem with social and cognitive skills.
2. Its focus on providing meaningful and relevant academic content and building opportunities for purposeful communication motivates L2 learning.
3. Exposure to content enables learners to map new language onto meaning and thought.
4. It provides exposure to structural and functional variation in different contexts of use, thus enabling L2 learners to acquire forms that are authentic and useful.
5. It facilitates opportunities for learners to link what is new to already known ideas and skills, thus providing opportunities for deeper learning.

Some additional benefits include the fact that CBI provides a meaningful context for the language items being presented and serves as an organizing principle for decisions about the selection and sequencing of language items. It also provides rich opportunities for L2 acquisition to occur by providing the input that learners need, creating opportunities for negotiation of meaning about meaningful content, and pushing students to develop appropriate and accurate output. Finally, it exposes students to high-level academic content and encompasses work on academic skills that can transfer to other academic disciplines. See Crandall (2012) and Fitzsimmons-Doolan, Grabe, and Stoller (this volume) for an extended discussion of research support for CBI.

The Three Prototype Models of CBI |||

As noted, in *Content-Based Second Language Instruction* (Brinton, Snow, & Wesche, 1989) we attempted to capture the three primary models of CBI that existed at the time: (1) theme-based instruction, (2) sheltered instruction, and (3) adjunct instruction. Recognizing that the approach needed to remain flexible, we identified these as "prototype" models, leaving room for practitioners to adapt the models to their own instructional contexts. Though today many additional models of CBI exist, these three models (see Figure 1.1) remain central to the approach and are thus deserving of further examination here.

Figure 1.1: The Three Prototype Models of CBI

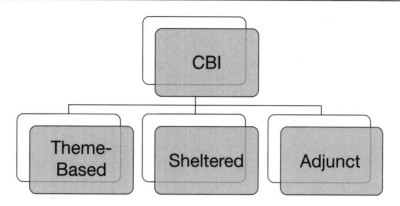

Theme-Based Instruction

Theme-based instruction refers to instruction that focuses on specific themes of interest and relevance to the learners. The themes (e.g., Heroes, Save the Environment, or Online Romance) create the organizing principle for the course and provide the point of departure for skill- and language-based instruction. Themes can vary from a four-page treatment in the students' textbooks to extended or sustained treatment of content over several weeks or even an entire term (Murphy & Stoller, 2001). The thematic texts and associated interactive tasks provide the language rich environment that allows learners to acquire the L2 through sustained content language teaching (SCLT).

Theme-based instruction is possible at virtually any level of instruction (from beginning to advanced), though probably most suitable for students at intermediate and above levels of language proficiency. To locate an example of theme-based instruction, one has only to look at the many multi-skills textbooks on the market today that have adopted this approach as their organizing principle. Listed in the textbooks' table of contents are chapter titles such as Extreme Sports, Voluntourism, Endangered Species, Smart Cars, and the like. The course designer's challenge is to find suitable themes for the students in question and level-appropriate texts to provide input. An additional challenge is to determine the language and skill foci that are appropriate to cover in each thematic module and how to best integrate and sequence these items in the overall course.

Hauschild, Poltavtchenko, and Stoller (2012) describe a theme-based unit that merged a focus on environmental education with a focus on academic language preparation. Entitled "Going Green," the unit was designed for students enrolled in an academic preparation program, although it could be adapted to a variety of levels and teaching contexts. The focus on environmental education taught students how to contribute to a more sustainable environment and heightened students' interest in contemporary issues. Targeted tasks and authentic materials helped to promote language acquisition and prepared students for meaningful communication. The four skills of listening, speaking, reading, and writing and an emphasis on critical thinking and autonomous learning were integrated throughout the unit.

Another option for theme-based instruction is the use of theme-based writing modules. This approach is most often found in EAP courses. One such example is an advanced ESL writing module centered on the theme of homelessness in the U.S. and designed for students in a program for matriculated ESL students at UCLA (C. Holten, personal communication). In this five-week module that stressed critical-thinking skills, Holten exposed students to numerous authentic source materials such as essays from university-level sociology texts, documentary videos, newspaper and journal articles, and excerpts from academic texts as well as a short story to acquaint students with the issue of homelessness. They also received targeted instruction in writing for academic purposes and produced a multi-draft essay in which they critically evaluated competing theories of homelessness.

Sheltered Instruction

The second model, *sheltered instruction,* refers to instructional models in which students who are still developing their L2 are separated from native speakers for the purpose of content instruction, which is delivered in the students' L2. The original sheltered content courses were developed at the bilingual University of Ottawa where Introduction to Psychology was offered to non-native speakers of English and taught by a native English–speaking psychology professor; a separate section of *Introduction á la Psychologie* was offered to non-native speakers of French and taught by a French-speaking professor (Brinton, Snow, & Wesche, 1989). As an incentive for taking the course, students received unit credit for the Psychology course and satisfied their foreign language requirement. The professors in their respective courses were assisted by an English or French language instructor who spent about 15–20 minutes before each class reviewing the readings and preparing students for upcoming topics. Evaluation of the sheltered courses revealed that the sheltered L2 students made significant gains in both English and French, respectively, that were equal to or greater than the gains of students in well-taught ESL and French as a Second Language classes at comparable proficiency levels (Edwards, Wesche, Krashen, Clément, & Kruidenier, 1984; Hauptmann, Wesche, & Ready, 1988). The original sheltered courses "convincingly demonstrated that subject matter teaching can be language teaching as well" (Brinton, Snow, & Wesche, 2003, p. 54).

Over the years since the original sheltered model was designed at the University of Ottawa, the model has seen widespread implementation at the elementary and secondary levels in the U.S. and in some EFL settings. The instructor is typically a content specialist, for example, a secondary school science teacher, who has specialized training in "sheltering" techniques, also referred to as Specially Designed Academic Instruction in English (Reynolds, 2015), for making the content comprehensible (e.g., via the use of visuals, pre-reading tasks, lexical accommodation, strategy instruction, and frequent comprehension checks). In this manner, instructors assist students with their language skill development and help them to access academically challenging content material. Exposure to rich academic language and complex concepts coupled with sensitive instructional delivery provide the necessary conditions for L2 acquisition to occur.

An example of sheltered instruction at the primary level involved a sheltered science class where elementary school students in a bilingual program were engaged in a unit about the rainforest (U.S. Department of State, Office of English Language Programs, 2007). In the video accompanying the unit, we can see that one corner of the classroom was transformed into a rainforest, complete with improvised hanging vines and a rainforest canopy affixed to the ceiling. We can also see the teacher conducting a warm-up activity where students sang the "water cycle" song (to the tune of "Oh My Darling, Clementine"); the teacher then reviewed and reinforced key vocabulary (adjectives, nouns, verbs, and adverbs), and guided the students to produce creative sentences about the creatures who live in the rainforest (e.g., "Big yellow jaguars fight madly on the ground" "Small poisonous monkeys scratch quickly in the canopy"). The class ended with students writing three sentences about rainforest creatures in their journals.

At the secondary level, Bright (2010) describes a ninth grade sheltered mathematics class at a large suburban high school in Virginia, just outside of Washington, DC. More than 20 percent of the school population was qualified for English to Speakers of Other Languages (ESOL) services. Education at this school was standards-based; the teacher of the sheltered math class was also certified in ESOL and built active production and receptive understanding into the lesson. In her account, Bright describes ways in which the mathematics teacher created a supportive learning environment for her L2 learners and encouraged risk taking. By systematically foregrounding language issues in the mathematics curriculum, she helped students to acquire key vocabulary and to develop their academic register.

The best-known sheltered model is the Sheltered Instruction Observation Protocol (SIOP) (Echevarría, Vogt, & Short, 2017). SIOP is a comprehensive, field-tested model of sheltered instruction that specifies the features of high-quality sheltered lessons for teaching content to L2 students. The protocol has eight components including: lesson preparation (e.g., designing content and language objectives); building students' background knowledge; comprehensible input; instructional strategies; interactional grouping configurations; practice/application; lesson delivery; and review and assessment. SIOP offers an extensively researched tool for observing and quantifying teachers' implementation of sheltered instruction. In a recent study of the academic literacy of secondary English learners (ELs) whose teachers had participated in professional development using SIOP, ELs made significant gains in reading, writing, and oral proficiency compared to similar students whose teachers had not received SIOP training (Short, Fidelman, & Louguit, 2012).

Adjunct Instruction

Finally, *adjunct instruction* refers to instructional models in which two courses (a content course and a language course are paired, with the content and language instructors collaborating to merge or dovetail their instructional objectives. Often, L2 students are separated for the purpose of language instruction but combined with mainstream students in the content course. The content course typically provides the point of departure for decisions about what to teach in the language class; language objectives are identified with respect to students' linguistic needs in the content class. L2 acquisition occurs through exposure to high-level, challenging language in the content course and through the systematic academic language instruction provided in the language course (Brinton, Snow, & Wesche, 2003). This model offers students "two for one"—that is, increased language proficiency as well as in-depth mastery of the content material.

Perhaps the most frequently cited example of adjunct instruction is UCLA's Freshman Summer Program (FSP), which we described in *Content-Based Second Language Instruction* (Brinton, Snow, & Wesche, 2003). In this summer bridge program, first-year L2 students who had been identified by university admissions as "high risk" took an EAP course paired with a content-area course that fulfilled one of the students' general education requirements (e.g., Introduction to Psychology). In collaboration with the Psychology professor and teaching assistants, the EAP instructors identified language objectives that would assist students in their reading and writing assignments for the content course. They also stressed academic preparation skills with a view toward preparing students for the general demands of academia. Former FSP students ranked the academic skills they had learned (e.g., taking lecture notes, preparing reading guides, using in-class essay/exam strategies) highly; however, above all "adjusting to UCLA" was the highest rated benefit of the adjunct experience (Snow & Brinton, 1988).

A second example of adjunct instruction involves an English/Philosophy adjunct course offered at an English-medium private university in Turkey (Spring, 2010). In this instance, the adjunct course was part of a larger initiative at the university to enrich sophomore-level EAP classes. Students in their sophomore year attended linked English and Philosophy courses, with the language component organized around the Philosophy topics and texts, which provided the point of departure for the language syllabus. The ultimate goal was to broaden students' intellectual background knowledge and cognitive skills and expose them to unabridged primary source texts.

As may already be clear, the three prototype models of CBI place differential amounts of emphasis on language and content. Met (1999) used the labels *content-driven* and *language-driven* to capture the degree of emphasis on language and content which underlies different CBI models. This difference is excellently captured by van Lier (2005) in his sliding scale of language and content (see Figure 1.2).

According to van Lier, "The chart… is a simple reminder that CBI is a continuum, not an either-or choice" (p. 15). Falling on the left-hand side of the scale (e.g., at Point A) are

Figure 1.2: van Lier's Scale of Language and Content

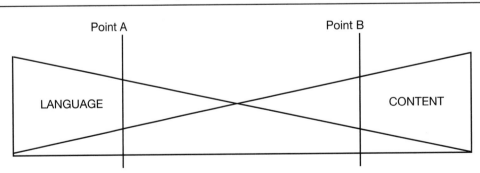

From van Lier, L. (2005). The bellman's map: Avoiding the "perfect and absolute blank" in language learning. In R. M. Jourdenais & S. E. Springer (Eds.), *Content, tasks and projects in the language classroom: 2004 conference proceedings* (p. 15). Monterey, CA: Monterey Institute of International Studies. Used with permission.

courses where "language takes precedence over content" (p. 16). The clearest example of this type of course would be *theme-based instruction*, where content (in the form of a theme) is a carrier topic for the language being presented and practiced. On the right-hand side of the scale (e.g., at Point B) are courses where "content takes precedence over language" (p. 16). An example of such courses would be *sheltered instruction*, where mastery of content is primary and L2 development occurs through exposure to contextualized language and subject matter. Finally, at the midpoint on the scale, we could place *adjunct instruction*, where the two courses combined provide a balanced emphasis on both language and content.[1]

The Emergence of Newer Hybrid Models of CBI ‖‖

Surveying the landscape of CBI today, some 30-plus years after the appearance of Mohan's (1986) *Language and Content*, we cannot help but be struck by the variety of new and/or hybrid models of CBI. As we have indicated in the title of this chapter, the "architecture" of CBI continues to "flex" or evolve as new contexts emerge where the application of CBI is relevant. This lack of a prescribed form, in fact, can be considered one of CBI's most obvious strengths as well as one of the primary reasons for the enduring nature of the model. Figure 1.3 provides an updated visual representation or "map" of the most documented variants of CBI on the language teaching scene today.

As we can see, the three prototype models of theme-based, sheltered, and adjunct instruction are still very much present on the scene. However, for all three prototypes we see offshoots of the original models indicating ways in which CBI has evolved to accommodate specific student populations, teaching settings, and local resources/logistics.

Sustained Content Language Teaching

The first of these accommodations, SCLT, was briefly mentioned. Sustained content courses, taught by a language instructor, are a form of theme-based instruction. According to Murphy and Stoller (2001), the two major components of SCLT include a focus on the explora-

Figure 1.3: An Updated Map of CBI

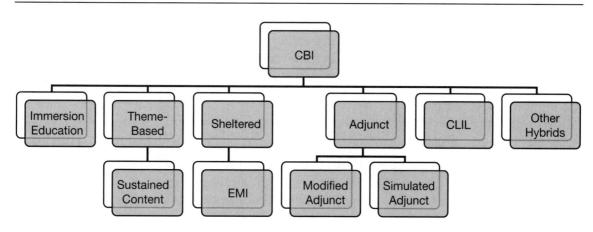

tion of a single content area or carrier topic over the course of a unit along with a complementary focus on L2 learning and teaching. The authors document these advantages of SCLT over more traditional theme-based instruction:

1. Topics are "stretched" over a whole term or an entire school year—thus avoiding the pitfalls of the theme-based "potpourri" approach (Jacobs, 1989) where content is presented in bits and pieces with no obvious connections in terms of content or language selection.
2. The use of sustained content simulates the conditions and demands of the subject matter classroom.
3. Learners engage with the content more deeply, in the process acquiring advanced academic vocabulary and language skills.
4. There is a dual focus on content (including critical-thinking, cognitive and metacognitive strategies, and study skills) and language development (including the four skills, grammar, vocabulary, and pronunciation).

Brinton (2001) provides an example of an elective literature course taught to advanced L2 students at the tertiary level. This example of SCLT, Focus on the City of Angels, revolved around the single extended theme of the city of Los Angeles. Opting to depart from the traditional format for literature courses in which students read excerpts from great works of literature, Brinton instead organized the course around works dealing with life and urban issues in Los Angeles. Students read essays, autobiographies, poems, short stories, and a novel; in all of these, the city took on a central role and exerted its unique influence on character and plot. Integral to the course were activities that acquainted students with literary devices (e.g., plot, setting, character development); however, equally important were activities (e.g., guided discussions, response journals, stylistic analysis of word choice) that used the content to enhance students' language and critical-thinking skills.

Content and Language Integrated Learning (CLIL)

The turn of the century saw the emergence and exponential growth of CLIL, particularly in Europe. According to Marsh (2003), CLIL:

> . . . refers to any dual-focused educational context in which an additional language, thus not usually the first language of the learners involved, is used as a medium in the teaching and learning of non-language content. It is dual-focused because whereas attention may be predominantly on either subject-specific content or language, both are always accommodated. (Introduction, para. 1)

CLIL, then, is a dual language model that involves the delivery of certain subject matter courses in the students' L2 or additional language and that represents a response to the multilingual needs and goals of global economies. With its goal of creating global citizens, CLIL lends itself to settings (e.g., the European Union) where a language other than the students' home language serves as a lingua franca or language of wider communication (Coyle, Hood, & Marsh, 2010). Since its beginnings, CLIL has spread rapidly throughout Europe and elsewhere worldwide.

CLIL shares key features with other forms of CBI, especially (partial) immersion and sheltered instruction. In both of these approaches, students study subject matter delivered in a language other than that of their L1; SLA occurs as a "by-product" of the rich exposure to meaningful language in the subject matter classroom. Additionally, in both approaches, language and content aims are integrated and the instructor's task is to both make content comprehensible to the L2 student population and to support language acquisition. So-called "hard" CLIL is a form of subject teaching in the L2 that emphasizes academic achievement in the subject matter and treats language development as a kind of "bonus." "Soft" CLIL, on the other hand, may be offered for a shorter period (half a year) and places emphasis on both subject matter achievement and language development (Ball, Kelly, & Clegg, 2015).

However, there are important differences as well. From our North American perspective, CLIL (at least "hard" CLIL) seems most closely related to sheltered instruction, but constructive discussions in the course of preparing this book have led us to give it a distinct classification as a separate model of CBI. Cenoz, Genesee, and Gorter (2013), however, point out that "definitions of CLIL and the varied interpretations of this approach within Europe indicate that it is understood in different ways by its advocates" (p. 244).[2] For one, CLIL is largely driven by a language policy that embraces the development of multilingual/multicultural individuals who can function in today's global society. Students' exposure to L2 subject matter instruction is systematically "phased in" over time, with the number of hours of L2 content instruction increasing with grade level. Sheltered instruction, on the other hand, is typically driven by pressing educational needs in settings such as the U.S. where large numbers of school-age children speak home languages other than the language of school and may enter the school system at any time during the academic year. Its end goal is to transition students from the sheltered to the mainstream classroom. Most ELs in U.S.-sheltered programs have very different sociolinguistic profiles than CLIL students; they typically come from immigrant families and are adjusting to life in their new country. CLIL, in contrast, is often seen as an elite programmatic option with "high social value for parents" (Ball et al., 2015, p. 11). See Dalton-Puffer, this volume, for a more thorough discussion of CLIL.

English-Medium Instruction (EMI)

Often referred to as the tertiary education variant of CLIL, EMI refers to content instruction delivered in the students' L2.[3] Central to the appeal of EMI are the dual aims of creating multilingual citizens and internationalizing tertiary institutions—that is, to appeal to international students for whom EMI courses are an enrollment incentive and thus a financial boon to the institution (Doiz, Lasagabaster, & Sierra, 2013). EMI course offerings have multiplied exponentially in recent years, not only in Europe but also in many other parts of the globe, with more than 60 percent of all post-graduate courses in Europe currently being offered through EMI (Macaro, 2015).

That being said, the implementation of EMI differs widely from country to country, as well as from institution to institution. In particular, this variation pertains to the degree to which language support or an intentional focus on language skills is present. In what might be termed the "weak" version of EMI, L2 students are exposed to content delivered in English with little or no attention paid to language skills, as described by Dueñas (2003):

> In [EMI], language aims are not contemplated as part of the curricular formulations of the given courses; in fact classes of this kind normally proceed without specific instructional emphasis on language analysis and practice, and without making adjustments to adequate the discourse to the level of proficiency of students. The context, however, provides valuable opportunities for language learning as it involves intensive exposure to highly contextualized language of particular relevance to the academic interest of students. These [students] therefore manage to advance their language competence by developing receptive and productive skills though in an unplanned, unsystematic way. (Section 4, Second Language Medium Courses)

On the other end of the spectrum, Brinton (2007) describes language-enhanced (also known as language-sensitive) English-medium courses in which the content and language goals are intentionally aligned and where there is an explicit focus on developing language skills as well as increasing content knowledge.

Whatever approach is selected, those who implement EMI are bound to encounter many of the same challenges that surface in other forms of integrated language and content learning, for example, the requisite threshold level of L2 proficiency needed for both students and faculty to participate successfully in and benefit from EMI; effective means of assessing this proficiency; faculty familiarity with and buy-in to the EMI model; and training of faculty to assist them in delivering content effectively to L2 students. (For more details, see Issues in Implementation. See also the chapters by Kling and Stillwell, this volume.)

Modified and Simulated Adjunct Models

In the prototype model of adjunct instruction, the instructors of two separate classes (a content and a language class) coordinate their instructional aims, with the content class driving curricular decisions and the language class narrowing in on the linguistic skills that students need to function in the content course. Numerous modifications have been made to this model to make it more responsive to setting variables. Iancu (2002), for example, describes an adaptation of the adjunct model to the Intensive English Program (IEP) setting; in this case, an introductory-level university content course was adjuncted to four separate skill-based IEP courses (listening and note-taking, reading, academic writing, and speech). This modification allowed the model to be used with students at a lower level of English language proficiency and was therefore well suited to the IEP setting. Snow and Kamhi-Stein (2002) describe another modification at the university level in which general education content courses were paired instead with a study group, co-taught by a language specialist and a peer study group leader (i.e., an undergraduate student who had previously successfully completed the content course). In this modification of the adjunct model, extensive faculty development took place with faculty of the targeted general education courses redesigning their courses to make the content more accessible to language minority students and to teach the language skills needed to meet the demands of the content assignments (Snow, 1997; Srole, 1997).

Finally, Brinton and Jensen (2002) describe a "simulated adjunct model" (p. 125) in which video excerpts of university content lectures and the accompanying course readings formed the core of sustained content units in the university's EAP program. Selected from a cross-curricular sampling of general education courses (such as Introduction to Sociology, Communication Studies, and Atmospheric Sciences), the units also contained language and academic skills development materials along with other theme-related enrichment activities (e.g., political cartoons, newspaper articles, short story excerpts) that complemented the content of each unit.

Other Hybrid Models

One difficulty of describing other hybrid models is that many variants or "twists" of the CBI model that have arisen to respond to local contexts and student needs are neither widely reported nor captured in print. One notable exception, however, are writing intensive (WI) courses. Such courses, which are offered in various discipline areas across the curriculum, typically have the following characteristics (Townsend, 2001): The student to instructor ratio is small, ensuring more attention to student writing; courses are taught by senior content-area faculty who have attended writing across the curriculum workshops; a specified number of writing assignments are required for the course to qualify as WI; and writing assignments require multiple drafts, span a variety of genres, and constitute a specified percentage of students' final grade in the content course. Jensen reports on one such WI course, An Introduction to Language Learning and Language Teaching, designed for multilingual writers and offered through the Department of Applied Linguistics at the University of California, Los Angeles (L. Jensen, personal communication, 2010). In the course, students completed four multi-draft written assignments: a personal reflection on their L2 learning experiences; an analysis of observations conducted in second language classrooms; a review of a recent ESL or EFL language textbook, written to publication specifications; and a research paper examining a popular conception of language learning that drew on a minimum of three sources. In addition to these formal writing assignments, the students also posted and responded to weekly reading reaction journals on the course management site.

Issues in Implementation |||

As Brinton, Snow, and Wesche (2003) note, there are numerous issues that impact the successful implementation of CBI. These include but are not limited to: administrative issues (e.g., where the impetus for implementing CBI comes from and who carries responsibility for the program's implementation); program design issues (e.g., whether the primary objective is to teach language or to teach content and how far-reaching the planned changes are); student issues (e.g., students' L2 proficiency level, their prior educational background, and their needs and interests); staffing issues (e.g., whether instructors have the necessary linguistic proficiency and background in CBI and whether they are willing to take on new roles in their teaching); and, finally, program evaluation issues (e.g., student achievement and the quality of the curriculum and materials). According to research studies in CBI, however, there appear to be three primary issues that are mentioned repeatedly as impacting the implementation of CBI. These include: (1) the lack of attention to form in CBI; (2) the balance of attention to language and attention to content; and (3) the power imbalance between language and content instructors.

With respect to the first of these issues, Eskey (1997) notes that CBI tends to "come down hard" on the side of fluency, thus often paying inadequate attention to form. This is echoed in research conducted by Brinton and Holten (2001), who note that language instructors often spend more classroom time reviewing content than focusing on language. They term this phenomenon "content envy." Lyster (2007), in his research in language and content integrated classrooms, documents similar findings—that is, that the focus on language is often incidental. And finally, Valeo (2013), in a controlled study, notes that a focus on form approach resulted in significant gains in language as well as in content mastery. (See also Lyster, this volume.)

Next, as pertains to achieving a balance of language and content in the integrated classroom, research yields the following findings: Davison (2005), in a study of "subject English" as a content course, notes that the definition of what is language and what is content can shift according to the disciplinary community—that is, that the very notions of language and content are subject to interpretation. Creese (2005), in her study of collaborating teachers in U.K. secondary school classrooms, concludes that language work in the content classroom is typically given low status. Tan (2011), in her study of math, science, and language teachers in the Malaysian context, documents that teachers' beliefs about their role as "only a language/content teacher" limited the effectiveness of CBI. And Cammarata and Tedick (2012), examining the practices of three immersion teachers, conclude that the teachers should engage in "pedagogical awakening" as they struggle to balance language and content. (See also Baecher, Ediger, & Farnsworth, this volume.)

A final area that impacts the successful implementation of CBI models is the perennial issue in CBI of power relations between content and language teachers. A classic in its own right, Goldstein, Campbell, and Clark Cummings' (1997) research highlighted the subservient position that many language instructors take to content instructors in adjunct contexts. Accordingly, the authors dubbed the phenomenon they observed "the flight attendant syndrome." (See Goldstein, this volume, for an updated discussion.) Arkoudis' (2005) research applied insights from appraisal and positioning theory to examine teacher power relationships in planning sessions. These relationships were shown to negatively impact teachers' efforts to balance language and content in their courses. Similarly, Tan (2011) found that overall, the mathematics and science instructors in her study tended to dismiss the importance of language instruction for the conceptual learning of their students. Lastly, Pawan and Ortloff (2011) in their research noted tensions between language and content faculty.

They conclude with a call to faculty from both disciplines for interprofessionality. (See also Pawan & Greene, this volume).

Conclusions |||

At this point, it is appropriate to ponder the future of CBI, which is still a vibrant force in the field of SFL teaching. Snow (2014) ventures the following thoughts on the issue:

> The teaching of language through content is not so much a method as a reorientation to what is meant by *content* in language teaching. The literature offers strong theoretical support for content-based approaches and abundant examples of successful programs in SFL settings... As [it] enters its fifth decade, we share Wesche's (2010) positive outlook that [content-based language teaching] "...is likely to continue to flourish, particularly in contexts where learners' main opportunity for developing advanced L2 proficiency is a school or post-secondary context and where they need to develop academic L2 ability." (p. 452)

As we have touched on in this chapter (and as will be discussed in greater length elsewhere in the volume), there remain a number of challenges that are pervasive in CBI. These include the collaboration of content and language faculty, the willingness and ability of content faculty to assume responsibility for language instruction, effective means of sheltering content delivery for L2 learners, the threshold level of proficiency needed for learners to function in the various models of CBI, and appropriate means of assessing both language and content in an integrated approach. These challenges notwithstanding, we contend that CBI is a highly flexible approach that provides a powerful means of structuring the syllabus for both general purpose and EAP courses. In this chapter, we have also attempted the perhaps foolhardy task of classifying the various approaches to CBI that have evolved. Classification is tricky business, especially given that we readily admit that the models are constantly evolving. We are, however, less interested in hard and fast boundaries than offering a helpful schema that delineates similar and contrasting features as a way of demonstrating the rich array of CBI possibilities.

APPLYING WHAT YOU LEARNED
Questions and Tasks

1. CBI first appeared on the scene in the early to mid-1980s.

   a. To what do you attribute the enduring nature of the approach?

   b. Do you believe, as do the authors, that CBI will continue to be a viable approach to L2 teaching and learning in the future? Why or why not?

2. Review the updated map of CBI in Figure 1.3. The authors have characterized CBI as an umbrella term for a variety of different models and created the classification based on key similarities and differences in the various models discussed.

   a. Summarize the major similarities that justify their overall classification as models of CBI.

   b. Summarize the major differences that set them apart.

   c. Can you think of any other similarities or differences that are not mentioned in the chapter?

   d. Do you know of any other programs that integrate language and content to some degree that are not included in Figure 1.3? What are they? Where would you place them?

3. The authors mention three often-cited issues that threaten the successful implementation of CBI.

   a. Summarize the three issues.

   b. Which of the three do you believe poses the greatest challenge? Why?

   c. Can you think of other issues that pose additional threats to successful implementation?

   d. Can you suggest any ways in which these challenges could be mitigated or eliminated?

4. Adamson (1993) describes a ninth grade English literature class. The class, which adheres to the mainstream syllabus, contained non-native English–speaking students from 13 different countries. Students read well-known short stories and an abridged version of Dickens' *Great Expectations*. The instructor, who had received special training in working with nonnative speakers, included additional vocabulary exercises and provided students with extra study questions. Finally, she frequently had students work in groups.

   a. Which of the three CBI prototype models does this scenario illustrate?

   b. Describe the distinct characteristics of the model as depicted in the scenario.

   c. What specific challenges would you expect the students to experience? The instructor?

   d. What do you consider to be the strengths of this program? The potential weaknesses?

ENDNOTES

1. van Lier (2005) reminds readers that courses at the far ends of the scale are not conceivable since "language is ... always about something, and content is (at least partly) expressed in language" (p. 16).
2. Note that Dalton-Puffer, Llinares, Lorenzo, and Nikula (2014), in fact, do not even classify CLIL as a type of CBI because CLIL "is timetabled as content lessons" and is "taught by content-trained teachers who also assess it 'as content'" (p. 215). They do, however, encourage researchers to be less concerned about labels and more concerned about promoting all forms of additive bilingual programs.
3. Increasingly, the term Integrating Content and Language in Higher Education (ICLHE) is being used, either synonymously with EMI or to refer to a form of EMI that is more language-enhanced / language-sensitive.

REFERENCES

A language for life: Report of the committee of inquiry appointed by the secretary of state for education and science under the chairmanship of Sir Alan Bullock F. B. A. (1975). London, England: Her Majesty's Stationery Office.

Adamson, H. D. (1993). *Academic competence—Theory and classroom practice: Preparing ESL students for content courses*. White Plains, NY: Longman.

Arkoudis, S. (2005). Fusing pedagogic horizons: Language and content teaching in the mainstream. *Linguistics and Education, 16,* 173–187.

Ball, P., Kelly, K., & Clegg, J. (2015). *Putting CLIL into practice*. Oxford, England: Oxford University Press.

Bright, A. (2010). Opening the door: Making mathematics accessible to English language learners. In J. Nordmeyer & S. Barduhn (Eds.), *Integrating language and content* (pp. 109–115). Alexandria, VA: TESOL.

Brinton, D. M. (2001). A theme-based literature course: Focus on the City of Angels. In J. Murphy & P. Byrd (Eds.), *Understanding the courses we teach: Local perspectives on English language teaching* (pp. 281–308). Ann Arbor, MI: University of Michigan Press.

Brinton, D. M. (2007). Two for one—Language-enhanced content instruction in English for academic purposes. In *Teaching English for specific purposes: Meeting our learners' needs* (pp. 1–16). Alexandria, VA: TESOL.

Brinton, D. M., & Holten, C. (2001). Does the emperor have no clothes? A re-examination of grammar in content-based instruction. In J. Flowerdew & M. Peacock (Eds.), *Research perspectives on English for academic purposes* (pp. 239–251). Cambridge, England: Cambridge University Press.

Brinton, D. M., & Jensen, L. (2002). Appropriating the adjunct model: English for academic purposes at the university level. In J. Crandall & D. Kaufman (Eds.), *Content-based instruction in higher education settings* (pp. 125–138). Alexandria, VA: TESOL.

Brinton, D. M., Snow, M. A., & Wesche, M. B. (1989). *Content-based second language instruction*. New York, NY: Newbury House.

Brinton, D. M., Snow, M. A., & Wesche, M. B. (2003). *Content-based second language instruction* (Classics ed.). Ann Arbor, MI: University of Michigan Press.

Cammarata, L., & Tedick, D. J. (2012). Balancing content and language in instruction: The experience of immersion teachers. *The Modern Language Journal, 96*(2), 251–269.

Cenoz, J., Genesee, F., & Gorter, D. (2013). Critical analysis of CLIL: Taking stock and looking forward. *Applied Linguistics, 35*(3), 243–262.

Coyle, D., Hood, P., & Marsh, D. (2010). *CLIL: Content and language integrated learning*. Cambridge, England: Cambridge University Press.

Crandall, J. (2012). Content-based instruction and content and language integrated learning. In A. Burns & J. C. Richards (Eds.), *The Cambridge guide to pedagogy and practice in second language teaching* (pp. 149–160). New York, NY: Cambridge University Press.

Creese, A. (2005). Is this content based language teaching? *Linguistics and Education, 16*, 188–204.

Dalton-Puffer, C., Llinares, A., Lorenzo, F., & Nikula, T. (2014). "You can stand under my umbrella": Immersion, CLIL, and bilingual education. A response to Cenoz, Genesee & Gorter (2013). *Applied Linguistics, 35*(2), 213–218.

Davison, C. (2005). Learning your lines: Negotiating language and content in subject English. *Linguistics and Education, 16*, 219–237.

Davison, C., & Williams, A. (2001). Integrating language and content: Unresolved issues. In B. Mohan, C. Leung, & C. Davison (Eds.), *English as a second language in the mainstream: Teaching, learning and identity* (pp. 51–70). Harlow, England: Longman.

Doiz, A., Lasagabaster, D., & Sierra, J. M. (Eds.). (2013). *English-medium instruction at universities: Global challenges*. Bristol, England: Multilingual Matters.

Dueñas, M. (2003). A description of prototype models for content-based instruction in higher education. *BELLS: Barcelona English Language and Literature Studies, 12.* Retrieved from http://www.publicacions.ub.edu/revistes/bells12/

Duff, P. A. (2014). Communicative language teaching. In M. Celce-Murcia, D. M. Brinton, & M. A. Snow (Eds.), *Teaching English as a second or foreign language* (4th ed., pp. 15–30). Boston, MA: National Geographic Learning/Heinle Cengage Learning.

Echevarría, J., Vogt, M. E., & Short, D. J. (2017). *Making content comprehensible for English learners: The SIOP model* (5th ed.). Boston, MA: Pearson.

Edwards, H. P., Wesche, M., Krashen, S., Clément, R., & Kruidenier, B. (1984). Second language acquisition through subject matter learning: A study of sheltered psychology classes at the University of Ottawa. *Canadian Modern Language Review, 41*(2), 268–282.

Eskey, D. E. (1997). Syllabus design in content-based instruction. (1997). In M. A. Snow & D. M. Brinton (Eds.), *The content-based classroom: Perspectives on integrating language and content* (pp. 132–141). White Plains, NY: Longman.

Genesee, F. (1987). *Learning through two languages: Studies of immersion and bilingual education.* Rowley, MA: Newbury House.

Genesee, F., & Lindholm-Leary, K. (2013). Two case studies of content-based language education. *Journal of Immersion and Content-Based Language Education, 1*(1), 3–33.

Goldstein, L., Campbell, C., & Clark Cummings, M. (1997). Smiling through the turbulence: The flight attendant syndrome and writing instructor status in the adjunct model. In M. A. Snow & D. M. Brinton (Eds.), *The content-based classroom: Perspectives on integrating language and content* (pp. 331–339). White Plains, NY: Longman.

Hauptmann, P. C., Wesche, M. B., & Ready, D. (1988). Second language acquisition through subject matter learning: A follow-up study of sheltered psychology classes at the University of Ottawa. *Language Learning, 38*(3), 439–482.

Hauschild, S., Poltavtchenko, E., & Stoller, F. L. (2012). Going green: Merging environmental education and language instruction. *English Teaching Forum, 2,* 2–13.

Hymes, D. (1971). On communicative competence. Philadelphia, PA: University of Pennsylvania Press.

Iancu, M. (2002). To motivate and educate, collaborate and integrate: The adjunct model in a bridge program. In J. A. Crandall & D. Kaufman (Eds.), *Content-based instruction in higher education settings* (pp. 139–153). Alexandria, VA: TESOL.

Jacobs, H. H. (Ed.). (1989). The growing need for interdisciplinary content. In *Interdisciplinary curriculum: Design and implementation* (pp. 1–11). Alexandria, VA: Association for Supervision and Curriculum Development.

Krueger, M., & Ryan, F. (Eds.). (1993). *Language and content: Discipline- and content-based approaches to language study.* Lexington, MA: D. C. Heath and Company.

Lambert, W. E., & Tucker, G. R. (1972). *The bilingual education of children: The St. Lambert Experiment.* Rowley, MA: Newbury House.

Lyster, R. (2007). *Learning and teaching languages through content: A counterbalanced approach.* Amsterdam, The Netherlands: Benjamins.

Macaro, E. (2015). English medium instruction: Time to start asking some difficult questions. *Modern English Teacher, 24*(2), 4–7.

Marsh, D. (2003, April). The relevance and potential of content and language integrated learning (CLIL) for achieving MT+2 in Europe. *ELC Information Bulletin, 9.* Retrieved from http://userpage.fu-berlin.de/elc/bulletin/9/en/marsh.html

Met, M. (1999, January). Content-based instruction: Defining terms, making decisions. *NFLC Reports.* Washington, DC: The National Foreign Language Center. Retrieved from http://carla.umn.edu/cobaltt/modules/principles/decisions.html

Mohan, B. (1986). *Language and content.* Reading, MA: Addison-Wesley.

Murphy, J. M., & Stoller, F. L. (Eds.). (2001, Summer/Autumn). Sustained-content language teaching: An emerging definition. *TESOL Journal, 10*(2/3), 3–5.

Parker, R. (1985). The "language across the curriculum" movement: A brief overview and bibliography. *College Composition and Communication, 36*(2), 173–177.

Pawan, F., & Ortloff, J. H. (2011). Sustaining collaboration: English-as-a-second-language, and content-area teachers. *Teaching and Teacher Education, 27,* 463–471.

Reynolds, K. M. (2015). *Approaches to inclusive English classrooms: A teacher's handbook for content-based instruction.* Bristol, England: Multilingual Matters.

Short, D. J., Fidelman, C. G., & Louguit, M. (2012). Developing academic language in English language learners through sheltered instruction. *TESOL Quarterly, 46*(2), 334–361.

Snow, M. A. (1997). Teaching academic literacy skills: Discipline faculty take responsibility. In M. A. Snow & D. M. Brinton (Eds.), *The content-based classroom: Perspectives on integrating language and content* (pp. 290–304). White Plains, NY: Longman.

Snow, M. A. (2014). Content-based and immersion models of second/foreign language teaching. In M. Celce-Murcia, D. M. Brinton, & M. A. Snow (Eds.), *Teaching English as a second or foreign language* (4th ed., pp. 438–454). Boston, MA: National Geographic Learning/Heinle Cengage Learning.

Snow, M. A., & Brinton, D. M. (1988). Content-based language instruction: Investigating the effectiveness of the adjunct model. *TESOL Quarterly, 22*(4), 553–574.

Snow, M. A., & Brinton, D. M. (Eds.). (1997). *The content-based classroom: Perspectives on integrating language and content.* White Plains, NY: Longman.

Snow, M. A., & Kamhi-Stein, L. D. (2002). Teaching and learning academic literacy through Project LEAP. In J. A. Crandall & D. Kaufman (Eds.), *Content-based instruction in higher education settings* (pp. 169–181). Alexandria, VA: TESOL.

Spring, J. (2010). Sustained content-based academic English teaching through paired English and philosophy courses. In J. Nordmeyer & S. Barduhn (Eds.), *Integrating language and content* (pp. 219–230). Alexandria, VA: TESOL.

Srole, C. (1997). Pedagogical responses from content faculty: Teaching content and language in history. In M. A. Snow & D. M. Brinton (Eds.), *The content-based classroom: Perspectives on integrating language and content* (pp. 104–116). White Plains, NY: Longman.

Tan, M. (2011). Mathematics and science teachers' beliefs and practices regarding the teaching of language in content learning. *Language Teaching Research, 15*(3), 325–342.

Tedick, D. J., Christian, D., & Fortune, T. W. (2011). *Immersion education: Practices, policies, possibilities.* Buffalo, NY: Multilingual Matters.

Townsend, M. (2001). Writing intensive courses and WAC. In S. H. McLeod, E. Miraglia, M. Soven, & C. Thaiss (Eds.), *WAC for the new millennium: Strategies for continuing WAC programs* (pp. 233–258). Urbana, IL: NCTE.

U.S. Department of State, Office of English Language Programs. (2007). Bilingual primary. *Shaping the way we teach English.* Washington, DC: Author. Retrieved from http://www.youtube.com/watch?v=caOXPCIGFyM

Valeo, A. (2013). The integration of language and content: Form-focused instruction in a content-based language program. *The Canadian Journal of Applied Linguistics, 16*(1), 25–50.

van Lier, L. (2005). The bellman's map: Avoiding the "perfect and absolute blank" in language learning. In R. M. Jourdenais & S. E. Springer (Eds.), *Content, tasks and projects in the language classroom: 2004 conference proceedings* (pp. 13–22). Monterey, CA: Monterey Institute of International Studies.

Wesche, M. B. (2010). Content-based second language instruction. In R. Kaplan (Ed.), *The Oxford handbook of applied linguistics* (2nd ed., pp. 275–293). Oxford, England: Oxford University Press.

Chapter 2

Research Support for Content-Based Instruction

Shannon Fitzsimmons-Doolan, William Grabe, & Fredricka L. Stoller

In second language[1] settings around the world, many language teachers find themselves in traditional classrooms, perhaps teaching sequences of grammar points and/or discrete skills across the curriculum. Some of those teachers feel a need to change their ways of teaching to increase students' motivation, their engagement in more cognitively demanding lessons, and their preparation for more authentic uses of English. These teachers may have read articles and attended conference presentations about various models of CBI. They may have been impressed by the fact that such classrooms make a dual commitment to language and content learning. They may be curious about effective ways to integrate skills in content-based classes as well as steps that teachers can take to integrate (a) engaging content, (b) project work, (c) scaffolding, (d) cooperative learning, and (e) synthesis tasks. These teachers realize that they need access to relevant research and reported content-based classroom outcomes that they can share with peers, supervisors, and program administrators. They want convincing arguments for transitioning to some form of CBI in their teaching contexts. This chapter explores such research, outcomes, and arguments.

Research Support for Content-Based Instruction |||

Content-based approaches to language teaching and learning vary across instructional settings, target student populations, and students' purposes for studying new languages (see Brinton & Snow, this volume; see also Lyster & Ballinger, 2011; Snow, 2014; Stoller & Fitzsimmons-Doolan, 2017). Despite the variations that exist across content-based approaches to language teaching, these approaches share an underlying premise: Specifically, they are designed to facilitate students' grasp of subject matter (content) while also developing students' language skills. It is assumed that the learning of content contributes to the learning of language, that language mastery gives learners easier access to content, and that learning language in classroom environments with coherent content is motivating for students (Grabe, 2009; Lightbown, 2014; Snow, 2014). Content-based courses, in their various configurations, reflect both this shared language- and content-learning foundation as well as the unique parameters of the educational settings in which they are offered.

Over the past few decades, the benefits of CBI have been examined and reported by researchers, classroom teachers, and curriculum designers. In this chapter, we examine research from a range of fields that argues, directly and indirectly, for the benefits of CBI. (See Grabe & Stoller, 1997, for an earlier review of research support for CBI.) We begin by reviewing support from empirical research conducted in the fields of SLA, cognitive psychology, and educational psychology. We then move on to support that emerges from CBI frameworks themselves and reports of CBI outcomes in various instructional settings. Findings such as those reported here can assist teachers, like those identified at the beginning of the chapter, in making a persuasive case for (a) transitioning to content-based approaches in their classrooms and/or (b) fine-tuning their content-based approaches to meet their students' language- and content-learning needs. We conclude with the identification of areas related to CBI in need of further study, with the hopes of establishing a research agenda that will lead to further insights into the benefits of CBI.

Support from Empirical Research in Second Language Acquisition |||

A major source of support for CBI comes from SLA research, beginning with studies that have emphasized the importance of input (i.e., target language that learners are exposed to through reading or listening), output (i.e., language, spoken or written, produced by learners), and interaction (i.e., student-student and student-teacher communication) in L2 learners' classroom experiences. In many cases, SLA theories for more effective language learning may not identify CBI as a preferred translation to instruction, but the SLA theories noted here are strongly compatible with tenets of CBI implementation.

Beginning with input-based theories, evidence gathered over four decades suggests that higher frequencies of repeated input facilitate language acquisition (Ellis, 2008). Because most content-based teachers structure curricular units around sustained content (i.e., content explored over time rather than in short textbook units), learners encounter more frequent uses of lexical and morphosyntactic items specific to target content and related genres than they would in traditional language classes. In addition to the importance of input, Swain's (1995) output hypothesis reinforces the value of explicit attention to productive language skills (speaking and writing); these skills are easily incorporated into CBI.

The Interaction Hypothesis (Long, 1996) convincingly theorizes that interaction facilitates SLA through modified output, attention to form, and negotiation of meaning (i.e., the process during which speakers work to understand each other—indicating, for example, understanding or lack of understanding, helping each other to express ideas, making corrections when necessary) (see also Ellis, 2008). Dalton-Puffer (2011) notes that the negotiation-of-meaning concept provides "an excellent basis for a content-and-language approach" (p. 191). In content-based classes, students tend to engage in more negotiation sequences than in lessons delivered in their L1. Most importantly, information gaps negotiated in CBI contexts are almost always based on a real need to find out what another student knows on a complex topic. In CBI classes, there is no need to create contrived information-gap activities. In addition, Lyster (2007), in investigations of teacher-student interactions in immersion and other content-based settings, noted that prompting and other teacher-feedback strategies in negotiations of form can "push" learners to develop their L2 (p. 114). Thus, SLA theories of input, output, and interaction support CBI curricula to the extent that CBI classes provide plentiful opportunities for meaningful input, output, and interaction.

Further support for CBI comes from studies examining the role of motivation in second language acquisition. Past research has documented the positive relationship between language-learning motivation and L2 achievement (Gardner, Tremblay, & Masgoret, 1997) in addition to factors that influence changes in language-learning motivation over time (Dörnyei, 2005). Recent conceptualizations of language-learning motivation are grounded in complex, dynamic models of language use, which maintain the importance of motivation in long-term L2 learning processes (Dörnyei, MacIntyre, & Henry, 2015). Because content-based classes are typically more intensive than traditional foreign language classes, students are able to witness their linguistic progress more clearly, which may positively affect motivation (Lightbown, 2014).

Wu and Chang (2010) found that the use of CBI, in a two-week Mandarin summer camp (with content centered on Chinese-American history and students' personal experiences), increased motivation among (self-reported) unmotivated heritage-language speakers—speakers with some proficiency in a language learned from and used in familial and/or community settings. Summer-camp students not only engaged in the use of Mandarin in (required) and out (not required) of camp, but they also reported intentions to attend the camp the following year. Furthermore, in an investigation of motivation in an English-based CLIL program in Spain, Doiz, Lasagabaster, and Sierra (2014) reported that across years of the program, students who were enrolled in CLIL courses exhibited higher levels of several motivational constructs (e.g., instrumental motivation, intrinsic motivation, and motivational strength)[2] than did non-CLIL students.

In addition to studies linking student motivation to common CBI practices, studies of the roles of form and meaning in language instruction have supported the implementation of CBI, specifically when CBI includes explicit attention to both form and meaning. Lyster (2007), in a detailed exploration of form-focused instruction (FFI)[3] in CBI, called for "intentional and systematic" (p. 58) approaches to FFI, including "reactive" instruction, as language is used in real time, and "proactive" instruction, which is planned in advance (see also Lyster, this volume). In a review of previous FFI research, Spada and Lightbown (2008) found that FFI—both integrated into and isolated from communicative activities—facilitated language learning in content-based classes. They drew upon: (a) Long's (1996) Interaction Hypothesis and studies of meta-talk[4] (e.g., Swain & Lapkin, 2013) to support integrated FFI and (b) VanPatten's (2004) work on form-meaning mapping[5] to support isolated FFI. This body of research supports the linkage of content and language objectives to promote explicit foci on meaning and form, characteristic of many CBI models (e.g., Echevarría, Vogt, & Short, 2017).

Further support for CBI follows from Cummins' (1984, 2000) notion of Cognitive Academic Language Proficiency (CALP) (Echevarría, Vogt, & Short, 2017; Lightbown, 2014; Snow, 2014; Walqui & Van Lier, 2010) and more recent developments in the study of academic language. Cummins argues that students take much longer to develop CALP than Basic Interpersonal Communication Skills (BICS).[6] Placing language learners in content-based classes, as opposed to traditional language classes, provides learners with more extended, varied, and contextualized exposure to academic language, thereby improving students' CALP. The fact that language use varies by content area, at all levels of education, has been robustly documented (e.g., Biber, 2006; Gardner, 2004; Nagy & Townsend, 2012; Schleppegrell, 2008). Content-based courses not only provide sustained access to disciplinary language in context but also promote the application of instructional strategies necessary for helping students navigate and appropriate such language.

Sociocultural approaches to SLA provide additional theoretical and empirical support for CBI (Donato, 2016). Briefly, sociocultural approaches to SLA, grounded in the work of Vygotsky (Lantolf & Poehner, 2008), theorize that language is both the object of learning and a tool for communication (and ultimately thought). Furthermore, they suggest that learning, more generally, and language learning, more specifically, are facilitated by scaffolding (i.e., deliberate, dynamic support) in the Zone of Proximal Development—a collaborative space where multiple individuals of varying proficiencies work together (Swain & Lapkin, 2013; Walqui, 2006). Walqui and van Lier (2010) link sociocultural theories with CBI because these theories "promise" to move students toward independent engagement in authentic academic language and tasks (p. 12). Snow (2014) and Dalton-Puffer (2011) suggest that CBI provides the appropriate context for scaffolding, as advocated by sociocultural approaches to SLA. Lightbown (2014) reinforces this claim by pointing out that the collaborative, interactive nature of many content-based courses supports scaffolding. Nguyen and Kellogg (2010) report how collaborative language use—in a university-level sustained content course focused on civil rights in the U.S.—assisted students in their use of language as well as their grasp of content.

Support from Empirical Research in Cognitive and Educational Psychology |||

In addition to SLA scholarship, research in cognitive and educational psychology continues to offer some of the most persuasive support for CBI. Of particular interest is research focused on cognitive theories of learning, depth-of-processing, discourse comprehension processing, motivation, attribution, interest, and expertise.

More general cognitive theories of learning specify various interrelated cognitive processes to account for learning, generally, and language learning, more specifically. Central to these processes are automaticity and implicit learning. Automatic processes are those that tend to be "unintentional, goal independent, uncontrolled, autonomous, and purely stimulus driven" while implicit learning can be described as acquiring new knowledge without awareness of that acquisition (Eysenck & Keane, 2010, p. 195). One cognitive learning theory that draws on the concepts of automaticity and implicit learning, which support CBI, is Anderson's (2010) Adaptive Control of Thought (ACT) learning theory. As described in Grabe (2009), Anderson posits that all learning, including language learning, begins with explicit, cognitive learning, then moves to implicit, associative learning that develops through practice and repeated formal and content exposure, and concludes with autonomous learning in which automaticity is developed. Many CBI frameworks (including Sheltered Instruction Observation Protocol [SIOP] and Concept-Oriented Reading Instruction [CORI], described in more detail later) advocate lesson sequences that guide students along this learning trajectory. For example, SIOP lessons begin with (a) an explicit description of content and learning objectives and (b) the presentation of new information, then move to activities that permit student practice with content and language, and finally transition to tasks in which students apply new knowledge and recycle already introduced knowledge without instructor support (Echevarría, Vogt, & Short, 2017).

Depth-of-processing research argues that the presentation of coherent and meaningful information (that we see so often in CBI) leads to deeper processing, which, in turn, results in better recall (Anderson, 2010; Eysenck & Keane, 2010). One technique for promoting depth-of-processing in L2 reading is Elaborative Interrogation—a teaching strategy that entails asking students multiple follow-up *why* questions to support reading comprehension and recall (Grabe, 2009). Brantmeir, Callender, and McDaniel (2011), for example, gave university-level L2 readers passages with and without embedded *why* and *what* questions. Recall was significantly higher for passages with embedded questions. Stoller and Grabe's Six Ts Approach to CBI (see Stoller & Grabe, this volume) reveals how well-planned content-based courses—through deliberate choices of themes, texts, topics, threads, tasks, and transitions—provide meaningful, coherent content for students, thereby inviting depth of processing.

Discourse comprehension processing research identifies characteristics of text types that are "considerate" (Grabe, 2009, p. 253)—that is, easier to comprehend—as well as instructional techniques for helping students recognize discourse structures, thereby making inconsiderate texts more considerate. Teacher selection of texts with considerate features (a) helps students retrieve appropriate prior knowledge and (b) provides clear signaling of main ideas and other discourse structures (Grabe, 2009). This line of research provides strong support for discourse structure awareness training, which involves the use of graphic organizers, the identification of explicit discourse signaling language, and practice with reading strategies (Grabe & Stoller, 2011). These research results provide a strong justification for CBI, which typically makes a commitment to L2 reading comprehension, strategic reading, and strategic-reader training (Grabe, 2009).

Motivation, positive attributions, and interest—studied from the perspective of cognitive psychology—have been identified as factors that strongly support (a) student success with challenging informational activities and (b) students' learning of complex skills, two important goals for CBI. Motivation is considered an important component of self-regulated learning (Efklides, 2011). Like the study of motivation in SLA, research in cognitive psychology explores changes in motivation over time and multiple motivational dimensions, including goals, expectations, and interest (Zimmerman, 2008). Grabe (2009) recommends supporting L2 reading motivation by means of (a) opportunities for learning success, (b) interesting instructional texts, (c) strategy instruction, and (d) social collaboration and relationship building for academic tasks (see also Komiyama, 2013). Flow, which increases motivation, is the state of optimal experiences that occurs when personal skills match the task challenge, leading to total absorption in an activity, a sense of timelessness, and a temporary lack of awareness of personal problems (Csikszentmihalyi, 2014; see also Dörnyei & Ushioda, 2011). CBI, with its focus on task complexity that is supported and increased over time, provides opportunities for students to engage in flow and to experience increased intrinsic motivation while learning both content and language.

Finally, studies on the nature of expertise within cognitive psychology also provide support for CBI. Research on expert performance seeks to identify how experts engage in "consistently superior performance" (Ericsson & Ward, 2007, p. 347). Outcomes from such investigations have led to an understanding that experts hone their skills over no less than 10 years of intense practice, that experts develop models of their skill that allow them to "plan, monitor, and reason" about performance in multiple situations, and that top performance comes from mastery of skills related to one's area of expertise rather than advantages in more generalized abilities such as memory or intelligence (Ericsson & Ward, 2007, p. 348). These findings echo aspects of the ACT theory advanced by Anderson (2010), which emphasizes the importance of (a) implicit learning through practice, (b) metacognition, (c) and automaticity in specific skills relative to the performance domain. CBI is compatible with research on expertise in that it emphasizes learning that is focused on a specific content domain. At the same time, CBI affords opportunities for large quantities of contextualized implicit practice of language skills and explicit strategies training, integrated with sustained content. In this way, research on the nature of expertise supports the implementation of CBI.

Support from CBI Frameworks |||

Approaches to CBI vary by focus (e.g., content, language, strategies), context, and teacher expertise (language or content); nonetheless, attempts have been made to specify and standardize CBI within particular frameworks. Research related to the applications of such frameworks offers support for CBI.

The SIOP model of sheltered CBI may be the most well-known, widely used, and well-researched CBI framework in the United States (Reynolds, 2015). For many educators, it is emblematic of CBI. The model is intended for use in both mainstream content classes, in which language learners are enrolled, and content classes designed exclusively for language learners in a variety of contexts, including ESL, dual language, and foreign language immersion (Echevarría, Vogt, & Short, 2017). The SIOP Model involves the implementation of 30 instructional features (e.g., specific applications of content and language objectives, frequent opportunities for student interaction, learning-strategy use) (Echevarría, Vogt, & Short, 2017). Under investigation since the late 1990s, research on the efficacy of the SIOP Model usually explores language-minority students learning the language of wider communication. A series of studies, conducted by SIOP Model designers, has found significant improvement in students' writing abilities and oral proficiency when taught by SIOP Model-trained teachers (Short, Echevarría, & Richards-Tutor, 2011) as well as a positive relationship between teachers' fidelity to SIOP Model implementation and student performance on content and academic-language assessments (Echevarría, Richards-Tutor, Chinn, & Ratleff, 2011).

CLIL is a CBI framework that originated in Europe in the mid-1990s; CLIL programs teach content through a foreign or additional language, often English (Lyster & Ballinger, 2011;

Wolff, 2009). Some scholars work from the premise that CLIL itself is synonymous with CBI (Cenoz, 2015a) and/or immersion (Genesee & Lindholm-Leary, 2013). One particular CLIL conceptualization (Mehisto, Frigols, & Marsh, 2008) looks much like the SIOP Model organizationally in that it presents 30 instructional features—including support for language learning in content classes, extensive student-student interaction (rather than student-teacher interaction), and the fostering of creative and critical thinking—that are grouped into six overarching categories (i.e., active learning, scaffolding, cooperation, authenticity, multiple focus, and safe and enriching learning environment). Navés (2009) has identified "substantially greater and better exposure to the target language" (p. 36) as the one feature that all efficient CLIL programs share. With regard to research support for CLIL, Coyle, Hood, and Marsh (2010) note that most performance studies of CLIL students to date have focused on language outcomes (rather than content-learning outcomes); they report clear language benefits for CLIL students (see also Dalton-Puffer, 2011; Nikula, Dalton-Puffer, & Llinares, 2013; Ruiz de Zarobe & Jiménez Catalán, 2009). Dalton-Puffer (2007), in her descriptive study of language use in Austrian secondary school CLIL classrooms using English as the medium of instruction, found that lexical items were the subject of most errors, yet the area in which teachers identified the most linguistic growth. Wolff (2009) reports that CLIL students learn content to the same extent as students who study content in their L1s. (See also Dalton-Puffer, this volume.)

Two additional content-based frameworks place great importance on strategies instruction: the Cognitive Academic Language Learning Approach (CALLA) and CORI. CALLA emerged in the late 1980s and is a sheltered CBI framework that makes a commitment to language, content, and strategies instruction (Chamot, 2009). Non-experimental research on CALLA has shown that students receiving CALLA instruction tended to make gains on content achievement measures (Chamot, 2007). The CORI framework, while structured around specific content domains and student-generated research questions, promotes reading across multiple texts, strategy instruction, and project work for content and language development (especially reading comprehension improvement) and motivation. While the extensive research on CORI focuses mainly on L1 Grade 3–9 readers, it can be supported by much of the same academic theory that supports CBI frameworks for L2 learners (Grabe, 2009). A meta-analysis of 11 empirical CORI studies (focused on students in Grades 3–5) found positive outcomes for (a) reading comprehension on standardized tests and (b) the use of reading strategies among students receiving CORI. In addition, a significant outcome was found for students' content knowledge acquisition (Guthrie, McRae, & Klauda, 2007). Outcomes from CALLA and CORI suggest that such approaches facilitate content learning and the development of specific language and literacy learning strategies.

Support from Reported CBI Program Outcomes |||

Additional support for CBI follows from outcomes of disparate programs that demonstrate successes with combined language and content instruction. Although there have been few controlled empirical studies demonstrating the effectiveness of CBI programs, outcomes in terms of SLA and content mastery have been reported in K–12 and post-secondary classrooms in second and foreign language (FL) contexts.

There is a well-documented tradition of scholarship on K–12 CBI programs across L2 contexts and populations. In a review of findings for French L2 learners in Canadian immersion programs, Genesee and Lindholm-Leary (2013) report that, generally, immersion students perform at the same level as do students receiving L1 instruction on measures of content mastery, including higher-level content such as advanced mathematics. They also report that immersion students outperform students in traditional French instruction on measures of all language skills. Lindholm-Leary and Genesee (2014) note that while the amount of exposure to the L2 accounts for some L2 proficiency gains, other pedagogical factors inherent in strong content-based approaches (e.g., student-centered instruction) also contribute to proficiency gains. Furthermore, they report that decades of research on two-way immersion programs[7] show that language-minority students outperform mainstream peers in L2 acquisition and content achievement. Finally, Lindholm-Leary and Borsato's (2006) synthesis of studies examining K–12 content instruction in L2 contexts reveals that particular features of CBI enhance content-learning outcomes; these features include positive meaning-focused interactions between students and teachers, collaborative group work, and the use of a wide variety of materials and texts.

Research conducted in immersion contexts continues to dominate CBI outcome studies in K–12 settings in FL contexts. In an analysis of EFL immersion in Hungary between 1989 and 1993, Duff (1997) reported English language proficiency at "near-ceiling" levels on standardized measures after one to two years and "considerably" higher than average acceptance rates into post-secondary schools based on content-assessment performance (pp. 34–36). In Hong Kong, Tsang (2008) compared secondary students in Chinese-medium courses with students in English immersion courses with respect to achievement scores on a series of university gatekeeping exams measuring both language and content. He concluded that English immersion students were much more likely to gain entry into the University of Hong Kong. In another Hong Kong study, Kong (2014) focused on a late-immersion history class taught in English; she found that (a) collaboration between a content teacher and language expert and (b) the implementation of writing tasks designed to integrate language and content learning resulted in improved history essay writing, with students writing more on their own, rather than copying from their textbooks (as is common practice). Finally, more broadly, Cenoz (2015b) reports that 70 percent of Hong Kong secondary students receive at least one course of CBI and that Hong Kong's 2012 scores on the Program for International Student Assessment (PISA) test for math, reading, and science were among the top five in the world.

In post-secondary L2 settings, CBI outcomes are generally reported at the class rather than program level. Over a five-year period, Song (2006) compared community college ESL students who enrolled in a set of content-linked courses during their first semester with matched students who did not. He found that the students who had enrolled in the content-linked classes received significantly higher grades in their ESL courses. In addition, significantly more content-linked students passed their English proficiency tests. An examination of the long-term effects and outcomes of the content-linked experience revealed that the content-linked group had higher grade point averages, higher retention rates, and higher graduation rates than students who did not begin their tertiary studies with content-linked classes. James (2006) examined the transferability of outcomes from a theme-based, engineering content-based course in a Canadian university. Using a case-study design, James found evidence of learning transfer—in terms of listening and reading comprehension skills, speaking, writing, study skills, and affect—from a content-based course to subsequent university coursework. These findings, though less robust than those at the K–12 level, suggest positive generalized academic outcomes for L2 CBI instruction at the post-secondary level.

In post-secondary CBI in FL contexts, CBI plays an arguably more important role than in L2 contexts, by greatly increasing students' meaningful exposure to the FL; however, little empirical data supporting the efficacy of CBI in post-secondary FL settings exist. Nonetheless, the Modern Language Association has strongly advocated the integration of content-based cultural coursework throughout post-secondary FL curricula (especially in the U.S.) (Byrnes, 2008). Yueming (2008) describes a content-based Chinese curriculum at Carnegie Mellon University in the U.S. She notes that course foci across four years bridge both language and content aims, which include "comprehensive ability in the Chinese language" and "awareness and understanding of Chinese culture and tradition" (p. 303). In Howard (2006), a rationale for and descriptions of CBI curricula for multiple languages at the Monterey Institute of International Studies (now Middlebury Institute of International Studies at Monterey) are presented. Howard notes that students' need for high levels of professional FL proficiency and faculty buy-in support the "Monterey Model." Howard reports that program outcomes reveal improvements in students' rate of language and content acquisition. In an exemplary study within a post-secondary FL context, Lin and Chen (2006) examined the effects of different graphic organizers on the content comprehension of 86 EFL learners in Taiwan; they found that the integration of advanced organizers, combined with the use of questions, significantly increased students' comprehension scores on three content measures.

Research Agenda ||

The research reported in this chapter provides support for different forms of CBI in a range of instructional settings. Nonetheless, additional quantitative and qualitative investigations of CBI are needed to expand our understanding of the benefits and nuances of integrating language- and content-learning aims in terms of both program outcomes and classroom practices. Gaining further insights into the extent to which CBI frameworks lead to improved content and language learning, language-skill mastery, strategy use, motivation, and autonomy could be helpful. Table 2.1 includes a sampling of research questions that could guide such inquiries.

Beyond the research areas noted in Table 2.1, the state of current research begs more evidence documenting what transpires in successful CBI classrooms. In particular, practices in classrooms effectively using CBI should be documented. Persuasive case studies—with detailed descriptions of feedback type, use of L1 or translanguaging (see D. Reynolds, this volume), collaboration across disciplines, and policy support (at school, district, state, and

Table 2.1: CBI Areas Meriting Further Investigation and Possible Research Questions

Areas Meriting Further Research	Possible Research Questions
Vocabulary and language structures	1. Do students make larger gains in vocabulary knowledge in CBI courses than in comparable non-CBI contexts? 2. Do students gain better control of language-structure use in CBI courses than in comparable non-CBI contexts? 3. Do students enrolled in CBI courses approach challenging language-learning tasks with greater awareness of vocabulary and language structures than students in comparable non-CBI contexts? 4. Do students in CBI courses gain better mastery of content information than in comparable non-CBI language learning contexts?
Intrinsic and extrinsic motivation, interest, and persistence	5. How can we measure gains in motivation, interest, and attributions for success in CBI contexts? 6. Do students in CBI courses show increased motivation for learning over students in non-CBI contexts? 7. Do students in CBI contexts show greater interest in learning than students in comparable non-CBI contexts?
Strategic-learner training	8. How well can language- and content-learning strategies be taught and learned in a CBI context and then transferred to new instructional settings? 9. Do students in CBI contexts demonstrate greater strategic awareness when addressing challenging language-learning tasks than students in more traditional classrooms?
Combinations and sequences of content and language-learning aims	10. What combinations of content and language emphases maximize language learning? 11. How can CBI learning activities/tasks be most effectively sequenced to maximize language learning? How does this "most effective sequence" change depending on content, student proficiency, learning goals, and specific task mastery?
Content-based materials	12. How do CBI teachers successfully adapt and supplement materials written for native speakers to promote content and language learning? 13. How can standard ESL/EFL course books be adapted to promote the aims of CBI classrooms?
Assessing CBI learning outcomes	14. How do teachers balance assessment of content learning and language learning most effectively in different instructional contexts? 15. What are the most effective ways to assess language-learning gains in CBI contexts? 16. How can CBI courses assess the development of more strategic awareness with challenging tasks?

other governmental levels) that facilitates student language and content development—would also be welcome. Though studies presenting rich descriptions of some of these practices are emerging (e.g., Alford & Windeyer, 2014; Milla & Mayo, 2014; Tavares, 2015), the efficacy of practices described in relation to language and content development deserves further attention.

The research emphases introduced here represent just some of the areas related to CBI meriting further research. The hope is that results from future research, in these areas and others, will add to the current research literature, which provides considerable evidence that argues forcefully for the effectiveness of integrated language and content learning.

APPLYING WHAT YOU LEARNED
Questions and Tasks

1. This chapter has presented numerous forms of support for integrating content and language in instruction. Which make the most sense to you? Identify the five forms of support that you find the most compelling. Then, share your list with a partner; listen to your partner's list; and, together, determine the eight best reasons for offering content and language integrated instruction.

2. Observe a content-based class or examine a textbook designed to support content-based instruction. Spend a few minutes recording what you observe. After reflection, which research reported in this chapter best aligns with what you noticed students and/or teachers doing? Explain.

3. Imagine that you have been asked to design an action-research project focused on CBI, either at your school or in a neighboring school. What area(s) explored in this chapter might you focus on? What might your research questions be? Action research is a form of teacher-initiated inquiry that involves teachers looking critically and systematically at their own classrooms (or the classrooms of others) for the purposes of improving their own teaching and enhancing the quality of learning that takes place there. The cyclical action-research process typically involves establishing a purpose and topic, posing a guiding research question, gathering relevant data, analyzing the data, generating practical solutions (to enhance classroom teaching and learning), and then experimenting with the solutions. (Refer to Burns, 2010; Grabe & Stoller, 2011; and Richards & Farrell, 2015, for more on action research and typical action-research cycles.)

ENDNOTES

1. In this chapter, the term *second language* (L2) is used to refer to second, foreign, and additional languages. When a distinction among the three needs to be made, the terms *second, foreign,* or *additional language* are used.
2. *Instrumental motivation* is associated with language learning for practical purposes (e.g., earning a good grade, obtaining employment); *integrative motivation* is associated with language learning driven by the goal of developing relationships with speakers of the target language and/or integrating oneself into the target-language community; *intrinsic motivation* refers to the enjoyment of language learning itself; and *motivational strength* refers to the amount of effort a learner might expend learning a language (Gardner, 1985).
3. *Form-focused instruction* (*FFI*) entails instruction that draws learners' attention to linguistic features—or forms—of their new language (Ellis, 2008).
4. *Meta-talk* refers to the language used to talk about language.
5. *Form-meaning mapping* refers to the association of a particular form with a particular meaning (Spada & Lightbown, 2008).
6. CALP and BICS refer to the language and skills needed for academic achievement and interpersonal oral communication, respectively.
7. Two-way immersion programs enroll students from two language groups who study the regular school curriculum in both languages (English and Spanish, for example).

REFERENCES

Alford, J., & Windeyer, A. (2014). Responding to national curriculum goals for English language learners: Enhancing reading strategies in junior high school content areas. *Journal of Immersion and Content-Based Language Education, 2*(1), 74–95.

Anderson, J. R. (2010). *Cognitive psychology and its implications* (7th ed.). New York, NY: Worth.

Biber, D. (2006). *University language: A corpus study of spoken and written registers.* Amsterdam, The Netherlands: Benjamins.

Brantmeir, C., Callender, A., & McDaniel, M. (2011). The effects of embedded and elaborative interrogation questions on L2 reading comprehension. *Reading in a Foreign Language, 23*(2), 187–207.

Burns, A. (2010). *Doing action research in English language teaching: A guide for practitioners.* New York, NY: Routledge.

Byrnes, H. (2008). Perspectives. *Modern Language Journal, 92,* 284–292.

Cenoz, J. (2015a). Content-based instruction and content and language integrated learning: The same or different? *Language, Culture and Curriculum, 28*(1), 8–24.

Cenoz, J. (2015b). Discussion: Some reflections on content-based education in Hong Kong as part of the paradigm shift. *International Journal of Bilingual Education and Bilingualism, 18*(3), 345–351.

Chamot, A. U. (2007). Accelerating academic achievement of English language learners: A synthesis of five evaluations of the CALLA Model. In J. Cummins & C. Davison (Eds.), *International handbook of English language teaching* (Part 1, pp. 317–331). New York, NY: Springer.

Chamot, A. U. (2009). *The CALLA handbook: Implementing the Cognitive Academic Language Learning Approach* (2nd ed.). New York, NY: Pearson.

Coyle, D., Hood, P., & Marsh, D. (2010). *CLIL: Content and language integrated learning.* Cambridge, England: Cambridge University Press.

Csikszentmihalyi, M. J. (2014). *Flow and the foundations of positive psychology: The collected works of Mihaly Csikszentmihalyi.* New York, NY: Springer.

Cummins, J. (1984). *Bilingualism and special education: Issues in assessment and pedagogy.* Clevedon, England: Multilingual Matters.

Cummins, J. (2000). *Language, power and pedagogy: Bilingual children in the crossfire.* Clevedon, England: Multilingual Matters.

Dalton-Puffer, C. (2007). *Discourse in content and language integrated learning (CLIL) classrooms.* Amsterdam, The Netherlands: Benjamins.

Dalton-Puffer, C. (2011). Content-and-language integrated learning: From practice to principles. *Annual Review of Applied Linguistics, 31*, 182–204.

Doiz, A., Lasagabaster, D., & Sierra, J. M. (2014). CLIL and motivation: The effect of individual and contextual variables. *The Language Learning Journal, 42*(2), 209–224.

Donato, R. (2016). Sociocultural theory and content-based foreign language instruction: Theoretical insights on the challenge of integration. In L. Cammarata (Ed.), Content-based foreign language teaching: Curriculum and pedagogy for developing advanced thinking and literacy skills (pp. 25–50). New York, NY: Routledge.

Dörnyei, Z. (2005). *The psychology of the language learner: Individual differences in second language acquisition.* Mahwah, NJ: Erlbaum.

Dörnyei, Z., MacIntyre, P. D., & Henry, A. (2015). *Motivational dynamics in language learning.* Bristol, England: Multilingual Matters.

Dörnyei, Z., & Ushioda, E. (2011). *Teaching and researching motivation* (2nd ed.). New York, NY: Routledge.

Duff, P. (1997). Immersion in Hungary: An EFL experiment. In R. K. Johnson & M. Swain (Eds.), *Immersion education: International perspectives* (pp. 19–43). Cambridge, England: Cambridge University Press.

Echevarría, J., Richards-Tutor, C., Chinn, V., & Ratleff, P. (2011). Did they get it? The role of fidelity in teaching English learners. *Journal of Adolescent and Adult Literacy, 54*(6), 425–434.

Echevarría, J., Vogt, M. E., & Short, D. J. (2017). *Making content comprehensible for English learners: The SIOP Model* (5th ed.). Boston, MA: Pearson.

Efklides, A. (2011). Interactions of metacognition with motivation and affect in self-regulated learning: The MASRL model. *Educational Psychologist, 46*(1), 6–25.

Ellis, R. (2008). *The study of second language acquisition* (2nd ed.). Oxford, England: Oxford University Press.

Ericsson, K. A., & Ward, P. (2007). Capturing the naturally occurring superior performance of experts in the laboratory. *Current Directions in Psychological Science, 6*(16), 346–350.

Eysenck, M. W., & Keane, M. T. (2010). *Cognitive psychology: A student's handbook* (6th ed.). New York, NY: Psychology Press.

Gardner, D. (2004). Vocabulary input through extensive reading: A comparison of words found in children's narrative and expository reading materials. *Applied Linguistics, 25*(1), 1–37.

Gardner, R. C. (1985). Social psychology and second language learning: The role of attitudes and motivation. London, England: Arnold.

Gardner, R. C., Tremblay, P. F., & Masgoret, A. (1997). Towards a full model of second language learning: An empirical investigation. *Modern Language Journal, 81*(3), 344–362.

Genesee, F., & Lindholm-Leary, K. (2013). Two case-studies on content-based language education. *Journal of Immersion and Content-Based Language Education, 1*(1), 3–33.

Grabe, W. (2009). *Reading in a second language: Moving from theory to practice.* Cambridge, England: Cambridge University Press.

Grabe, W., & Stoller, F. L. (1997). Content-based instruction: Research foundations. In M. A. Snow & D. M. Brinton (Eds.), *The content-based classroom: Perspectives on integrating language and content* (pp. 5–21). White Plains, NY: Longman.

Grabe, W., & Stoller, F. L. (2011). *Teaching and researching reading* (2nd ed.). New York, NY: Routledge.

Guthrie, J. T., McRae, A., & Klauda, S. L. (2007). Contributions of Concept-Oriented Reading Instruction to knowledge for interventions about motivation for reading. *Educational Psychologist, 42*(4), 237–250.

Howard, J. (2006). Models of integrating content and language learning. *Journal of the National Council of Less Commonly Taught Languages, 3*, 61–85.

James, M. A. (2006). Transfer of learning from a university content-based EAP course. *TESOL Quarterly, 40*(4), 783–806.

Komiyama, R. (2013). Factors underlying second language reading motivation of adult EAP students. *Reading in a Foreign Language, 25*(2), 149–169.

Kong, S. (2014). Collaboration between content and language specialists in late immersion. *Canadian Modern Language Review, 70*(1), 103–122.

Lantolf, J. P., & Poehner, M. E. (2008). *Sociocultural theory and the teaching of second languages*. London, England: Equinox.

Lightbown, P. (2014). *Focus on content-based language teaching*. Oxford, England: Oxford University Press.

Lin, H., & Chen, T. (2006). Decreasing cognitive load for novice EFL learners: Effects of question and descriptive advance organizers in facilitating EFL learners' comprehension of an animation-based content lesson. *System, 34*, 416–431.

Lindholm-Leary, K., & Borsato, G. (2006). Academic achievement. In F. Genesee, K. Lindholm-Leary, W. M. Saunders, & D. Christian (Eds.), *Educating English language learners: A synthesis of research evidence* (pp. 176–222). New York, NY: Cambridge University Press.

Lindholm-Leary, K., & Genesee, F. (2014). Student outcomes in one-way, two-way, and indigenous language immersion education. *Journal of Immersion and Content-Based Language Education, 2*(2), 165–180.

Long, M. (1996). The role of the linguistic environment in second language acquisition. In W. C. Ritchie & T. K. Bhatia (Eds.), *Handbook of second language acquisition* (pp. 413–468). New York, NY: Academic Press.

Lyster, R. (2007). *Learning and teaching languages through content: A counterbalanced approach*. Amsterdam, The Netherlands: Benjamins.

Lyster, R., & Ballinger, S. (2011). Content-based language teaching: Convergent concerns across divergent contexts. *Language Teaching Research, 15*(3), 279–288.

Mehisto, P., Frigols, M. J., & Marsh, D. (2008). *Uncovering CLIL: Content and language integrated learning in bilingual and multilingual education*. Oxford, England: Macmillan Education.

Milla, R., & Mayo, M. P. G. (2014). Corrective feedback episodes in oral interaction: A comparison of a CLIL and an EFL classroom. *International Journal of English Studies, 14*(1), 1–20.

Nagy, W., & Townsend, D. (2012). Words as tools: Learning academic vocabulary as language acquisition. *Reading Research Quarterly, 47*(1), 91–108.

Navés, T. (2009). Effective content and language integrated learning (CLIL) programmes. In Y. Ruiz de Zarobe & R. M. Jiménez Catalán (Eds.), *Content and language integrated learning: Evidence from research in Europe* (pp. 22–40). Bristol, England: Multilingual Matters.

Nguyen, H. T., & Kellogg, G. (2010). "I had a stereotype that American were fat": Becoming a speaker of a culture in a second language. *Modern Language Journal, 94*, 56–73.

Nikula, T., Dalton-Puffer, C., & Llinares, A. (2013). CLIL classroom discourse: Research from Europe. *Journal of Immersion and Content-Based Language Education, 1*, 70–100.

Reynolds, K. M. (2015). *Approaches to inclusive English classrooms: A teacher's handbook for content-based instruction*. Bristol, England: Multilingual Matters.

Richards, J. C., & Farrell, T. S. C. (2005). *Professional development for language teachers: Strategies for teacher learning.* New York, NY: Cambridge University Press.

Ruiz de Zarobe, Y., & Jiménez Catalán, R. M. (Eds.). (2009). *Content and language integrated learning: Evidence from research in Europe.* Bristol, England: Multilingual Matters.

Schleppegrell, M. J. (2008). Grammar, the sentence, and traditions of linguistic analysis. In C. Bazerman (Ed.), *Handbook of research on writing: History, society, school, individual, and text* (pp. 673–692). Mahwah, NJ: Erlbaum.

Short, D. J., Echevarría, J., & Richards-Tutor, C. (2011). Research on academic literacy development in sheltered instruction classrooms. *Language Teaching Research, 15*(3), 363–380.

Snow, M. A. (2014). Content-based and immersion models of second/foreign language teaching. In M. Celce-Murcia, D. M. Brinton, & M. A. Snow (Eds.), *Teaching English as a second or foreign language* (4th ed., pp. 438–454). Boston, MA: National Geographic Learning/Heinle Cengage Learning.

Song, B. (2006). Content-based instruction: Long-term effects and outcomes. *English for Specific Purposes, 25,* 420–437.

Spada, N., & Lightbown, P. (2008). Form-focused instruction: Isolated or integrated? *TESOL Quarterly, 42*(2), 181–207.

Stoller, F. L., & Fitzsimmons-Doolan, S. (2017). Content-based instruction. In N. Van Deusen-Scholl & S. May (Eds.), *Encyclopedia of language and education: Second and foreign language education* (Vol. 4, 3rd ed., pp. 71–84). Berlin, Germany: Springer.

Swain, M. (1995). Three functions of output in second language learning. In G. Cook & B. Seidlhofer (Eds.), *Principle and practice in applied linguistics: Studies in honour of H. G. Widdowson* (pp. 125–144). Oxford, England: Oxford University Press.

Swain, M., & Lapkin, S. (2013). A Vygotskian sociocultural perspective on immersion education: The L1/L2 debate. *Journal of Immersion and Content-Based Language Education, 1*(1), 101–129.

Tavares, N. J. (2015). How strategic use of L1 in an L2-medium mathematics classroom facilitates L2 interaction and comprehension. *International Journal of Bilingual Education and Bilingualism, 18*(3), 319–335.

Tsang, W. K. (2008, May). Evaluation research on the implementation of the medium of instruction guidance for secondary schools. *Hong Kong Institute for Educational Research Newsletter 24,* 1–7. Retrieved from http://www.fed.cuhk.edu.hk/~hkier/content/document/publications/newsletter/newsletter24.pdf

VanPatten, B. (2004). Input processing in SLA. In B. VanPatten (Ed.), *Processing instruction: Theory, research, and commentary* (pp. 5–31). Mahwah, NJ: Erlbaum.

Walqui, A. (2006). Scaffolding instruction for English language learners: A conceptual framework. *The International Journal of Bilingual Education and Bilingualism, 9*(2), 159–180.

Walqui, A., & van Lier, L. (2010). *Scaffolding the academic success of adolescent English language learners: A pedagogy of promise.* San Francisco, CA: WestEd.

Wolff, D. (2009). Content and language integrated learning. In K. Knapp & B. Seidlhofer (Eds.), *Handbook of foreign language communication and learning* (pp. 545–572). Berlin, Germany: Mouton de Gruyter.

Wu, M. H., & Chang, T. M. (2010). Heritage language learning and teaching through a macro-approach. *Working Papers in Educational Linguistics, 25*(2), 23–33.

Yueming, Y. (2008). Restructuring foreign language curricula to meet the new challenge. *Modern Language Journal, 92,* 301–303.

Zimmerman, B. J. (2008). Investigating self-regulation and motivation: Historical background, methodological developments, and future prospects. *American Educational Research Journal, 45*(1), 166–183.

Part II

Program, Curriculum, and Lesson Design in Content-Based Instruction

Chapter **3**

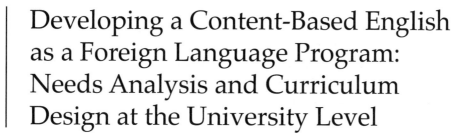

Developing a Content-Based English
as a Foreign Language Program:
Needs Analysis and Curriculum
Design at the University Level

Tetsuo Harada

||| A Glimpse into the Content-Based Classroom

About 600 undergraduate students (150 each year) are enrolled in the School of Education's Department of English Language and Literature at Waseda University. Waseda is a private, competitive university in Japan. One-third of the students are in the Teaching Certificate program with a future career as teachers in mind, while the remaining 70 percent (despite being in the School of Education) are not enrolled in the Certificate program and plan to work in major businesses. The existing departmental curriculum for this student population is composed of upper-division content courses in English and American literature, linguistics, and English language teaching, almost all taught in Japanese. The only exception to this are the five lower-division required general English courses taught mostly in English.

Among the faculty teaching in this program, there has for some time now been general dissatisfaction with this curriculum, particularly regarding their B.A. recipients' ability to function in English, both in the classroom and the workplace. Reinforcing this notion, a student questionnaire was administered, revealing that many of the students were not fully satisfied with their English ability. One of the more serious problems is that many students cannot reach a professional or even functional level of English for both general and academic purposes because of their limited use of English inside and outside of class. On the other hand, the societal expectation in Japan is that undergraduate students will have a professional command of English upon completion of their B.A. degree. Finally, the Japanese government now requires secondary school teachers to teach English courses using the medium of English—a fact particularly relevant to the Department's future teacher population, most of whom do not feel comfortable using English in their classes.

Due to the spread of English caused by globalization and related societal demands, the Department's faculty members determined that the curriculum should be revised to reflect the need for increased English language proficiency. As Department Head at the time of these discussions, I proposed that to address these problems and meet societal needs, the Department undertake a major revision of the curriculum, adopting the concept of CBI. Accordingly, a curriculum working group was convened to conduct a thorough needs analysis and to propose major revisions to the curriculum. In essence, the plan involved transitioning to EMI for the upper-division content courses and preparing students for these courses at the lower-division level via content-based "bridge" courses in EAP.

CBI in an EFL Setting |||

CBI is an umbrella term for a curricular approach for both majority- and minority-language students, ranging from theme-based, sheltered, and adjunct models to bilingual education including immersion programs (e.g., Lightbown, 2014; Snow, 2014). Widely adopted in North America, CBI is often referred to as content and language integrated learning (CLIL), mainly in Europe and some other areas of the world. The two terms are often used interchangeably, implying that they are in essence the same thing.[1] For the purposes of this chapter, I will equate the two, and use the more general term of CBI, assuming that the central tenet of both CBI and CLIL is that language and content are integrated.

Before discussing the key concepts of needs analysis and curriculum development, it is relevant to first briefly discuss how CBI has been introduced in elementary, secondary, and higher education in Japan. In the 1990s, CBI started as a form of immersion education at a private elementary school in Shizuoka (Bostwick, 2001); subsequently, several private elementary schools developed the immersion model into a secondary education program leading to the Middle Years Program and/or the Diploma Program accredited by the International Baccalaureate® (IB).[2] These IB programs have helped set some clear goals (e.g., career goals, general education goals, as well as language learning goals) for both teachers and students, and have led the schools' English immersion programs to success. In addition to the immersion programs, in 2011 Japan's Ministry of Education, Culture, Sports, Science and Technology (MEXT) introduced English in the elementary curriculum, requiring that fifth and sixth graders in public school be exposed once a week to English through activities such as games and songs; it also recommended that English activities be related to what children have learned in other subjects (e.g., Japanese language, music, and arts and handicrafts) (MEXT, 2010). In accordance with this recommendation and encouraged by the CLIL movement in Europe (e.g., Coyle, Hood, & Marsh, 2010), a limited number of both elementary and secondary schools (e.g., Tokyo Gakugei University International Secondary School) have begun developing content and language integrated curricula leading to the IB Diploma Program.[3]

In higher education, though several Christian universities (e.g., International Christian University) have a long history of EMI,[4] it was not until recently that both public and private universities have started to offer EMI undergraduate programs in different fields.

These programs target international students as well as domestic students who are highly motivated to learn English and want to prepare for their future careers in today's globalized world. Akita International University,[5] a public university in Japan, has two undergraduate programs (Global Business and Global Studies) in which almost all courses are taught entirely in English (Taguchi, 2014). When students are admitted as freshmen, they are required to take the TOEFL®[6] to place them into the appropriate level of EAP courses. After completion of the courses, they take basic education courses and go on to study in their major field. Further, all students must study abroad for a year. Similar programs are also available in private universities (e.g., The School of International Liberal Studies, Waseda University).[7] This current trend in primary, secondary, and higher education in Japan shows that despite the limited number of schools, the concept of CBI and EMI is quite widespread.

The rationale behind this trend is grounded in terms of second language acquisition (SLA) theories (e.g., Lightbown, 2014; Lyster, 2011; Snow, 2014; see also Fitzsimmons-Doolan, Grabe, & Stoller, this volume). A common problem in EFL settings is that students lack both the appropriate, meaningful contexts and adequate motivation to use English. They are also not motivated by the goals of using English in the global world of the future. What does appear to work is to provide students with relevant academic content requiring them to use English in a meaningful context and to provide them with a sufficient amount of comprehensible input (Krashen, 1982; Lyster, 2011), pushed output (Swain, 1985, 1993, 2005),[8] and opportunities for interaction (Gass, 1997; Long, 1983, 1996; Pica, 1994). By adopting CBI and EMI in EFL settings, we can maximize the amount of input that students receive through listening to lectures and reading assignments, have them negotiate for meaning in pair/group interactions about subject matter, and provide them with more opportunities for pushed output via cognitively demanding tasks. More recently, Swain (2000) draws on sociocultural theory, emphasizing collaborative dialogues in which "language use and language learning can co-occur" (p. 97) and in which language use mediates language learning, thus combining cognitive and social activity. CBI is an ideal option for both language use and language learning because the CBI classroom easily promotes collaborative work, both in the cognitive and social domains.

The other rationale behind adopting the integration of content and language concerns the learners' mindset. In today's technological age, young people are exposed to mobile phones, text messaging, social networking, the internet, and games at an early age; therefore, they are likely to "learn as you use, use as you learn," as opposed to the older generation's view of "learn now for use later" (Coyle, Hood, & Marsh, 2010, p. 10). As an example of this trend, we need look no further than any technological device available on the market today. Rarely do we see a detailed user's manual accompanying a smart phone, for example; instead, we are expected to learn the new phone's many functions while attempting to use it. Young people with this mindset will undoubtedly find a content-based curriculum very beneficial for learning a foreign language. Their mindset is also related to the concept of transfer appropriate processing (Roediger & Guynn, 1996), that is, the notion that people can more easily use what they have learned in psychologically authentic conditions than what they have done otherwise. This requires that learning be done in conditions similar to those of actual use, and this need can be accommodated by CBI, where students are exposed to actual language use while learning the content under conditions where both learning and use are aligned (Larsen-Freeman, 2014; Lightbown, 2014).

Next, we will look at several key issues in designing a CBI curriculum in an EFL setting.

Issues in CBI Curriculum Design |||

Curriculum planning is the very foundation of every educational activity. The curriculum provides teachers, students, administrative personnel, and other stakeholders an overview of what the program is like—that is, how teachers plan and conduct their classes, and how they assess their students' outcomes. In second/foreign language teaching, Christison and Murray (2014) provide three main stages of curriculum design: (1) understanding the context, (2) developing curriculum relevant to the context, and (3) evaluating the curriculum. Graves (2014) provides a slightly more detailed scenario in which curriculum design is seen as consisting of six stages: (1) guiding principles, (2) contextual factors, (3) learner needs, (4) program goals, (5) program content, and (6) assessment. In fact, these two analyses of the curriculum design process share much in common. Graves' Stages 1–3 can be seen as roughly equivalent to Christison and Murray's Stage 1 while Graves' Stages 4–5 can be equated to their Stage 2. Finally, Graves' Stage 6 equates to Christison and Murray's Stage 3.

To elaborate on Graves' analysis, guiding principles refer to how curriculum developers view language, language learning, learners, teachers, and content. This process comprises different views of language and/or teachers/learners—for example, whether or not the curriculum planners believe that language is rule based, whether they see teachers serving as facilitators, whether they believe that learners are receptive vessels, etc. Obviously, all of these factors can greatly impact the content of the curriculum. Therefore, the first stage of curriculum development involves the stakeholders putting everything relevant to learning and teaching on the table, sharing their beliefs and experiences with each other, and hopefully reaching a certain level of consensus on the direction of the new curriculum. In the scenario at the outset of this chapter, we see the faculty of the Department of English Language and Literature considering research in the field along with societal demands for English language proficiency, discussing problems in their current curriculum, and determining how content and language could be integrated to better meet the needs of their students.

Graves' second stage is contextual analysis, during which the social, economic, political, and institutional factors that affect the curriculum are analyzed (see also Richards, 2001). The opening scenario of this chapter shows working group members considering how both the societal pressure for higher education in Japan to train students to reach a professional or functional level of English and the government's proposal that English teachers in secondary school teach English only through English might impact their curriculum planning.

Third, learner needs analysis focuses on the learners. This phase of the process identifies what is not working well for learners in the current curriculum, which goals of English and content learning they have in mind, what their current levels of English are, and/or whether they are adequately motivated to enroll in content courses in English. In general, the most common way to analyze student needs is to give them a questionnaire and/or to conduct an extensive needs analysis through focus-group interviews about the current and future curriculum. In addition, as motivation plays a crucial role in successful language learning, the questionnaire should include items relevant to students' motivation—for example, the degree to which their motivation is integrative, and what their orientations and attitudes toward L2 learning are.

Fourth, both the contextual and needs analyses will help determine the program goals for the curriculum, including the type of knowledge and skills students are expected to acquire; guidelines for teachers, learners, and materials writers; and the specific focus of instruction (Richards, 2001). For instance, the working group members found that due to the lack of English input, the current curriculum did not provide adequate opportunities for students to improve their English skills. Thus, the working group reached a consensus that it should design two preparatory content-based courses on English language and literature, which would help to bridge the gap between students' limited English skills and the skills required for their upper-division EMI courses. The program goals are twofold: (1) to determine the English language skills students need to attain and (2) to delineate the content courses students are required to take for completion of their degree. The former goal clearly defines what students are expected to do in both general and academic English, specifying the typical tasks in four skills instruction (phrased as "can-do" statements) whereas the latter goal identifies the special knowledge and skills required in the field of English and American literature, English Linguistics, or English language teaching.

Stage 5 (Graves, 2014) concerns deciding upon and organizing program content, including what should be taught, how the content should be divided into courses, and how the courses will be leveled and sequenced. For example, in our curriculum for English majors, we have divided the four-year program into these six modules:

1. required English foundation courses for both general and academic purposes including Tutorial English (i.e., oral skills course) and Academic Writing (Year 1)

2. two CBI bridge courses, one in Literature and Culture and the other in Language and Communication, in which students are exposed to the academic skills required to succeed in the elective EMI content courses they must take in their junior and senior years (Year 1)

3. four required introductory courses on both History of American and English Literature and Linguistics and Applied Linguistics, all of which will be conducted in Japanese (Year 2)

4. elective EMI content courses, many of which are relevant to Applied Linguistics and will be taught in English (Years 3 and 4)

5. short-term study abroad (Years 1–4) and internship programs (Years 3 and 4)

6. additional elective English skills courses (e.g., Current Affairs in English, TOEFL® Preparation) (Years 1–4).

The final element of the curriculum development process entails assessing students' L2 outcomes and evaluating the entire program. The curriculum planning process is cyclic

(Brown, 1995) in that after the assessment and program evaluation, we return to the previous stages to make major or minor changes that further enhance the curriculum. As seen in the scenario, we are planning to administer four different assessments. The one within the program is a university-based English placement exam (i.e., listening, reading, vocabulary, and grammar) at the beginning and end of the first year to measure students' general English development. Further, to objectively measure the development of academic writing, we chose to introduce the Criterion® Online Writing Evaluation tool[9] to assist students with the writing process and to measure the development of their writing skills within our writing courses. Additionally, we opted to measure their speaking ability using the Versant English test.[10] Finally, to obtain an objective assessment of their academic English skills, the TOEFL IPT® test will be administered every year. Multiple measurements of students' skills derive from the necessity of examining each of the four skills in detail for both placement and diagnostic purposes. It is crucial for both teachers and students to monitor students' development of L2 skills. Depending on the results of the tests, students may be placed in a different course level.

Next, we will look at the actual EFL curriculum for the university-level CBI and EMI content courses designed for students in the Department of English Language and Literature. The whole program is summarized in Figure 3.1.

The School of Education at Waseda University consists of seven departments including the Department of English Language and Literature,[11] which recently initiated the newly designed CBI/EMI program in April 2016. As previously discussed, the major function of the CBI portion of the curriculum is to prepare freshman and sophomore English majors to take the upper-division EMI content courses in TESL and Applied Linguistics.

The School of Education currently has an in-house EFL program designed for all its matriculated students across the curriculum in the school. For the current revision of the curriculum, this in-house program remains as is. It offers about 160 EFL courses, in which no less than 4,800 students are enrolled, with four proficiency levels of English (English for false beginners, elementary, intermediate, and advanced learners).[12] Matriculated students who are English majors are required to take five two-credit courses each (including two advanced courses) in this EFL program and can select their five courses from the Communication, Comprehension and Preparation for TOEIC® courses.

In addition to these EFL core courses, the Department decided to offer the English majors (1) required foundation courses, (2) elective Japanese-medium major courses, and (3) elective EMI major courses. The required foundation courses include: (1) one general English tutorial course, in which students are primarily expected to develop their oral skills in a small group format (maximum five students enrolled); (2) two content-based bridge courses, in which such academic skills as lecture listening and note-taking will be taught; (3) two communicative writing courses; and (4) two academic writing courses. The primary goal of the content-based bridge courses is to give students as much scaffolding as possible in both in-class and out-of-class content-based activities. The class size is limited to 15 students so as to ensure interactions with the instructor and among students. All these courses are offered in English only. In addition, students are required to take two courses on the history of British literature, two on the history of American literature, and two introductory courses (on

Figure 3.1: Components of the Curriculum for English for General Purposes (EGP), English for Academic Purposes (EAP), and English-Medium Instruction (EMI)

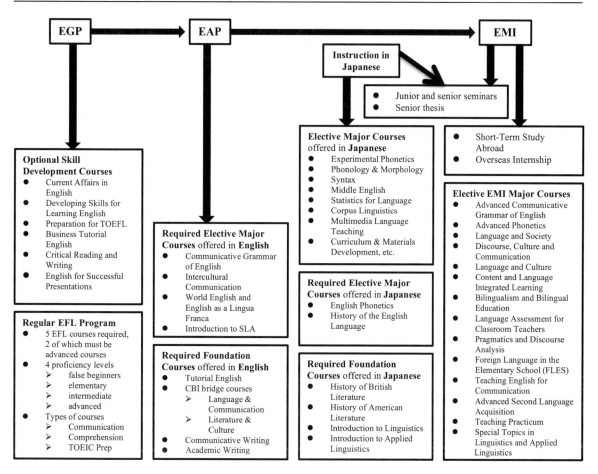

Note: Generally, the courses in the lower box should be taken earlier than the ones in the upper box.

linguistics and applied linguistics, respectively). All of these courses are offered in Japanese since developing academic literacy in the students' L1 and understanding the selected area thoroughly in the L1 is viewed as supporting and accelerating content learning in English.

By the end of the first year, once students have completed the required courses, they will select one of two tracks: (1) Literature and Culture or (2) Linguistics and Applied Linguistics. It is important for students to get familiarized with the genres of a specific discipline and to have a positive attitude toward their specialization. Comparing journal articles on Literature and (Applied) Linguistics, for example, we find different writing styles required. The elective major courses are designed for students to establish a solid foundation for the track they have selected as a major field. Some courses are conducted in Japanese, whereas others are conducted in English. For the purpose of this chapter, we will focus on the second of these two tracks. The elective major courses in the Linguistics and Applied Linguistics track consist of English Phonetics and History of the English Language (which are taught in Japanese) and the Communicative Grammar of English, Intercultural Communication, World Englishes and English as a Lingua Franca, and Introduction to Second Language Acquisition (all of which are offered in English).

Further, the required major courses include two junior and two senior seminars on either linguistics or applied linguistics, which students must select at the end of the second year. In their senior year, they are required to write a 30-page senior thesis in their selected field, which may be written either in English or in Japanese, at the students' discretion.

Finally, the elective EMI major courses are taught by several faculty members in the Department. In these EMI courses, no scaffolding of language is provided since students are expected to be autonomous learners. The requirements of the courses are similar to ones required in an English-speaking country (i.e., lectures, materials, reading assignments, essays, exams, projects). All the faculty members in the Department of English Language and Literature are specialists in their field with considerable experience teaching EFL as well as teaching content; therefore, the Department has unique human resources and ideal circumstances that help support the implementation of CBI and EMI, with some of the faculty members having received their PhD in either linguistics or applied linguistics in an English-speaking country. The elective EMI courses are listed in Figure 3.1.

In addition, for those students who want to further develop their English skills, some optional courses are offered along with a short-term study-abroad program and an overseas internship program so that students can benefit from an overseas, hands-on experience using English. Students in study-abroad programs are reported to demonstrate increased confidence in using English and a more positive attitude toward the target language (e.g., Davidson, 2010). For the overseas internship program, for example, after taking a course on bilingualism and bilingual education, students can participate in a teacher assistantship program in an English-Japanese two-way immersion school in the United States.

Challenges

Designing an innovative CBI and/or EMI curriculum in an EFL setting is a complex venture. As Department Head and as an active member of the working group, I identified three main challenges: human, budgetary, and administrative. The most crucial human constraint involved the need for faculty members to arrive at common beliefs and ideas about the curriculum. Despite faculty members sharing fields of similar expertise (i.e., all being specialists in literature, language, or communication), their teaching philosophies varied greatly and a substantial number of compromise solutions and agreements were necessary for consensus to be reached. For instance, it was proposed that with sufficient training in academic writing during the first two years, we could require students to write a senior thesis on their specialization in English. But some professors held the view that the university is responsible for having students consider and deeply discuss serious academic issues in their native language. Others were afraid that it would be too time-consuming to supervise students with developing English proficiency to write a senior thesis in English. The compromise solution was that each student could opt to write the senior thesis in Japanese or English. Another human constraint was the heavy workload for those faculty members who were most involved in the complex process of curriculum reform, which took almost five years from the start of the initial proposal to final approval from the School of Education. During this entire period of time, certain faculty members, especially the department heads and the working group members, had to spend a great deal of time creating various documents and discussing both major and minor issues relevant to the new curriculum, sometimes late at night at the expense of research and personal time. Other human constraints that are typical in EFL settings include the often complex process of hiring content lecturers who feel comfortable delivering their lectures in English, the challenge of ensuring a comprehensive understanding of CBI and EMI curricular principles by part-time lecturers, and the difficult process of training faculty new to the concept of how to integrate language with content.

Another serious issue concerns budget constraints. In order to offer courses dealing with newly developing areas and topics in the field, we planned to increase the number of part-time instructors, but due to university-wide budget constraints, we had to develop the new curriculum within the budget allocated for the current number of part-time instructors and had to decide to offer some content courses every other year. Further, for the diagnostic and summative assessment of students' language outcomes, we finalized a comprehensive assessment plan that included administering a variety of assessment instruments: the university-wide English proficiency test, the Criterion®, TOEFL®, and the Versant speaking test. However, in order to do so, we were forced to raise academic fees, which had to be approved by the School of Education.

The last challenge concerns administrative constraints. As mentioned earlier, the Department is charged with administering the regular EFL program in the School of Education with an enrollment of about 4,800 students from various disciplines along with the new departmental program for around 600 undergraduate English majors. Despite the fact that the Department has three administrative assistants, the Department Head has always found it very challenging to manage the many levels of administrative work involved in the development of the new curriculum, including the approval by several committees, the appointment of full-time and part-time faculty members to many current and new courses, discussions with administrative personnel, and the scheduling of courses.

Despite these challenges, the faculty members, instructors, and administrative staff firmly believe the CBI/EMI curriculum revision project to have been well worth their considerable efforts. In the next section, the principles that underlie the needs analysis and curriculum design are presented.

Underlying Principles ||

Revisiting the scenario at the beginning of this chapter, we can trace the principles of designing an EFL university-level content-based curriculum that will prepare freshman and sophomore English majors for their EMI content courses in their junior and senior years. In this scenario, a unique advantage is that out of 19 faculty members in the Department of English

Language and Literature, seven are specialists in applied linguistics or TESOL and the remaining professors of British and American literature or linguistics are familiar not only with content teaching but also with language teaching due to their prior English language teaching experiences. The primary goal of the curriculum design project is to determine the needs of undergraduate English majors and to design several content-based EAP courses that help better prepare the students for the EMI content courses they will take as part of their major in their junior and senior years. Table 3.1 summarizes the principles underlying the needs analysis and design of the CBI/EMI curriculum in this setting.

These observations do not represent a linear process but rather a cyclical or back-and-forth process. For example, in the midst of the curriculum development, there may be the need for another working group to hire additional part-time lecturers or to promote faculty development. Or, at every stage, we may need departmental meetings to discuss details regarding the implementation of the curriculum.

Research Agenda |||

Though numerous studies have been conducted on CBI and CLIL in North America and Europe, respectively (Dalton-Puffer, 2011; Genesee & Lindholm-Leary, 2013; Kasper, 2000; Lindahl, Baecher, & Tomas, 2013; Lyster, 2011; Ruiz de Zarobe & Catalan, 2009; Smit & Dafouz, 2012), research in EFL settings, which is not yet full-fledged, is characterized by issues not typically found in ESL settings, such as students' language use in and out of class, the preponderance of—in both content and language courses—teachers who are non-native speakers of English, the unique motivations of EFL students in CBI courses (Sylven & Thompson, 2015), and the sociocultural context of the country in which CBI/EMI is being implemented. As detailed next, the area of content and language integrated instruction in EFL is ripe with research possibilities.

In the EFL settings, since university students have limited exposure to English outside of class and are primarily exposed to English in CBI and/or EMI courses, they may lack oral skills, expressions, and vocabulary used in daily language. Thus, one suggested area of research is to examine how students' limited exposure to English outside of class affects both L2 outcomes and their understanding of content courses. Important precedents for this research are found in studies on language and content outcomes in CBI and CLIL courses (e.g., Dalton-Puffer, 2007; Smit & Dafouz, 2012); however, more systematic research is required, especially in Asian countries where CBI and EMI are being implemented. In Japan, both CBI and EMI classes at the university tend to be taught by Japanese-speaking professors or instructors. With the development of English as a lingua franca (ELF) and non-native issues in the profession (e.g., Braine, 2010; Jenkins, 2013; Seidlhofer, 2009), it is well worth examining the roles of both content and language teachers who are non-native speakers and investigating how the non-native speaking instructors influence students' understanding of the content and their performance in English.

Another recommended area for intensive research concerns students' affective factors. In Japan, most students study and view English as a school subject only and have little occasion to use English as a tool in authentic situations. When they experience CBI or EMI

Table 3.1: Activities and Principles in the Process of the CBI/EMI Curriculum Development

Activities	Underlying Principles
1. The Department Head asks the colleagues to form a working group in charge of guiding the curriculum reform.	The working group is responsible for taking the initiative in proposing the curriculum revision, an involved and lengthy design process. For a large program, like the one described in the scenario, without such a group, no curricular revision is possible.
2. The working group carries out a questionnaire survey targeting both the faculty members and students, and conducts interviews and focus groups to determine whether or not the curriculum revision is necessary, and if so, how it should be revised.	Needs analysis is an essential tenet of curriculum design. The findings obtained from both the questionnaire and interviews help working group members to understand the contextual factors and needs involving both students and faculty.
3. The Department administers a proficiency test that measures the four skills required for both the content-based bridge courses and academic content courses taught in English.	It is crucial to assess students' proficiency accurately as they enter the program. The scores on the proficiency test allow us to triangulate data from the questionnaire and interviews to understand how to organize the various curricular components to best scaffold the students' learning experience.
4. Based on the contextual and needs analysis, the faculty members (and on occasion departmental administrative staff) discuss the feasibility of the potential content-based and EMI curriculum proposed by the working group as it relates to their views of language learning and teaching.	The core element of curriculum development is for the stakeholders to share common pedagogical philosophies and assumptions about the curriculum. Many meetings in small groups, at the departmental level, and even in the college or school are required to determine the program goals for a new curriculum. Without this effort, the curriculum revision will not be accomplished and its goals will not be universally embraced.
5. The working group proposes some organizing principles of the curriculum and decides on its detailed content (e.g., what should be taught, how many courses are needed, and how they should be leveled and sequenced).	This serves as a blueprint for the implementation of the new curriculum; therefore, several meetings involve not only the faculty members but also part-time instructors and the administrative staff and assistants.
6. As a pre-implementation stage, the Department Head as well as the working group complete the necessary administrative procedures, with support from both faculty and administrative personnel in other departments.	Good coordination of the Department with other departments and the administrative staff is a must. In some universities, college-level approval of the new curriculum may be required, in addition to some essential administrative work (e.g., the hiring of new part-time instructors, faculty development, course descriptions, syllabus preparation including learning outcomes, course scheduling, etc.). This process is time-consuming and tedious, but it plays an important role in ensuring the success of the new curriculum.
7. The Department assesses students' language and content outcomes and evaluates the entire curriculum.	The assessment and program evaluation help to further improve the quality of the curriculum for the following semester or year. Both formative evaluation during courses and summative evaluation at the end of courses are required. In addition, questionnaires and interviews provide other ways of evaluating the overall curriculum.

courses at the university for the first time, they tend to experience a shock factor—getting completely lost in lectures, feeling extremely anxious about using English in class, and even completely losing their motivation for learning the content in English. Several preliminary studies have been conducted on the effects of an EMI program on Japanese-speaking students' anxiety (Suzuki, 2013) and culture shock (Yamazaki, 2014). However, more studies of this nature are called for.

Another possible research agenda concerns the effects of a CBI/EMI curriculum in the home country on study abroad. With the popularity of research on study abroad (e.g., Davidson, 2010), some universities in Japan have integrated CBI/EMI programs into their curriculum that are taken by students prior to going on their study-abroad program. It is generally assumed that these programs are of great benefit to students. However, very little research has been conducted on the psychological and social effects of such programs on students' study-abroad experiences.

Finally, the disciplines of discourse and conversation analysis and ethnographic studies can help to clarify the nature of interactions in CBI/EMI courses with language or content teachers who are not native speakers or among L2 learners. Through such studies (e.g., Copp Mokkonen, 2013; Henderson & Palmer, 2015; Nikula, Dalton-Puffer, & Garcia, 2013), many interesting aspects of language and content learning can be identified (e.g., the nature of corrective feedback, instances of scaffolding, input quality, negotiation of meaning, discourse practices, and power relationships).

This chapter has discussed one process of developing a CBI curriculum at a university level in an EFL setting. First, it has given a brief introduction of CBI in primary, secondary, and higher education in Japan, and the rationale behind the curriculum. Then, some procedures in the curriculum development and the actual examples have been described with some challenges. The chapter has concluded that the design and implementation of CBI in EFL situations is still in its nascency and more research is called for.

APPLYING WHAT YOU LEARNED
Questions and Tasks

1. Reflecting back on the university-level content-based instruction described in this chapter, which aspects of CBI curriculum development do you believe to be unique to the EFL setting?

2. Design several interview questions to ask a few international students who were in a CBI program in an EFL country about how the program impacted their English language learning and what issues or problems they encountered (e.g., motivation, anxiety). If possible, administer the interview to a few of the students, and based on the students' perspective, discuss several important issues that curriculum designers should keep in mind.

3. Do web research on an EAP program leading to EMI courses in an EFL country and identify key issues in the curriculum such as those described in the chapter (e.g., guiding principles, contextual factors, analysis of learner needs, program goals, program content, assessment issues). If possible, visit the school to observe one or two EAP courses and interview the director or a teacher about these key issues.

4. Suppose you are designing a CBI curriculum for university EFL students. First, brainstorm as many guiding principles and contextual factors as you can in pairs or groups, and then design several questionnaire items to analyze learner needs. With some hypothetical questionnaire findings in mind, discuss program goals and content and how you would go about evaluating the outcomes of students' language in each course and the whole program.

Acknowledgments

I thank the faculty members, the curriculum development working group; the administrative personnel and assistants; and above all, the department heads, Profs. Akiko Kimura and Yasuyo Sawaki in the Department of English Language and Literature, the School of Education at Waseda University, Japan for spending a great amount of time discussing and supporting the development of the CBI and EMI curriculum. Without their understanding of the new curriculum and sincere cooperation on its implementation, I could not have written this chapter.

ENDNOTES

1. Many CLIL practitioners and researchers would disagree with this assessment. Dale and Tanner (2012), for example, note differences in the goals of CLIL and CBI curricula, their implementation, the assessment of content and language, and the teachers' roles. In the same vein, Dalton-Puffer (2011) identifies CLIL as "a foreign language enrichment measure packaged into content teaching" (p. 184), further clarifying that CLIL lessons tend to be offered as content courses while the target language continues to be taught as subject matter (see also Dalton-Puffer, this volume).
2. See www.ibo.org.
3. See www.iss.oizumi.u-gakugei.ac.jp/en/.
4. See www.icu.ac.jp/en/.
5. See web.aiu.ac.jp/en/.
6. See www.ets.org/toefl.
7. See www.waseda.jp/sils/en/.
8. *Pushed output* (Swain, 1985) refers to instances where the act of producing the target language triggers L2 learners to notice syntactic or lexical gaps in their oral or written production and therefore to pay more attention to the way in which they are expressing their meaning. CBI provides rich opportunities for pushed output and has been found to result in more noticing of lexical items, increased listening comprehension, and greater grammatical accuracy in students' L2 writing (e.g., of past tense in Spanish) (Leeser, 2008).

9. This tool has been developed by Educational Testing Service (ETS) (www.ets.org/criterion).

10. This test was published by Pearson (www.versanttest.com).

11. See www.waseda.jp/fedu/edu/en/.

12. In EFL settings, students must develop general English skills as well as academic English skills. This is especially important at our university, since two-thirds of the students attending our courses for matriculated students get hired into a company upon graduation. These students typically have deficiencies in certain areas, especially listening and speaking skills.

REFERENCES

Bostwick, M. (2001). English immersion in a Japanese school. In D. Christian & F. Genesee (Eds.), *Bilingual education* (pp. 125–137). Alexandria, VA: TESOL.

Braine, G. (2010). *Nonnative speaker English teachers: Research, pedagogy, and professional growth.* New York, NY: Routledge.

Brown, J. D. (1995). *The elements of language curriculum: A systematic approach to program development.* Boston, MA: Heinle & Heinle.

Christison, M. A., & Murray, D. E. (2014). *What English language teachers need to know. Designing curriculum (Volume III).* New York, NY: Routledge.

Copp Mokkonen, A. (2013). An ethnographic study of language socialization and choice in a first and second grade English medium classroom in Finland. *Journal of Immersion and Content-Based Language Education, 1,* 279–295.

Coyle, D., Hood, P., & Marsh, D. (2010). *CLIL: Content and language integrated learning.* Cambridge, England: Cambridge University Press.

Dale, L., & Tanner, R. (2012). *CLIL activities: A resource for subject and language teachers.* New York, NY: Cambridge University Press.

Dalton-Puffer, C. (2007). *Discourse in content and language integrated learning (CLIL) classrooms.* Amsterdam, The Netherlands: Benjamins.

Dalton-Puffer, C. (2011). Content-and-language integrated learning: From practice to principles? *Annual Review of Applied Linguistics, 31,* 182–204. doi:10.1017/S0267190511000092

Davidson, D. E. (2010). Study abroad: When, how long, and with what results? New data from the Russian front. *Foreign Language Annals, 43,* 6–26. doi:10.1111/j.1944-9720.2010.01057.x

Gass, S. M. (1997). *Input, interaction, and the second language learner.* Mahwah, NJ: Lawrence Erlbaum.

Genesee, F., & Lindholm-Leary, K. (2013). Two case studies of content-based language education. *Journal of Immersion and Content-Based Language Education, 1,* 3–33.

Graves, K. (2014). Syllabus and curriculum design for second language teaching. In M. Celce-Murcia, D. M. Brinton, & M. A. Snow (Eds.), *Teaching English as a second or foreign language* (4th ed., pp. 46–62). Boston, MA: National Geographic Learning/Heinle Cengage Learning.

Henderson, K. I., & Palmer, D. K. (2015). Teacher scaffolding and pair work in a bilingual pre-kindergarten classroom. *Journal of Immersion and Content-Based Language Education, 3,* 77–101.

Jenkins, J. (2013). *English as a lingua franca in the international university: The politics of academic English language policy.* New York, NY: Routledge.

Kasper, L. F. (with M. Babbitt, R. W. Mlynarczyk, D. M. Brinton, J. W. Rosenthal, P. Master, S. A. Myers, J. Egbert, D. A. Tillyer, & L. S. Wood.). (2000). *Content-based college ESL instruction.* Mahwah, NJ: Erlbaum.

Krashen, S. D. (1982). *Principles and practice in second language acquisition.* Oxford, England: Pergamon Press.

Larsen-Freeman, D. (2014). Teaching grammar. In M. Celce-Murcia, D. M. Brinton, & M. A. Snow (Eds.), *Teaching English as a second or foreign language* (4th ed., pp. 256–270). Boston, MA: National Geographic Learning/Heinle Cengage Learning.

Leeser, M. J. (2008). Pushed output, noticing, and development of past tense morphology in content-based instruction. *Canadian Modern Language Review, 65,* 195–220.

Lightbown, P. (2014). *Focus on content-based language teaching.* Oxford, England: Oxford University Press.

Lindahl, K., Baecher, L., & Tomas, Z. (2013). Teacher language awareness in content-based activity design. *Journal of Immersion and Content-Based Language Education, 1,* 198–255.

Long, M. H. (1983). Native speaker/non-native speaker conversation and the negotiation of comprehensible input. *Applied Linguistics, 4,* 126–141.

Long, M. H. (1996). The role of the linguistic environment in second language acquisition. In W. Richie & T. Bahtia (Eds.), *Handbook of second language acquisition* (pp. 413–468). San Diego, CA: Academic Press.

Lyster, R. (2011). Content-based second language teaching. In E. Hinkel (Ed.), *Handbook of research in second language teaching and learning* (Vol. 2, pp. 611–630). New York, NY: Routledge.

Ministry of Education, Culture, Sports, Science and Technology (MEXT). (2010). *The course of study for elementary school: Foreign language activities.* Retrieved from http://www.mext.go.jp/component/a_menu/education/micro_detail/__icsFiles/afieldfile/2010/10/20/1261037_12.pdf

Nikula, T., Dalton-Puffer, C., & Garcia, A. L. (2013). CLIL classroom discourse: Research from Europe. *Journal of Immersion and Content-Based Language Education, 1,* 70–100.

Pica, T. (1994). Research on negotiation: What does it reveal about second-language learning conditions, processes, and outcomes? *Language Learning, 44,* 493–527.

Richards, J. C. (2001). *Curriculum development in language teaching.* New York, NY: Cambridge University Press.

Roediger, I., & Guynn, M. (1996). Retrieval processes. In E. Bork & R. Bork (Eds.), *Memory* (pp. 197–236). New York, NY: Academic Press.

Ruiz de Zarobe, Y., & Catalan, R. M. J. (2009). *Content and language integrated learning: Evidence from research in Europe.* Bristol, England: Multilingual Matters.

Seidlhofer, B. (2009). *Understanding English as a lingua franca.* Oxford, England: Oxford University Press.

Smit, U., & Dafouz, E. (Eds.). (2012). Integrating content and language in higher education: Gaining insights into English-medium instruction at European universities [Special issue]. *AILA Review, 25.*

Snow, M. A. (2014). Content-based and immersion models of second/foreign language teaching. In M. Celce-Murcia, D. M. Brinton, & M. A. Snow (Eds.), *Teaching English as a second or foreign language* (4th ed., pp. 438–454). Boston, MA: National Geographic Learning/Heinle Cengage Learning.

Suzuki, N. (2013). *An investigation of Japanese students' foreign language speaking anxiety in an undergraduate English-medium instruction (EMI) program* (Unpublished master's thesis). The Graduate School of Education, Waseda University, Tokyo, Japan.

Swain, M. (1985). Communicative competence: Some roles of comprehensible input and comprehensible output in its development. In S. M. Gass & C. Madden (Eds.), *Input and second language acquisition* (pp. 235–256). Rowley, MA: Newbury House.

Swain, M. (1993). The output hypothesis: Just speaking and writing aren't enough. *Canadian Modern Language Review, 50,* 158–164.

Swain, M. (2000). The output hypothesis and beyond: Mediating acquisition through collaborative dialogue. In J. Lantolf (Ed.), *Sociocultural theory in second language learning* (pp. 97–114). Oxford, England: Oxford University Press.

Swain, M. (2005). The output hypothesis: Theory and research. In E. Hinkel (Ed.), *Handbook of research in second language teaching and learning* (pp. 471–483). Mahwah, NJ: Erlbaum.

Sylven, L. K., & Thompson, A. S. (2015). Language learning motivation and CLIL: Is there a connection? *Journal of Immersion and Content-Based Language Education, 3,* 28–50.

Taguchi, N. (2014). Pragmatic socialization in an English-medium university in Japan. *International Review of Applied Linguistics in Language Teaching (IRAL), 52,* 157–181.

Yamazaki, E. (2014). *A qualitative study on culture shock: The shock symptoms and coping strategies of first year "Jun-Japa" students in English-medium instruction* (Unpublished master's thesis). The Graduate School of Education, Waseda University, Tokyo, Japan.

Chapter **4**

Building Coherence into the Content-Based Curriculum: Six Ts Revisited

Fredricka L. Stoller & William Grabe

||| A Glimpse into the Content-Based Classroom

Scenario 1: The teacher looks out at the classroom and sees puzzled looks on students' faces as the class moves from a textbook chapter on air pollution to one on the history of the potato. The students had been quite engaged in discussions of air pollution (drawing from multiple sources of information) and would probably have enjoyed moving on to an exploration of other forms of pollution, but the curriculum obliges the teacher to move on to the potato. Despite the potato's interesting journey from the high Andes in South America to Europe in the 1500s, the students are uninterested. Furthermore, because the content vocabulary for the two units is so distinct, the teacher cannot (a) recycle content-specific vocabulary to consolidate learning of language and content or (b) assign synthesis tasks to prepare students for their academic futures.

Scenario 2: The class has just finished a unit on upcycling and is now turning its attention to related topics, introduced in new sets of readings and YouTube videos, focused on the uses of tomatoes for car parts and old vinyl records for decorative household items. The class is animated; students are working in groups comfortably, using concepts associated with upcycling to explore these related topics. Students are willingly tackling challenging tasks that require them to (a) identify connections among upcycling, tomatoes, and vinyl records and (b) define projects of interest that will lead to a deeper understanding of upcycling and its consequences for the environment and economy. Throughout the unit, students use strategies introduced and practiced in previous lessons to (for example) preview new passages, repair faulty comprehension, reread for well-defined purposes, and communicate effectively with each other.

A Rationale for Building Coherence in the Content-Based Classroom ||

CBI, in its many configurations (Snow, 2014), is shaped by students' current needs and future goals, institutional expectations and constraints, available resources, teacher abilities, and expected final-performance outcomes. Despite these variations, we know that learners make the greatest gains in content and language learning when they connect new with known, when there is sufficient content for meaningful tasks, when they make use of skill-specific and learning strategies for authentic purposes, and when learning is embedded in a coherent curriculum. The value of curricular coherence is not limited to CBI contexts; in fact, coherence is important across educational settings. Effective teacher-preparation courses serve as good illustrations; whether their emphases are on teaching methods, second language acquisition, or curriculum design, teacher-preparation courses are typically characterized by a carefully sequenced set of topics, texts, and tasks that are linked by the assumption of a coherent overarching theme (typically captured by the course title). Similarly, at the other end of the educational spectrum, elementary school classrooms are usually organized around carefully sequenced thematic units that serve as a basic curricular structure (Díaz-Rico, 2004, 2012; see also Coyle, Hood, & Marsh, 2010; Echevarría, Vogt, & Short, 2012).

In this chapter, we revisit the Six Ts approach to CBI (Stoller & Grabe, 1997), an approach that is predicated on the importance of coherence as an effective means to promote students' language, content, and strategy learning. Our thinking on curricular coherence, in the context of CBI, was influenced early on by the work of Walmsley (1994) and Johns (1997). More recently, we have been influenced by Guthrie and his colleagues (e.g., Guthrie, Wigfield, & Klauda, 2012; Guthrie, Wigfield, & Perencevich, 2004; Swan, 2003), who have focused on Concept-Oriented Reading Instruction (CORI). CORI emphasizes instruction centered around sustained thematic units (see also Murphy & Stoller, 2001), which (a) support student motivation and engagement, (b) increase students' self-efficacy, (c) permit selection of abundant informational texts that are related and relevant, (d) allow for scaffolded[1] academic text-related tasks that increase in complexity over time, (e) accommodate integrated skills and meaningful strategy instruction, (f) promote student choice and collaboration, and (g) set students up for success.

The Six Ts approach was developed initially in reaction to what we perceived as less-than-effective course design features observed in early renditions of CBI and commercial textbook materials. These features are itemized in Table 4.1 (and suggested in Scenario A at the beginning of this chapter, where we witness a major disjuncture between the units on air pollution and the history of the potato).

It is worth noting that we initially envisioned the Six Ts approach for CBI settings in which teachers had the freedom to select content emphases (distinct from settings in which content is predetermined by adopted textbooks or curricular specifications decided by, for example, language program administrators, school districts, and Ministries of Education). Over decades now, we have observed that the Six Ts planning framework is applicable across a much wider range of CBI settings. In the next sections, we introduce the six Ts individually, explore their interrelationships, and conclude with underlying principles that

Table 4.1: Less-than-Effective Course Design Features That Led to Early Conceptualizations of the Six Ts Approach

▪ thematic units used to deliver more traditional, *segmented* language instruction	▪ an assortment of *weakly* related texts and tasks
▪ *fragmented* instructional units in which connections are either missing or *shallow*	▪ *limited* numbers and types of content resources
▪ the *superficial* consideration of content because of the dominance of language-learning objectives	▪ assumptions that language-learning processes and knowledge can and should be divided into *discrete* skills and language forms
▪ use of themes and/or topics that are *uninteresting* or *irrelevant* to students	▪ language-learning goals that are *detached* from the demands of content resources used in class
▪ exploration of *disconnected* topics in a thematic unit	

can guide CBI teachers, materials writers, and curriculum designers in their efforts to create effective learning conditions for students in second, foreign, and additional language CBI classrooms.

Perspectives on CBI: Six Ts for Building Coherence in the Content-Based Classroom |||

The Six Ts approach to CBI—defined by the integration of *themes, topics, texts, tasks, transitions,* and *threads*—has evolved over more than three decades; it started out with five Ts and was then expanded to include Six Ts (with *texts,* surprisingly in retrospect, being the last T to be incorporated into the approach). At different points in time, we contemplated the incorporation of additional Ts into our model (e.g., *teaching, teamwork, temerity, tension, testing, timing, tolerance, training, transfer,* and *trouble-shooting*) in response to what we heard from teachers, teacher trainers, material developers, and curriculum designers in different instructional contexts.[2] We ultimately decided to retain just Six Ts as a way to create a simple-to-remember, but conceptually intricate, planning framework that can guide novice and experienced teachers in the creation (or fine-tuning) of coherent instruction with a dual commitment to language and content learning.[3] Our goal has always been to devise a user-friendly planning framework that improves upon less-than-effective CBI design features (see again Table 4.1). As should become apparent in our description of each T and their interrelationships, the Six Ts approach is meant to turn around what we have perceived as sometimes less-than-satisfactory CBI practices and, at a minimum:

- ▪ encourage the creation of coherent content-based curricula, broadly speaking, and coherent thematic units, more specifically
- ▪ facilitate meaningful conceptual connections across themes, topics, texts, and tasks
- ▪ integrate a variety of conceptually linked content resources (i.e., texts) to introduce students to and engage students with various genres and information sources

- recognize the value of assisting students in learning interesting content and holding students accountable for content learning
- acknowledge that knowledge evolves over time and that it requires more than a cursory exposure to topic- (or theme-) related texts and tasks
- assist students in grappling with and generating knowledge through text-responsible tasks
- promote the natural integration of language skills
- enable the natural use of language learning strategies in the context of academic language learning
- validate the importance of content, alongside language, when planning language-learning activities.

In addition, our aim has been to create a framework that is flexible enough to be applicable in a wide range of CBI contexts, including (a) second, foreign, and additional language classrooms; (b) elementary, secondary, and adult contexts; (c) university-preparation programs; (d) programs in which content is mandated by a central curriculum plan; (e) programs that do not presuppose institutional pre-selection of target content; and (f) programs that make a strong commitment to content learning (e.g., immersion) or language learning (e.g., topic-based classrooms).

To begin, we introduce each T in turn. The order of presentation should not be construed as an inflexible set of curricular components; in actuality, a great deal of interplay exists among the Six Ts. Their uses require a flexible, dynamic, interactive, and cyclical process.

Themes are the central ideas that organize major curricular units; they are chosen to be appropriate to student needs and interests, institutional expectations, standards, program resources, and teacher abilities. Themes are designated or selected because they are important and worth knowing about (Brophy, 2008; Pappas, Kiefer, & Levstik, 2006). They are substantive enough to promote systematic and reflective inquiry and broad enough to allow students to connect and relate ideas in important ways. Depending on the instructional setting, themes can be abstract (e.g., liberty, adolescence) or more concrete (e.g., United Nations Declaration of Human Rights, rain forests). They might be tied to mainstream curricula (in immersion, sheltered, and linked CBI) or be selected because of their potential relevance to target students (in, e.g., theme-based CBI). In some settings, students explore one sustained theme (or school content area) in depth for an entire semester or school year (Bigelow, Ranney, & Hebble, 2005). For example, a course might be structured around the content area of U.S. Social Studies in a year-long middle-school course; the themes of human behavior (Espeseth, 2012; Seal, 2012) or American culture (Delk, 2008) in a semester-long university-preparation program; and mathematics, as a school content area, in an immersion setting (Genesee & Lindholm-Leary, 2013). In many CBI settings, students explore multiple themes, each one for a few class sessions or weeks at a time (e.g., MacIntyre & Bohlke, 2015). The focus of themes (Figure 4.1), the number of themes, and the amount of time devoted to each are variable, depending on the setting and curricular expectations.

Figure 4.1: Sample Themes for Different Instructional Settings

Sample Themes		Possible Instructional Setting
Insects Weather	⇨	Elementary school classroom
The solar system U.S. history (1945–present)	⇨	Secondary school classroom
Demography Ecosystems	⇨	University-preparation program
Citizenship Health care	⇨	Adult basic education

Topics are the sub-units of content that permit the exploration of more specific aspects of the theme. They are selected to complement curricular objectives; student interests and needs; content resources (i.e., *texts*, as described next); and, in some settings, teacher interests. Topics are developed to generate maximum coherence for the thematic unit and provide non-contrived opportunities to explore both content and language. Thematic units evolve differently depending on the specific topics that define them. For example, a thematic unit on North American indigenous peoples could lead to the exploration of the Navajo, Hopi, and Apache (each tribe representing a different topic for the thematic unit); conversely, the same theme could be characterized by a different set of topics that permits an exploration of tensions that exist in contemporary Native American communities, with topics such as rural versus urban living, traditional versus contemporary religious practices, and values of younger and older generations. These examples (and those in Figure 4.2) are meant to illustrate how thematic units can vary when defined by different coherent sets of topics— whether mandated by the curriculum, defined by an adopted textbook, selected by the teacher, and/or negotiated with students.

Texts, defined in a broad sense here, are the written, aural, and visual (e.g., photos, maps) content resources that permit (a) the exploration of themes and related topics, (b) the use of strategies to comprehend and connect texts, and (c) the meaningful use and development of language. Text selection depends on a number of criteria. A first set of text-selection criteria includes relevance to themes, topics, and other curricular specifications; student interest; and instructional appropriateness (in terms of, e.g., comprehensibility, cross-cultural issues, length, plausible linkages, students' maturity levels and ages, syntactic complexity, vocabulary). Format appeal, availability, and cost represent important secondary criteria. The goal is to have sufficient numbers of related texts to permit *tasks* that involve comparisons, rankings, purposeful rereading, information gaps and information transfer, questioning, re-organization of information graphically, summaries, and syntheses, among other tasks. The numerous types of texts used in CBI, as is shown in Figure 4.3, may be selected, compiled, and/or created in different ways, depending on the instructional setting.

Figure 4.2: Sample Sets of Topics That Characterize Coherent Thematic Units

Theme	Coherent Topics: Set A	Coherent Topics: Set B
Insects	a. Insects that pollinate b. Insects that support ecosystem development c. Insects that are harmful	a. Ants b. Bees c. Caterpillars
Solar system	a. Technology in space b. Research in space c. The international space station	a. Mercury b. Earth c. Mars d. Pluto
Demography	Impact of population on a. air b. water c. natural resources	Population trends a. in developing countries b. in developed countries c. and their impact on the environment

Figure 4.3: Types of Texts (i.e., Content Resources) Used in CBI, Organized by Text Sources

Text Source	Example Text Types
Institution-mandated texts	Primary textbook(s) and workbook(s)
Instructor-compiled texts	Primary textbook(s), (supplementary) readings in various genres, YouTube clips, audiotapes, videos, websites, and visuals (e.g., maps, tables, graphs, posters, pictures, line-drawings)
Instructor-generated texts	Lectures, worksheets, bulletin board displays, webpages, audio-recordings of reading passages
Task-generated texts	Class or small-group discussions; problem-solving tasks; completed graphic organizers; library/internet searches; in-class debates, surveys, and questionnaires; free-writes; simulations
External texts	Guest speakers, field trips

Tasks are the basic units of instruction through which the Six Ts approach is realized day to day. Tasks are the instructional activities, inextricably linked to texts and course goals, that are utilized for content, language, and strategy instruction. They include activities for (a) teaching and consolidating content knowledge; (b) teaching and reinforcing language skills (i.e., reading, writing, speaking, listening), language structures, and study skills; (c) teaching and recycling vocabulary; (d) teaching and providing practice with relevant learning and skill-specific strategies (e.g., establishing a purpose for reading, predicting, checking predictions, connecting text information to background knowledge, rereading (see Grabe, 2009; Grabe & Stoller, 2011); and (e) engaging students in cooperative learning. Content-rich instructional units—resulting from well-defined themes, connected topics, and plentiful related texts—allow for progressions of well-sequenced tasks that begin with motivating initiating tasks and lead to culminating thematic-unit tasks or project outcomes (Stoller, 2006). Culminating tasks that require the synthesis of content, stemming from various text sources, help students develop the academic skills, strategies, and critical thinking abilities that they will need in future academic endeavors. Equally important is the fact that meaningful culminating activities provide students with a sense of successful completion and pride. They also create closure for the thematic unit, thereby preparing students psychologically to move onto the next unit. Finally, major tasks, within and across topics and texts in a thematic unit, can be designed with higher levels of complexity as students move from one thematic unit to the next and as teachers work toward realizing curricular goals. In Figure 4.4, we list a sampling of tasks, organized by instructional foci, that can be integrated into CBI, assuming that they complement both the texts being used and the course objectives. (See also Nunan, this volume.)

Figure 4.4: Sample Tasks Organized by Instructional Foci

Focus of Instruction	Sample Tasks
Academic language, language skills, content, and strategy integration	Pre-, during-, post-reading activities; reading strategy training (e.g., establish a purpose, tap prior knowledge, predict, check predictions, summarize, critique the author); reading fluency training
	Process writing (brainstorming, drafting, revising, editing); writing fluency tasks (e.g., speed-writes, free-writes); writing from sources (e.g., using proper citation conventions, paraphrasing, and understanding the serious consequences of plagiarism)
	Conversational gambit practice (e.g., using polite expressions to show agreement, express disagreement, offer an alternative viewpoint); spontaneous speeches; oral presentations (with or without PowerPoint slides)
	Listening to mini-lectures (for main ideas, for details, for making key inference connections); directed listening for specific information
Vocabulary building	Learning from definitions and dictionary consultation; raising consciousness about connotations, collocations, cognates; word family exercises; semantic clustering; arranging words in lexical sets and classification activities; word-wall activities; collecting words
Discourse organization	Filling in graphic organizers while reading; ordering strip stories; exploring how text organization supports comprehension; scanning/listening for signal words and predicting contents
Communicative interaction	Role-plays, simulations, debates, problem-solving activities, surveys and interviews, group work, cooperative learning; supported by instruction and feedback on pronunciation
Study skills	Listening to lectures, note-taking, and use of notes for authentic purposes (e.g., writing a paper, studying for a quiz); test-taking strategies; library work; internet searches; identification of key information; time management (e.g., to complete parts of a project)
Synthesis of content materials	Project work, problem-solving, synthesis papers, oral presentations, poster displays
Grammar	Inductive and deductive grammar tasks focused on key structures needed for main-idea comprehension in core texts; review, practice, and production

Transitions and *threads,* the fifth and sixth Ts, are explicit mechanisms for building coherence in content-based curricula. *Transitions* represent explicitly planned linkages (a) across *topics* in a thematic unit and (b) across the *texts* and *tasks* within them. For example, the teacher may say something like this: "We've now explored fracking and its possible impact on the land. Let's now look at off-shore oil drilling and its impact on seas and shorelines." Transitions, like this one, provide constructive entrees for new topics, tasks, and texts within a thematic unit (see Figure 4.5) in addition to meaningful opportunities for, at a minimum, connecting new with known information, recycling content and language knowledge, rereading purposefully, revisiting content in light of new information, synthesizing information from multiple sources, and building student expertise. (See Appendix 4A for a sample sequence of transitions, texts, and tasks in a thematic unit on demography.)

Threads, unlike transitions, are linkages across themes that create greater curricular coherence. They are not necessarily directly tied to the central idea controlling each thematic unit. Rather, in many CBI contexts, threads are relatively abstract concepts (e.g., alternative choices, contrasts, ethics, health, obstacles, power, responsibility, traditions) that provide means for (a) linking diverse themes, (b) reviewing and recycling important content and language across themes, and (c) practicing learning strategies. The use of threads is a par-

Figure 4.5: Transitions among Topics, Tasks, and Texts That Contribute to Instructional Coherence

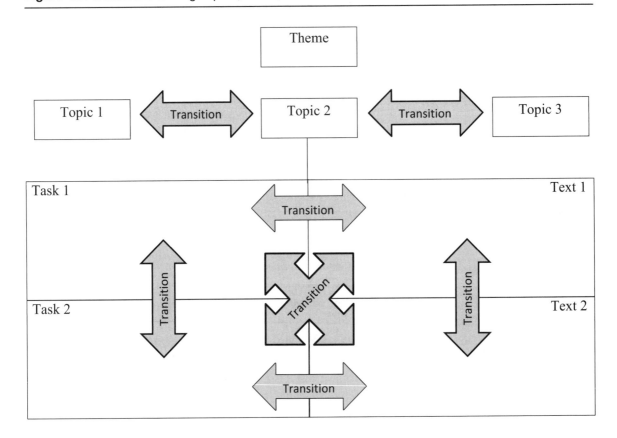

ticularly important bridging mechanism in content-based contexts defined by disjointed themes (e.g., a textbook with themes such as robots, fast food cultures, and toxic wastes). A single thread or multiple threads can link thematically diverse content, providing opportunities to revisit previously encountered content, make connections, synthesize information, and build new knowledge. In other CBI settings, more concrete threads (e.g., recycling materials) permit logical linkages among more cohesive sets of thematic units (e.g., distinct units on plastics, paper, aluminium, and glass as forms of pollution and environmental waste). Threads can be planned ahead of time by the instructor, though some of the most effective threads are those that emerge in class as a result of students' comments, observations, questions, and personal experiences. Figure 4.6 illustrates how one abstract thread (i.e., responsibility at individual, community, regional, societal, national, and/or international levels) could serve as a link across five distinct thematic units.

How teachers make use of the Six Ts framework to enhance their instruction varies from setting to setting. In almost all settings, teachers are responsible for incorporating relevant *transitions* (to link topics, tasks, and texts) and *threads* (to link themes) into their lessons to create as much curricular coherence as possible; rarely are transitions and threads explicitly incorporated into commercial content-based materials. With regard to *themes, topics, texts,* and *tasks* (the other four Ts), teachers' roles vary. In settings where, for example, themes, topics, texts, and tasks are mandated by a centralized curriculum committee or Ministry of Education, the teacher, when permissible, may want to examine the curriculum to determine where coherence may be lacking and/or where it could be improved. The teacher could, in such cases, supplement mandated content resources (texts) to expose students to other genres and alternative viewpoints, devise additional tasks that are linked to the richer text set, and/or plan for staged project work. With more content-rich curricula, the teacher can plan sequences of tasks that better simulate the types of tasks that students may encounter in future studies.

At the other end of the continuum are teachers who work in programs that have made a commitment to CBI, without specifying any of the Ts. In such settings, teachers (often teams of teachers) have total responsibility for conceptualizing and designing their content-based

Figure 4.6: Sample Thread That Provides Logical Linkages among Diverse Themes

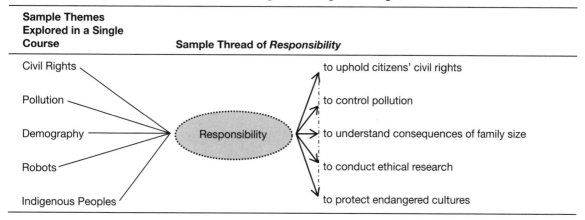

curricula. They are granted the freedom to select appropriate themes, topics, and texts and then devise tasks to bring the course to life. While such an approach can be laborious, it permits course designers to work toward real coherence from the outset by using the Six Ts to guide them. (See Appendix 4B for a description of other settings in which teachers can creatively make use of the Six Ts to enhance their course planning and instruction.)

Underlying Principles |||

The Six Ts planning framework has evolved over time, with the ever-present goal of creating an approach that contributes to a sense of seamlessness in CBI. Table 4.2 juxtaposes (a) classroom design features that emerge from the approach and promote opportunities for meaningful content and language learning and (b) associated principles underlying the Six Ts approach.

Research Agenda |||

As suggested in Fitzsimmons-Doolan, Grabe, and Stoller (this volume), the field could benefit from additional quantitative and qualitative research on CBI and a thoughtful translation of results into practice. Empirical investigations into the efficacy of the Six Ts approach as a whole, the individual Ts, and their relationships in different settings (with different students, teachers, and materials) could prove worthwhile. The extent to which the Six Ts (individually or as a set) lead to improved content and language learning, language-skill mastery, academic-task completion, strategy use, motivation, and autonomy is worthy of investigation as well. Case studies with detailed descriptions of effective practices related to the Six Ts are encouraged. Action research focused on textbook adaptations, materials development, and task creation, as related to one or more of the Six Ts, could prove insightful. Because instructional approaches, in general, are typically only as effective as the teachers who adopt them (Pressley, 2006), it would be worthwhile to conduct research (as has been done with the Sheltered Instruction Observation Protocol, e.g., Echevarría, Richards-Tutor, Chinn, & Ratleff, 2011; Short, Echevarría, & Richards-Tutor, 2011) on the training of teachers to use the Six Ts and the outcomes of that training (in terms of teacher effectiveness and student learning).

APPLYING WHAT YOU LEARNED
Questions and Tasks

1. Describe a teaching context and decide which of the Six Ts presented in this chapter are most important for creating curricular coherence. Provide a rationale for your answer.

2. Evaluate a content-based textbook from the perspective of the Six Ts. Which Ts are present? Which are absent? Which Ts could be improved upon? How might you supplement the textbook, keeping the Six Ts in mind, to maximize coherence and meaningful content- and language-learning opportunities for students?

Table 4.2: Six Ts Approach: Classroom Design Features and Underlying Principles

Classroom Design Features	Underlying Principles
1. Teachers link elements at topic, theme, lesson, and curricular levels. Teachers purposefully use *transitions* to link topics, texts, and tasks and *threads* to link themes.	Coherent curricula (a) promote a sense of seamlessness as teachers and students move from one instructional element to the next; (b) permit a range of meaningful *tasks* that contribute to students' content and language learning; and (c) add meaningful complexity to course content, a key for developing students' more advanced language skills and strategies.
2. Teachers use plentiful related texts in order to promote meaningful content and language learning. To achieve these teaching and learning conditions may require the adoption, adaptation, and/or creation of supplementary content resources for thematic-unit instruction.	Content-based curricula are enhanced when sufficient, varied, and related content resources (i.e., *texts*) are used.
3. Teachers guide students in comprehending and making use of content from multiple content sources. Teachers design *tasks* that require students to, at a minimum, pose questions, find connections, reread, synthesize, and extend their knowledge.	Content learning requires more than a cursory exposure to *topic*- and *theme*-related *texts*.
4. *Tasks* are inextricably linked to the *texts* being assigned. Whether the focal point of the *task* is grammar, strategic reading, vocabulary, and/or language-skill development, *tasks* build upon the content and key features of core texts (e.g., discourse organization, grammatical structures, vocabulary).	Teachers recognize the importance of content when planning language-learning *tasks*; that is, language and language-skill foci should be guided, at least in part, by what course content and *texts* offer.
5. Teachers examine mandated materials to identify their strengths and weaknesses from the Six Ts perspective. Teachers enhance instruction (or make up for deficiencies) by bringing in the missing or underexploited Ts.	Commercial content-based materials do not typically address all Six Ts (*themes, topics, texts, tasks, transitions, threads*) in an explicit manner.
6. Teachers plan well-sequenced *tasks*, centered on core *texts*, to promote a natural integration of skills.	Content-based instruction lends itself naturally to integrated-skill instruction.
7. Teachers connect *themes*, and the *topics* within them, to students' interests, experiences, and needs. Students are given some choices (of *texts* and *tasks*) as a way of giving them responsibility for their own learning.	Students have the best chances of succeeding when they are motivated to learn; appropriate student choices enhance motivation.
8. Teachers begin thematic units with carefully orchestrated and motivating initiating tasks; then they engage students in a series of activities. These activities culminate with a well-defined task requiring students to synthesize information from multiple sources, possibly generate new knowledge, and develop academic language skills.	Thematic units benefit from motivating initiating activities and meaningful culminating tasks.

3. Briefly identify a target group of students (age, language proficiency, purpose for studying the target language, setting). Select a theme that would be of interest and relevance to the student group. Identify two different coherent sets of topics (a minimum of three topics in each set) that would result in thematic units with different trajectories. Consider the types of texts that could bring each set of topics (and related thematic unit) alive for the target setting.

4. Imagine that you teach in an instructional setting that endorses a content-based approach. You've noticed some shortcomings in the programmatic approach, many linked to the less-than-effective features identified in Table 4.1. What might you propose to your colleagues to turn those shortcomings around, thereby making a stronger commitment to content and language learning? For each suggestion, identify the Ts that are involved.

5. Identify an instructional setting of interest. Find a pair of related texts on the internet that would be of potential interest to students in the target setting and that are level-appropriate with respect to language. Consider the two texts as a point of departure for thematic-unit development. Identify the theme, state two to three related topics that could easily emerge from the theme, list five possible academic tasks that could link your two texts, suggest transitions, and propose a thread to another theme.

ENDNOTES

1. Scaffolding entails deliberate teacher (or peer) assistance that is gradually removed as students' skills improve and as students take on more responsibility for their own learning.
2. We acknowledge colleagues Kathi Bailey, Natalie Hess, Ann Johns, and others who have contributed to our thinking about the Six Ts approach and the various Ts that could be incorporated into the framework.
3. Kathi Bailey has described the Six Ts framework using a quilt metaphor. A quilt is an artistic blanket made up of different pieces of cloth, a backing, and padding between the layers of cloth. The Six Ts framework too brings together six different elements to create a cohesive whole.
4. We acknowledge Kathi Bailey for having envisioned relationships among components of the Six Ts Approach in this way.

REFERENCES

Bigelow, M., Ranney, S., & Hebble, A. M. (2005). Choosing depth over breadth in a content-based ESOL program. In D. Kaufman & J. A. Crandall (Eds.), *Content-based instruction in primary and secondary settings* (pp. 179–193). Alexandria, VA: TESOL.

Brophy, J. (2008). Developing students' appreciation for what is taught in school. *Educational Psychologist, 43*, 132–141.

Carson, J. G. (2000). Reading and writing for academic purposes. In M. Pally (Ed.), *Sustained content teaching in academic ESL/EFL* (pp. 19–34). Boston, MA: Houghton Mifflin.

Coyle, D., Hood, P., & Marsh, D. (2010). *CLIL: Content and language integrated learning*. Cambridge, England: Cambridge University Press.

Delk, C. L. (2008). *Discovering American culture* (2nd ed.). Ann Arbor, MI: University of Michigan Press.

Díaz-Rico, L. T. (2004). *Teaching English learners: Strategies and methods*. Boston: Pearson.

Díaz-Rico, L. T. (2012). *Strategies for teaching English learners* (3rd ed.). Boston: Pearson.

Echevarría, J., Richards-Tutor, C., Chinn, V., & Ratleff, P. (2011). Did they get it? The role of fidelity in teaching English learners. *Journal of Adolescent and Adult Literacy, 54*(6), 425–434.

Echevarría, J., Vogt, M. E., & Short, D. J. (2012). *Making content comprehensible for English language learners: The SIOP model* (4th ed.). Boston, MA: Allyn and Bacon.

Espeseth, M. (2012). *Academic encounters, human behaviour, level 4: Listening and speaking* (2nd ed.). New York, NY: Cambridge University Press.

Genesee, F., & Lindholm-Leary, K. (2013). Two case studies of content-based language education. *Journal of Immersion and Content-Based Language Education, 1*(1), 3–33.

Grabe, W. (2009). *Reading in a second language: Moving from theory to practice*. Cambridge, England: Cambridge University Press.

Grabe, W., & Stoller, F. L. (2011). *Teaching and researching reading* (2nd ed.). New York, NY: Routledge.

Guthrie, J. T., Wigfield, A., & Klauda, S. L. (Eds.). (2012). *Adolescents' engagement in academic literacy.* Retrieved from www.cori.umd.edu/research-publications/2012_adolescents_engagement_ebook.pdf

Guthrie, J. T., Wigfield, A., & Perencevich, K. C. (Eds.). (2004). *Motivating reading comprehension: Concept-oriented reading instruction*. Mahwah, NJ: Erlbaum.

Johns, A. M. (1997). *Text, role and context: Developing academic literacies*. Cambridge, England: Cambridge University Press.

MacIntyre, P., & Bohlke, D. (2015). *Reading explorer 2* (2nd ed.). Boston, MA: National Geographic Learning.

Murphy, J. M., & Stoller, F. L. (2001). Sustained-content language teaching: An emerging definition. *TESOL Journal, 10*, 3–5.

Pappas, C. C., Kiefer, B. Z., & Levstik, L. S. (2006). *An integrated language perspective in the elementary school: An action approach* (4th ed.). New York, NY: Pearson.

Pressley, M. (2006). *Reading instruction that works* (3rd ed.). New York, NY: Guilford Press.

Seal, B. (2012). *Academic encounters, human behaviour, level 4: Reading and writing* (2nd ed.). New York, NY: Cambridge University Press.

Short, D. J., Echevarría, J., & Richards-Tutor, C. (2011). Research on academic literacy development in sheltered instruction classrooms. *Language Teaching Research, 15*(3), 363–380.

Snow, M. A. (2014). Content-based and immersion models of second/foreign language teaching. In M. Celce-Murcia, D. M. Brinton, & M. A. Snow (Eds.), *Teaching English as a second or foreign language* (4th ed., pp. 438–454). Boston, MA: National Geographic Learning/Heinle Cengage Learning.

Stoller, F. L. (2006). Establishing a theoretical foundation for project-based learning in second and foreign language contexts. In G. H. Beckett & P. C. Miller (Eds.), *Project-based second and foreign language education: Past, present, and future* (pp. 19–40). Greenwich, CT: Information Age Publishing.

Stoller, F. L., & Grabe, W. (1997). A six-T's approach to content-based instruction. In M. A. Snow & D. M. Brinton (Eds.), *The content-based classroom: Perspectives on integrating language and content* (pp. 78–94). White Plains, NY: Longman.

Swan, E. A. (2003). *Concept-oriented reading instruction: Engaging classrooms, lifelong learners*. New York, NY: Guilford Press.

Walmsley, S. A. (1994). *Children exploring their world: Theme teaching in elementary school*. Portsmouth, NH: Heinemann.

APPENDIX 4A
Sample Sequence of Transitions, Texts, and Tasks in a Thematic Unit on Demography

Students read a graph depicting population trends (**Text 1**) and work with a classmate to interpret the trends (**Task 1**).

Transition 1: Student pairs share their interpretations of the graph with another pair. Then these groups of four identify one or more of the trends suggested in **Text 1** to explore further (**Task 2**).

Transition 2 and **Task 4:** Students create a new graph by hand, initially, that combines information from **Text 1** and the new text(s) found (**Text 2**).

Task 3: In groups of four, students search the internet for more detailed information about the interesting trends identified in **Task 2**. Students read the websites found (**Text 2**) and identify information that is new and that supports and/or contradicts **Text 1.**

Transition 3: Students reconstruct the handwritten graph on the computer. Then individually they write an interpretation of the new graph (**Task 5**) and embed the graph into their written work, labelling and making reference to the graph in an academic manner (**Task 6**).

APPENDIX 4B
T Specifications in Different Settings and Possible Teacher Actions

Teachers make use of the Six Ts framework differently, depending on the CBI settings in which they teach. The discussion in the chapter has focused mainly on instructional settings (a) in which themes, topics, texts, and tasks are clearly specified or (b) where there is a commitment to a content-based curriculum but without an organizing principle such as the Six Ts. Teachers may find themselves, however, in other settings with different configurations of elements present. We list a sampling of instructional contexts in which different combinations of Ts are specified, along with possible actions that teachers can take to create more coherent CBI curricula.

T Specifications in Different Settings	Possible Teacher Actions
Theme-only specified	In such CBI settings, teachers are told what subject matter (i.e., *themes*) to cover, but they are given the freedom to select relevant *topics*, *texts*, and *tasks*.
Tasks predetermined	In language programs with *task*-based orientations, CBI course goals may be stated in terms of the tasks that students should master (Carson, 2000). Teachers in such settings oftentimes find themselves in the position of having to select appropriate *themes*, *topics*, and *texts* to achieve task-oriented course goals. In tertiary contexts, sometimes introductory university-level textbooks are adapted for CBI use.
Texts specified in terms of target genres	In CBI contexts that adopt a genre-based approach, *texts* may be organized by genre, rather than themes or topics. To achieve a different type of curricular coherence, teachers (a) examine mandated *texts*, (b) do their best to cluster them by relevant *topic* and/or *theme*, and (c) devise *tasks* that build upon the features of the *texts* to achieve language- and content-learning course goals.
Topics, texts, and tasks established by commercial content-based textbook(s) adopted for classroom use, but overall content can be fairly limited and fragmented	Commercial CBI textbooks typically endorse one of three approaches: (a) a sustained content approach (with one theme and multiple topics that run across the entire textbook); (b) a thematic approach (with multiple, and oftentimes disconnected, themes); or (c) a topical approach (with more limited content). Teachers should examine adopted textbooks to identify ways in which they can be enhanced. Teachers may supplement textbook materials—to create more coherence and robust learning experiences—with additional *texts* (carefully chosen to complement the already designated themes, topics, and/or texts) and/or *tasks* that are devised to hold students responsible for text information (i.e., text-responsible tasks). With topical materials, teachers may (a) supplement *topics* with additional *texts* and *tasks* and (b) connect *topics* with overarching *themes*, the latter connected by one or more abstract *threads*. In this way, the teacher can create opportunities for more meaningful language use, content learning, purposeful strategy use, and critical thinking.

Chapter 5

Strategic Curriculum Planning: Standards and Objectives in Content-Based Instruction

Kate Mastruserio Reynolds

||| A Glimpse into the Content-Based Classroom

At Longfellow Elementary School in Eau Claire, Wisconsin, a sheltered content course for fourth and fifth grade English learners (ELs) is centered around building learners' literacy skills, in keeping with school district guidelines for this population of learners. The learners are mostly second- or third-generation descendants of Hmong or Vietnamese immigrants who struggle in their academic learning due to weak literacy skills. A small minority of the ELs are from China or Russia. Their parents are in the U.S. on international exchanges; thus, they are recent arrivals to the U.S. educational context. This population is less orally proficient, but has strong L1 literacy and some L2 literacy. In this particular sheltered content course, no native speakers of English are integrated; however, the ELs share other grade-level academic courses with native speakers. The teacher, Kate, has overarching aims for the sheltered content course: to build vocabulary, word recognition, reading fluency, and reading strategies while engaging in intensive and narrow extensive reading activities. As part of their goal to build literacy skills, Kate and the bilingual paraprofessional Mrs. Yer, who works with her in the sheltered course, have created a mystery genre study emphasizing a variety of reading instruction formats (such as guided reading, independent reading, read-alouds, and paired reading).

Curriculum Planning in CBI |||

Graves (2014) defines a curriculum as "…a dynamic system of interconnected processes" that include "…planning, enacting, and evaluating" (p. 49). She explains that these processes interrelate in lessons, units, courses, and programs, and result in the creation of "curriculum products such as syllabi, lesson plans, and assessment instruments" (p. 49). A curriculum serves school districts as an overarching plan of shared instructional goals, which helps teachers to organize and sequence instruction in a logical and step-wise manner and gauge both learning and learners' progress. Without a thoughtfully designed curriculum, a teacher: (1) is subjected to the curriculum provided by the selected textbook(s), which may or may not meet learners' academic or linguistic needs; (2) relinquishes control of the learning progress and thus has reduced flexibility or creativity to engage the learners; and, (3) may be without direction, leading to disjointed information and potentially shallow learning for the students.

A CBI curriculum may include a series of units ranging in duration from several weeks to a full term, depending on the topic. Designing curricula for any CBI model—whether sheltered content, adjunct, or any other CBI program type—follows similar processes (see Brinton & Snow, this volume). Modifications based on the population of learners are factored into the design process through differentiation. Differentiation in curriculum or lesson development can be accomplished by modifying content information, instructional processes or products, activity/task expectations, language skills, or supports provided (Reynolds, 2015).

The design process advocated in this chapter is known as *backward design* (Wiggins & McTighe, 2005). The premise of backward design unifies the academic standards being taught with the content and language required on the final assessments. In CBI, educators at the K–12 (elementary through secondary levels) must consider the academic *and* language standards that guide instruction, so CBI educators have a dual focus during the backward design process. Figure 5.1 illustrates an educator starting with the relevant grade-level academic standards (Step 1) and beginning to draft preliminary objectives (Step 2). Then, the educator gauges the objectives against what the learners need to know and be able to do (i.e., content and linguistic knowledge and skills) for success on the term-end assessment(s) (Step 3). The educator next analyzes the textbook for the content and linguistic concepts taught in relation to the objectives (Step 4). In Figure 5.1, this step is represented by the gray rectangle with lines and xs; the lines represent the content or linguistic concepts present in the text, while the small xs represent quizzes or chapter tests from the textbook. The lines beneath the rectangle represent the enabling academic or linguistic concepts (enabling objectives) that are not present in the textbook and must be added by the teacher. It is vital that the teacher analyze the concepts present in the textbook (whether content or language) in relation to the objectives and assessments in order to be able to build the knowledge and skills necessary for learners' academic success (Step 5). Once each of these areas has been considered, the educator can sequence the finalized unit objectives and begin to develop activities, find supplemental readings, create presentations of new information, and prepare other supplementary materials.

Figure 5.1: Modified Backward Design Process

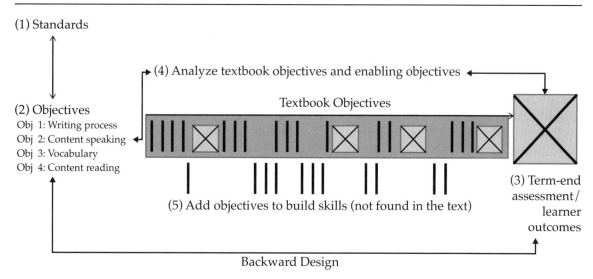

The backward design process may become more complex when one factors in standards, such as the Common Core State Standards (CCSS) (National Governors Association Center for Best Practices, Council of Chief State School Officers, 2010) for English language arts and literacy. Another layer of complexity is added when one factors in the World Class Instructional Design and Assessment (WIDA) standards (World Class Instructional Design and Assessment Consortium, 2012). WIDA's ESL standards outline proficiency levels of second language learners from beginning to advanced levels. The learners' proficiency levels may be different in each language skill (speaking, listening, reading, and writing). In other words, what the learner can comprehend (read/listen) and produce (write/speak) increases at higher proficiency levels, but reading and writing may be stronger than speaking and listening, for instance. Not all skills will be equally strong even if the composite score passes the learners' proficiency at one level. Other notable language standards include the Common European Framework of Reference (CEFR) (Cambridge University Press, 2013), the American Council of Teachers of Foreign Languages Proficiency Guidelines (ACTFL) (ACTFL, 2012), and TESOL's PreK–12 English Language Proficiency Standards (2006) (see Appendix 5A for more detailed information about these language standards).

To illustrate the symbiotic relationship between standards and assessments, fifth grade students might need to work toward this CCSS (2010) Language Arts standard:

CCSS.ELA-LITERACY. R1.5.3: *Explain the relationships or interactions between two or more individuals, events, ideas, or concepts in a historical, scientific, or technical text based on specific information in the text.* (p. 14)

In a unit on animal characteristics, for example, the final assessment(s) would evaluate learners' understanding (listening and/or reading) and ability to produce (speaking and/or writing). The learners, therefore, should be taught to read, write, speak, and listen to comparisons of animal characteristics as well as attend to oral and written phrases and structures and the required grammatical features (comparative language and adjectives). The backward design process requires the content and language knowledge and skills expected on the final assessments to be articulated as unit learning outcome objectives and to be taught explicitly. This backward design process facilitates the teacher's writing of the unit and, ultimately, helps to clarify lesson objectives.

Learning outcome objectives are the forms that unit and lesson objectives take. They are written with the focus on what the student will learn during the instructional process and not on the teacher, the teaching process, or the unit activities. In the past, objectives tended to be written describing what the teacher planned to do. For example, the objective would say "The teacher will explain common past tense irregular verb forms," whereas now it would focus on what the students would be learning: "Students will be able to write and speak using four common past tense irregular forms when conveying a personal narrative." In order to emphasize the learning, learning outcome objectives are written in a formulaic manner using the sentence frame: At the end of instruction, *students will be able to* [observable action verb] *in* [context]." If the learning outcome is measurable for accuracy, a degree of accuracy should be included. For example: *Students will be able to write and speak using four common past tense irregular forms with 90% accuracy when conveying a personal narrative.*

During the backward design unit process, the teacher also considers any other knowledge and skills that learners need to be successful on the final unit assessments, even if they are not directly part of the standard. For example, if learners are studying animal characteristics and are expected to write a paragraph comparing two different animals on the final test, they need to learn content about animal characteristics (e.g., habitat, behavior, physical descriptions) as well as knowledge and practice in academic paragraph writing, including process writing, timed writing, paragraph format, topic sentences, declarative sentences, main ideas, supporting details, subject verb agreement, simple and irregular present tense forms, comparative adjectives, etc.

To ensure that ELs will be successful, educators must identify learners' language competencies and abilities while also analyzing the enabling skills necessary to complete a task. In the animal characteristics example, enabling skills could include prewriting (e.g., planning and organizing thoughts), sentence-level grammatical knowledge (e.g., word order, verb tense, use of pronouns, etc.), discourse-level knowledge (e.g., comparative transitions), and/or vocabulary knowledge (i.e., content terms such as *mammal, reptile, woodland, desert* and general language terms such as *swim, burrow, climb)* (Bernier, 1997).

Once the educator has identified the assessment objectives or test specifications (i.e., the list of academic and linguistic knowledge and skills as well as the enabling skills to be directly or indirectly assessed on an exam, a writing assignment, or a performance assessment), he/she then evaluates these instructional and assessment objectives against those present in the textbook(s) as depicted in Figure 5.1.

Often overlooked areas are the ELs' writing skills and their background experience in oral language. In content-area classes with native speakers, educators tend to assume that students have learned the essentials of academic writing in their language arts classes and that these skills can be applied to their content classes. Native speakers also have orality, or the background of oral language, to assist them in their writing whereas non-native speakers do not necessarily have this fund of knowledge to assist them. Non-native speakers are consequently practicing the second language competencies they are in the process of acquiring when engaged in an academic literacy task. Therefore, such knowledge and skills cannot be assumed for non-native speakers.

Perspectives on CBI: An Example from a Sheltered ESL Class ||

Kate and Mrs. Yer were given the overarching goals of developing reading fluency and reading strategies. To motivate their fifth graders, they combined the reading goals with English language arts to develop the ELs' literary knowledge (i.e., formats, plot, and characterization) through mystery genre study (i.e., study of the specific stylistic characteristics of the mystery genre such as characterization and plot). The linguistic needs of this differentiated group of ELs (newcomers and Hmong/Vietnamese residents) were generally to build social and academic vocabulary and to improve word recognition, speaking, listening, and writing skills. The CCSS English Language Arts/Literacy Standards were employed to address the reading development needs of ELs, as required by elementary schools in most U.S. states, including Longfellow Elementary, the school depicted in the scenario at the beginning of the chapter.

The relevant WIDA standards were: Standard 1: *communication for social, intercultural and instructional purposes* for the new arrivals, and Standard 2: *academic language in language arts* for the residents and new arrivals. The CCSS standards which the fifth grade EL students' needed to work on pertained to the domains of reading, writing, speaking, listening, and vocabulary acquisition and were integrated into the unit presented in Figure 5.2.

Each year, public school districts in Wisconsin assess ELs' language abilities (i.e., speaking, listening, reading, writing, and composite literacy and orality scores) using the WIDA Measure of Developing English Language (MODEL) test (WIDA, 2008). This test describes proficiency levels from (1) Entering (the lowest); (2) Emerging; (3) Developing; (4) Expanding; (5) Bridging; to (6) Reaching (the highest). The ELs in Kate's class had overall proficiency levels ranging from 1–3. The newcomers scored lower on the WIDA assessments for oral language, whereas the residents had greater literacy needs. Kate took these proficiency levels into account when deciding which objectives would be appropriate for each learner.

From the standards described earlier and from the needs of the learners as identified from WIDA scores and teachers' reports, Kate developed the unit objectives, a selection of which are listed in the first column of Figure 5.2. The curricular plan sequence helped her organize the topics developmentally and provide enough time for instruction and practice. The second through the fifth columns show the modifications to the objective or scaffolds provided to learners at each level of proficiency so that they may achieve the objective. The final column indicates when the objective is taught in the unit sequence.

Figure 5.2: Mystery Unit Objectives Differentiated by Proficiency Level

Objectives	WIDA Levels					Curricular Plan Sequence
At the conclusion of instruction, students will be able to...	Level 1	Level 2	Level 3	Level 4	Level 5	
Employ mystery vocabulary correctly to describe characters, events and symbols when speaking or writing. (Language arts) (Linguistic competence/word level) WIDA Standard 2	Meet objective (5–8 word mastery) with the support of a graphic organizer and word bank	Meet objective (10 word mastery) with the support of a graphic organizer	Meet objective (15–18 word mastery)	Meet objective (20 word mastery)	Meet objective (20 word mastery)	Weeks 1–4
Utilize discourse markers (first, then, next; however, although, in addition, similarly, etc.) 80 percent correctly when narrating a mystery in speaking or writing. (Language arts) (Linguistic competence/word level) WIDA Standard 1	Meet objective (accurately uses 2–3 discourse markers) with the support of a cloze passage	Meet objective (accurately uses 4–5 discourse markers)	Meet objective (accurately uses 5–8 discourse markers when appropriate)	Meet objective (accurately uses discourse markers when appropriate)	Meet objective (accurately uses discourse markers when appropriate)	Weeks 5–6
Use decoding and word analysis skills to comprehend texts when reading or listening. (Language Arts) (Linguistic competence/word level) WIDA Standard 2	Meet objective with support of a word analysis strategy prompt	Meet objective with support of a word analysis strategy prompt	Meet objective	Meet objective	Meet objective	Weeks 1–6
Write mystery narratives (setting, plot, characters, and conclusion) through process writing. (Discourse competency; Linguistic competency) WIDA Standard 2	Meet objective (3–4 sentences)	Meet objective (2–3 paragraphs)	Meet objective (1–1.5 pages)	Meet objective (1.5–2 pages)	Meet objective (2–2.5 pages)	Weeks 2–8
Summarize mystery narratives that were read or watched for key elements (setting, characters, plot, conclusion, symbols). (Discourse competency) WIDA Standard 2	Identify orally main characters, important events, and conclusion with support of a graphic organizer and word bank	Identify orally setting, characters, important events, and conclusion with support of a graphic organizer	Retell mystery narratives (setting, characters, plot, conclusion)	Retell mystery narratives (setting, character and roles, plot, conclusion)	Summarize mystery narratives that were read or watched for key elements (setting, characters and roles, plot, conclusion, symbols)	Weeks 1–5
Identify speakers' and writers' assertions and support with textual evidence. (Strategic competency; Linguistic competency) WIDA Standard 2	Identify explicit claims in passages with guidance	Identify explicit claims in passages with guidance	Identify explicit authorial claims while referring to specific passages	Identify explicit and implicit authorial claims while referring to specific passages	Identify explicit and implicit authorial claims while referring to specific passages	Weeks 2–6

Formative assessments occurred throughout the term, and students were provided feedback on the various stages of their written assignments, from brainstorming, organizing, drafting, editing, etc. The most important end-of-term reading assessment was conducted using the Developmental Reading Assessment (DRA) (Beaver & Carter; 2006). The final writing assessment was a mystery narrative of two pages written in the first person, which required students to accurately use key mystery vocabulary and transition words, among other objectives, measured according to an analytical rubric. Hmong, Vietnamese, Chinese, and Russian students also read their stories aloud to the class and listened to their peers' stories. This was followed by a class discussion of the stories, which helped Kate to assess their oral skills.

Underlying Principles |||

In the opening scenario, Kate and Mrs. Yer were charged with the development of reading skills (i.e., to build vocabulary, word recognition, reading fluency, and reading strategies) while engaging in intensive and narrow extensive reading activities. They were given the MODEL assessment scores for their ELs, which revealed the learners' differing needs. Other than the test scores, they were given no other guidelines for creating their curriculum. They developed their mystery genre unit based on the theoretical and instructional principles of backward design, sequencing instruction, differentiated instruction according to proficiency level, integration of language skills, text analysis, and combinations of English language arts and WIDA standards (Table 5.1).

Research Agenda |||

In the literature on differentiation, there is little written about differentiation by language proficiency level, despite the fact that it is an essential approach to meeting the widely varied needs of second language learners in CBI environments. Many authors write about differentiation by learning style (Landrum & McDuffie, 2010; Pritchard, 2013) and by ability (e.g., struggling readers, students with special needs or giftedness) (Heacox, 2012; Tomlinson, 2001, 2014). Differentiating by proficiency level, and specifically language skill strengths and weaknesses, is not often examined in the research. When educators choose to provide a scaffold for ELs at a certain proficiency level, they can investigate the effectiveness of the scaffold. For example, does a simplified reading assist learners in developing their reading fluency? Questions about the learners' language abilities and content knowledge can be asked and answered on a micro level to ascertain whether learners at WIDA Level 1, for example, are making the same or greater linguistic and content gains as their peers at other levels.

Another area ripe for research is investigation of the design of language and content textbooks. Along with the implementation of CCSS, content-area educators need to integrate the skills of writing and speaking into their academic instruction. Many textbooks that are geared to mainstream students have been modified to include skills needed by ELs, for instance, including the writing process and pre- and post-reading discussion topics. However, the receptive skills that the ELs need (i.e., reading and listening) tend not to

Table 5.1: Principles That Informed the Mystery Genre Curriculum Design

Planning and Classroom Procedures	Underlying Principles
1. Standards and final assessments are analyzed in relation to each other to derive the objectives of the unit.	The backward design process is employed to ensure that all academic and language knowledge and skills required for success on the final assessment inform the development of the CBI unit objectives.
2. The mystery unit design integrates the four language skills plus grammar, vocabulary, and pronunciation as well as communicative competencies (e.g., linguistic, discourse, and sociocultural competencies).	The learners' linguistic needs in each domain are considered as they relate to the content objectives and the final assessment.
3. The natural connections between the content objectives and what learners need to be able to communicate about them are considered, so that language skills are intertwined with the content objectives.	Language skills and content topics need to be balanced so that neither the academic content nor the language learning content is overshadowed.
4. Teachers determine which reading materials to use and which they will need to develop or find to support the unit learning objectives. Not all content and language objectives will be met by the materials provided by the district.	Text analysis is employed in the development of the unit to determine what academic and language content is presented in the textbook and what needs to be supplemented by the teacher.
5. Each objective is analyzed against the proficiency level descriptors. The teacher considers what aspect(s) of the objective is achievable and the scaffolds needed to support student learning.	In order to meet the varied needs of the resident ELs in comparison to those of the newcomers, academic and linguistic objectives by language proficiency are delineated.
6. Discovery/inquiry learning, task-based instruction, and cooperative learning techniques are all employed in the unit since they enhance interaction.	The methodology in this unit is based on constructivist and interactionist theories of language learning, which support the ELs' SLA. All instructional activities for each language skill are designed to be student-centered, interactive, and meaningful.
7. General language terms and content terms are systematically introduced and integrated thoroughly into all curricular activities.	Explicit instruction of content and general academic vocabulary aids ELs to notice new vocabulary and to develop their academic language.
8. The writing process is presented in such a way that students learn each stage of the process (planning, researching, organizing, drafting, revising) and have ample practice time. They are then expected to write a mystery narrative for part of the final assessment.	Sequenced instruction of process writing stages with time and activities allocated for each stage is built into the curricular plan as it was not part of the original textbook-provided materials.

be explicitly taught in these new texts. Research on the integration of language skills into core academic textbooks can yield vital information for educators, so that an analysis of textbooks in the curriculum design process is less of a burden for the teacher. Furthermore, research into what continues to be needed for ELs in terms of textbook content would raise awareness of reading and listening development and strategies as well as assist educators in adding these much needed skills into their curriculum and instruction.

APPLYING WHAT YOU LEARNED
Questions and Tasks

1. How might one describe the process of backward design when taking into account district-required textbooks, enabling objectives, and final assessments that are not developed for the specific texts or EL populations?

2. What do you think are the most challenging parts of the process of developing unit objectives in alignment with standards, assessments, and materials, and differentiating them by proficiency level?

3. Work with a partner to choose a core content standard appropriate for your target grade level and work through Figure 5.2.

4. Are there other approaches to differentiation by proficiency level? What would those approaches look like?

5. How do you determine mastery of an objective?

6. What are some of the challenges that a preK–12 educator might experience when constructing his/her own units to meet learners' needs?

REFERENCES

American Council on Teaching Foreign Languages. (2012). *ACTFL proficiency guidelines 2012*. Alexandria, VA: Author. Retrieved from http://www.actfl.org/publications/guidelines-and-manuals/actfl-proficiency-guidelines-2012

Beaver, J. M., & Carter, M. A. (2006). *The developmental reading assessment* (2nd ed.) Upper Saddle River, NJ: Pearson.

Bernier, A. (1997). The challenge of language and history terminology from the student optic. In M. A. Snow & D. M. Brinton (Eds.), *The content-based classroom: Perspectives on integrating language and content* (pp. 95–103). White Plains, NY: Longman.

Common European Framework of Reference. (2013). *Common European framework of reference for languages: Learning, teaching, assessment*. Cambridge, England: Cambridge University Press.

Graves, K. (2014). *Syllabus and curriculum design for second language teaching*. In M. Celce-Murcia, D. M. Brinton, & M. A. Snow (Eds.), *Teaching English as a second or foreign Language* (4th ed., pp. 46–62). Boston, MA: National Geographic Learning/Cengage.

Heacox, D. (2012). *Differentiating instruction in the regular classroom: How to reach and teach all learners (Updated anniversary ed.)*. Minneapolis, MN: Free Spirit.

Landrum, T. J., & McDuffie, K. A. (2010). Learning styles in the age of differentiated instruction. *Exceptionality, 18*(1), 6–17.

National Governors Association Center for Best Practices, Council of Chief State School Officers. (2010). *Common core state standards*. Washington, DC: Authors. Retrieved from http://www.corestandards.org/

Pritchard, A. (2013). *Ways of learning: Learning theories and learning styles in the classroom*. New York, NY: Routledge.

Reynolds, K. M. (2015). *Approaches to inclusive English classrooms: A teacher's handbook for content-based instruction*. Bristol, England: Multilingual Matters.

Teachers of English to Speakers of Other Languages. (2006). *PreK–12 English language proficiency standards*. Alexandria, VA: Author.

Tomlinson, C. A. (2001). *How to differentiate instruction in mixed-ability classrooms*. Alexandria, VA: Association for Supervision and Curriculum Development.

Tomlinson, C. A. (2014). *The differentiated classroom: Responding to the needs of all learners* (2nd ed.). Alexandria, VA: Association for Supervision and Curriculum Development.

Wiggins, G., & McTighe, J. (2005). *Understanding by design* (2nd ed.). Alexandria, VA: Association for Supervision and Curriculum Development.

World Class Instructional Design and Assessment Consortium. (2008). *WIDA model*. Madison, WI: Board of Regents of the University of Wisconsin System.

World Class Instructional Design and Assessment Consortium. (2012). *2012 Amplification of the English language development standards, kindergarten–grade 12*. Madison, WI: Board of Regents of the University of Wisconsin System. Retrieved from https://www.wida.us/get.aspx?id=540

APPENDIX 5A
Four Language Learning Standards

There are many differing sets of standards being applied internationally in core academic or language fields. For example, in the U.S., the Common Core State Standards (CCSS) (National Governors Association Center for Best Practices, Council of Chief State School Officers, 2010) is a set of public school preK–12 standards that combine English language arts (for native English speakers) with history/social studies, science, and technical subjects. There is a separate set of Common Core mathematics standards. Other countries have their own set of academic standards. Which sets of standards are employed in conjunction with academic content standards depends on the school district or institution, state, or country.

Four influential models of language learning standards are described:

I. American Council on Teaching Foreign Languages. (2012). *ACTFL proficiency guidelines 2012*. Alexandria, VA: Author. Retrieved from http://www.actfl.org/publications/guidelines-and-manuals/actfl-proficiency-guidelines-2012

The American Council on Teaching Foreign Languages (ACTFL) standards were the first set of language proficiency guidelines established. They were developed in the U.S. and focus on learners' progress in language proficiency in modern languages, such as Spanish, French, Italian, and German. As originally conceived, the standards focused on speaking proficiency and were used to help educators determine oral communication abilities. Later, ACTFL created written proficiency standards. The receptive skills, listening and reading, are subsumed into the speaking and writing proficiency standards, respectively. The range of assessed abilities includes: novice low, mid, high; intermediate low, mid, high; advanced low, mid, high; and distinguished.

II. Teachers of English to Speakers of Other Languages. (2006). *PreK–12 English language proficiency standards*. Alexandria, VA: Author.

TESOL's *PreK–12 English Language Proficiency Standards* integrate the four language skills into five areas of focus: one in social, intercultural, and instructional language; and four in academic areas (language arts, math, science, and social studies). The range of proficiency is described as Level 1–Starting, Level 2–Emerging, Level 3–Developing, Level 4–Expanding, and Level 5–Bridging. Appropriate grade-level clusters are also important contributions of the *PreK–12 English Language Proficiency Standards*. TESOL first developed the *ESL Standards for PreK–12 Students* in 1997. The subsequent revision in 2006 was developed in tandem with the WIDA (2004) standards, so there are many similarities between these two sets of standards. For more information on how to obtain the standards visit www.tesol.org/advance-the-field/standards/prek-12-english-language-proficiency-standards.

III. World Class Instructional Design and Assessment Consortium. (2012). *2012 Amplification of the English language development standards, kindergarten–grade 12*. Madison, WI: Board of Regents of the University of Wisconsin System.

The WIDA standards concentrate on the development of academic language for preK–12 learners as well as the cognitive development that occurs in conjunction. The standards focus on social and academic areas (language arts, math, science, and social studies). The range of proficiency is described as Level 1–Starting, Level 2–Emerging, Level 3–Developing, Level 4–Expanding, and Level 5–Bridging. The WIDA standards differentiate language learning by grade-level clusters as well as linguistic competencies at the discourse, sentence, and word/phrase levels. For more information on the 2012 WIDA Standards, see www.wida.us/standards/eld.aspx.

IV. Common European Framework of Reference. (2013). *Common European framework of reference for languages: Learning, teaching, assessment*. Cambridge, England: Cambridge University Press. Retrieved from www.coe.int/t/dg4/linguistic/Source/Framework_EN.pdf

The Common European Framework of Reference (CEFR) standards have been developed over the last 20 years. They are generic standards that can be used for instruction of the different languages taught in Europe and are being widely employed in EFL contexts as well. All four language skills are integrated into the CEFR proficiency guidelines, called "can do" indicators, which span the following proficiency ranges: Breakthrough (A1), Waystage (A2), Threshold (B1), Vantage (B2), Effective Operational Proficiency (C1), and Mastery (C2). These indicators require approximately 240 hours of instruction to progress from bands A to C. The CEFR also includes other language competencies: linguistic, sociolinguistic, and pragmatic. They factor different contexts into the guidelines as well: public domain (i.e., socially distant, interpersonal), personal domain (i.e., socially close, interpersonal), educational domain, and occupational domain.

APPENDIX 5B
Common Core State Standards Employed in the Mystery Unit

This appendix details all the Common Core State Standards chosen for the mystery unit broken into categories: reading, writing, speaking/listening, and vocabulary. It is useful to categorize these objectives in order to verify that vital language skills are not overlooked. At the end of each standard is the communicative competence area being addressed by the standard.

Reading
- Phonics and Word Knowledge—(3) *Know and apply grade-level phonics and word analysis skills in decoding words.* [Linguistic competence at the word level]
- Fluency—(4) *Read with sufficient accuracy and fluency to support comprehension.* [Linguistic, Discourse, and Strategic competencies]

Writing
- Text Types and Purposes—(3) *Write narratives to develop real or imagined experiences or events using effective technique, descriptive details, and clear event sequences.* [Discourse competence]

Speaking and Listening
- (2) *Summarize a written text read aloud or information presented in diverse media and formats, including visually, quantitatively, and orally.* [Discourse competence]
- (3) *Summarize the points a speaker makes and explain how each claim is supported by reasons and evidence.* [Strategic competence]

Vocabulary Acquisition and Use
- (4a) *Use context (e.g., cause/effect relationships and comparisons in text) as a clue to the meaning of a word or phrase.* [Linguistic competence at the sentence level and Strategic competence]
- (6) *Acquire and use accurately grade-appropriate general academic and domain-specific words and phrases, including those that signal contrast, addition and other logical relationships (e.g., however, although, nevertheless, similarly, moreover, in addition)* [Linguistic competence at the word level]

Chapter **6**

Teacher Planning in Content-Based Instruction: Supports for Developing Novice Teachers' Language Awareness

Laura Baecher, Anne Ediger, & Tim Farnsworth

||| A Glimpse into Teacher Planning for Content-Based Instruction

In their urban middle school, several ESL teachers gather during a common planning period to design a content-based unit they will use with eighth grade students (13- to 14-year-olds) they see during the students' English language arts (ELA) period. The school has recently prescribed the use of a single textbook for all eighth grade ELA students—and the textbook is designed for native English–speaking students. The ESL teachers are concerned about how to create meaningful, context-rich yet language-appropriate lessons using this textbook. They question how they will be able to make the literary passages in the textbook accessible to their English learners (ELs), who come from a variety of first language backgrounds and who have lived from a few months to a few years in the U.S. They puzzle aloud over how the writing tasks will be doable for their EL students without significant linguistic support. They realize that they will need to spend some time reviewing literary devices themselves, in order to make sense of the content demands of literary analysis that are prevalent in the student writing assignments of the text. At the end of their meeting, the ESL teachers wonder how they will be able to make space for language teaching within this content.

Topics in CBI: Focusing on Language and Content

Multilingual students in the U.S. prekindergarten through Grade 12 (PreK–12) context face the challenge of mastering rigorous academic content in social studies, mathematics, science, and literature in a language other than their mother tongue. As a way to support these learners, many researchers and EL advocates have pointed to CBI as an effective way for ELs to gain access to content knowledge, thus avoiding falling behind in earning grade-level credits towards promotion and graduation (Council of Great City Schools, 2014; Snow & Brinton, 1997). In terms of language learning, CBI has been shown to be more efficient, more motivating, and more likely to enable students to achieve higher levels of second language proficiency (Lightbown, 2014). CBI in the U.S. is generally provided via an ESL teacher teaching solo or through co-teaching partnerships between ESL teachers and classroom content teachers, who are often underprepared for EL instruction (de Oliveira & Schleppegrell, 2015; Menken & Antunez, 2001). When ESL teachers do work collaboratively with content teachers to co-plan content and language instruction, they can support ELs by adapting instructional techniques and "sheltering" content material to help ELs understand the academic content while also providing specialized support for learning both language and content together (Echevarría, Vogt, & Short, 2017).

However, whether the instruction is provided by an individual teacher or through co-teaching, many teachers struggle with providing equivalent, or even integrated treatment of the language and the content components of CBI. At one end of the continuum, teachers have been found to teach language at the expense of, or in isolation from, content (Cammarata, 2009) while at the other end, they have been found to neglect language in their teaching (Lyster, 2007). More often than not, language goals end up being sacrificed for content-learning goals due either to the dominant role of the content teacher in the co-teaching relationship (Arkoudis, 2006) or to the ESL teacher's focus on sheltering content rather than language planning (Lindahl, Baecher, & Tomaš, 2013). Teaching both language and content in a closely integrated fashion is a highly complex task.

Although there is still considerable disagreement in SLA research about how teachers should focus on language form in classrooms (Ellis & Shintani, 2014), there is broad agreement that language instruction that also shelters content requires a highly systematic and intentional focus on language itself (Doughty & Williams, 1998; Goldenberg, 2013; Spada, 2011). In addition, with the Common Core State Standards[1] (National Governors Association Center for Best Practices & Council of Chief State School Officers, 2010) raising the expectations of native English–speaking and EL students alike:

> the ESL teacher clearly needs to provide leadership and linguistic expertise in analyzing academic language demands and designing relevant instruction. We need to address both content standards and English Language Development standards, and design language objectives for content-based lessons in order to bring about a balance of language, literacy and content in instruction. (Ranney, Schornack, Maguire, & Dillard-Paltrineri, 2014, p. 1)

For many ESL teachers educated in approaches to ESL instruction emphasizing comprehensible input (cf. Krashen, 1982), this means rethinking how they approach language teaching and developing a new understanding of the qualities and demands of academic language (Ranney, 2012). So how do ESL teachers design language-focused instruction (along with content) in a CBI context, and how well are teacher education programs able to prepare them to do this?

Planning for Language Instruction in CBI ||

One way to investigate how teachers address language within a CBI approach is to focus on the pre-teaching phase in which teachers specify what and how they intend to teach—the design and planning of lesson objectives focusing on language. In lesson planning, teachers envision a lesson that brings together their prior learning and teaching experiences, their beliefs and understandings of their students, their pedagogical content knowledge, and knowledge they have about the content they are teaching (Warren, 2000). It is in this planning phase of the teaching process that teachers enact their beliefs about how students learn, what students are interested in, how they should teach the subject, and what sorts of activities they will engage in (Bullough, 1992). By focusing on teachers' development of learning objectives as part of lesson planning, one can shine a spotlight on what teachers feel the focus of a lesson should be, and what they intend their lessons to achieve. While describing clear objectives may not be the same as actually delivering the instruction and assessment for achieving these objectives, the organization and articulation of language-focused instruction is a critical developmental skill for educators of ELs. If teachers are not intentionally organizing instruction focused on language learning, how, then, are ELs provided with instruction that actually targets their language development needs?

Thus, a key element of ESL teachers' knowledge base is the ability to plan lessons in terms of determining appropriate language objectives. The design of language objectives is one way in which teachers conceptualize and begin to lay out what and how they will teach language purposefully for student language development. Teachers who cannot design clear and effective language objectives risk treating students' language learning needs haphazardly, if they are addressed at all. Therefore, by looking at what teachers intend to teach, we can begin to see at least what they intend for their students to learn. Research on setting clear objectives in the general education literature shows a link between clarity of objectives and learner outcomes (Echevarría, Short, & Powers, 2006).

In order to be able to design effective language instruction, teachers of language and content need an understanding of and empathy for their students; an ability to assess their students' needs; and specific to language teaching, they require a high degree of teacher language awareness (TLA) (Andrews, 2007; Lindahl, 2013). TLA includes "considering such factors as the potential linguistic demands of the task and the linguistic capacity of the learners to cope with those demands" (Andrews, 2007, p. 33). According to Andrews, TLA:

> affects the teacher's ability to specify the most appropriate learning objectives, and to select materials and tasks which are most likely to serve those objectives, ensuring that they are appropriate in terms of the learners' age, previous learning, and present stage of inter-lingual development, and that they serve the desired learning outcomes. (p. 41)

While there is already a significant body of research on the collaborative processes involved in content area and ESL teachers' co-planning (see Pawan & Greene, this volume), there have been relatively few studies of how teachers specifically plan language objectives within the teaching of content. Popko's (2005) case studies of teachers' planning and teaching began to show that teachers struggled to connect their declarative ("explicit knowledge that we can report and of which we are consciously aware") and their procedural language knowledge ("knowledge of how to do things, . . . often implicit") (Robinson, 1997, p. 47). Language teachers in Popko's study were not able to make connections between what they had learned about language in their teacher education coursework and their instructional decisions, falling back instead upon the learning and teaching experiences they themselves had had in the classroom.

Lyster (2007) highlights the dangers in this lack of intentionality, noting that "content-based instruction that only alludes to language incidentally falls short of full-fledged integration, and decontextualized grammar instruction, by definition, precludes integration" (p. 26). Similarly, Ellis (2006) reviews what second language acquisition (SLA) research has to say about optimal grammar teaching, reaching several critical conclusions about first, whether grammar should be taught, and then, if so, which ways are optimal. Ellis (2006) makes three specific recommendations:

1. A case exists for teaching explicit grammatical knowledge as a means of assisting subsequent acquisition of implicit knowledge. Teaching explicit knowledge can be incorporated into both a focus-on-forms and a focus-on-form approach.[2] In the case of a focus-on-forms approach, a differentiated approach involving sometimes deductive and sometimes inductive instruction may work best.

2. An incidental focus-on-form approach is of special value because it affords an opportunity for extensive treatment of grammatical problems (in contrast to the intensive treatment afforded by a focus-on-forms approach).

3. Corrective feedback is important for learning grammar. It is best conducted using a mixture of implicit and explicit feedback types that are both input based and output based. (p. 102)

Ellis found that most SLA researchers agree that implicit knowledge helps for using the L2, but in these conclusions he addresses whether explicit grammar knowledge has any value, and how implicit and explicit knowledge are best taught. For Ellis, *explicit* knowledge includes *analyzed knowledge* ("a conscious awareness of how a structure works") and *metalinguistic explanation* (the "knowledge of grammatical metalanguage and the ability to understand the explanation of rules"), while *implicit* knowledge is "procedural, is held unconsciously, and can only be verbalized if it is made explicit" (p. 95). Ellis concludes that teaching explicit knowledge facilitates students' development of implicit knowledge, and recommends using each type, both deductively and inductively, for different types of students. He also recommends using incidental approaches—unplanned, occurring as needed during a lesson—because teachers can address multiple structures in a lesson, compared to planned instruction, where generally only a single predetermined structure is taught. Finally, Ellis stresses the importance of providing both implicit and explicit feedback, through both input- [listening and reading] and output-based [speaking and writing] activities.

A growing number of empirical studies build upon a belief in the value of TLA, focusing on the nature of explicitly stated language objectives, including Bigelow and Ranney (2005), Bigelow (2010), Fisher and Frey (2010), Regalla (2012), and Baecher, Farnsworth, and Ediger (2014). Fisher and Frey (2010) analyzed hundreds of language objectives by practicing mainstream teachers who had completed coursework on teaching ELs, English language development, and ESL methodologies, categorizing the language objectives into three categories: those that focused on vocabulary, language structure, and language function. The most common focus of language objectives was discipline-specific vocabulary (50 percent overall)—most commonly focused on by single-subject teachers—which the authors found "both understandable and problematic" (p. 330). The next most common focus was structure (30 percent overall), for example, using past tense verbs, of which about 15 percent involved the use of sentence frames. Finally, the remaining category of objectives focused on language functions (20 percent), such as justification, persuasion, and description. Interestingly, many of the so-called language objectives were actually activity descriptions, from which Fisher and Frey concluded that teachers might not understand clearly how certain activities lead to specific learning outcomes.

Bigelow and Ranney (2005) investigated how ESL teacher candidates designed language objectives, starting from either the language or the content goal. Although the teachers initially focused their attention on such issues as the pacing and timing of portions of their lessons, as they became more skilled, they reported the need to pay more attention to the classic challenge of CBI: the conflict between focusing on language versus content. Generally, the teacher candidates were more successful when they started with the content and sought out language goals to support it; however, "the content often eclipse[d] the language objectives of the lesson" (p. 195). The teacher candidates struggled to identify specific language objectives other than vocabulary, particularly if a lesson, text, or cooperating teacher did not designate explicit language issues to focus on, or teacher candidates felt they did not have adequate metalinguistic knowledge or knowledge of their learners' language needs. In general, they struggled to teach language in other than the deductive (i.e., providing explicit rules), decontextualized way (e.g., a grammar worksheet not connected to the content material) in which they themselves had been taught a foreign language, and no matter where the teacher candidates began their planning (from the content or from the language goals), they tended to address only a very limited variety of linguistic forms, with most addressing verb forms.

Bigelow (2010) also investigated K–12 ESL teacher candidates across a wide range of practicum teaching settings, looking at their choices and reflections on those choices as they planned language objectives within their content-based lesson plans. The elementary teachers in her sample had more form-focused language objectives than did the secondary teachers. Bigelow also found that the teacher candidates tended to design objectives in a very narrow fashion, focusing primarily on vocabulary and grammar points (mainly past tense verbs), and teaching the productive language skills (speaking and writing) rather than focusing on listening and reading.

Like Bigelow, Regalla (2012) found teachers focusing on vocabulary as their main language objective focus. Regalla focused on the Sheltered Instruction Observation Protocol (SIOP) model[3] (Echevarría, Short, & Powers, 2006). The SIOP Model of instruction is a commonly used approach to teaching content such as science or mathematics in English to students who are not yet proficient in English. In this approach, teachers are directed to identify and teach the key language demands of a content unit, including but not limited to specialized vocabulary, and to present the material in such a way as to make it more easily comprehensible to English learners. Regalla (2012) examined the effects of workshops presented to a small group of elementary student teaching interns with ELs mainstreamed in their classes. The focus of the workshops was to provide the interns with training in strategies to support their ELs, including instruction on teaching language objectives according to the SIOP model. Results showed that the interns' teaching of language objectives was limited to teaching vocabulary by creating context and using visual supports. This suggests that although the teaching of key vocabulary is an important component of the SIOP model, language objectives cannot be limited to teaching word knowledge alone.

Most recently, Baecher, Farnsworth, and Ediger (2014) investigated the ability of preK–12 teacher candidates to design language objectives within content lessons, based upon an analysis of their lesson plans from a practicum course taken at the end of an MA in TESOL program. Building upon the findings from the previously mentioned studies, the study employed a qualitative analysis of content and language objectives designed by TESOL teacher candidates, which were then reviewed through descriptive statistics. The results were analyzed to determine salient patterns of clear and problematic objectives among different subject areas, grade levels, and language foci.

The data analysis was conducted in two phases. First, in an exploratory phase, a sample of lesson plans was examined and discussed in order to arrive at a taxonomy of issues and descriptors of clear lesson objectives. Second, in a validation phase, 107 plans from 43 teacher candidates were examined using the taxonomy to further test and refine the instrument, and to analyze the frequency of various problematic issues in the plans. Definitions of successful/acceptable objectives for both content and language objectives were drafted. These categories roughly describe the problems encountered with the language and content objectives:

- **Vaguely/broadly worded:** These objectives were considered unclear due to vagueness or overly broad descriptions of the understandings they described. For example, one content objective stated: "Students will use the scientific method."

- **Undigested standard:** Some objectives merely quoted verbatim a portion of the state content-area learning standards, which, while useful, did not in general describe understandings at the lesson level of achievement. For example, one ELA content objective stated, "Students will be able to read, write, listen, and speak for information and understanding, literary response and expression, critical analysis and evaluation and social interaction."

- **Not feasible in a single period of instruction:** Some objectives were clearly not feasible within a single period of instruction, which was at the core of the definition. For example, one lesson had as its language objective, "Students will make and support inferences about information and ideas with reference to features in oral and written text. Such features include vocabulary, format, facts, sequence, register, and relevance of details."

- **Describes an activity rather than a learning goal:** The objectives described what students would do during the lesson instead of what they would learn. For example, one plan stated, "Students will describe pictures and situations using the present progressive tense."

- **Describes an ELA rather than an ESL goal, where it should be clearly distinct:** The objectives did not include any understandings that would be unique to or particularly appropriate for ESL learners as opposed to general education students. For example, one lesson objective stated, "Students will understand that authors write with different purposes."

- **Clear mismatch between content objectives and language objectives:** The language and content objectives bore no logical or functional relationship to each other. For example, one language objective stated, "Students will identify parts of speech," whereas the content objective stated, "Students will understand why Beowulf is characterized as an epic hero."

In addition to analyzing the objectives, the specific language focus of the plans was categorized by establishing definitions for the following foci: (1) vocabulary; (2) grammar (and the specific grammar focus); (3) language function; (4) language strategy use; (5) subskill of reading, writing, listening, or speaking (and what subskill); and (6) sentence frame or starter. The majority of the plans analyzed had an ELA content-area focus. Within content objectives, ELA objectives were clear less often than those of other subjects. This may indicate that ELA content-based lesson plans pose unique challenges for TESOL teacher candidates in that the content and language are sometimes difficult to distinguish. Content objectives were judged as clear more often than language objectives were: 55 percent versus 38 percent for language objectives.

Objectives for elementary grades were rated satisfactory more often than those for secondary grades, for both language and content. Overall, the number of satisfactory language objectives was low—38 percent of the total. The number of satisfactory language objectives in mathematics and in social studies was only about 30 percent combined, which may indicate that crafting language objectives in these content domains is particularly challenging for teacher candidates. In secondary grades, ELA not ESL (the objective had no connection to ESL instruction specifically) was a bigger challenge than it was in elementary grades. The "activity, not goal" problem—where language objectives describe classroom activities to be completed rather than student competencies or understandings to be addressed—was persistent across grades and subject areas. So, too, was the problem of objectives that were "too vague." Of the plans that were problematic in multiple areas (more common with language objectives), the most common difficulties involved being "too vague" and "ELA not ESL."

Finally, the language objectives were further analyzed to determine if they focused on vocabulary, structure, function, strategy, subskill within modalities—such as "using context clues in reading"—or sentence frames. Plans most commonly focused on the four skills rather than on other aspects of language, such as grammatical structure. The four skills were generally covered throughout a unit, but within a single lesson plan, only one was the focus. The second most common focus was vocabulary. Overall, there was little focus on language function or strategy use. When grammar was a focus, it was only on a limited range of structures, and primarily on verb tenses or adjectives. The only other structures featured— several more than once—were transition words (either sequence words or comparison/contrast words), identifying parts of speech (noun, verb, adjective, adverb only), and sentence structure (involving peer correction of sentences in writing). When specific language skills/modes were focused on, reading and writing were most commonly addressed, possibly due to the current strong emphasis on development of literacy skills in K–12 schools.

Taken together, these studies illustrate persistent problems in the way that novice and even some experienced teachers conduct language planning within the CBI context. First of all, as often noted, the language component of the lesson can easily become lost in the demands of teaching content, certainly in the case of K–12 CBI classrooms. Secondly, teachers, especially novices, tend to focus on a narrow range of language structures, such as vocabulary and verb tenses, and to neglect the treatment of language from a functional perspective (e.g., how to ask for clarification). This may be partially due to teacher candidates' lack of confidence in or metalinguistic knowledge of a wider range of language structures and functions (Ediger & McCormack, 2015). Thirdly, many teachers seem to confuse the activity students will engage in (e.g., reading a specific text) with the desired learning outcomes of a lesson (e.g., greater fluency in sight word recognition or understanding of typical structures within a text). While these may also be problems outside of CBI contexts in traditional stand-alone ESL classrooms, the dual demands of the CBI classroom may exacerbate these problems. (See also Gibbons, this volume.)

In the next section, we propose some principles of sound lesson planning in CBI classrooms that are both research based and practitioner friendly. Language objectives need not get lost in the CBI classroom shuffle, nor be limited to a list of vocabulary items or verb tenses that EL students are likely to encounter in a content-area lesson.

Underlying Principles ||

Whether a class for ELs is taught by a content teacher, an ESL specialist, or is co-taught, there are several key features of effective planning that support English language development. These principles can support the teachers' efforts to keep language at the forefront of their planning process. Table 6.1 illustrates six of these key principles.

Using a Lesson-Planning Template ||

Another particularly effective approach we have used for guiding teacher candidates in developing integrated language and content objectives in their student teaching practicum is through a lesson planning template that requires them to plan for both areas in parallel fashion (see Appendix 6A). This template, developed collaboratively with input from TESOL and other subject-area faculty in the School of Education at Hunter College, requires candidates to focus on both the larger teaching context of an entire unit of instruction, bringing in such considerations as the "big idea" in the content, relevant content and language learning standards, and the larger language function, together with the more detailed content and language objectives of individual lessons. By providing detailed questions for teacher candidates to answer in each cell in the template, we can guide them toward the specific issues they must plan for at each point in their lesson structure. All TESOL program candidates are required to submit a completed lesson plan template to a supervisor for feedback before that lesson is observed by the supervisor.

Research Agenda ||

Various aspects of the juxtaposition of language and content in integrated instruction suggest the need for more research, first at the K–12 level, but also for other age levels in a similar fashion. First of all, since planning for and teaching both in an equal and integrated fashion is so challenging, helpful future investigations could address some of these questions:

- How do experienced or master teachers integrate language and content, not only in the planning stage but also in broader curriculum design, materials development, and assessment?
- Exactly what aspects of TLA are needed for effective integration of language and content?
- How do teachers actualize the teaching of their language objectives, and what is the relationship between how they are taught and the language objectives planned for those lessons?
- How do teachers over time develop understandings and skills for operationalizing content and language planning as they move from abstract understanding of language to applying it to the design and execution of instruction?
- How should teacher education best prepare teachers to integrate language and content?

Table 6.1: Core Principles in Designing Language Objectives in Content-Based Instruction

Recommended Practices	Underlying Principles
1. Plan at the unit rather than at the lesson level to balance content and language development.	When planning for language and content, it is important to be realistic about what can be accomplished in a single lesson. Usually, in a single lesson it is difficult to foreground both language and content. Instead, one or the other generally takes the lead. Therefore, if teachers plan at the mini-unit level—for example, one or two weeks of instruction, it is possible to see on which days content will be foregrounded and on which days there are language development opportunities. Often, at the start of a new unit, ELs need heavy sheltering of content and those initial lessons may be heavy in content that has been adapted to create maximum accessibility. That can include use of the native language in materials or discussions, modified materials, and extensive use of visual supports. Toward the middle and end of the instructional cycle, more space can be created for focus on language development as students move towards their end of unit performance task.
2. Design the performance task around a relevant language function.	Using a backwards planning approach (Wiggins & McTighe, 2011), once the content goal is clear, teachers can spend time thinking through the performance task that students will need to complete in order to demonstrate their understanding of the content learned. This performance task is generally carried out in an expressive modality of speaking or writing, and falls into a particular language function. For example, in a content unit on healthy eating habits, students might be asked to deliver a persuasive speech to their classmates that would convince them to make healthier diet choices. Note that the performance task naturally fits with the content, and that there is an authentic audience for the language output. Once the type of language needed for performing this task is identified, the language objective as well as the time and place for instruction on it can be developed through backwards planning. (See also K. Reynolds, this volume.)
3. Examine the language students will need for the performance task by doing the task yourself first.	Once a performance task has been selected, it is very helpful for teachers to then try to write it out or do the task themselves. This helps teachers "see" the actual language needed for the task and supports their language awareness of what students will need to be taught and practice over the course of the unit of study. At this point, teachers can create a simple rubric that can be used to provide feedback to students on the performance task with attention to the content understanding as well as the language use expected. By setting down the performance task and developing an associated rubric at the beginning of the unit, teachers can find it easier to set daily language objectives. Oftentimes it is the process of deciding what *not* to teach that can be more difficult than determining what *to* teach. Planning with the end in mind makes for more coherent lesson design and helps the teacher see what language must be addressed in order for students to be successful on the performance task.
4. Consider the language that students will need in order to discuss the content.	Starting with a consideration of the core content vocabulary ensures that students will have enough practice with the content-obligatory language (Snow, Met, & Genesee, 1989) to express their content understanding. This vocabulary will consist of academic words with particular meanings in the content area (e.g., *table* for mathematics) and technical language always associated with particular disciplines (e.g., *carbohydrates* for science). Most content teachers, however, present vocabulary as single words rather than presenting them in common word strings. Using online corpus-based tools[3] can aid in the process of planning to present and model content language within usable chunks (e.g., *complete the table*; *reduce the amount of carbohydrates*). In addition, making choices about which vocabulary (strings) students will need to use in their performance task can also help in the editing process so that a smaller number of high-frequency terms can be incorporated into lesson plans.

Table 6.1 (*continued*)

Recommended Practices	Underlying Principles
5. Plan for instruction and practice with the language students will need to carry out the language function.	The language other than the content vocabulary will include the general language needed to accomplish the function, set out in the performance task. In the example of the persuasive speech on healthy eating, the language function may call for the use of modals, parallel structures, or use of rhetorical questions (see, e.g., www.gympcentss.eq.edu.au/classwork/cs2_7/pdf/Week10/LanguageFeaturesOfPersuasiveTexts.pdf). This language is what Snow, Met, and Genesee (1989) refer to as content-compatible, meaning the language that travels across content areas and works to support academic language functions in various disciplines. When teachers are able to clarify which language is content-obligatory and which is content-compatible, they can then re-integrate those in the planning of the unit of study.
6. Make the language focus take the form of both *planned* and *incidental* instruction.	Language instruction can take place in multiple ways—it can be designed and presented from the outset as mini-lessons intended to create awareness of new language forms or address specific, anticipated needs of the students (planned instruction) for comprehending readings, or expressing particular functions in their writing or speaking. It can also take the form of corrective feedback or simple noticing of how language is used—right at the point when it is encountered (i.e., through incidental instruction) (Ellis, 2001, 2006). This latter focus on language is not presented as an explicit lesson, but rather, occurs in response to students' language production, misunderstandings, or difficulties in conveying intended meaning.

Thus far, much of the research into integrated language and content has approached this issue from the viewpoint of ESL teachers and their preparation, but approaching it from the view of how content teachers might also incorporate language instruction would also be helpful, including looking into some of these questions:

■ How do novice content-area teachers integrate language instruction into their content when they have EL students in their classes?

■ When preparing content-area teachers to help ELs by integrating language in their CBI classrooms, what should this preparation optimally include?

■ What sorts of impact might preparing content-area teachers to integrate language in their instruction have on student content and language learning outcomes?

Future research into any of these issues could provide valuable insights by making use of a wider range of types of data, including:

■ think-aloud data from teachers during lesson planning

■ observational or discourse data from classroom interaction around language (though some already exists—see, e.g., Simard & Jean, 2011)

■ outcome data assessing the impact of instruction focusing on language in CBI contexts.

Clearly, there will continue to be much interest and concern about the various ways in which language and content can (or should) be integrated, as well as how such knowledge might be built into ESL and content-area teacher preparation programs in the future.

APPLYING WHAT YOU LEARNED
Questions and Tasks

1. The scenario at the outset of this chapter represents a common challenge of the content-based syllabus in course design for ELs. Comment on how this challenge takes on different aspects depending on the context for teaching, taking into account these factors:

   a. the student population

   b. the faculty

   c. the content area of the course

   d. the degree and type of language support available

   e. the primary goal(s) of the course

2. How does the process of instructional planning differ when you begin with content versus beginning with language in mind? How are the two mutually supportive?

3. If the content-based English lessons described in the opening scenario were delivered through collaboratively taught lessons between an English teacher and an ESL teacher, how would the planning process ideally take place?

4. If you are currently teaching, what are the challenges you encounter in planning for language and content? What part of these challenges is due to the structures and expectations of your institution and what part has to do with the complexity of the work?

5. Look at the Sample Template for Designing CBI Units of Study provided in Appendix 6A. How does this template incorporate the suggestions given in this chapter? How could you use such a template in your (or your teacher candidates') lesson plan preparation? Would you need to change any aspects of this template for use in your particular teaching context, or to fit your philosophy of teaching/learning? Which aspects?

6. Obtain either a text in a content area to be taught to a class of EL students or an ESL student's essay. From the text, identify several possible language focus points that you could address with these students to assist them in understanding the content of the text. From the essay, identify several language points that the student (1) already appears to understand well (and upon which future instruction could be built) and (2) still needs some instruction on in order to express his/her intended meaning in this essay more effectively.

ENDNOTES

1. The Common Core State Standards (National Governors Association for Best Practices, 2010) are a set of learning standards for language arts and mathematics that have been adopted by most U.S. states as of this writing. These standards are the closest thing the U.S. has to national learning standards or curriculum, in contrast to most other developed nations. The Common Core standards in language arts place a heavier focus on reading non-fiction texts, being able to cite and analyze textual evidence, and producing academic writing than most states' previous standards.

2. Ellis (2006) distinguishes a "focus-on-forms" from a "focus-on-form" approach by saying that "'[f]ocus-on-forms' refers to instruction involving a structure-of-the-day approach, where the students' primary focus is on form (i.e., accuracy) and where the activities are directed intensively at a single grammatical structure. This approach, then, involves teaching grammar in a series of separate lessons." In contrast, " 'focus-on-form' entails a focus on meaning with attention to form arising out of the communicative activity. This focus can be planned, where a focused task is required to elicit occasions for using a predetermined grammatical structure…" or it could also be "incidental, where attention to form in the context of a communicative activity is not predetermined but rather occurs in accordance with the participants' linguistic needs as the activity proceeds. In this approach, it is likely that attention will be given to a wide variety of grammatical structures during any one task and thus will be extensive. Focus on form implies no separate grammar lessons but rather grammar teaching integrated into a curriculum consisting of communicative tasks" (pp. 100–101).

3. Some useful corpus-based resources include: The Corpus of Contemporary American English (COCA) (http://corpus.byu.edu/coca/); collocational dictionaries (e.g., Oxford Learners' Dictionaries, www.oxfordlearnersdictionaries.com; the Collins COBUILD Dictionary, www.collins-dictionary.com/dictionary/english); and concordancers (e.g., Lextutor, www.lextutor.ca)

REFERENCES

Andrews, S. (2007). *Teacher language awareness*. Cambridge, England: Cambridge University Press.

Arkoudis, S. (2006). Negotiating the rough ground between ESL and mainstream teachers. *International Journal of Bilingual Education & Bilingualism, 9*(4), 415–433.

Baecher, L., Farnsworth, T., & Ediger, A. (2014). The challenges of planning language objectives in content-based ESL instruction. *Language Teaching Research, 18*(1), 118–136.

Bigelow, M. (2010). Learning to plan for a focus on form in CBI: The role of teacher knowledge and teaching context. In J. Davis (Ed.), *World language teacher education: Transitions and challenges in the twenty-first century* (pp. 35–56). Charlotte, NC: Information Age Publishing.

Bigelow, M., & Ranney, S. (2005). Pre-service ESL teachers' knowledge about language and its transfer to lesson planning. In N. Bartels (Ed.), *Applied linguistics and language teacher education* (Vol. 4, pp. 179–200). New York, NY: Springer Science/Business Media.

Bullough, R. V. (1992). Beginning teacher curriculum decision-making, personal teaching metaphors, and teacher education. *Teaching and Teacher Education, 8*(3), 239–252.

Cammarata, L. (2009). Negotiating curricular transitions: Foreign language teachers' learning experience with content-based instruction. *Canadian Modern Language Review/La Revue Canadienne Des Langues Vivantes, 65*(4), 559–585.

Council of Great City Schools. (2014). *A framework for raising expectations and instructional rigor for English language learners.* Retrieved from http://www.cgcs.org/cms/lib/DC00001581/Centricity/Domain/4/Framework%20for%20Raising%20Expectations.pdf

de Oliveira, L., & Schleppegrell, M. (2015). *Focus on grammar and meaning.* New York, NY: Oxford University Press.

Doughty, C., & Williams, J. (1998). *Focus on form in classroom SLA.* Cambridge, England: Cambridge University Press.

Echevarría, J., Short, D., & Powers, K. (2006). School reform and standards-based education: An instructional model for English language learners. *Journal of Educational Research, 99*(4), 195–210.

Echevarría, J., Vogt, M., & Short, D. J. (2017). *Sheltered content instruction: Teaching English-language learners with diverse abilities* (5th ed.). Boston, MA: Pearson.

Ediger, A., & McCormack, B. (2015, May). *Teacher language knowledge as applied to error analysis and design of instruction.* Paper presented at the CARLA Language Teacher Education Conference, Minneapolis, MN.

Ellis, R. (2001). Investigating form-focused instruction. In R. Ellis (Ed.), *Form-focused instruction and second language learning* (pp. 1–46). Malden, MA: Blackwell.

Ellis, R. (2006). Current issues in the teaching of grammar: An SLA perspective. *TESOL Quarterly, 40*(1), 83–107.

Ellis, R., & Shintani, N. (2014). *Exploring language pedagogy through second language acquisition research.* New York, NY: Routledge.

Fisher, D., & Frey, N. (2010). Unpacking the language purpose: Vocabulary, structure, and function. *TESOL Journal, 1*(3), 315–337.

Goldenberg, C. (2013). Unlocking the research on English learners: What we know—and don't yet know—about effective instruction. *American Educator, 37*(2), 4–11.

Krashen, S. D. (1982). *Principles and practice in second language acquisition.* Oxford, England: Oxford University Press.

Lightbown, P. (2014). *Focus on content-based language teaching.* Oxford, England: Oxford University Press.

Lindahl, K. M. (2013). *Exploring an invisible medium: Teacher language awareness among preservice K12 educators of English language learners* (Unpublished doctoral dissertation). The University of Utah, Salt Lake City.

Lindahl, K., Baecher, L., & Tomaš, Z. (2013). Teacher language awareness in content-based activity design. *Journal of Immersion and Content-Based Language, 1*(2), 198–225.

Lyster, R. (2007). *Learning and teaching languages through content: A counterbalanced approach.* Amsterdam, The Netherlands: Benjamins.

Menken, K., & Antunez, B. (2001). *An overview of the preparation and certification of teachers working with limited English proficient (LEP) students.* Washington, DC: National Clearinghouse for Bilingual Education.

National Governors Association Center for Best Practices, Council of Chief State School Officers. (2010). *Common core state standards.* Washington, DC: Author. Retrieved from http://www.corestandards.org/

Popko, J. (2005). How MA-TESOL students use knowledge about language in teaching ESL classes. In N. Bartels (Ed.), *Applied linguistics and language teacher education* (Vol. 4, pp. 387–403). New York, NY: Springer Science/Business Media.

Ranney, S. (2012). Defining and teaching academic language: Developments in K–12 ESL. *Language and Linguistics Compass, 6*(9), 560–574.

Ranney, S., Schornack, M., Maguire, C., & Dillard-Paltrineri, B. (2014, Spring). Academic language demands: Texts, tasks, and levels of language. *Minnetesol Journal*. Retrieved from http://minnetesoljournal.org/spring-2014/academic-language-demands-texts-tasks-and-levels-of-language

Regalla, M. (2012). Language objectives: More than just vocabulary. *TESOL Journal, 3*(2), 210–230.

Robinson, P. (1997). Individual differences and the fundamental similarity of implicit and explicit adult second language learning. *Language Learning, 47*(1), 45–99.

Simard, D., & Jean, G. (2011). An exploration of L2 teachers' use of pedagogical interventions devised to draw L2 learners' attention to form. *Language Learning, 61*, 759–785.

Snow, M. A., & Brinton, D. M. (Eds.). (1997). *The content-based classroom: Perspectives on integrating language and content.* White Plains, NY: Longman.

Snow, M. A., Met, M., & Genesee, F. (1989). A conceptual framework for the integration of language and content in second/foreign language instruction. *TESOL Quarterly, 23*(2), 201–217.

Spada, N. (2011). Beyond form-focused instruction: Reflections on past, present and future research. *Language Teaching, 44*, 225–236.

Warren, L. L. (2000). Teacher planning: A literature review. *Educational Research Quarterly, 24*(2), 37–42.

Wiggins, G. P., & McTighe, J. (2011). *The understanding by design guide to creating high-quality units.* Alexandria, VA: Association for Supervision and Curriculum Development.

APPENDIX 6A
Sample Template for Designing CBI Units of Study

Overview of Learning Segment: Respond to the prompts below (**no more than 2 single-spaced pages, including prompts**) by typing your responses within the brackets following each prompt.

Content Curriculum Standard(s)	English Language Proficiency Standard(s)
Which content area standards is this WHOLE learning segment driving towards? Choose no more than 2—may be from Common Core State Standards and/or relevant state standards. [student teachers fill in here]	*Which language skills is this learning segment teaching, practicing, and assessing? Choose no more than 2—use WIDA or ESL Progressions or standards.* [ ]

Big Idea	Content Understanding(s)	Language Function	Target Vocabulary	Performance Assessment
What essential questions or big ideas does the larger unit address? Where does this learning segment sit within the larger unit of study? THIS SHOULD ALIGN TO THE CONTENT AREA [ ]	*What is the content understanding you want to develop in this learning segment? Choose 1–2 clear and focused content understandings.* THESE MUST BE LIT-SCI-MATH-SS, NOT A LANGUAGE or LITERACY SKILL GOAL [ ]	*What is the language function that students will be working towards in this learning segment? Choose 1 language function.* SUGGESTED LANGUAGE FUNCTIONS INCLUDE: DESCRIBE, COMPARE, CONTRAST, EXPLAIN, JUSTIFY [ ]	*Content-specific: What are the content/discipline words in this learning segment (1–3)?* [ ] *Cross-content: What are the words in this learning segment that cross disciplines (1-3)?* [ ] VOCABULARY SHOULD BE PRESENTED IN WORD STRINGS OF FREQUENT COLLOCATIONS, NOT AS SINGLE WORDS	*What will students produce for you to assess both content understanding and language skills at the end of this learning segment? It should be in one modality—L, S, R or W.* THIS MUST PARALLEL THE LANGUAGE FUNCTION—*and is not part of the learning segment plans but will occur when they are finished.* [ ]

Lesson Plan Day 1: Respond to the prompts below (**no more than 3 single-spaced pages, including prompts**) by typing your responses within the brackets following each prompt.

Content Objective	Language Objective
What will students leave the lesson understanding that they didn't know before? STATE THE CONTENT LEARNING GOAL, NOT THE CONTENT ACTIVITY THAT YOU WILL DESIGN TO BRING STUDENTS THERE NOR THE ASSESSMENT OF THAT LEARNING. "CONTENT" MEANS LITERATURE, SCIENCE, SOCIAL STUDIES, OR MATH—NOT ELA SKILLS. [ ]	*What language will the students be asked to practice/learn in this lesson?* STATE THE LANGUAGE OBJECTIVE IN TERMS OF THE SKILL (L-R-S-W) AND THE TARGET FORMS (VOCABULARY PLUS GRAMMAR) STUDENTS WILL USE. [ ]

APPENDIX 6A *(continued)*

Materials		
List all of the textual, visual, auditory materials, technology, etc. that will be called upon for use in this lesson. [ ]		

Opening		
Do Now/Starter with Anticipatory Set/Motivation		**Time (approx. # of minutes)**
How will you get students started as they enter the room? What will be the first task they must engage in to capture their interest? SHOW SOMETHING THAT SPARKS THINKING ON THE LANGUAGE OR CONTENT OF THIS LESSON [ ]		5 [ ]

Introduction to New Material (I Do/We Do)		
Statement of Lesson Objectives		**Time**
How will you express to students what the learning goals for the lesson are? (What language will students understand?) [ ]		2 [ ]
Guided Practice of Lesson Task		**Time**
How will you show students what you want them to engage in? *What will you model in terms of language forms/target language?* *How will you set them up to "notice" some language?* SHOW STUDENTS THE LANGUAGE THEY NEED TO PRACTICE IN THIS LESSON. [ ]		5 [ ]
Checking for Understanding of Task (Informal Assessment)		**Time**
How will you assess that students are ready to begin the independent work portion of the lesson? [ ]		3 [ ]

Independent Practice (You Do)		
Differentiation of Lesson Task		**Time**
What will students be engaged in for the major work portion of the lesson? *How will it be differentiated for students at different proficiency levels (in terms of process/product/content)?* *How will students be grouped/paired?* *What choices will students have about their learning?* SHOW WHAT STUDENTS WILL BE GIVEN TO DO DIFFERENTLY IF THEY ARE HIGH vs. LOW PROFICIENCY (e.g., different materials, different linguistic supports, different task set up, different level of teacher or peer support). [ ]		20 [ ]

APPENDIX 6A *(continued)*

Feedback on Lesson Task (Informal Assessment)	Time
What will you do to watch and provide on-the-spot feedback on language use to students as you circulate or target a particular group? *What language do you want to see or hear being used in this portion of the lesson? Did you try performing this same task yourself to determine this?* *What possible difficulties/errors/misconceptions can you predict may come up? How can or have you built these into your original guided practice?* *What are some model answers you are expecting?* SHOW YOUR METHOD FOR COLLECTING DATA ON STUDENTS HERE *(iPad, student roster, rubric, notecards).* [ ]	*During above*

Closing	
Students' Reflection on Learning/Homework Extension	Time
What will you do to invite students to share back what they did or learned during the lesson? *How do you intend to create awareness about what they have learned? Will learning be on display in the classroom or in an online forum?* *What will they be asked to practice when they go home related to the lesson?* [ ]	10 [ ]

Impact on Student Learning (Informal Assessment)
What data did you collect during or at the conclusion of the lesson to review in order to ascertain where students are in their language and content learning? [ ]

Lesson Plan Day 2: Respond to the prompts below (**no more than 3 single-spaced pages, including prompts**) by typing your responses within the brackets following each prompt.

Copy/Paste the blank lesson template.

Lesson Plan Day 3: Respond to the prompts below (**no more than 3 single-spaced pages, including prompts**) by typing your responses within the brackets following each prompt.

Copy/Paste the blank lesson template.

Note: To request an electronic copy of the template, email Laura Baecher (lbaecher@hunter.cuny.edu).

Chapter 7

Bringing Together Academic Language and Subject Learning in Elementary and Secondary Schools

Pauline Gibbons

A Glimpse into the Content Classroom in School

A not uncommon scenario in New South Wales, Australia, concerns the English-medium classroom in which students from diverse ethnic and cultural backgrounds are enrolled. In our case, we are visiting two classrooms—a primary/elementary classroom with students in their fifth year of school and a secondary science classroom with students in their first year. Both sets of students are in "mainstream classrooms," meaning that students follow the regular curriculum and are integrated with English-speaking students. In both classrooms, 90–95 percent of the students come from a background where a language other than English is spoken at home, although, depending on their backgrounds, they vary widely in their ability to speak, read, or write it. In the primary classroom there is no majority language, although in the secondary classroom most students speak various dialects of Arabic. A few students have developed literacy in their mother tongue prior to arriving in Australia, and undoubtedly this is a major advantage in their development of English.

The students in both classrooms are very diverse in their populations. However, all students have in common a need to learn subject content through English, a language in which most are not, as yet, fluent. More specifically, they are developing English for learning; that is, the academic language and literacies associated with subject learning. A major issue for the two teachers of these classrooms, therefore, is how to develop subject content hand in hand with subject-related language.

Neither the class teacher (in the case of the primary school) or subject teacher (in the case of the secondary school) is a qualified English language specialist, although both are experienced teachers of English language learners. In both schools, however, there are two specialist English language teachers whose role in the school includes not only direct teaching of identified students but also co-planning and sometimes co-teaching with non-specialist teachers, with the aim of providing language support for all English language learners across the curriculum. This collaborative model is used in both classrooms.[1]

In Australia, Britain, Canada, New Zealand, and the United States, and often as a result of economic and political upheavals, almost all schools have increasingly large numbers of school-aged students for whom English is a second, or subsequent, language. Although often referred to as English as an additional language (EAL) or English language (EL) learners, it is important that these labels do not mask the fact that EL learners are not a homogenous group. They may be immigrants or refugees who have had minimal or disrupted schooling. They will have widely differing levels of spoken and written English and may or may not have literacy in their dominant language.

This chapter addresses a key issue for all teachers of EL learners in similar school contexts, namely how to integrate subject-related language across all curriculum areas. Many of the principles on which the chapter is based are in common with other content-based approaches: the value of learning through subject content, a focus on the social context of language use, and the engagement and participation of students in the process of learning. But unlike some English language learning contexts, subject content in an English-medium school cannot be viewed only as a vehicle for language learning. Neither language nor curriculum content can be compromised, and so all teachers of EAL learners need to address both within regular subject teaching.

The chapter draws on a model of language that facilitates integration in the school context, because it enables teachers to recognize the ways in which language varies according to the registers and genres demanded by a particular subject context and for different purposes and audiences. With its dual focus on meaning and form, it provides a tool for teachers to develop specific language goals in relation to the planning, teaching, and assessment of content learning. In turn teachers are then better able to provide targeted scaffolding to support EL learners in developing the language of school, hand in hand with subject knowledge.

An Approach to Language Integration in the Classroom |||

The approach to content-based language teaching suggested in this section draws on three broad areas of research: (1) a systemic functional model of language, drawing on the extensive work of Michael Halliday and others who have applied it within education; (2) a broadly sociocultural approach to learning; and (3) current research and practice in schools with large numbers of EL learners in mainstream classrooms. The chapter focuses primarily on how a functional approach to language can be used for integrating content and language. Some of the features of a functional approach to language are briefly discussed. For a fuller description of the systemic functional model, see Derewianka and Jones (2012) and for further examples of how it is used in a classroom context, see Gibbons (2009, 2015).

Halliday's work has been influential in language education (and many other fields) around the world, but it is in Australia where his work has probably had most influence in language education. Referred to as systemic functional linguistics, or simply as functional grammar, it is a socially oriented, functional theory of language that has at its heart the notion that language varies according to context, and that it varies, not randomly, but systematically, according to the purpose for which it is used and the social context in which it occurs (see, e.g., Halliday & Matthiessen, 2013). This model provides both EL specialist teachers as well as subject teachers with the linguistic tools to relate the content of a curriculum topic to very specific language, and so it is a rich model for CBI, for student assessment, and for more targeted and responsive scaffolding. A functional approach to language thus highlights the role of language in mediating the construction of knowledge.

In the context of subject teaching, the approach goes far beyond content-specific vocabulary. It includes consideration of the role of spoken language in learning, the relationship of spoken language to literacy, an understanding of how different social contexts affect the register of a spoken or written text, the subject-based written genres and their key features, and the major grammatical features of academic and written language. The next section illustrates how the two teachers in the scenario drew on functional grammar to inform their planning, programming, and classroom practices.

Content-Based Learning in the Classroom ⏐⏐

One of the biggest changes in education over the past decade has been the emphasis on the need for an intellectually challenging curriculum for *all* learners. We know that such a curriculum leads to better outcomes for all students and that all students are more engaged in an intellectually demanding curriculum. It also appears that achievement gaps tend to be reduced between students who are potentially educationally disadvantaged (e.g., because of language, dialect, or socioeconomic background) and those who arrive at school with greater educational advantage (Hammond, Gibbons, Michell, Dufficy, Cruickshank, & Sharpe, 2007; Newmann & Associates, 1996; Newmann, Marks, & Gamoran, 1996).

When an intellectually challenging curriculum also includes targeted language scaffolding from the teacher, EL learners are given multiple opportunities for language learning. A "high challenge, high support" curriculum has an emphasis on inquiry, collaborative learning, and problem solving along with high-level literacy expectations; for EL learners, this offers many affordances for language learning, especially compared to more traditional linear or simplified curricula. For example, students will hear and use language in highly contextualized situations. Group problem-solving often leads to key language being repeated and makes it more likely that it will be comprehensible to EL learners, especially where other semiotic systems (such as diagrams or symbols) are at play. There is a real purpose for learners to make their language comprehensible to others, and they are likely to have their own language resources "stretched" (Swain, 2000) as they engage in problem-solving with others.

As Lantolf and colleagues (2000) illustrate, there is a wide range of ways in which language and content integration is planned and organized. Through three examples of classroom practices, this section highlights the significance of teachers' language understandings in a content classroom within an intellectually challenging curriculum and the consequent choices they make with respect to planning and classroom practices. All the examples are taken from classrooms where over 80 percent of students were EL learners, and all included several students who were recent arrivals to Australia. The teachers had a good working knowledge of functional grammar, as can be seen from the three examples. The students' enthusiasm and engagement in the tasks, and the spoken and written outcomes, attest to the success of the classroom practices described (Gibbons, 2008).

Before each example is a description of the context in which it occurred. Note that the term *topic* or *unit of work* is used to refer to an area of study within a broader subject curriculum, for example, Colonizing Other Planets (secondary science including physics and ecology); Medieval Europe (history); or Myths and Legends (primary/elementary English).

Example 1: What Constitutes the Scientific Method? (Science)

This example is taken from the science class in the first year of secondary school (approximately 13 years of age) that we encountered in our opening scenario. The students in this class were studying one of the first science units in the secondary science curriculum focusing on the scientific method. Figure 7.1 is an overview of both the science and language outcomes planned for a unit of work that lasted for approximately four weeks. The overview and the teaching program were collaboratively produced and taught as the result of ongoing collaborative planning and co-teaching between the science teacher and the specialist EL teacher.

As part of the unit of work, students collaboratively designed their own experiments in ongoing small-group work. They needed to argue for the scientific validity of their design and also to incorporate appropriate variables. Their final assessment task was to write a scientific report. The report needed to discuss what the experiment showed and critique the design to suggest how it might be improved.

Figure 7.1: A Planning Format for Integrating Content and Language in Science

Science Outcomes	Language Outcomes
Students will - develop an understanding of what constitutes the scientific method - carry out independent investigations to prove or disprove common myths - develop understandings about the kinds and functions of variables, and the need for replication, in the context of developing a method, carrying out practical experiments, observing, recording, and interpreting results, and drawing conclusions - complete an experimental report detailing their investigations (assessment task)	Students will write an experimental report, using - an appropriate organizational structure - appropriate grammar (nominalizations and nominal groups, use of cause-and-effect structures, use of passive voice as appropriate) - time connectives - correct technical vocabulary (e.g., *controlled, dependent, independent variables, replicate, replication*)

Rationale for the Focus Language

Of course not all the language that will occur in a unit of work can be predetermined, nor can every piece of language that is likely to occur be listed. Rather, the "focus" language represents the language that is essential to learning and participating in a particular unit of work. In this example, the teachers made a conscious choice to focus *only* on the written report (although there was much else they could have focused on). As they pointed out, the report itself, and the science understandings it represented, would remain relevant for students in their science studies far beyond that class: It represented a piece of "enduring" and relevant learning central to the subject. In addition, it related to the final assessment task, and in the teachers' words "we wanted to set students up for success."

During some of the science classes, and throughout the four weeks, the written report that students were to produce at the end of the unit was carefully scaffolded, with the teacher working with the whole class. In the process of modeling the report, students studied a range of science reports and then, with the help of the teacher, analyzed what an effective report looked like, focusing on the key points listed in Figure 7.1.

Activities for this language focus included:

- reordering a report that had been cut up into paragraphs
- highlighting key language such as connectives and conjunctions
- taking part in pairs in a barrier crossword puzzle[2] based on the key vocabulary, including that listed in Figure 7.1
- underlining grammatical structures to express cause and effect and suggesting alternatives.

After becoming familiar with the structure and grammatical patterns associated with a science report, the class took part in a jointly constructed report based on a whole class experiment carried out with the teacher. A joint construction is a heavily scaffolded piece of writing that involves the teacher scribing on the whiteboard as the students offer wording. The teacher acts as "editor," questioning unclear wording or grammatical or scientific errors, and getting the students to regularly reread what they had written. A joint construction models both the *process* of writing and the *product* (here, the science report).

After this scaffolding, the students wrote a report as a group, based on their group-designed experiments, and only after this were they expected to write individually. When the students were asked what helped them in the task, a number of them commented, "We knew what to do!" One implication of this approach is that making language explicit to students requires an understanding by the teacher of, in this case, the key criteria for a successful science report.

Example 2: Food for Health in Our Multicultural Community (Health/Social Studies)

Example 2 illustrates the primary level planning format for content/language integration. In this unit of work, the fifth grade primary class that we encountered in the opening scenario was studying nutrition. Figure 7.2 presents the health activities/outcomes and the language outcomes.

Rationale for the Focus Language

At two points in the unit of work, students needed to express similarity or difference. First, given the multicultural nature of the class, the classroom teacher wanted students to understand that, while different ethnic groups may eat different foods, the need for a healthy diet is a common factor for all human beings. She discussed with the children what a healthy diet might consist of, using an illustrated "food pyramid" (referred to as Food Pyramid 1). The base of the triangle showed grains, fruits, and vegetables; then proteins and dairy products; and, finally, "sweets and treats." Second, since she wished to encourage a critical perspective on the material, she also showed a food pyramid illustrating what many of the poorest children in developing countries typically eat (Food Pyramid 2, based on data from a major charity). This second pyramid showed only a small amount of grain and some bananas. As the result of what students learned in the unit, the teacher planned to have students develop a recipe book based upon a range of different foods that they ate at home. The scaffolding for this writing followed a similar process as that described in Example 1.

Since collaborative group work played a major part in this unit, the teacher also wanted to focus on the kind of interpersonal language that facilitates successful group work, such as showing agreement, disagreeing politely, building on another student's ideas, encouraging

Figure 7.2: A Planning Format for Integrating Content and Language in Health

Health Activities and Outcomes	Language Outcomes
Students will ■ learn how culture and climate shape what we eat ■ share some international food ■ learn about and show respect for cultural differences in food choices ■ understand that a need for good nutrition is important for everyone (Food Pyramid 1) ■ write a recipe for healthy food ■ understand that not everyone in the world has enough to eat (Food Pyramid 2) and express how they feel about this ■ evaluate what they have learned	Key Vocabulary ■ *grains, fruit and vegetables, proteins, dairy products,* "sweets and treats," *processed, fresh.* Writing a Recipe (Procedural text) Connectives of Comparison ■ Saying what's the same: *similarly, in the same way, the same as* ■ Saying what's different (e.g., healthy and unhealthy food; different cultural choices; adequate and inadequate diets): *however, on the other hand, but, whereas* Use of Appropriate Interpersonal Language in Group Work ■ *yes, I agree; I don't think that's quite right; because; can you explain that a bit more, so what we are saying is…; maybe we could say…*

quiet students to contribute, or summarizing the group's ideas. Such language is often not explicitly addressed in the classroom, yet it is a prerequisite for productive group work. The context for this language was a progressive brainstorm focusing on what children saw as their most important learning in the unit. On a large sheet of paper, groups of students, each with a different colored pen, wrote down their ideas organized as a mind map (a type of graphic organizer). Every five minutes, moving in the same direction, the students moved on to another group's table, leaving their paper behind but taking their pen. Now responding to the other group's ideas, they extended them or added additional items.

Example 3: From Spoken to Written Language (Science)

In another example from the secondary-level science class, the students had begun the unit by watching a video from the "MythBusters" Discovery Channel series. The program showed a series of experiments that the scientists carried out to prove or disprove the myth that wearing a tongue stud increases one's chances of being struck by lightning.[3] Example 3 is an interaction between the teacher and the class after they had watched the program. The teaching is focusing here on the notion of *replication*.

S1:   They have to do it [*the experiment*] **many times** so they can see if there are any changes.

T: Yes so they can see if they get similar results.

S2:   And see if the myth is busted. It wasn't getting busted but then they **kept doing it** until it got busted.

T: So they did the experiment **many times**. Your experimental method should be **repeated a number of times** too…so that a more accurate conclusion can be made. This is called **replicating** the experiment. …. OK so they **repeated** their experiments many times.

S3:   They **kept on doing** it.

T: They **kept on doing** it. And this is what you have to do as well in your experiments. You have to **replicate** the experiment, you're going to **repeat** it several times, **replicate** it. And why do we have to do that? So that we get…?

S2:   An accurate ?

S3:   So that we get more accurate results

T: Right, and doing the same experiment **many times**, that's what we call **replication.**

Rationale for the Interaction

Here the teacher introduces some key science vocabulary (*replicate, replication*) by appropriating the students' responses into her own talk, for example, repeating *kept doing it and many times*. During the course of the interaction, she recasts these in more formal and science-appropriate language (*repeat, replicate*) and finally introduces the term *replication*. Linguistically, she moves along a spoken-written continuum, building on the informal language that is already familiar to the students in order to introduce the academic language associated with a central concept for this unit of work: *kept doing it, many times, repeat, replicate, replication.*

These three examples from the two classrooms in the opening scenario offer some insight into the practical implications of a curriculum informed by functional linguistics, namely the relationship between language and context in content-based classrooms. The next section offers further examples.

Observations and Underlying Principles |||

Table 7.1 presents selected classroom activities with their corresponding underlying principles.

Research Agenda |||

This chapter has illustrated the symbiotic relationship between language and learning in school. Language is not a "conduit" that "channels" content, but rather, it is the medium through which content itself is constructed. Without the explicit teaching of academic language, it remains the hidden curriculum of schooling for many learners (not only EL learners) who are then denied full access to subject learning. Language in this context is not the "icing on the cake," but an essential ingredient of it. One of the implications is the need for all teachers, not simply EL teachers, to have some knowledge of how language is related to subject learning. Yet while most educators agree that "every teacher is a teacher of language," the reality is that most general classroom and subject teachers have not been specifically trained as language teachers.

Two related research areas are suggested. First, there is a need to closely examine the classroom discourse (including both teacher to student, and student to student) and the teaching and learning practices that characterize an intellectually challenging curriculum. Second, there is a need to identify the ways in which these classroom practices afford opportunities for EL learners' development of the registers and literacies of school. Such research would draw on the fields of classroom discourse and second language development in the context of an intellectually challenging curriculum. This requires a cross-disciplinary approach and a functional approach to language. In recent years, there has been some research in this area in relation to EL learners (e.g., Hammond et al., 2007; Walqui & van Lier, 2010), but much more is needed. These studies have illustrated the potential of longer-term classroom-based research with teachers as co-researchers, as well the teacher professional learning that results. The findings of such interdisciplinary and classroom-based research would be relevant for university teacher training courses and in ongoing teacher development contexts.

Table 7.1: Observations and Underlying Principles in Academic Language and Subject Learning

Classroom Practices	Underlying Principles
1. At the beginning of the unit, the whole class watched a MythBusters video that showed how the scientists designed a series of experiments to test whether a myth was true or false.	Watching the video created a shared experience for the class that the teacher could later build on in order to model some aspects of academic language (see dialogue in Example 3). In addition, the video built up the knowledge of the *field* that the students would be drawing on later.
2. After a shared whole-class experiment, students formed small groups in order to design a valid experiment to prove or disprove a common myth (e.g., *Toast always falls on the butter side down.*)	The hands-on activities allowed students to use informal spoken language to begin to develop an understanding of the scientific principles required for designing a valid experiment. This informal talk helped to develop students' understandings of the *field*.
3. After carrying out their experiments, each group reported back to the whole class about how they set up their experiment and what they had learned about designing an experiment. Each group looked at a different myth.	This context required the reporters to take account of the needs of their listeners, who had not shared that group's earlier discussions. The reporters next had to reconstruct for their listeners, through language alone, what they designed, and why. Therefore, the talk had to be more explicit and more "written-like" in its register. This more written-like spoken language (or "literate spoken language") provided scaffolding for the later written report. Since some of the language was still relatively new to students, it also provided an opportunity for students to use "stretched" language in a context where the speakers also needed to pay attention to their own language use ("comprehensible output") (Swain, 2000).
4. In this overview, the teacher focused on some key connectives that were integral to the unit (*similarly, in the same way, however, but, whereas*).	Connectives and conjunctions play a major part in structuring a piece of writing, but are often a late development in EL students' learning, probably because they are associated with written language and therefore less easily "noticed." Explicit teaching of connectives and conjunctions in the context of whole texts is therefore an important part of developing literacy, both in reading and writing.
5. Students did a progressive brainstorm about what they had learned.	This required students to share ideas in the initial group, using some of the key vocabulary. As each group moved on, there was another opportunity for further discussion and further practice in talking about the topic, and opportunity to reinforce both content and language learning.

APPLYING WHAT YOU LEARNED
Questions and Tasks

1. How would you respond to subject teachers of EL learners who say it is not their job to teach English?

2. Consider in what ways functional grammar differs from traditional grammar. Why does the author claim that functional grammar is an appropriate model of language for content/language integration in schools?

3. How important is spoken language in literacy learning? Why does the author emphasize the need for "literate" spoken language in the classroom?

4. Register describes the relationship between content and language. The register of a text is influenced by the *field* (the subject matter) and the *mode* (whether it is spoken or written). Mode is of particular significance in the development of literacy at all levels, since more formal written language is very different from informal spoken language. Consider the relationship between these examples (each from a more extended piece of language). They share a similar *field* (science/ magnetism):

   A. *Look it's making them move . . . those are not sticking . . . doesn't work.*

   B. *We found out the pins stick on the magnet, but the plastic clip didn't stick.*

   C. *Our experiment showed that magnets attract some metals.*

   D. *Magnetic attraction occurs only between ferrous metals.*

   E. *Well-known magnetic materials that exhibit easily detectable magnetic properties include nickel, iron . . .and their alloys.*

   Texts A, B, and C occurred in an elementary classroom with a group of 8- to 9-year-old EL learners talking in a small group about the properties of magnets; Text D was taken from a middle school textbook, and Text E from written university materials.

   a. What do you notice about the *register* in these examples?

   b. Do you notice any differences in *mode* in the five examples? If so, in what ways?

5. The written genres (or kinds of writing) in school will vary depending on the curriculum subject, whether they occur at elementary or secondary level, and the age of the students. Each particular genre can be

considered in terms of its overall structure, the likely connectives and conjunctions used to organize ideas within that genre (for example, in a discussion text, connectives might include *first, second, in addition, on the other hand, however*), and the kind of grammatical patterns and vocabulary that are likely to occur. One particularly significant feature of most academic registers is *nominalization*. Nominalization enables a writer to refer to a process as a concept, to turn it into a noun, and to use it as the theme of a sentence, as in this example:

A. The rain ***washed away*** *(verb) the soil.*

B. The rain ***eroded*** *(verb)* the soil.

C. ***The erosion*** *(noun)* was caused by the rain.

Nominalization allows a writer to move away from a description of a particular event (as in A) to a focus on the process itself (as in C), and thus to use language in far more abstract ways. It is also a way of packing information into a single word. In a school curriculum there are numerous examples of nominalizations. But ELs do not automatically "pick up" these higher-level understandings about language or the grammar pattern behind them. Nominalizations also assume a high level of background knowledge and can cause unseen texts to be hard to read.

a. Look through a content-area textbook (for the educational level you are interested in), newspaper, or a magazine such as *Scientific American* or *National Geographic* or similar magazine. Find examples of nominalization. Share them with your group or class.

b. How would you teach this concept to students? How could you develop an instructional unit or part of an instructional unit on the topic of nominalization that goes beyond treating nouns (such as Example C) as simply vocabulary items?

ENDNOTES

1. Although outside the scope of this chapter for discussion, it is worth mentioning that both pairs of teachers find this mode of working has increased their own professional learning.
2. A barrier crossword is a vocabulary game in which a pair of students each has one half of a completed crossword (either the down-words or the across-words). They give each other clues about their own words, or definitions, in order for their partner to fill in the blanks on their own crossword. The purpose is for both students to complete the crossword.
3. The MythBuster series can be found at: www.discovery.com/tv-shows/mythbusters/videos/ or www.youtube.com/watch?v=_-g1md7jCRQ&list=PL0A5590CEE7F2EC3B

REFERENCES

Gibbons, P. (2008). "It was taught good and I learned a lot": Intellectual practices and ESL learners in the middle years. *Australian Journal of Language and Literacy, 31*(2), 155–173.

Gibbons, P. (2009). *English learners, academic literacy, and thinking: Learning in the challenge zone.* Portsmouth, NH: Heinemann.

Gibbons, P. (2015). *Scaffolding language, scaffolding learning: Teaching English language learners in the mainstream classroom* (2nd ed.). Portsmouth, NH: Heinemann.

Halliday, M. A. K., & Matthiessen, C. (2013). *Halliday's introduction to functional grammar* (4th ed.). Oxford, England: Routledge.

Hammond, J., Gibbons, P., Michell, M., Dufficy, P., Cruickshank, K., & Sharpe, M. (2007). *Challenging pedagogies: Engaging ESL Students in intellectual quality.* Sydney, Australia: Australian Research Council and Multicultural Programs, New South Wales.

Lantolf, J. (Ed.). (2000). *Sociocultural theory and second language learning.* Oxford, England: Oxford University Press.

Newmann, F. M., & Associates. (1996). *Authentic achievement: Restructuring schools for intellectual quality.* San Francisco, CA: Jossey-Bass.

Newmann, F., Marks, H., & Gamoran, A. (1996). Authentic pedagogy and student performance. *American Journal of Education, 104*(4), 280–312.

Swain, M. (2000). The output hypothesis and beyond: Mediating acquisition through collaborative dialogue. In J. Lantolf (Ed.), *Sociocultural theory and second language learning* (pp. 97–114). Oxford, England: Oxford University Press.

Walqui, A., & van Lier, L. (2010). *Scaffolding the academic success of adolescent English language learners: A pedagogy of promise.* San Francisco, CA: West Ed.

Chapter 8

Language-Focused Instruction in Content-Based Classrooms

Roy Lyster

||| A Glimpse into Immersion Classrooms: Two Perspectives on Language in Content-Based Instruction

Scenario 1: Michel, a seventh grade immersion teacher, often begins science lessons by drawing on his students' knowledge to introduce the textbook material, but without encouraging much discussion or exploration of students' answers. He speaks clearly and provides a good model of the immersion language, while elaborating very little and without encouraging students to expand their answers. Students rarely give more than one-word or one-phrase answers, which Michel repeats or rephrases and then writes on the board while students take notes. There is little interaction among students, as language is used for communication mainly between the teacher and the students.

Scenario 2: Claudette's seventh grade immersion classroom is a veritable arena of language-rich science communication. Her students engage in both "doing" science and collaboratively talking about it, as she gives them increasing responsibility for their learning. Claudette encourages students to speculate, justify, and be comfortable with the view that there might be "no right answer" to some questions, even though she has specific learning objectives and structures her classes accordingly. Many opportunities for students to produce the immersion language and to communicate with one another appear to arise inherently out of what is being learned, fusing language and science into a unified whole and enabling students to use a wide variety of language functions and structures.

---

ransmission model of teaching in which lecturing is important and the role

These two very different scenarios are both from Day and Shapson's (1996) observational studies of French immersion classrooms, which revealed clear differences in instructional strategies employed by immersion teachers during science lessons. The first scenario corresponds to a transmission model of teaching in which lecturing is important and the role of students is relatively passive. It assumes that language learning is achieved more through comprehension than through production. In contrast, students in the second scenario are more actively engaged in learning both language and content, as they are encouraged to explore content in more depth in ways that extend their language abilities. In the second scenario, the fusion of language and content enriches the learning of both.

Research in immersion and other CBI classrooms has indeed revealed a wide range of instructional approaches, with some teachers focusing more on content than on language and others able to integrate a focus on both. This chapter is based on the premise that improvement in the language learning outcomes of immersion and CBI programs is contingent on a more systematic integration of language-focused instruction and suggests ways that this can be achieved.

Rationale for Language-Focused Instruction in CBI |||

Considerable differences among teachers were also observed in a large-scale study of 23 Grades 1–3 immersion classrooms in Newfoundland by Netten and Spain (1989). An intriguing result of their study is that a low-ability class actually excelled in L2 performance compared to a higher-ability class. The success of these students was attributed to their teacher's instructional practices, which included the following:

- teacher-student interaction using a question/answer technique rather than a lecture format
- opportunities for meaningful interaction among peers rather than only listening to the teacher
- use of language rather than non-verbal clues to convey meaning
- explicit rather than implicit correction.

Netten and Spain (1989) argued strongly in favor of more language-oriented immersion classrooms that "encourage active and purposeful communication on the part of as many pupils as possible" (p. 500). Teachers who orchestrate opportunities for students to engage with language in these ways are more apt than others to succeed in moving their students' L2 development forward.

One of the reasons for encouraging a greater focus on language in CBI stems from the results of immersion programs revealing that students attain high levels of comprehension skills and communicative ability but lower-than-expected levels of production abilities with respect to grammatical accuracy, lexical variety, and sociolinguistic appropriateness (Harley, Cummins, Swain, & Allen, 1990). It has become clear that many target language features, especially (but not limited to) those involving morphosyntax, are not learned "by osmosis" and instead require a more intentional instructional focus.

These findings led to the assertion that content teaching on its own is not necessarily good language teaching and needs to be manipulated and complemented in ways that maximize target language learning (Swain, 1988). Otherwise, use of the target language to teach content has limitations in terms of the range of language forms and functions to which it exposes students. A good example of this is the distribution of verb tenses used by French immersion teachers: 74–75 percent in the present tense or imperative forms, 14–15 percent in the past tense, and 3 percent in the conditional (Lyster, 2007; Swain, 1988). The disproportionate use of present tense and imperative forms helps to explain gaps in French immersion students' L2 development, especially their limited use of conditional forms and their inaccurate use of past tense forms.

Another concern about content teaching on its own is that it can take on a lecture format without providing sufficient opportunities for interaction and student production. A driving force underlying CBI has been the notion of comprehensible input whereby language acquisition occurs when learners are able to understand language containing structures that are a bit beyond their current competence (Krashen, 1982). Early observations of immersion classrooms revealed that students had limited opportunities to produce the language (Swain, 1985) as teachers strove to expose students to comprehensible input, drawing attention especially to vocabulary to facilitate comprehension.

Yet Swain (1985) argued that exposure to comprehensible input via subject-matter instruction engages comprehension strategies that enable students to process language semantically but not necessarily syntactically, allowing them to bypass structural information and to rely instead on pragmatic and situational cues. The limits of a comprehension-based approach to language instruction are now well known, especially in the long-run and for learners aspiring to reach beyond beginner-levels of proficiency and to develop literacy skills in the target language.

Researchers now agree that content-based programs need to be carefully planned from a language perspective. As Lightbown (2014) summed it up: "After decades of research on language acquisition in CBLT [content-based language teaching] in a variety of educational and social contexts, it is clear that language acquisition does not 'take care of itself'" (p. 129). Contrary to initial conceptualizations of immersion programs, CBI should not preclude language instruction but needs rather to promote its integration. The goal is to strengthen students' metalinguistic awareness, which, in turn, enables them to detect grammatical patterns in the input and facilitates language analysis (i.e., breaking language down into smaller units). Being aware of language in this way helps learners to benefit from content-based input as a source of L2 learning and to engage with increasingly complex language, which is key to academic literacy and school success.

Many researchers now advocate a more systematic integration of language across content areas. The integration of content-based and language-based instruction creates opportunities for students to notice and use specific target language features (otherwise misused, unused, or unnoticed in classroom discourse) in the context of content-based activities (Lyster, 2007) or other meaning-oriented tasks (Ellis, 2003). It thus differs from traditional language instruction, which isolates language from any content other than the mechanical workings of the language itself. Integrating a focus on language in immersion and other contexts of CBI without resorting to decontextualized language instruction requires a great deal of systematic planning and does not come easily to many teachers, who may still believe that their mandate is to focus mainly on content and to expect language to emerge incidentally. (See also Dalton-Puffer, this volume, for discussion of this issue in the CLIL context.)

Perspectives on Language-Focused Instruction in CBI | | |

This section outlines a proactive approach to content and language integration that requires planning for noticing and awareness activities followed by opportunities for guided and autonomous practice. Planning for content and language integration in this way aims to shift learners' attention to language in the context of content instruction in cases where they would not otherwise process the language at the same time as the content.

The noticing phase establishes a meaningful context related to content, usually by means of a text in which target features have been contrived to appear more salient (i.e., typographical enhancement such as bolding and underlining) or more frequent (i.e., input flood). This phase is based on the premise that, for L2 learning to occur, learners need to notice target features in the input and their ability to do so is mediated by factors such as frequency and perceptual salience (Schmidt, 1990, 1994). The awareness phase then encourages the students to reflect on and manipulate the target forms in a way that helps them to restructure their interlanguage representations. Also known in the literature as consciousness-raising tasks (Sharwood Smith, 1981, 1993), awareness activities require some degree of analysis or reflection by means of rule-discovery tasks, metalinguistic exercises, and opportunities for pattern detection. The practice phases then provide opportunities for students to procedur-alize their (re)analyzed representations of the target language by "engaging in an activity with the goal of becoming better at it" (DeKeyser, 2007, p. 50). The guided practice phase engages students' metalinguistic awareness by pushing them to use the target features in a meaningful yet controlled context with opportunities to receive corrective feedback in order to develop automaticity and accuracy. The sequence then comes full circle at the autono-mous awareness phase by returning to the content area that served as the starting point. Similar to guided practice, autonomous practice requires the use of the target language fea-tures but in a disciplinary or thematic context with fewer constraints in order to encourage more autonomous use of the target language.

To illustrate the implementation of this instructional sequence, two examples are pro-vided here from Lyster's (2016) resource book for French immersion teachers. Both are intended for social studies classes, the first with a focus on pronouns at the Grade 8 level and the second with a focus on grammatical gender in Grade 5.

Object Pronouns in Social Studies

This instructional unit has both content and language objectives, as follows:

Content Objectives

- Students will understand the causes and effects of Clifford Sifton's campaign at the turn of the 20th century to solicit Europeans to immigrate to western Canada.
- Students will compare the different social realities motivating Sifton's campaign and Canada's current campaign to receive Syrian refugees.

Language Objectives

- Students will notice the differences between direct and indirect third-person object pronouns and will use them appropriately.
- Students will understand that *lui* as an indirect object pronoun is gender neutral.

To appreciate why object pronouns might be integrated into social studies, one first needs to understand why object pronouns in French are a source of difficulty for many immersion students, particularly concerning the use of third-person direct and indirect object pronouns. Third-person object pronouns are more complex than their equivalents in English in at least three important ways.

First, different forms are used in French to distinguish direct object pronouns from indirect object pronouns (*le*, *la*, and *les* vs. *lui* and *leur*). In contrast, in English, the object pronouns *him*, *her*, and *them* are used invariably as direct and indirect pronouns. Second, although both English and French follow basic Subject-Verb-Object (SVO) word order, this is the case in French only when the object following the verb is a noun. When the object is a pronoun, the order changes in French, but not in English, from SVO to Subject-Object-Verb (SOV).

Daniel (S) is watching (V) the hockey game (O). ⇒ Daniel (S) is watching (V) it (O).

Daniel (S) regarde (V) le match de hockey (O). ⇒ *Daniel (S) le (O) regarde (V).*

Probably influenced by English to some extent, but also by French itself which requires SVO in declarative (statement) phrases when the objects are nouns and also in imperative (command) phrases when the objects are pronouns, many L2 learners of French have problems using object pronouns before the verb, particularly in the case of third-person pronouns. Third, although third-person singular pronouns have different masculine and feminine forms when used as subjects (*il* vs. *elle*), direct objects (*le* vs. *la*), and objects of a preposition (*lui* vs. *elle*), this is not true of third-person singular reference to an animate indirect object, in which case the pronoun *lui* can be either masculine or feminine. Perhaps due to its saliency as a stressed pronoun meaning *him*, which can stand on its own (*Lui, il regarde le match de hockey*), immersion students, from an early stage, equate *lui* almost exclusively with *him*. Consequently, *lui* is often used by immersion students invariably as either a direct or indirect pronoun and, in both cases, the referent tends to be male.

Noticing Phase

At the noticing phase, students read a letter written to them by their teacher about the upcoming arrival of a new student: a Syrian refugee named Liliane. The letter provides many suggestions for making Liliane feel welcomed in her new classroom (an English translation appears in Appendix 8A). The letter is replete with multiple instances of third-person subject and object pronouns, which become the focus of attention during the awareness phase. During the noticing phase, the content of the letter is in the foreground and is used to engender a discussion about welcoming newcomers to Canada, a theme that will be revisited later in the sequence.

Chers élèves,

Nous accueillerons bientôt une nouvelle élève dans la classe. Elle s'appelle Liliane. <u>Elle</u> et sa famille sont des réfugiés syriens récemment accueillis au Canada. Que pourriez-vous faire pour faciliter l'arrivée de Liliane?

Les réfugiés sont susceptibles de se sentir isolés dans leur pays d'accueil où presque tout peut sembler étrange à prime abord. De plus, comme ils ont beaucoup souffert pendant la guerre civile en Syrie, il est très important d'être très sensibles à cet égard.

Quant à Liliane, il est important de <u>la</u> compter parmi vos amis dès son arrivée. Il suffit de <u>lui</u> parler, de <u>la</u> consoler au besoin et de jouer avec <u>elle</u> sans <u>lui</u> demander trop de détails sur ce qui <u>lui</u> est arrivé durant la guerre civile dans son pays. C'est parce qu'une guerre civile entraine habituellement des atrocités inimaginables et alors des traumatismes dont il est difficile de se remettre. Soyez donc sensibles mais pas indiscrets. Si <u>elle</u> vous en parle, écoutez-<u>la</u> attentivement et essayez de <u>la</u> réconforter. Et profitez de l'occasion pour <u>lui</u> suggérer d'en parler à d'autres en qui <u>elle</u> a confiance.

Si <u>elle</u> a des difficultés de compréhension en français ou en anglais, offrez-<u>lui</u> de l'aide. Quant à ses études, ce sera à <u>elle</u> de décider dans quelles matières elle a le plus besoin d'aide. Conseillez-<u>lui</u> de ne pas abandonner si <u>elle</u> a des difficultés. De plus, parlez-<u>lui</u> des différentes activités parascolaires auxquelles <u>elle</u> pourrait se joindre pour se faire de nouveaux amis à l'extérieur de la classe. Félicitez notre nouvelle élève pour son courage et accueillez-<u>la</u> chaleureusement dans son nouveau pays et à sa nouvelle école! De mon côté, je vais <u>l'</u>accueillir à bras ouverts et <u>lui</u> offrir toute l'aide dont <u>elle</u> a besoin.

Awareness Phase

The letter lends itself well to an analysis of the form/function mappings of third-person pronouns in a meaningful context. First, the teacher can simply ask students to identify third-person singular pronouns and can then initiate a metalinguistic discussion that helps them to identify these patterns.

First, it is important for students to notice the repeated use of *lui* as indirect object pronoun combined with *elle* as subject pronoun—and that both refer both to a girl:

Lui	Elle
Et profitez de l'occasion pour <u>lui</u> suggérer And take the opportunity to suggest to <u>her</u>	
	d'en parler à d'autres en qui <u>elle</u> a confiance. to talk to others whom <u>she</u> trusts.
Offrez-<u>lui</u> de l'aide Offer to help <u>her</u>	
	si <u>elle</u> a des difficultés de compréhension. if <u>she</u> has difficulties understanding.
Conseillez-<u>lui</u> de ne pas abandonner Encourage <u>her</u> not to give up	
	si <u>elle</u> a des difficultés. even if <u>she</u> has difficulties.
Parlez-<u>lui</u> des différentes activités parascolaires Tell <u>her</u> about the different extracurricular activities	
	auxquelles <u>elle</u> pourrait se joindre. that <u>she</u> could join.
Je vais <u>l'</u>accueillir à bras ouverts et <u>lui</u> offrir I will welcome <u>her</u> with open arms and offer <u>her</u>	
	toute l'aide dont <u>elle</u> a besoin all the help <u>she</u> needs.

Depending on the level of the students, the teacher can also draw their attention to the distinctions between direct and indirect object pronouns:

Direct Objects	Indirect Objects
« *essayez de <u>la</u> réconforter…* » "try to comfort <u>her</u>"	« *sans <u>lui</u> demander trop de détails…* » "without asking <u>her</u> too many details"
« *je vais <u>l'</u>accueillir à bras ouverts…* » "I will welcome <u>her</u> with open arms"	« *profitez de l'occasion pour <u>lui</u> suggérer…* » "take the opportunity to suggest to <u>her</u>"

Finally, the teacher can point out that direct and indirect objects precede the verb in declarative phrases but follow the verb in imperative phrases.

	Direct Objects	**Indirect Objects**
Declarative phrases	« de _la_ consoler au besoin » "console <u>her</u> when needed"	« il suffit de _lui_ parler » "just talk to <u>her</u>"
Imperative phrases	« écoutez-_la_ attentivement » "listen to <u>her</u> carefully"	« offrez-_lui_ de l'aide » "offer <u>her</u> help"

The difficulties that immersion students and other L2 learners encounter with respect to third-person object pronouns in French can all be addressed in this single text. Yet the analysis of a single text will not be enough to sensitize students to the use of third-person object pronouns and so teachers need to identify or create other texts in which these pronouns are numerous and essential to understanding. More important, students need opportunities not only to notice these pronouns but also to use them in meaningful contexts, which is the objective of the next phases.

Guided Practice

While studying about the settlement of Western Canada at the turn of the 20th century, students will learn about Clifford Sifton and his campaign to draw European immigrants to settle on the prairies. In the guided practice activities that follow, students are asked to speculate on what they would have said and to whom during this period, thus creating obligatory contexts for the use of third-person object pronouns and opportunities for corrective feedback.

After reading a text about Clifford Sifton's campaign, students are asked what they might say as Canadian officials to prospective immigrants in Europe at that time to convince them to leave their homeland to help settle Western Canada. Based on what they have studied about this campaign, students are asked to speculate on what they would say, using phrases such as:

- _D'abord, je <u>leur</u> expliquerais que... (First, I would explain to <u>them</u> that...)_
- _Ensuite, je <u>leur</u> proposerais de... (Then, I would propose to <u>them</u>...)_
- _Enfin, pour <u>les</u> convaincre, je <u>leur</u> offrirais des avantages sociaux tels... (Finally, to convince <u>them</u>, I would offer <u>them</u> social benefits such as...)_

Students are then asked to imagine being the prospective immigrants and to reflect on the questions they would like to ask of the Canadian officials in order to decide whether or not to immigrate to Canada. Model phrases include the following:

- _Je <u>leur</u> demanderais si... (I would ask <u>them</u> if...)_
- _Je <u>leur</u> demanderais de <u>nous</u> expliquer comment... (I would ask <u>them</u> to explain to <u>us</u> how to...)_
- _Je <u>leur</u> poserais des questions à propos de... (I would ask <u>them</u> questions about...)_
- _Nous <u>leur</u> demanderions de <u>nous</u> assurer que... (We would ask <u>them</u> to assure <u>us</u> that...)_

To complete the activity, students need to demonstrate an understanding of many of the historical issues at stake during this campaign. At the same time, teachers need to provide students with the kind of scaffolding and feedback they need in order to maintain an accurate use of third-person pronouns, which are otherwise easy to avoid or misuse.

Autonomous Practice

During this phase, the content focus switches to what went wrong with this campaign. That is, history shows that some of the European immigrants who were encouraged to settle on the prairies felt duped by the campaign, such as expressed by this woman's testimonial:

À l'époque, le Canadien Pacifique inondait le pays d'images de magnifiques champs de blé dans les grandes prairies de l'Ouest. Tout le monde pouvait faire fortune en trois ans, sans compter les promesses chatoyantes de terres pratiquement données. L'espoir était grand. De sorte que nous, pauvres idiots, sommes tombés dans le piège. (Leblanc & Sarrasin, 2004, p. 33)

(At the time, the Canadian Pacific Railway was inundating countries with images of beautiful wheat fields in the western prairies. Everyone could make a fortune in three years, and there were promises of practically free land. The hopes were so great that we, poor fools, fell into the trap.)

After studying this and other testimonials, students are asked what they would say to the settlers in terms of gratitude, apology, or advice, specifically to respond to the woman's description of their difficult experience, using phrases such as the following:

- *D'abord, je <u>lui</u> dirais que... (First, I would tell <u>her</u> that...)*
- *Ensuite, je <u>lui</u> expliquerais que... (Then I would explain to <u>her</u> that...)*
- *Enfin, je <u>lui</u> conseillerais de... (Finally, I would advise <u>her</u> to...)*

Students are then asked to reenact an interview with this person and/or other settlers in which the settlers express what they would like to say to Clifford Sifton, in light of what they had been initially told versus how the events actually unfolded. Some model phrases might be:

- *Je <u>lui</u> dirais que... (I would tell <u>him</u> that...)*
- *Je <u>lui</u> décrirais les difficultés que nous avons vécues, telles... (I would describe to <u>him</u> the difficulties we experienced such as...)*
- *Je <u>lui</u> expliquerais que nous avons l'impression d'être « tombés dans le piège » en ce sens que... (I would explain to <u>him</u> that we had the impression of having fallen into a trap in the sense that...)*
- *Nous <u>l'</u>avertirions d'un certain ressentiment dans la région envers le gouvernement canadien causé par... (We would warn <u>him</u> of a certain resentment in the area against the Canadian government as a result of...)*

Again, to complete these tasks, students need to demonstrate a solid understanding of the causes and effects of this campaign. For their part, teachers need to support students in their dual focus on both social studies content and the target language forms.

To conclude the instructional sequence, students are asked to engage either in an oral discussion or a written text to compare the different social realities that motivated Sifton's campaign to populate the prairie provinces at the beginning of the 20th century and those motivating the campaign to welcome Syrian refugees in the 21st century.

Grammatical Gender in Social Studies

The next example illustrates form-focused instructional activities targeting grammatical gender that were embedded in the children's social studies materials. The content objective aimed to develop students' awareness of the hardships of life in New France while the language objective aimed to develop their awareness of how certain noun endings predict grammatical gender (e.g., nouns ending in –*tion* are feminine; nouns ending in –*ment* are masculine). The activities briefly mentioned here serve to illustrate the instructional sequence and do not represent the entire scope of the five-week unit (see Lyster, 2004).

Noticing activities drew students' attention to noun endings as predictors of grammatical gender. For example, in the context of learning about the founding of Quebec City in 17th century New France, endings of target nouns and their determiners had been highlighted in bold. Target words and related patterns were key to the content of the lessons. For example, *la fourrure* ("fur") was a key noun because of the pivotal role of the fur trade in New France, and so was the noun *la nourriture* ("food") because of the lack of food in the colony that led to a serious outbreak of scurvy.

The ensuing awareness activities required students then to detect the patterns by classifying the target nouns according to their endings and indicating whether nouns with these endings were masculine or feminine. In the case of *la fourrure* and *la nourriture*, students were expected to identify them both as feminine nouns because of their common ending –*ure*.

Then for guided practice in attributing the right gender marker to target nouns, a set of riddles was used to review the challenges experienced by settlers in New France while eliciting target nouns from students. For example, the riddle (provided in French), "*I am what covers certain mammals and can be made into warm coats,*" was intended to elicit the noun phrase *la fourrure* but, to stay in the game, a student needed to say the right gender-specific determiner, which is no small feat for young learners of French for whom grammatical gender markers, despite their frequency, are notoriously difficult.

Finally, for autonomous practice, teachers returned to an emphasis on content objectives by asking students to reflect on some of the differences between life in the 17th century and life today, especially with respect to social realities and values. For example, students were asked to compare the attitudes of people in New France with those of people today concerning the fashionability of fur. Even though the subject-matter goal was to have students question and compare different social realities, teachers maintained a secondary focus on language by ensuring correct use of gender at least with key topic words such as *la fourrure*.

This instructional sequence allows for variable emphases to be placed on content and language, as is illustrated in Figure 8.1. This figure is reminiscent of Gibbons' (2015) hour-

Figure 8.1: Instructional Sequence Integrating Language and Content
(adapted from Lyster, 2016, p. 58)

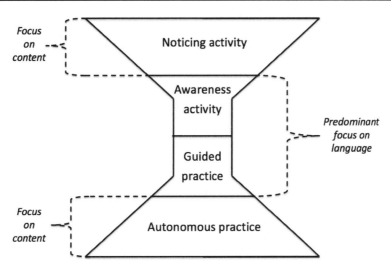

glass figure illustrating how mainstream teachers can focus on language as an object of study with English learners (ELs). Gibbons proposes a progression from "learning through language" to "learning about language" and then back to "learning through language" (p. 227). In the case of Figure 8.1, the sequence begins with a primary focus on content during the noticing phase and then zooms in on language during the awareness and guided practice phases. During the autonomous practice phase, the primary instructional focus is again on the content that served as the starting point.

Underlying Principles |||

Language-focused instruction can be integrated into CBI through a proactive approach, as illustrated in the previous section. A proactive approach includes pre-planned activities that draw students' attention to language features by means of noticing and awareness activities followed by opportunities to use the features during guided and autonomous practice.

Language-focused instruction can also be integrated through a reactive approach. A reactive approach includes scaffolding techniques that serve to support student participation while ensuring that classroom interaction is a key source of learning. A reactive approach can take the form of (a) teacher questions intended to increase both the quantity and quality of student output and (b) corrective feedback that serves to negotiate both form and meaning. Questioning and feedback techniques together provide learners with the scaffolding they need in order to understand and engage with content that they are learning through their L2.

For optimal effectiveness, proactive and reactive approaches are best implemented in tandem in the CBI classroom. Table 8.1 outlines the main components of a proactive approach and presents a reactive approach as "ongoing scaffolding" that is interwoven throughout the instructional activities.

Table 8.1: Language-Focused Instructional Phases in CBI and Their Underlying Principles

Instructional Activities	Underlying Principles
1. Noticing phase	Noticing activities serve as catalysts for drawing learners' attention to problematic target features that have been contrived to appear more salient and/or frequent in oral and written input. Target forms can be made more salient and thus more readily noticed by learners through input enhancement, which includes typographical enhancement of written input or intonational stress in oral input.
2. Awareness phase	Awareness activities require learners to do more than merely notice enhanced forms and instead to engage in some degree of analysis, which includes inductive rule-discovery tasks and opportunities to compare and contrast language patterns, followed by different types of metalinguistic information. In some cases, the contrasted patterns may entail differences between students' L1 and their L2.
3. Guided practice phase	Students are pushed to use the features in a meaningful yet controlled context with opportunities to receive corrective feedback in order to develop automaticity and accuracy. Guided practice is designed to engage students' metalinguistic awareness in a way that helps them move beyond their use of inaccurate interlanguage forms and away from their reliance on communication strategies.
4. Autonomous practice phase	In a context related to content, students are encouraged to use the features in more open-ended ways to develop fluency, motivation, and confidence. Autonomous practice engages learners in more open-ended and meaning-focused tasks with fewer constraints to ensure accuracy, providing a safe playing field for students to experiment with the more advanced language they need in order to engage with content.
5. Ongoing scaffolding	A reactive approach includes oral scaffolding provided in an ongoing manner by teachers to enable their students to engage with content in a language they know only partially. One type of scaffolding entails lots of linguistic and non-linguistic support that enables students to understand content as they draw on the contextual clues provided in the scaffolding and on prior knowledge. Another type of scaffolding includes well-planned questions and feedback that support students' use of the L2 while helping to move their L2 development forward.

Research Agenda |||

There is a consensus in the CBI literature that "teachers who teach content through their students' L2 require considerable professional development to effectively do so" (Lyster & Tedick, 2014, p. 219). Consequently, many of the future directions for research and development in CBI are linked to teacher education and professional development.

The instructional integration of language and content continues to prove challenging for teachers (Cammarata & Tedick, 2012) and needs to be systematically addressed through pre-service teacher education and ongoing professional development. The underlying questions include what skills teachers need in order to integrate language and content instruction effectively and also how teachers can collaborate to facilitate language and content integration. An interesting area to explore in this regard is the extent to which discipline-specific language (i.e., the language of science, of mathematics, of history, etc.) can be identified in ways that help teachers to integrate language and content (Llinares, Morton, & Whittaker, 2012). A pivotal question that remains open for further investigation is how teachers can most effectively implement CBI in ways that scaffold content learning while ensuring continued development in the target language.

The purpose of immersion and other CBI programs has been to create an environment in which exposure to the target language and opportunities to use it are optimal. However, there is a growing research interest in examining the role of the L1 as a cognitive tool for L2 learning and also for subject-matter learning through the L2. Yet context is a determining factor in making decisions about L1 use in CBI. On the one hand, minority-language students in contexts of CBI such as sheltered instruction or transitional programs for ELs in the U.S. are certain to benefit from use of their L1 to help them make sense of the content. On the other hand, majority-language students whose L1 is English are unlikely to benefit as much from use of their L1 given its high status in an English-dominant society that tends to militate against use of non-English languages. In contexts where English L1 students are learning a minority language, sustained use of the non-English language is likely more beneficial for pushing its development forward (given sufficient scaffolding to sustain its use) than recourse to English. A pressing issue for continued research, therefore, is to identify the scaffolding techniques other than English L1 support that teachers can use to enable students to engage with increasingly complex content in the target language.

Research on the effects of CBI has hitherto tended to measure L2 development more than content knowledge, leaving open many questions about the feasibility and effectiveness of focusing on language during subject-matter instruction. Specifically, we still need to know whether content knowledge is enhanced or possibly compromised by a greater focus on language during content instruction. In the specific case of two-way immersion programs where speakers of the first and second language are enrolled, we need to know more about how a language focus can be adapted to accommodate different groups of learners with different language learning needs (e.g., Spanish-dominant, English-dominant, bilingual; see Tedick & Young, 2014). Finally, while there is still a need to explore effective ways of integrating a greater focus on language in content-driven classrooms, there is also a need to continue exploring ways of integrating CBI in language-driven classrooms, such as theme-based instruction, as a means of enriching classroom discourse and increasing opportunities for purposeful communication.

APPLYING WHAT YOU LEARNED
Questions and Tasks

1. What is your experience as a language learner with instruction that focused on accuracy? What did you learn in this chapter that your second or foreign language teachers could have used?

2. What new ways of thinking about language-focused instruction did you learn from this chapter that you can use in your L2 teaching?

3. Identify a topic in a content area or a language arts theme that you teach. Then identify a language feature related to this topic or theme that you believe L2 learners find challenging. Based on the instructional sequence illustrated in this module, design a content-based unit that integrates a focus on your selected target feature(s). The instructional sequence should include at least four inter-related activities:

    a. A noticing activity designed to make the language features more salient and/or frequent in a content-related text.

    b. An awareness activity that requires learners to manipulate or reflect on the language features in a way that engages them in some degree of analysis or inductive rule discovery.

    c. A guided practice activity that pushes students to use the features in a meaningful yet controlled context with feedback in order to develop automaticity and accuracy.

    d. An autonomous practice activity related to content that encourages students to use the features in more open-ended ways to develop fluency, motivation, and confidence.

REFERENCES

Cammarata, L., & Tedick, D. (2012). Balancing content and language in instruction: The experience of immersion teachers. *The Modern Language Journal, 96*, 251–269.

Day, E., & Shapson, S. (1996). *Studies in immersion education.* Clevedon, England: Multilingual Matters.

DeKeyser, R. (Ed.). (2007). *Practice in a second language: Perspectives from applied linguistics and cognitive psychology.* Cambridge, England: Cambridge University Press.

Ellis, R. (2003). *Task-based language learning and teaching.* Oxford, England: Oxford University Press.

Gibbons, P. (2015). *Scaffolding language, scaffolding learning: Teaching second language learners in the mainstream classroom* (2nd ed.). Portsmouth, NH: Heinemann.

Harley, B., Cummins, J., Swain, M., & Allen, P. (1990). The nature of language proficiency. In B. Harley, P. Allen, J. Cummins, & M. Swain (Eds.), *The development of second language proficiency* (pp. 7–25). Cambridge, England: Cambridge University Press.

Krashen, S. (1982). *Principles and practice in second language acquisition.* New York, NY: Pergamon.

Leblanc, G., & Sarrasin, L. (2004). *En temps et lieux. Géographie, histoire et éducation à la citoyenneté, 3e cycle. Module 4, La conquête de l'Ouest vers 1905.* Montréal, Canada: Chenelière/McGraw-Hill.

Lightbown, P. (2014). *Focus on content-based language teaching*. Oxford, England: Oxford University Press.

Llinares, A., Morton, T., & Whittaker, R. (2012). *The roles of language in CLIL*. Cambridge, England: Cambridge University Press.

Lyster, R. (2004). Differential effects of prompts and recasts in form-focused instruction. *Studies in Second Language Acquisition, 26*, 399–432.

Lyster, R. (2007). *Learning and teaching languages through content: A counterbalanced approach*. Amsterdam, The Netherlands: Benjamins.

Lyster, R. (2016). *Vers une approche intégrée en immersion*. Montreal, Canada: Les Éditions CEC.

Lyster, R., & Tedick, D. J. (2014). Research perspectives on immersion pedagogy: Looking back and looking forward. *Journal of Immersion and Content-Based Language Education, 2*(2), 210–224.

Netten, J., & Spain, W. (1989). Student-teacher interaction patterns in the French immersion classroom: Implications for levels of achievement in French language proficiency. *The Canadian Modern Language Review, 45*, 485–501.

Schmidt, R. (1990). The role of consciousness in second language learning. *Applied Linguistics, 11*, 129–158.

Schmidt, R. (1994). Deconstructing consciousness in search of useful definitions for applied linguistics. *AILA Review, 11*, 11–26.

Sharwood Smith, M. (1981). Consciousness-raising and the second language learner. *Applied Linguistics, 2*, 159–168.

Sharwood Smith, M. (1993). Input enhancement in instructed SLA. *Studies in Second Language Acquisition, 15*, 165–179.

Swain, M. (1985). Communicative competence: Some roles of comprehensible input and comprehensible output in its development. In S. Gass & C. Madden (Eds.), *Input in second language acquisition* (pp. 235–253). Rowley, MA: Newbury House.

Swain, M. (1988). Manipulating and complementing content teaching to maximize second language learning. *TESL Canada Journal, 6*, 68–83.

Tedick, D., & Young, A. (2014). Fifth-grade two-way immersion students' responses to form-focused instruction. *Applied Linguistics*. doi:10.1093/applin/amu066

APPENDIX 8A
English Translation: A Teacher's Letter to Students and Liliane

Dear students,

We will soon welcome a new student in the class. Her name is Liliane. She and her family are Syrian refugees who have recently arrived in Canada. What can you do to make Liliane's arrival in class easier?

Refugees are likely to feel isolated in their new country at first, where almost everything may seem strange. And because of the suffering they experienced during the civil war in Syria, it is very important to be very sensitive in this respect.

As for Liliane, it is important to make friends with her right away. Just talk to her, console her when needed, and play with her without asking too many details about what happened to her during the civil war in her country. This is because a civil war usually leads to unimaginable atrocities from which it is difficult to recover. So be sensitive, but not indiscreet. If she talks to you about it, listen carefully and try to comfort her. And take the opportunity to suggest that she also talks to others that she trusts.

If she has difficulty understanding French or English, offer her help. As for her studies, it will be up to her to decide what she needs the most help in. Encourage her not to give up even if she has difficulties. Moreover, tell her about the different extracurricular activities that she could join to make new friends outside of class. Congratulate our new student for her courage and welcome her warmly into her new home and new school! For my part, I will welcome her with open arms and offer her all the help she needs.

Chapter **9**

The Integrated Syllabus: Content, Tasks, and Projects

David Nunan

‖‖ A Glimpse into the Project-Based Classroom

A group of 20 final-year business majors from a well-known Japanese university take part in a three-week summer course at the University of Hong Kong. The primary aim of the course is to provide an intensive enrichment experience (Cadd, 2015) for the students through a contact assignment over the three weeks. The three teachers responsible for the program decide that the theme of the course will be "Contemporary Life in Hong Kong," a sensible choice given the nature of the program and the students who are to take part in it. As Asia's "World City," Hong Kong provides many opportunities for students to carry out meaningful, real-world communicative tasks beyond the classroom. The teachers decide that the major learning outcome for the course will be a project on the theme of life in Hong Kong. After some discussion and debate, they decide that the project will be to create a website based on the life in Hong Kong theme. At the end of the course, the website will be uploaded to the internet and will be accessible in Japan for participants to share with their family, friends, and fellow students, providing an insight into their experience in Hong Kong. To complete the project, they will have to use English beyond the language classroom, not only off campus but also with the technical services department of the university, which will help them to create their website.

When the students arrive at the university, they expect "more of the same": classes on listening, speaking, reading, writing, grammar, and vocabulary in the context of business English communication. When introduced to the project, they are at first bemused and also intimidated, as they will be required to interact with both native speakers and non-native speakers of English in English. They are divided into four teams, and, as a first step, each team is required to come up with a sub-theme. As a class, the teams discuss options and come up with the four themes:

■ eating out in Hong Kong
■ tourist attractions
■ entertainment
■ historical Hong Kong

The course itself consists of in-class and out-of-class opportunities to practice and use English in authentic contexts. In-class work includes developing and polishing interview schedules, honing interview skills through role-plays and simulations, completing online searches for information on the four topic areas that the participants had selected, and so on. Participants also have meetings with the technical support staff at the university who assist and advise them in the construction of their website.

The Role of Content, Tasks, and Projects in Curriculum Design ||

The key terms that have relevant bearing on this chapter include curriculum, syllabus, content, task, project, and learning beyond the classroom. In a subsequent section, I shall explore options in integrating these elements into units of work. Many elements go into the construction of a comprehensive curriculum. In this chapter, I want to restrict my focus to just three of them: content, task, and project.

Curriculum has been broadly defined as all of the planned learning experiences in an educational setting and the totality of student experiences that occur in the educational process (Kerr, 1968). At a slightly less cosmic level, a particular curriculum will consist of three main components specifying the content to be covered, the learning procedures and processes through which the content will be delivered, and the means of assessing learners and evaluating the overall effectiveness of the curriculum (Nunan, 2015). Metaphorically, you can imagine the curriculum as a "pie" consisting of three slices (see Figure 9.1). The first slice is syllabus design and has to do with the selection, sequencing, and integrating of content. Methodology, the second slice, is concerned with the selection, sequencing, and integrating of learning processes and experiences. The final slice has two dimensions: (1) assessment, which is concerned with selecting and sequencing tools and techniques of judging learner performance, and (2) evaluation, which consists of procedures for determining the effectiveness of the curriculum.

Traditionally, curriculum planning, implementation, and evaluation have been thought of in terms of classroom-based pedagogy. Increasingly, however, curriculum specialists are turning their attention to the opportunities that exist for integrating in-class learning with language learning and use outside the classroom. The vignette at the beginning of this chapter illustrates one such possibility, but there are many others. Technology, travel, and the fact that we now live in a global "village" presents many challenges, but also, for language learners, many exciting opportunities. Out-of-class extensive reading clubs, teacher-student dialogue journals, language exchange websites, email tandem learning, in-country language villages, study abroad, home tutoring schemes: These are just some of the out-of-class projects described in a recently published book of case studies on out-of-class learning (Nunan & Richards, 2015).

In a slim but influential book published in 1976, David Wilkins drew a distinction between two basic syllabus types: synthetic syllabi and analytic syllabi (see also Brinton, this volume). A synthetic syllabus takes as its point of departure the individual linguistic elements (sounds, words, and grammar) that make up the language. These are "taught separately

Figure 9.1: The Three Components of Curriculum

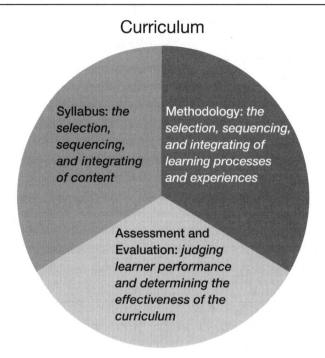

Curriculum

Syllabus: *the selection, sequencing, and integrating of content*

Methodology: *the selection, sequencing, and integrating of learning processes and experiences*

Assessment and Evaluation: *judging learner performance and determining the effectiveness of the curriculum*

and step-by-step so that acquisition is a process of gradual accumulation of parts until the whole structure of language has been built up" (Wilkins, 1976, p. 2). In contrast, analytic syllabi take as their point of departure an element or elements that are non-linguistic in nature. Content-based, task-based, project-based, and text-based syllabi are all analytic in nature.

Content-Based

Content refers to the "what" of instruction and therefore resides within the wedge of the curriculum labeled *syllabus*. It is useful to distinguish between linguistic content and experiential content. A syllabus driven by linguistic content will take as its point of departure lists of grammar, morphology, lexis, and sounds. Such syllabi fit into Wilkins' synthetic paradigm. An experiential syllabus fits the analytic paradigm and is organized around topics, themes, texts, contexts, and settings. (See also Snow's 2014 content-driven / language-driven continuum.)

In elementary and secondary school ESL contexts, there are two issues to be considered when developing experiential content-based instruction (as opposed to linguistic content-based instruction). The first is the actual content itself. The second has to do with the relationship of CBI to the rest of the school curriculum.

Content selection—that is, deciding on the themes and topics to be covered—can come from a number of sources. In school settings, themes and topics can come from other subjects in the curriculum—that is, from mathematics, science, environmental studies, and so on. In colleges and universities where ESP and EAP courses are increasingly common, the content is also usually derived from the academic disciplines being studied by the students. Brinton (this volume) provides two good example of this in her scenarios, one of which is taken from an ESL setting, and the other from an EFL setting in which English is the medium of instruction.

In EFL contexts, in general, as opposed to specific purpose courses, content is selected with reference to learners' current or projected communicative needs and interests. For young learners, topics may include family and friends, school life, shopping, parties, and entertainment. Even in these contexts, however, there is a trend towards including topics from other subjects in the school curriculum. For example, the series *Our Discovery Island* (Pearson Education, 2012), which is designed for elementary school learners, incorporates activities from art, social science, music, geography, science, history, technology, and mathematics.

As mentioned previously, in ESL school and college contexts, a major issue is how to fit CBI into the curriculum. Two prominent models are the sheltered and the adjunct model. In the sheltered model, second language students are separated from native speakers of the target language for the CBI lessons. In the adjunct model, students are simultaneously enrolled in a language class and a content class. There is close collaboration between the language teacher and the content teacher, and objectives and assessment are coordinated by both instructors. Scenario 2 in Brinton's chapter (this volume) is an example of the adjunct model. For this model to work, there has to be mutual respect and close collaboration between the language and the content instructors. This is not always readily achievable. All too often, content instructors take the view that the role of the language instructor is to "fix up the grammar" so that they can get on with the real work of teaching content. (For a detailed description and discussion of these and other content-based models, see Snow, 2014.)

Task-Based

Task-based language teaching (TBLT) developed during the 1980s as a methodological application of communicative language teaching (Candlin & Murphy, 1987; Nunan, 1989). In my book on TBLT (Nunan, 2004), I draw a distinction between target/real-world tasks and pedagogical tasks. A target task is something that people do in the world beyond the classroom. The number of target tasks is limitless. They include: obtaining goods and services (buying a movie ticket online, asking the way to the city center); socializing (exchanging personal information at a party); and using language for aesthetic purposes (writing a short story). A pedagogical task is carried out in the classroom. These can be ranged on a continuum from more-like-target task to less-like-target task (see Figure 9.2).

By rights, selecting and sequencing tasks belongs to the domain of methodology because they describe communicative procedures and thus relate to the "how" of the curriculum. However, in a syllabus in which the point of departure is an inventory of target tasks, the distinction between content and process becomes increasingly difficult to sustain. Because

Figure 9.2: Pedagogical Task Continuum

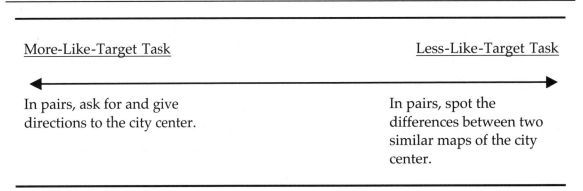

<u>More-Like-Target Task</u>   <u>Less-Like-Target Task</u>

In pairs, ask for and give   In pairs, spot the
directions to the city center.   differences between two
                                           similar maps of the city
                                           center.

these syllabi specify what learners should be able to do as a result of instruction, they are known as performance- or standards-based (Nunan, 2007).

It needs to be pointed out that not everything that is done in the classroom is a task. Sentence completion, fill-in-the gap, and similar form-focused exercises are not tasks. Nor are choral drills or reading a text and answering comprehension questions. This is not to say that these are not valuable classroom activities. They are just as likely to be found in classrooms that are based on principles of TBLT as in any other type of language classroom.

Despite their differences, the family of approaches that appear under the rubric of TBLT share a number of characteristics. To begin with, the focus is primarily on the exchange of meaning rather than the manipulation of form: Learners have to generate their own sentences and utterances rather than regurgitating those provided for them. Secondly, they have a series of steps that culminate in a concrete outcome that is couched in performance terms. Thirdly, the concrete outcome has a relationship, which may be relatively direct or indirect, to a target/real-world task.

Project-Based

A project contains most of the key characteristics of a task: It has a beginning, a middle, and an end; the focus is on the creation and exchange of meaning rather than the manipulation of form; there is a link between the classroom work and the world beyond the classroom; there is a concrete outcome or "product"; and completion of the project involves work through a series of steps or carrying out a number of subsidiary steps. In some ways, a project can be thought of as a "super-task." Examples of school projects are as follows:

1. organizing a beach cleanup day
2. designing a website
3. creating a visitor's guide to a local museum or market
4. producing a school play
5. planning, carrying out, and writing a science experiment

Projects can serve as capstones to a module or unit of work, or the project can make up the entire course of study (Legutke & Thomas, 1990). In their book-length treatment of projects in language learning, Ribe and Vidal (1993) emphasize the student-centered, whole-person value of projects, pointing out that they:

1. are open and flexible, and it is the students who occupy center stage.
2. involve the teacher and students negotiating objectives, planning together, monitoring, and evaluating processes and results.
3. incorporate the students' previous knowledge and personal experience.
4. appeal to the students' imagination, creativity, and affectivity.
5. can be quite extensive in terms of scope and length.
6. contain thematic content that is related to the students' immediate environment and interests.
7. require the use of all the language skills and organizational strategies.
8. approach language globally, not sequentially, according to the needs created by the task.

Content, Tasks, and Projects in the General English Classroom ||

In this section, I want to look at some of the ways in which interrelationships between the key curricular elements of *content, task,* and *project* might be articulated in the general English classroom. I want to do so with reference to the "glimpse into the classroom" that heads this chapter. I do not want to get bogged down in a discussion over demarcation lines between general English and ESP/EAP because this terrain has been extensively trodden elsewhere. Because the Japanese students who were taking part in the intensive summer program at the University of Hong Kong (HKU) had all done courses in EAP as well as ESP courses at their home university, the overall goal of the HKU program was to provide them with an opportunity to activate their general communication skills through contact with a range of native and non-native speakers of English in Hong Kong.

The content focus of the course is "Contemporary Life in Hong Kong." On the first day, the students, in consultation with the three teachers assigned to the courses, decide on the four subthemes mentioned in the chapter-opening scenario.

The teachers tell the students that the course itself will be organized around a project that will have to be completed over the three weeks in which they will be at the university. The project is to design and upload a website introducing eating out in Hong Kong, tourist sites, entertainment, and the historical aspects of Hong Kong. Each day, between the start of class and lunch, they will plan and develop their project assisted by their teachers. However, in the afternoon, they will be required to work independently, individually, or in small teams, gathering information for the project. This may involve internet search activities but will also require them to work off campus. In addition to the website, they will be required to keep a journal of their experiences over the three weeks. Within a month of returning to Japan, they will be required to submit a reflective assignment, drawing on their journals.

In their journals, the students document a wide variety of tasks that they carry out in the course of completing their project. These include:

1. constructing, field testing, and administering questionnaires
2. designing a questionnaire for tourists to Hong Kong about their experiences as well as their likes and dislikes
3. interviewing a Canto pop star
4. shadowing a chef in a popular restaurant for a day
5. researching and compiling a list of Hong Kong's top ten restaurants
6. conducting a group interview with several Hong Kong university exchange students
7. designing a walking tour of the Soho/Hollywood Road antiques and gallery district
8. taking part in an information scavenger hunt designed by their teachers
9. making digital video tours of several Hong Kong museums
10. making a video documentary of a trip to Cheung Chau Island.

This list is just a small sample of the many tasks that students completed during their three-week course. It is worth noting that some of these tasks, for example, "making a video documentary of a trip to Cheung Chau Island" could also be considered as projects in their own right, in that they have their own tasks embedded within them. One such embedded task was obtaining departure times of the slow ferry to Cheung Chau. (Students had been told that, if the weather was good, the slow ferry provided a better experience than the fast ferry because it was possible to sit on the deck rather than in an air-conditioned cabin.) A further point to note, and this marks a difference between projects and tasks, is that projects result in a physical product such as a clean beach, a video, a website, etc. Tasks typically result in a physical product, but this is not always the case. For example, tasks involving the collection of information may result in a physical product (where the information is written down), but they may not.

So far, I have described the three key elements in the intensive summer program undertaken by a group of undergraduate business majors from Japan: the content (topic(s)/theme(s), the project, and some of the tasks. So can this course best be described as content-based, project-based, or task-based? The answer, of course, is that all three terms fit the description. I find it impossible to imagine how one could have a content-based course without tasks, because one has to do something with the content. By the same token, it is impossible to imagine a task-based course without content. That said, I should point out that Ellis (2003) has proposed a task-based syllabus linked to linguistic rather than experiential content, although my reading of the literature on CBI (and not withstanding Snow's 2014 continuum) assumes that "content" refers to some form of experiential content.

Project-based instruction is probably the odd-one-out here. It is entirely possible to have content/task-based syllabi that are project-free. In fact, one does not have to search very far to find one. However, I find that the incorporation of a project, either as the capstone of a lesson or unit of work, provides coherence to a syllabus, textbook, or program that might otherwise be lacking.

If the argument that I am advancing here is accepted—that content, however conceived, and tasks are essential and that projects are highly desirable in terms of providing coherence—then the question is, what is the relationship between the three elements? Here we could conceive of two broad options: a blended option and a hierarchical option. In the blended option, all three elements have the same status, and all three are thrown into the syllabus "mix." Figure 9.3 illustrates this option. In design terms, all three elements have the same status within the syllabus.

In the hierarchical model, one of the elements forms the point of departure for the syllabus. One could begin with content and subsequently specify tasks then project, or project then tasks, or one could begin with a project and subsequently specify content and tasks, or tasks and content. Figure 9.4 illustrates one such option.

Although one can mix and match the three key syllabus elements that are the focus of this chapter, my own view is that one cannot get very far in the course design process by proceeding with one of the elements without reference to the others. Projects and tasks specify pedagogical and communicative procedures. However, they must be "about something." One cannot have content-free communication. While it is possible to develop detailed linguistic content specifications without reference to learning processes, it is difficult to get

Figure 9.3: An Illustration of the Blended Option

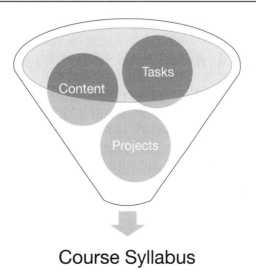

Course Syllabus

Figure 9.4: An Illustration of the Hierarchical Model

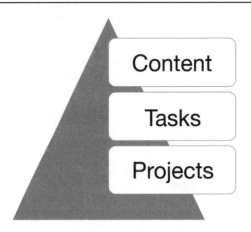

too far in the experiential content domain without reference to procedures. As Breen (1987) pointed out in the early days of communicative language teaching, language is a process, and in communicative syllabus design, content and process begin to merge. (It should be noted that in non-language areas, process is also becoming paramount. For example, these days, a major goal of history is not to have learners memorize and recite historical "facts" but to think and reason using historical methods. The goal of mathematics is to engender mathematical thinking.)

I have characterized the course described in the scenario at the beginning of this chapter as being project-based. When we designed the course, my fellow teachers and I decided that the principal learning outcome would be a website developed by the students. However, the website had to be about something. Given the nature of the summer course, "Contemporary Life in Hong Kong" was a natural topic. So, content and project issues were considered in tandem. Tasks were fleshed out as a second-order activity.

Observations and Underlying Principles |||

In Table 9.1, I make three observations on the course described in this chapter and identify three principles underlying these observations. The principles highlight the centrality of embracing an integrated approach to course design, the importance of embracing a learner-centered approach to instruction, and the value of weaving together in-class instruction with out-of-class activation.

Research Agenda |||

The terrain covered in this chapter provides fertile grounds for research. It raises many questions about the nature of, and relationship between, in-class and out-of-class language learning and use. In this section, I can only touch on a few of the research topics and questions raised by out-of-class, project-based learning.

Table 9.1: Observations and Underlying Principles Regarding the Business Enrichment Course at HKU

Observations	Underlying Principles
1. In designing the summer course, while the course could be described as project-based, it was not possible to flesh out details of the course without identifying a topic area and enabling tasks. The project that represented the overall learning outcome of the course and the course topic were identified at the same time. Some of the pedagogical and target tasks were subsequently developed. Other tasks were developed collaboratively between teachers and students once the course had begun and the students had begun fleshing out the project.	In an integrated approach, content specification and course outcome, specified in terms of a project, have to be developed in tandem. Enabling tasks are developed as a second-order activity.
2. In the summer course, learners had a central role in making decisions about content and processes as the course developed. The learners were responsible for identifying the sub-themes, deciding on the target tasks that they wanted to carry out to assemble data for the project, and carrying out the tasks themselves. They were, of course, also responsible for making decisions about the look of the website as well as the content to be incorporated into it.	A learner-centered approach to curriculum development will contain similar elements and procedures to traditional approaches. However, in a learner-centered approach, information by and from learners will be central to decisions about what will be taught, how it will be taught, and how it will be assessed (Nunan, 2013).
3. Language learning beyond the classroom and an integration between in-class (pedagogical) tasks and out-of-class (target/real-world) tasks were a major feature of the course. Learners had to carry out a wide range of target tasks such as interviewing Hong Kong residents (both local Chinese and expatriates) and visitors to Hong Kong, doing historical research, assembling and synthesizing media information on current affairs, ordering food and drink in restaurants and bars, shadowing people in the workplace and so on. These tasks are sometimes known as contact assignments.	Integrating in-class learning with collaborative out-of-class learning and language activation through use provides the optimal environment for language learning in both second and foreign language contents (Cadd, 2015).

The blending of in-class learning and out-of-class language use presents many opportunities for research. Questions in this area include:

1. What is the relationship between scaffolded learning in the classroom and language use beyond the classroom?

2. To what extent do in-class rehearsals (e.g., of interviews) transfer to and facilitate authentic out-of-class language use?

3. In those cases where learners struggle to transfer scaffolded in-class learning to independent language use beyond the classroom, what strategies can be employed to bridge the gap?

Another obvious area for research is comparative studies into the nature of student interlanguage in the classroom and beyond the classroom. Prior research has shown that classroom discourse tends to be structured and hierarchical. (This was first established in Sinclair and Coulthard's seminal 1975 study and subsequently elaborated upon by many other classroom researchers.) It involves simple rituals and routines as well as display language. Behavior and contexts of use are safe and predictable (McCarthy & Walsh, 2003). Discourse beyond the classroom, on the other hand, is relatively unstructured and its contexts of use generate complex rituals and routines resulting in authentic (rather than display) language. Behavior is unregulated, and communication is relatively risky and unpredictable. Comparing the discourse used by learners in the classroom and beyond the classroom could provide insights into the complex relationship between instructed language acquisition and language use.

In this blended learning model, research could investigate what opportunities exist for authentic input, opportunities for real conversations, a broader range of interactional contexts, and the provision of honest feedback.

Learner autonomy and independence has been widely researched (Benson, 2001). However, as new pedagogical models (such as the project-based approach presented in this chapter) are developed, a key question is to what extent models requiring independent language use foster autonomy.

Another aspect of the pedagogical model is the requirement for learners to collaborate with each other to achieve the learning outcome of developing a website. Qualitative case studies into collaborative learning based, for example, on learner diaries, could provide insights into the nature and impact of collaborative learning on learning outcomes.

APPLYING WHAT YOU LEARNED
Questions and Tasks

1. In this chapter, I have described an approach to syllabus design that integrates content, project, and tasks, illustrating it with reference to a summer intensive course for university-level Business English majors. Think of three to four other contexts that you are familiar with (e.g., a group of elementary post-beginning EFL learners in Korea). Would the approach work in these situations? Why or why not? Identify challenges and possible solutions to implementing the approach in these situations.

2. Create a project involving in-class learning and out-of-class interaction following the procedures described in this chapter. Describe the project, the topic(s)/theme(s), and some of the pedagogical and target/real-world tasks learners will need to undertake to complete the project.

3. Design an out-of-class assignment to be carried out by a specified group of learners. Provide details of the following variables.

    a. Location (e.g., *home, library, museum, park, cinema*)

    b. Modality (*speech vs. writing; face-to-face vs. email, "blended" modes*)

    c. Learning aims (*intentional vs. incidental; general vs. specific*)

    d. Control (*learning-managed, teacher-managed, other managed*)

    e. Type of interaction (*one way vs. two way*)

    f. Language register (*scripted, unscripted, casual, formal*)

    g. Logistics (*demanding, complex, simple*)

    h. Task demands (*listen, repeat, rephrase, respond, summarize, question, react, initiate conversation with native speaker, access community resources*)

    i. Manner (*individual, pair, group*)

    j. Means (*computer, mobile phone, television*)

REFERENCES

Benson, P. (2001). *Teaching and researching autonomy in language learning.* London, England: Longman.

Breen, M. (1987). Learner contributions to task design. In C. N. Candlin & D. Murphy (Eds.), *Language learning tasks* (pp. 26–46). Englewood Cliffs, NJ: Prentice-Hall.

Cadd, M. (2015). Increasing the linguistic and cultural benefits of studying abroad. In D. Nunan & J. C. Richards (Eds.), *Language learning beyond the classroom* (pp. 253–271). New York, NY: Routledge.

Candlin, C. N., & Murphy, D. (Eds.). (1987). *Language learning tasks.* Englewood Cliffs, NJ: Prentice-Hall.

Ellis, R. (Ed.). (2003). *Task-based language teaching and learning.* Oxford, England: Oxford University Press.

Kerr, J. (Ed.). (1968). *Changing the curriculum.* London, England: University of London Press.

Legutke, M., & Thomas, H. (1990). *Process and experience in language learning.* London, England: Longman.

McCarthy, M., & Walsh, S. (2003). Discourse. In D. Nunan (Ed.), *Practical English language teaching* (pp. 173–195). New York, NY: McGraw-Hill.

Nunan, D. (1989). *Designing tasks for the communicative classroom.* Cambridge, England: Cambridge University Press.

Nunan, D. (2004). *Task-based language teaching.* New York, NY: Cambridge University Press.

Nunan, D. (2007). Standards-based approaches to the evaluation of ESL instruction. In J. Cummins & C. Davison (Eds.), *International handbook of English language teaching* (Part 1, pp. 421–438). New York, NY: Springer.

Nunan, D. (2013). *Learner-centered English language education: The selected works of David Nunan.* New York, NY: Routledge.

Nunan, D. (2015). *Teaching English to speakers of other languages: An introduction.* New York, NY: Routledge.

Nunan, D., & Richards, J. C. (Eds.). (2015). *Language learning beyond the classroom.* New York: Routledge.

Pearson Education. (2012). *Our discovery island.* Harlow, England: Author.

Ribe, R., & Vidal, N. (1993). *Project work step-by-step.* Oxford, England: Heinemann.

Sinclair, J., & Coulthard, M. (1975). *Towards an analysis of discourse.* Oxford, England: Oxford University Press.

Snow, M. A. (2014). Content-based and immersion models of second/foreign language teaching. In M. Celce-Murcia, D. M. Brinton, & M. A. Snow (Eds.), *Teaching English as a second or foreign language* (4th ed., pp. 438–454). Boston, MA: National Geographic Learning/Heinle Cengage Learning.

Wilkins, D. (1976). *Notional syllabuses.* Oxford, England: Oxford University Press.

Part III

Innovative Applications of Content-Based Instruction

Chapter 10

From Human Rights to Conflict Resolution: Thematic Teaching for Peace and Cross-Cultural Acceptance

Mary Lou McCloskey

||| A Glimpse into the Content-Based Classroom

Good morning, Hungary. Jó reggelt.

Good morning, Montenegro. Dobro jutro.

Good morning, Serbia. Dobro jutro.

Good morning, Kosovo. Miremendjes.

Good morning, Croatia. Dobro jutro.

Good morning, Romania. Buono Diminaza.

Good morning, Slovakia. Dobre rano.

Good morning, Lithuania. Labas rytas.

Good morning, USA. Good morning!

So began the day at Teaching Tolerance through English (TTTE), a two-week program held for seven summers near Lake Balaton in central Hungary. This greeting at the morning circle provided a message of inclusion and respect for the middle school students and teachers speaking many languages, from many countries and cultures, all of whom came together to build a community to live, learn, and play together for two weeks in midsummer.

An afternoon, two-hour "English Club" is team-taught by two English teachers who met at camp, one a Croatian teacher from Croatia and the other an Albanian teacher from Kosovo. They have attended a daily morning session for teachers on teaching language through the content of peace, tolerance, and conflict resolution. They have explored today's theme, "Can differences be strengths?" through book talks by peers on relevant literature and through discussion of language-development-through-content strategies; they have also experienced these strategies playing the roles of students. They spent an hour planning how to implement what they have learned and are now working with a group of ten middle school learners from seven countries speaking five different home languages, with language levels ranging from beginning to advanced.

In today's club meeting, as the learners enter the room, they hear a recording of the song "Abiyoyo" and then practice singing the song. Teachers introduce a few key terms relevant to the lesson, with pictures, actions, and some translation, and learners enter terms they need to learn in their notebooks using "Word Squares." (See Appendix 10A for a summary of the language teaching strategies mentioned in this chapter.) Teachers do a "book walk" through the picture book *Abiyoyo* (Seeger & Hayes, 1994), introducing terms and asking questions at a variety of learner levels about what they see and what they believe might happen; the teachers then conduct an animated read-aloud, using different voices for each character. Teachers encourage learners to sing along when the Abiyoyo song comes up in the story. They lead a follow-up discussion using the Question, Answer, Relationship (QAR) technique (Raphael, 1986) to help learners address the plot, characters, theme, and author's intentions as well as help learners connect the theme of the day to the story and to their own lives. They refer to the "Conflict Resolution Wheel" from an earlier lesson (Kessler, McCloskey, Quinn, Stack, & Lee, 1994) and use it to discuss how the conflicts in the story were resolved. They conduct a brief action game of "I Have—Who Has?" reviewing vocabulary from the story. Teachers distribute a Readers Theater (Black & Stave, 2007) version of the story, and learners take different roles and voices as they read the story aloud. At the end of the lesson, teachers and learners discuss project options for sharing the literature that they have studied in their library project, which they will begin working on the next week. (Learners will each present a book in English to the local public library along with a project highlighting key learning from the books.) Teachers also introduce language frames, templates, and multi-level rubrics that will help support both the creation and assessment of the projects.

Learners walk out of class singing, "Abiyoyo, Abiyoyo!"[1]

Thematic Instruction in a Camp Setting |||

Craig Dicker, then Regional English Language Officer (RELO) at the U.S. Embassy in Budapest, Hungary, whose office served central and southeastern Europe and the Baltics, was looking for ways to help a region trying to heal from devastating ethnic war in the former Yugoslavia as well as the current discrimination of Roma communities in many of the regional countries. He believed that educators and youth could be invaluable resources in helping these countries and cultures formerly at war to live and work together peacefully. In addition, English was becoming a more and more important common language in the region, and teachers and learners would be attracted by the opportunity to improve their proficiency in an intensive program. He invited like-minded professionals—Mary Lou McCloskey, Lydia Stack, and Assistant RELO Gergo Santha—to work with him to develop a summer program that could build on that potential. And so, TTTE came to be as a program for middle school teachers and students from the region. The theme-based, English–

language medium program was designed for four primary purposes, all of which align with the rationale for CBI:

1. **Develop an ongoing community.** In CBI, learners develop language skills in combination with social and cognitive skills. Through the rich experiences of working, playing, living, and learning together, we sought to develop a supportive, collaborative learning community with the goal of providing a model that would help participants see this as a possibility. We also hoped that teachers and students would forge links and maintain contact to support one another in replicating or adapting aspects of the model for developing and spreading the concepts of interactive English language teaching (McCloskey & Levine, 2014) and peace-making beyond the camp.

2. **Promote content learning about living peacefully together.** CBI focuses on meaningful and relevant academic content. We hoped to help teachers to develop their students' understandings and skills regarding the following: respect for others' cultures; human rights; civil rights; standing up for our own rights and those of others; responding to bullying, hate, and bigotry; and resolving conflict (Eisler & Miller, 2004).

3. **Introduce active, interactive teaching approaches and tools.** CBI provides rich opportunities for language acquisition by providing opportunities for comprehensible input and negotiation of meaning. Because of the power of active, interactive, engaging approaches and strategies for learning both language and content, we wanted to offer these to teachers for the purpose of developing English language through content teaching (Gibbons, 2009; see also Gibbons, this volume). Our constructivist approach incorporated:
   - research-based communicative learning and cooperative learning
   - literature-focused, values-based learning using multicultural, theme-relevant literature from the United States and around the world[2]
   - active, interactive language development strategies to teach English
   - strategies for differentiation to support multilevel learners of English into, through, and beyond (Brinton & Holten, 1997) content reading selections and media.

4. **Increase English language proficiency.** By language immersion, including language instruction, content instruction through scaffolding language, and the use of English as the common language of communication in the camp, and by the experience of living, working, and playing in many different multicultural, multilingual groups, we aimed to improve the communicative competence in English of both learners and teachers.

CBI in the Classroom |||

TTTE shares characteristics of content-based language teaching and learning in the U.S. (Levine & McCloskey, 2012) by providing interactive learning and teaching of language using relevant grade-level content and incorporating elements of active engagement, cultural relevance, learner collaboration, content integration, and many forms of scaffolding to provide access to new language. The project, in its European setting, also has elements of the European Union's approach, CLIL (Banegas, 2012; Pérez Cañado, 2012; see also Dalton-Puffer, this volume), which Coyle, Hood, and Marsh (2010) define as "a dual-focused educational approach in which an additional language is used for the learning and teaching of both content and language" (p. 1). Within that definition of CLIL as an approach, Cenoz, Genesee, and Gorter (2014) point out that some scholars view CLIL as a set of instructional techniques in the classroom to promote foreign language learning, while others see CLIL in curricular terms, ranging from early partial or total immersion (teaching new learners in English 100 percent of the time) to modular subject program segments. Coyle, Hood, and Marsh (2010) assert that "there is neither one approach nor one theory of CLIL" (p. 101).

TTTE can best be described as a short-term, theme-based CBI project. All instruction and most of the interaction throughout the program were provided in English—the shared language (at some level) of all participants. The target population for language development was young adolescents (with some peripheral language development of their already proficient teachers); the content objectives involving tolerance, conflict resolution, and peace-making were directed toward both teachers and students. The professional development objectives were intended for teachers alone. The syllabus was an analytic one, with the organization provided by content and the language goals designed to help learners internalize and acquire the holistic content. English language goals focused primarily on improving speaking and reading fluency and listening ability, though writing was frequently integrated with those objectives.

Scaffolding was provided through:

- a variety of supports including lesson sequences that connected to learners' previous experiences and differentiated tasks for the various levels in the group.
- a wide choice among readings and activities centered around a certain topic such as human rights or conflict resolution.
- a range of strategies used to help learners interact with readings.
- authentic response tasks and texts that were accessible at a variety of grade levels.
- strategies for use of program texts to create authentic products (e.g., a book review, role-play, graphic display, or video responding to a text).
- vocabulary development strategies, including tools, games, and activities.
- a variety of interactive and cooperative strategies to promote social learning.
- availability of speakers of the students' first languages for scaffolding language learning and addressing urgent needs.

Appendix 10B includes a list of strategies provided for teachers and introduced during the teacher development portion of the days at TTTE, with brief descriptions.

Underlying Principles |||

Table 10.1 displays examples of the underlying principles of selected classroom strategies implemented in TTTE and how they relate to principles of CBI.

Table 10.1: Classroom Strategies and Underlying Principles of the TTTE Program

Classroom Strategies	Underlying Principles
1. Teachers help learners develop "Picture Life Histories" and use the pictures for pair-share activities.	This activity, an example of the many ways that learning can be scaffolded in a CBI environment, offers a supportive structure for social exchange along with a foundation for developing a learning community. The picture life history provides an opportunity for learners at all levels to share information about themselves; its goal is both to help elicit oral language and to develop community. Learner-drawn illustrations provide a visual reference to scaffold follow-up conversations with peers. The pair-share structure offers learners multiple opportunities to think, listen, and respond to their peers. They gain a shared sense of meaning of the text or content (Snow, Burns, & Griffin, 1998), connect their own experience to new information, and gain from the experience of their peers as well, all as they negotiate meaning (Swain & Lapkin, 2000). The teacher also has an opportunity to observe and informally assess students' introductory oral language levels.
2. Teacher reads aloud the picture book *Abiyoyo*, sharing pictures and leading retelling and discussion of the story.	The use of meaningful, relevant, and authentic texts, with scaffolding, supports both language and content development in this CBI environment. The story's theme is that of cross-cultural acceptance and conflict resolution. The illustrations, which include individuals from many cultures, reflect inclusion and acceptance of diversity. A picture walk-through, followed by reading aloud, allows learners to experience texts and language that they are not yet able to read on their own, provides an opportunity for teachers to share their interest and enthusiasm about reading and about particular texts, and provides an opportunity for addressing form by modeling the patterns and rhythms of English (Krashen, 2004; Trelease, 2013).
3. The teacher uses the QAR strategy to ask questions, scaffolding responses from learners at different levels.	The QAR strategy (Raphael, 1986) identifies four types of questions that students learn to ask and answer: (1) Right there; (2) Think and search, (3) Author and you, (4) On your own. (See Appendix 10B.)
4. The teacher leads the class in several Readers Theater performances of the *Abiyoyo* story, having students change roles each time.	Working with the same story in a different format provides structural and functional variation of content in different contexts. The use of Readers Theater has been shown to improve reading fluency (Carrick, 2006). By assigning parts according to language proficiency, the teacher challenges each learner. Through the inclusion of dramatic readings and acting, English language comprehension—plus stress and intonation—is enhanced.

Table 10.1 (*continued*)

Classroom Strategies	Underlying Principles
5. The teacher introduces the "Conflict Resolution Wheel" graphic organizer, provides role-play situations for discussing how conflicts are resolved, and uses the graphic organizer to discuss how the conflict in the story of *Abiyoyo* was resolved.	Graphic organizers provide opportunities to make thinking visible and to map academic labels onto concepts learners are acquiring. The Conflict Resolution Wheel graphic helps learners develop terminology and discuss and evaluate a rich repertoire of ways for dealing with conflict, including: Get Angry, Postpone, Compromise, Get Help, and Give In (Drew, 2004; Kessler et al., 1994). Understanding that we have choices about how we deal with conflicts gives us power over how conflicts are resolved and power in life. Opportunities to apply the knowledge through role-plays and story analysis offer learners the varied repetition that promotes deep learning of both language and content.
6. Learners are offered a menu of ways to respond to one of the books that will be given to the community library. Possibilities include: a map of culture elements in the story, a narrative structure map, a timeline graphic of the story, a discussion of conflict resolution in the story, a list of new words and meanings from the story, a comparison of the story to one from the students' culture, an analysis of a character in the story, or a "book talk" review of the story.	Because learners are acquiring language at different rates and in different ways in the CBI environment, we must provide differentiation through content, process, product, and language scaffolding. The activities to respond to a story: a. incorporate an authentic, meaningful purpose (i.e., the responses will be shared in the local library when the books are donated); b. provide choices that enable differentiation and empower learning (i.e., teachers support students in making choices that are attainable yet provide challenge); c. incorporate rich language-focused opportunities for learning and understanding (e.g., of vocabulary, character development, story sequence, elements of the story, story analysis); d. incorporate rich content-learning and application opportunities (e.g., looking at the cultural perspectives of the story, discussing the approach to problem-solving or conflict resolution); e. provide opportunities for learners to cooperate and collaborate (Johnson & Johnson, 1999; Johnson, Johnson, & Stanne, 2000).
7. The teacher provides models, practice, language frames, templates, and rubrics to scaffold learners' oral and written production.	There is tension in the CBI classroom between the desire to develop fluency and the need for accuracy and form in language development. By modeling, providing speaking and writing language frames, and making expectations explicit through templates and rubrics, teachers have the opportunity to shape the form of learners' language development.

Research Agenda |||

The program assessment and evaluation of the TTTE project were examples of action research, defined as: "a disciplined process of inquiry conducted by and for those taking the action. The primary reason for engaging in action research is to assist the 'actor' in improving and/or refining his or her actions" (Sagor, 2000, p. 1).

As part of the program, teachers and staff participated in action research to evaluate the program's effectiveness. Teachers conducted pre- and post-oral language assessments with learners, using an activity in which students tell a story from pictures, and also responded to a series of questions. Pre-tests were compared with post-tests. Combining the results of the last three years of the program, 120 of the 152 students demonstrated growth over the brief two-week session; 66 of them advanced by one level, 29 by two levels, and 1 by three levels. Twenty-four of the 25 students at the ceiling Level 4 on the pre-test maintained that Level 4 on the post-test while one student went to Level 3. Only 29 students showed no growth from pre-test to post-test.

Other formative data were collected during the program. Each evening, a student representative of each "team" met with camp staff at dinner to review the camp and the day, sharing what was going well or could be improved. Campers, teachers, and staff all completed surveys during the final days of camp regarding what they had learned and how they felt about the experience. We have rich testimonies regarding the high quality of their learning from our participants who wrote effusive evaluations at the end of their programs, who have stayed in touch with one another and with us years later, who have initiated a wide range of programs in their own countries, and who have had the confidence in their English to study in the U.S. Appendix 10B includes a list of follow-up projects of teachers, staff, and learners after their participation in TTTE.

The strength of field-based research is that it is authentic—it studies learning in the very situation and under the very circumstances in which it takes place. But field-based educational research is also messy. We are dealing with human subjects in places of learning, not in a laboratory where we can easily provide controls. Action research has a specific goal— that is, to improve the performance of the participants (in the case of TTTE, the teachers, leaders, and students who attended the camp). Because the participants are themselves collecting and observing the data, they have first-hand opportunities to use it to improve their performance. But because research is conducted by the participants themselves, it is subject to investigator bias.

We have evidence that our program made significant contributions toward the language development of the individuals that attended, as well as students who attended for the years that followed. We also have evidence that our participants gained the knowledge and skills to promote tolerance, peace, and effective conflict resolution in their communities. We have seen many examples of how that has been done (see Appendix 10B). Because our program was so multifaceted, however, it is difficult to determine exactly which variables led to this change.

There is little research that examines similar programs. Although there are many short-term language camps, few include a research component. Early research on Canadian French immersion programs, carried out over a longer period, demonstrated that learners could achieve near-native proficiency without sacrificing their L1 proficiency (Cummins, 1983; Genesee & Jared, 2008). Recent research (Slavin, Madden, Calderón, Chamberlain, & Hennessy, 2011) compared an immersion model with a transitional bilingual model in the U.S. and found that both could effectively develop both L1 and L2 reading.

Future research might try to separate the variables that lead to change in a theme-based program such as ours (these might include, e.g., staff training and practices, curriculum, the camp setting, the variety of languages of participants, or particular interest in the content in Central and Southern Europe). Researchers might include data collection with standardized instruments and by impartial individuals not involved in or invested in the program. Further qualitative research might use extensive interviews to document the outcomes of projects listed in Appendix 10B. Alternatively, similar action research could be used with replications of the TTTE experience (perhaps including projects like the follow-up activities) to see if results were replicated.

APPLYING WHAT YOU LEARNED
Questions and Tasks

1. In many ways, this learning situation was ideal—two weeks of living and learning together in a camp on a lake. What lessons from this summer camp experience might be applied in a classroom/course setting, perhaps one like your own?

2. In the TTTE program, the preliminary needs analysis was performed by an outside agency—the U.S. Regional English Language Teaching Office in Budapest, Hungary. What are the issues here? Should educators in the countries participating in the project have been included in determining the curriculum? If so, how might they have been included?

3. The program implements theme-based learning, where as the language teaching of the European Framework is frequently conducted through CLIL. How are these approaches similar and different? In your opinion, can they be effectively combined?

4. How would you describe this program: CBI? CLIL? ESP? Why? How are these types of programs different and the same? Consider the different categories of CBI programs described in Chapter 1 of this volume as you formulate your response.

5. The research in this project can be described as action research, defined previously as "a disciplined process of inquiry conducted *by* and *for* those taking the action. The primary reason for engaging in action research is to assist the actor in improving and/or refining his or her actions" (Sagor, 2000, p. 1). What are the strengths and weaknesses of this type of research in this setting? How might other research models be used in this context?

Acknowledgments

Many thanks to my collaborators in this project: Lydia Stack, who was co-director of teacher development; Craig Dicker, U.S. State Department RELO, who originated the program; Gergo Santha, Assistant RELO, who administered the camp; Jim Stack, who served as camp "grandfather" and also managed and analyzed our data; Molly Staeheli, camp director for four of the seven years; and all the other RELOs, staff members, participants, and students who made such important contributions to our program.

ENDNOTES

1. Zsuzsanna Kozak (2010) has created a charming film available on YouTube that tells the story of the TTTE camp through the eyes of a young participant from Romania.
2. Information on the literature and other resources provided for teachers in the program, along with an analysis of program results is available on the author's website at http://www.mlmcc.com.

REFERENCES

Banegas, D. L. (2012). Integrating content and language in English language teaching in secondary education: Models, benefits, and challenges. *Studies in Second Language Learning and Teaching, 2*(1), 111–136. Retrieved from http://www.ssllt.amu.edu.pl/images/stories/vol. 2.no.1.march. 2012/ SSLLT%2021%20111/136%20_Banegas.pdf

Black, A., & Stave, A. M. (2007). *A comprehensive guide to Readers Theatre: Enhancing fluency and comprehension in middle school and beyond.* Newark, DE: International Reading Association.

Brinton, D., & Holten, C. (1997). Into, through, and beyond: A framework to develop content-based material. *English Teaching Forum, 35*(4), 10–21.

Carrick, L. U. (2006). *Readers Theater across the curriculum.* In T. Rasinski, C. Blachowicz, & K. Lems (Eds.), *Fluency instruction: Research-based best practices* (pp. 209–230). New York, NY: Guilford.

Cenoz, J., Genesee, F., & Gorter, D. (2014). Critical analysis of CLIL: Taking stock and looking forward. *Applied Linguistics, 35*(3), 243–262.

Coyle, D., Hood, P., & Marsh, D. (2010). *Content and language integrated learning.* Cambridge, England: Cambridge University Press.

Cummins, J. (1983). Language proficiency, biliteracy and French immersion. *Canadian Journal of Education/Revue Canadienne de L'éducation, 8*(2), 117–138.

Drew, N. (2004). *The kids' guide to working out conflicts: How to keep cool, stay safe, and get along.* Minneapolis, MN: Free Spirit.

Eisler, R., & Miller, R. (2004). *Educating for a culture of peace.* Portsmouth, NH: Heinemann.

Genesee, F., & Jared, D. (2008). Literacy development in early French immersion programs. *Canadian Psychology, 49*(2), 140–147. Retrieved from http://www.psych.mcgill.ca/perpg/fac/genesee/19.pdf

Gibbons, P. (2009*). English learners, academic literacy, and thinking: Learning in the challenge zone.* Portsmouth, NH: Heinemann.

Johnson, D. W., & Johnson, R. T. (1999). Making cooperative learning work. *Theory into Practice, 38*(2), 67–73.

Johnson, D. W., Johnson, R. T., & Stanne, M. E. (2000). *Cooperative learning methods: A meta-analysis.* University of Minnesota, Minneapolis: Cooperative Learning Center. Retrieved from http://www.cooperation.org/pages/cl-methods.html

Kessler, K., McCloskey, M. L., Quinn, M. E., Stack, L., & Lee, L. (1994). *Making connections: Language through content for secondary ESOL, Book 2.* Boston, MA: Heinle.

Kozak, Z. (2010). *Teaching tolerance through English* [Video]. Budapest, Hungary: U.S. Department of State Regional English Language Teaching Office. Retrieved from https://www.youtube.com/watch?v=Y7A0ireuyuU

Krashen, S. (2004). *The power of reading* (2nd ed.). Westport, CT: Libraries Unlimited.

Levine, L. N., & McCloskey, M. L. (2012). *Teaching English language and content in mainstream classes: One class, many paths* (2nd ed). New York, NY: Pearson.

McCloskey, M. L., & Levine L. N. (2014). No water, no life, no blue, no green. In M. Gottlieb & G. Ernst-Slavit (Eds.), *Academic language in diverse classrooms: Promoting content and language learning* (pp. 131–176). Thousand Oaks, CA: Corwin.

McCloskey, M. L., Orr, J., Stack, L., & Kleckova, G. (2015). *Strategies for teaching English language, literature and content: A teacher's guide.* Atlanta, GA: Educo.

Pérez-Cañado, M. L. (2012). CLIL research in Europe: Past, present, and future. *International Journal of Bilingual Education and Bilingualism, 15*(3), 315–341.

Raphael, V. (1986). Teaching question-answer relationships. *The Reading Teacher, 39,* 516–520.

Sagor, R. (2000). *Guiding school improvement with action research.* Alexandria, VA: ASCD.

Seeger, P., & Hayes, M. (1994). *Abiyoyo.* New York, NY: Scholastic.

Slavin, R. E., Madden, N. A., Calderón, M. E., Chamberlain, A., & Hennessy, M. (2011). Reading and language outcomes of a five-year randomized evaluation of transitional bilingual education. *Educational Evaluation and Policy Analysis, 33*(1), 47–58.

Snow, C. E., Burns, M. S., & Griffin, P. (Eds.). (1998). *Preventing reading difficulties in young children.* Washington, DC: National Academy Press.

Swain, M., & Lapkin, S. (2000). Task-based second language learning: The uses of the first language. *Language Teaching Research, 4*(3), 251–274.

Trelease, J. (2013). *The read-aloud handbook* (7th ed.). New York, NY: Penguin.

APPENDIX 10A
Strategies and Activities for Teaching English Language Literature and Content

These are brief descriptions of the teaching strategies mentioned in the chapter. For more thorough explanations, with examples and references, see McCloskey, Orr, Stack, & Kleckova (2015) and/or Levine & McCloskey (2012).

Active Learning: Learning in which learners are physically active and cognitively engaged, frequently using language for speaking and writing.

Active Listening: Strategies for listening to partners that lead to mutual understanding. This might include withholding judgment or conclusions, rephrasing what a partner says to check comprehension, or asking questions for clarification.

Anticipation guide: The teacher presents a list of true/false questions to consider before students read a text and students make guesses. After reading, they return to the questions and answer them according to the text.

Book Walk: Before read-aloud or student reading of a fiction or non-fiction picture book, teachers and learners browse through the book, discussing each page. Teachers introduce new terms; clarify meanings; identify characters; develop hypotheses abut setting, plot, and theme of the text; and encourage questions about what will happen/what students will learn.

Brainstorming: Gathering ideas from everyone in a non-evaluative way. Teachers and learners often use graphic organizers such as bubble maps or spider maps to write and connect ideas during brainstorming.

Carousel: Questions are posted around the room. Small groups rotate from question to question at a signal. At each poster, they write their ideas and their responses to the ideas of others.

Conflict Resolution Wheel: A graphic organizer pie chart divided into sections labeled with ways of resolving conflicts, including: Get Angry, Postpone, Compromise, Get Help, and Give In. Learners use the wheel to analyze how problems are solved in literature and critical incidents and to role-play optional resolutions to problems that arise.

Dipsticking: A metaphor for quick ongoing checks on classroom learning. It can be carried out with cards, signals, oral questions, whiteboards, electronic devices, or observations.

Discussion Participation Rubric: Learners use a rubric to evaluate the quality of their discussion. Did they listen carefully without interrupting? Build on another's idea? Ask a question to include someone? Work to come to a mutual conclusion?

Exit Ticket: As a quick formative evaluation, the teacher gives students a short challenge as they leave the room. They may write an answer on a slip of paper, tell it orally, or show with a sign or symbol.

Fishbone Outline: A graphic organizer in the shape of a fish skeleton that shows cause and effect.

Give One—Get One: In response to a challenge (perhaps a review question), learners divide a paper into squares. They write several responses in squares. Then they mingle and choose a new partner at a signal. With each partner, learners share one idea and collect one idea, which they write in a blank square.

I Have—Who Has?: A whole-class card game. Teacher creates a series of cards with connected terms, concepts, etc. Each card connects to the next. Each student has one or more cards. The first student asks, "Who has____?" The student with the answer/match reads, "I have ____," and so on.

Index Card Life History: Learners draw pictures on an index card representing different aspects of their lives (name, family, favorite activities, goals, something they're good at, etc.). They use the drawings as an outline to introduce themselves to a partner; then they introduce the partner to others.

Inside/Outside Circles: Students each prepare different study cards for vocabulary, etc. Partners stand in concentric circles facing one another. They teach their partners what is on the card. On a signal, they trade cards and the outside circle rotates one person.

Into-Through-Beyond: An approach to a text that includes activities before reading (e.g., to build background and connect to students' previous experience), strategies for use during the reading (e.g., self-questioning), and activities to interact and reflect after the reading (e.g., QAR).

Jigsaw: A cooperative learning strategy in which a text or task is divided into sections. Small groups each study the section and prepare to teach others. Then they form groups with one "expert" on each section and teach one another about what they have learned.

Language Frames: Language frames are paper, oral, or written sentence stems, sentence starters, or organizers for paragraphs and longer pieces with model language to promote and support academic talk and writing. For example, to encourage active listening and oral comprehension, partners might use this language frame in a discussion: "I understand that you are saying _____, but I still have a question. Would you please clarify _____?"

Language Templates: Language templates are electronic or paper forms that provide examples of writing genres, structures, form, and content, using open-ended sentences, paragraphs, or spaces to encourage production and provide learners with opportunities to use appropriate format and structure in written or oral language production.

Lineup: Learners are asked to use language to find out something about one another (e.g., how long it takes the person to get to school or the person's birth month and day) and then that criterion is used to line up in order.

Literature Circles: A literature study strategy in which each learner brings a different product to the literature discussion, such as on a different aspect of the selection read, e.g., Questioner, Literary Luminary, Character Captain, Illustrator, Summarizer, Researcher, Vocabulary Wizard, Passage Picker, or Scene Setter.

Numbered Heads: A cooperative learning strategy in which small group members each have a number, e.g., 1–4. Groups are given a question or challenge. Students put their heads together to find the answer and prepare each member to share that answer. Then the teacher calls out a number and the person in each group with that number gives the group's answer.

Picture Life History: Learners are instructed to draw pictures in different areas of an index card describing personal information (e.g., family, favorites, goals, accomplishments). The drawings are then used in self-introductions and later in peer introductions.

Point of View: After reading a selection, learners think of questions to ask various characters (or things) in a reading. Then they take turns playing the roles and asking and answering the questions.

Question, Answer, Relationship (QAR): After reading a selection, students learn to answer (and, later, ask) four types of questions: (1) *Right there* (details from the text); (2) *Think and search* (connecting different parts of the text); (3) *Author and you* (considering the writer's craft) and (4) *On your own* (connecting the text to your life and/or other literature).

Quickwrite: To develop fluency, learners respond in 2–10 minutes to an open-ended question or prompt posed by the teacher.

Readers Theater: A story with rich dialogue is revised into a narrated play in which learners take parts and read aloud.

Reciprocal Teaching: Pairs of learners read a text together taking turns as student and teacher. Four kinds of questions help them focus intently on understanding and remembering what they read: predicting, questioning, clarifying, and summarizing.

Round Robin/Roundtable: In Round Robin, learners take turns responding to a challenge or prompt by passing a single paper around. In Roundtable, groups rotate from one table to the next to write on the paper there.

Rubric: A rubric is a scoring guide for evaluating the quality of student responses. A rubric might include a list of clearly stated criteria or a matrix describing performance on several criteria at different levels. Rubrics can be used effectively for student self-evaluation, reflection, and review as well as for teacher evaluation.

Sentence Maker: Several learners stand in a line in front of the room. The rest of the group takes turns asking them questions. The "line" responds in complete sentences in which each person can contribute only one word at a time, cycling back to the beginning of the line as needed.

Sunshine Outline: A graphic organizer for describing a narrative in which the "rays" of a picture of the sun are labeled with reporter's questions: who, what, when, where, why, and how.

T-List: A simple graph in which learners draw a T, label the two columns at the top (e.g., same/different; pro/con), and write responses under the appropriate column.

Think-Pair-Share: A cooperative learning strategy in which a question/challenge is posed, and students have time to think about (and/or write about) their responses. Then they share responses with a pair. In the final step, pairs join with a second pair and each person shares their partners' ideas with the group.

Using Picture Books: Picture books can be used effectively with beginners of all ages. Possible strategies include: Taking a "book walk" through the pictures of the book with oral discussion, developing the vocabulary, looking at the pictures, and making predictions about the story; showing the pictures and retelling the story in language appropriate for learners, reading aloud to learners; analyzing the story elements (e.g., character, setting, plot, theme, author's purpose, problem-solution); or making a story map or other graphic organizer to summarize the text. Many of the other strategies in this list are appropriate for picture books.

Word Squares: To learn and study a challenging new word, learners draw a square and divide it into four parts. In each part, they include an aspect of the word—for example, Square 1: Word and translation; Square 2: Picture illustrating the meaning of the word; Square 3: Sentence showing meaning of the word; Square 4: Antonym, or for words that don't have an antonym, a negative example of the word (e.g., a negative example of baseball is checkers).

APPENDIX 10B
Follow-Up Projects of Teachers and Learners after the Camp Experience

- International Day of Peace in Hungary
- International Day for the Elderly
- Translation of the Convention on Children's Rights into Albanian
- School presentations and trainings in multiple sites
- Replication of activities from camp in home schools: "The Spider's Web," Picture-Life History, Readers Theater
- Romanian course on teaching tolerance
- Tolerance Day; Tolerance Week
- Tri-National Drama team (Hungary, Serbia, Romania)
- Posters on conflict resolution
- Meetings to involve students and the community in the educational process
- Media reports on camp projects in several countries
- Project to integrate Roma into the Croatian community
- Kindergarten for Roma children in Serbia
- Democratic Education School in Hungary
- School Beautification Campaign in Bosnia and Herzegovina
- "Turn Bystanders into Upstanders" Anti-Bullying Education project in Greece
- Multinational Project for Empowerment of Girls
- The Global Village Project in the U.S.

Chapter 11

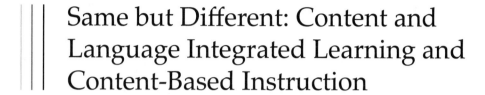

Same but Different: Content and
Language Integrated Learning and
Content-Based Instruction

Christiane Dalton-Puffer

||| A Glimpse into the CLIL Classroom

Scenario 1: We are visiting a class in a secondary school in a heavily built-up part of the larger Madrid area. The students in this CLIL geography lesson are 14–15 years old. All of the 11 girls and 7 boys have Spanish as their L1, although most other classes in their school include several immigrant students with family languages other than Spanish. The teacher, too, is a Spanish L1 speaker. She is a content specialist (geography and history) and has several years of experience teaching her subjects through the medium of English. In the following lesson extracts, a group of learners are presenting their project on urban planning and land use. The group had done a project on designing a skateboard park for a piece of unused land in the area.

<...>

S1:   This is the video presentation

S?:   Eh.. can you put it in full screen? ((silence)) No

S1:   ((She tries to do it))<L1 No se puede más creo L1> [you can't enlarge it further, I think]

S?:   <L1 Doble clic L1> [Double click] in the centre

  T: Double click in the centre ((T does so. The video starts and for a few seconds everybody is quiet)) Can you explain the location, please?

S1:   Eh.. the location.. <L1 es que no puedo L1>. The chalets and the other pa- and the other part of the park.

<...>

S2:   ...because is a good opportunity to eh.. to do something eh to tell all the.. it of the.. of the population, no only the young but because you said that is fav- it to... <L1 favorecer L1>

Sx: Favours

S2: favours to the young people but from the young young people it's not..

<..>

S1: but our project is just a skateboarding park. We can put it in a park that could be built in that zone because is eh..<x...x> that in a very big place like is the... ((she makes gestures)) <L1 no sé cómo se dice L1>

T: Flat area?

S1: Yes, in that flat area is not just for this because this in that area is a minimum part of it.

The extract shows students using L1 for signaling the need for help, or as an alternative route of expression when they need a lexical item. Support is provided by both peers and the teacher, and all interlocutors deftly move in and out of the linguistic codes they share. In this whole-class situation, all interlocutors always return to the CLIL language.

Scenario 2: We are in an upper secondary school of crafts and engineering in a town in Austria. This large school (1,000 students ages 15–20) offers five-year specializations in mechatronics, medical information technology, electronics, and automobile engineering. Besides their technical training, students also qualify for entrance to university. Teachers in the technical subjects have a background in the engineering industry plus a short post-graduate teaching qualification. Like in other schools of its type, the school ethos is one of "engineers educating the next generation of engineers." English (as a foreign language) is the only obligatory language subject apart from German (their L1) and is taught by language specialist teachers with a five-year integrated teacher education degree. Students that do not go on to university usually join local companies, many of which are small in size but often are highly specialized participants in a world market where English is the working language. About ten years ago, the school started to offer several theoretical and practical subjects in its electronics branch in English. "I want them to feel confident about explaining their appliances in English to people who aren't native speakers either and perhaps know even less English than they do," says one technology teacher in an interview. Another teacher says he wants students to be able to read the latest specialist literature with ease. New students express mixed feelings about the extra challenge in this high-pressure environment but after the first year, most of them feel "the fear of speaking English has gone." They say they manage because they study extra hard and teachers are often more supportive in CLIL classes than in the L1 subjects. They particularly like the fact that using English as a working language during technology lessons creates a sense of commonality between them and their teachers who sometimes also struggle for expressions, and whom they sometimes subtly correct "Sorry Mr X, but it's actually *so and so*, you know." Students whose English teacher sometimes co-teaches in electronics lessons remark that "in those lessons she's more like a colleague. You know, we are the technical experts and she is the language expert. That's cool, I like it." (extracts from Dalton-Puffer, Hüttner, Schindelegger, & Smit, 2009)

What Is CLIL? │|│

The term *CLIL* was a programmatic coinage in the 1990s by a group of European language educators wanting to stimulate policy measures that would encourage innovation in foreign language teaching. The overarching political aim, which is of high priority in the European Union (EU), lies in fostering multilingualism among the citizens of the Union, where 23 national (and many more minority) languages are spoken in the member states. The broader socio-educational context in which CLIL is embedded is thus one that aims at language enrichment and additive bilingualism, not only but especially among speakers of majority languages. (The term *additive bilingualism* refers to situations where an L2 is learned without detracting from the development of the L1. The aim is thus not to replace the L1 but to enlarge students' repertoire, to make monolinguals bilingual, or to add further languages to the repertoires of bilinguals. The opposite is *subtractive bilingualism.*) The notion of CLIL was concretized in an EU-level resolution (European Council, 2008) that content subjects should partly be taught to school-level learners via a language different from their usual medium of instruction/L1 in order to complement regular foreign language instruction, cater to a broader range of learning styles, and generally increase language awareness in students.

A widely accepted definition by Coyle, Hood, and Marsh (2010) says:

Content and Language Integrated Learning (CLIL) is a dual-focused educational approach in which an additional language is used for the learning and teaching of both content and language. That is, in the teaching and learning process, there is a focus not only on content, and not only on language. Each is interwoven, even if the emphasis is greater on one or the other at a given time. (p. 1)

This emphasis on the integration of language and content places CLIL at the crossroads of language teaching and content teaching and is mirrored in the formulation of learning goals that go beyond either type of subject. Among these additional goals are cognitive advantages through deeper content learning via the L2; access to knowledge that is being created and communicated internationally in the CLIL language; or enhanced cultural awareness, for instance, through gaining alternative perspectives on historical events. The overall socioeducational goals of the CLIL concept have been translated into a widely used pedagogical model, the 4 Cs Model, with the components content, culture, communication, and cognition (Coyle, 2007). This combination of components directly reflects the conception of CLIL as an approach that aims to transcend established pedagogical practices in both content and language education in order to create an innovative space where fields of learning separated by tradition can be brought together.

The actual implementation of CLIL is not tightly defined but is characterized by a multitude of forms and models, ranging from individual didactic units lasting a few lessons to several subjects of the regular school curriculum taught in the target language over several years. For instance, a Finnish biology teacher might decide to teach a two-week unit on transport across cell membranes in English and to include another three-week unit in the following term. Or a Romanian geography teacher might be asked by her principal to teach Grade 8 through the medium of German (the L2), with history taught through the medium of German to be added in Grade 9. The alternation of language of instruction within school subjects can be visualized in Figure 11.1.

These content-driven forms of CLIL resemble one-way immersion programs in the U.S. and have been referred to as Hard CLIL (Bentley, 2010) or Type A-CLIL (Massler, Stotz, & Queisser, 2014). Soft or Type B-CLIL, on the other hand, is integrated into foreign language lessons as theme-based projects, for instance, on the history and culture of target language societies, the main objective being language development. Optional theme-based courses taught by language teachers also fall in this category. Figure 11.2 summarizes this juxtaposition.

Figure 11.1: Visualization of Different Possible CLIL Implementations

School Year Grade 8

Topics	Units and Language of Instruction																
Biology	L1	L1	L1	L2	L1	L1	L1	L1	L1	L1	L2	L2	L2	L1	L1	L1	L1
Geography	L2	L2	L2	L2	L2	L2	L2	L2	L2	L2	L2	L2	L2	L2	L2	L2	L2
History	L1	L1	L1	L1	L1	L1	L1	L1	L1	L1	L1	L1	L1	L1	L1	L1	L1

School Year Grade 9

Topics	Units and Language of Instruction																
Biology	L1	L1	L1	L1	L1	L2	L2	L1	L1	L1	L1	L1	L1	L2	L2	L2	L2
Geography	L2	L2	L2	L2	L2	L2	L2	L2	L2	L2	L2	L2	L2	L2	L2	L2	L2
History	L2	L2	L2	L2	L2	L2	L2	L2	L2	L2	L2	L2	L2	L2	L2	L2	L2

Figure 11.2: Comparison of Hard CLIL/Type A and Soft CLIL/Type B

Hard CLIL–Type A-CLIL	Soft CLIL–Type B-CLIL
▪ Resembles content-driven CBI	▪ Resembles language-driven CBI
▪ Dominant objective: content learning	▪ Dominant objective: language development
▪ Content-subject curriculum applies	▪ Foreign language curriculum applies
▪ Taught by content teachers	▪ Taught by language teachers
▪ Assessment: content criteria	▪ Assessment: language (and some content) criteria

Interestingly, even though CLIL has become a stable phenomenon in many countries in Europe, Asia, and, increasingly, also in South America, few education systems in Europe have responded with firm regulations regarding its range, extent, or quality control,[1] so that more often than not, CLIL programs are defined by the contingencies of local grassroots contexts. Ideologies regarding the status of individual languages, availability of teachers, or parental pressure are only a few among the contingencies that shape concrete CLIL implementations.

Despite this high degree of variability, the following typical features are shared by many European CLIL programmes (Dalton-Puffer, 2011; Dalton-Puffer & Smit, 2013):

1. CLIL happens alongside foreign language teaching, which itself is firmly established in national curricula. At least one foreign language, which tends to be English, is obligatory from Grade 1 onwards.

2. CLIL addresses mainstream learners rather than linguistically vulnerable populations such as recent immigrants needing support with the majority language. Participation in CLIL programs has been mostly voluntary until now.

3. CLIL is timetabled as content lessons. Consequently, it is taught by content-trained teachers, who also assess it "as content." In some national contexts, teachers with a dual qualification in foreign language teaching and content teaching are available.

4. CLIL teachers are bilingual but usually are not native speakers of the target language. In some programs, they have the support of native-speaker co-teachers or foreign language specialists.

In sum then, CLIL can be seen as a foreign language enrichment measure packaged onto regular content teaching with the sociopolitical aim of additive bilingualism.

So far I have employed the general terms *foreign* or *target* language to stand for the first L (language) in the CLIL acronym. In non–English speaking countries the reality, however, tends to be that this L stands for English. This has nothing to do with the CLIL concept as such, but with current worldwide language ideologies. In today's world, English is unique in its degree of functionality in domains as diverse as international politics, business, academia, pop culture, and social media; it is therefore considered a highly desirable asset by many students and parents. Some researchers have even suggested that some of the success stories of CLIL might be owed to the real and imagined benefits of knowing English rather than the CLIL approach itself (Hüttner, Dalton-Puffer, & Smit, 2013). Other CLIL languages are very often major or minor international linguae francae (i.e., languages of wider communication; in Europe these would be mostly French, Spanish, German, or Russian) but less commonly spoken, regional, or minority languages can, of course, also be CLIL languages.

It is evident that, as an educational concept, CLIL shares fundamental assumptions with CBI, notably the idea that working with meaningful content in a target language facilitates learners' engagement, appropriation, and development (Cenoz, 2015). Among the different forms of CBI familiar to North Americans, I would see one-way foreign language immersion as that form which is most directly comparable with CLIL as it is currently practiced in Europe. Both address learner populations who are not multilingual by force or necessity and both aim at "academic achievement at or above grade level, additive bilingualism/biliteracy, and the development of cultural or multicultural competence," as formulated for North American immersion programs by Tedick and Wesely (2015, p. 26). An additional facet, however, is the extent to which upper-secondary students in many countries use English as their media and online lingua franca. In sum, I believe that even though the local contingencies of individual CLIL and CBI implementations should not be underestimated, numerous shared concerns provide ample space for mutual exchange and joint research.

Issues in CLIL | | |

The most important issues arising in CLIL go back to tensions built into the following constellation of facts: (1) the origins and main conceptual underpinnings of CLIL lie in fostering improved foreign language learning; (2) the CLIL concept invokes content and language *integration*; and (3) actual realizations of CLIL in schools and universities overwhelmingly anchor it in content teaching. Given the fact that institutional traditions treat the worlds of language and content as separate, paradoxes and tensions are bound to arise. Before looking at issues arising inside the classroom, I will discuss some contextual and organizational issues as they condition to a significant degree what goes on during lessons and how this is perceived by the participants.

Contextual Conditions

A first issue where the tensions play out is at the level of curriculum. As a rule, the binding curricular goals for Type A-CLIL learners are those of the content subject. Explicit language learning goals are rarely formulated at the curriculum level.[2] Some official documents mention rather unspecific language goals such as increased oral fluency, increased motivation, lower language anxiety, or larger specialist vocabulary and a promise of "added value" such as deeper cognitive processing, increased internationalization, and intercultural sensitivity (Coyle, Hood, & Marsh, 2010). At the end of the day, it is the content-subject learning outcomes that count for school grades and university entrance examinations. In consequence, many countries revert CLIL subjects to the national medium of instruction in the one or two final years before high school graduation. Worries about possible negative consequences of intensive CLIL on the development of learners' academic register in L1 have been voiced in many contexts, but only Swedish researchers have produced empirical evidence so far showing negative consequences on students' command of Swedish (Paulsrud, 2016). In the case of Type B-CLIL, where CLIL is part of the foreign language program, the curricular situation is, of course, different as binding learning goals refer to language competencies rather than subject content.

A second problematic issue concerns participants' underlying conceptualizations regarding language learning. For CLIL to deliver the anticipated L2 outcomes in the dominant content-driven constellation, one needs to rely on an exclusively input-based language learning theory. (This approach would be based on the assumption that rich input alone is enough to secure L2 development so that learners do not need to focus on language form or produce L2 output themselves to propel their learning.) The language learning/teaching field, however, has meanwhile come to an agreement that instruction does create an advantage for learners over exclusively naturalistic situations (Lyster, 2007; Norris & Ortega, 2000). Language instruction that is directly responsive to the cognitive and communicative needs of subjects like science or history, however, requires a specific kind of expertise, and so questions of teacher recruitment and teacher qualification (e.g., certified competence level in the CLIL language, training in language pedagogy, etc.) are important concerns in all CLIL implementations. Research has shown that when exclusively language-trained teachers teach CLIL, the content dimension becomes seriously diluted and thinned out, while content-qualified teachers are often unresponsive to their responsibility for the learners' language development (Kong, 2009). Interestingly, even teachers with dual qualifications self-report on wearing their content-teacher hat in Hard CLIL lessons and their language-teacher hat in Soft CLIL lessons (Dalton-Puffer, 2007). This means that specially qualified CLIL teachers are called for and post-graduate qualifications have been established in many places, but the education systems are reluctant to move beyond the established curricular categories.

The Learners

We saw in the second vignette that some novice CLIL students report increased levels of anxiety due to language pressure and that they also exhibit a reluctance to actively contribute to CLIL lessons to the same extent as to lessons delivered in the L1. On the other hand, we observed a tendency for learners and teachers to consider themselves to be in the same boat as L2 users, thereby bringing about subtle changes in teacher-student relations and a relaxed attitude towards language errors. This may be one of the reasons why students also tell of feelings of satisfaction and achievement vis-à-vis having mastered the difficult challenge of content learning in the L2 and also report eventually feeling relaxed about spontaneously using the CLIL language in and out of school—something that few of them felt they had achieved via traditional foreign language lessons. The affective balance for CLIL learners seems to be clearly positive (Hüttner, Dalton-Puffer, & Smit, 2013; Seikkula-Leino, 2007).

Learners' fulfillment of curricular goals has naturally been of great interest from the inception of CLIL. So far, most research attention has been paid to L2 attainment, and one should note that studies do not compare CLIL learners to native speakers of the medium of instruction, but to their peers—often attending the same school—who study the target language in traditional foreign language classes only. Since the CLIL students also continue their normal foreign language program and thus spend more time with the language than their peers, it is hardly surprising that they outscore those peers in language tests. Comparisons at entry level indicate, however, that CLIL learners already have a head start upon entering the program (such as a larger receptive vocabulary or higher language aptitude and motivation). Several recent studies show that the CLIL-learner advantage does not increase as one might expect because of the extra contact with the target language but remains stable over time (e.g., Rumlich, 2013; Verspoor, de Bot, & Xu, 2015). This entry-level advantage highlights an effect that is not part of the conception of CLIL as such, namely its attraction to more academically and linguistically gifted students from middle-class homes. This effect no doubt contributes to the generally encouraging findings concerning students' content-learning outcomes, which tend to be no worse than those of their peers who learn through the L1, as has also been found by studies on immersion programs (Tedick & Wesely, 2015). It remains to be seen how these aspects play out when CLIL is made obligatory, as has recently happened in Italy and in part of the Austrian education system (BMBF, 2011; MIUR, 2016).

Language Use in CLIL Lessons

Like all CLIL lessons, the CLIL geography lesson we visited in Madrid forms a discourse space that is utterly familiar to the learners. They have a lot of experience with lessons at their school and know all the rules of the game really well, a strong contrast to most situations of L2 use in out-of-school contexts. This sense of familiarity and low risk may well be an important source of the often-reported positive affect and feelings of success in CLIL learners (Hüttner, Dalton-Puffer, & Smit, 2013). So while CLIL classrooms are definitely a setting for meaning-focused naturalistic L2 use, they are definitely *classrooms* in terms of participant roles, physical setting, timing, and overall purpose. As such, they cannot directly prepare learners for all situational contexts.

It has been argued that several generic features of classroom interaction are well suited to support learners' L2 because they are designed to scaffold understanding per se. Among these are teacher questioning techniques; reformulations; peer playback; and, most important, the multimodal nature of a lot of classroom input. In the here-and-now of classroom interaction, teachers and peers support their utterances with gestures and body language; images and written materials complement the oral language that dominates most school lessons. The introduction of subject-specific technical and semi-technical vocabulary quite naturally gives rise to what, from a language teaching perspective, are language-directed episodes. For example, a Finnish history teacher says "apprentices—they are the ones who are being trained" during a lesson on medieval guilds and draws attention to linguistic form by pointing out the correct English pronunciation. Some instances are on record where students indicate to a teacher that his/her pronunciation is not quite correct, but other issues of linguistic correctness are routinely sidelined as long as "the meaning can be understood," which is usually possible because of the highly contextualized nature of oral classroom interaction. This tendency to downplay correctness may be especially prevalent for CLIL languages that serve as lingua francae among non-native speakers in international out-of-school contexts (which is especially true of English today), but no research to test this assumption has been conducted so far.

As we have seen in our visits to schools in Spain and Austria, the participants in CLIL lessons are bi-/multilinguals who also share another language, the majority language, which might be their L1 or L2. This opens up another scaffolding option, namely using the system-wide majority language at particular moments, as we saw during the Spanish students' presentation, when the L1 was used for appeals for help or to deal with technical matters. Classroom humor and attention to personal relationships are very often performed in the L1, but one can observe a great deal of variation in this respect among different learning groups. The question of "how much L1 use is alright" is hotly debated, much like it is in foreign language teaching. More recently, the notion of translanguaging (see also D. Reynolds, this volume) suggests that such practices should not be problematized but viewed as natural behavior of multilinguals using their full linguistic repertoire and should not be avoided but rather exploited for learning (Gierlinger, 2015; Lin, 2015).

Pedagogy and Classroom Discourse

As we have seen, in its conception CLIL was designed as a space for innovation where fields of learning separated by tradition could be brought together. The realities of content-driven L2-medium education, however, frequently speak otherwise. More often than not, the actual pedagogical design of everyday CLIL lessons is identical to the content lessons in the same subject taught in the regular majority language (the L1), which is not surprising if we remember that CLIL is mostly taught by regular subject-trained teachers. The expectation of content specialists that CLIL learners will simply "pick up the language" is very likely overly optimistic because the actual range of linguistic forms and functions one can experience in a classroom is contextually limited. So, any incidental language learning that CLIL learners will perform while working on content depends on subject educators, since it is their pedagogical decisions that determine the amount and quality of oral and written input and the opportunities for producing output during a lesson. For example, a comparison of different types of classroom tasks with regard to students' likelihood of expressing their own stance and thus drawing on linguistic resources of appraisal has shown a clear gradation (in descending order) of role-play, group work, student presentations, and whole-class discussion in that respect (Llinares & Dalton-Puffer, 2015). Interestingly, role-plays carried out in the L2 have been found to pay off also in terms of subject education. Learners in Swiss CLIL biology/ecology lessons seemed to consider the L2 as a kind of "mask" that enabled them to invest in role-plays on controversial topics without fear of face loss (Maillat, 2010).

As in many forms of CBI, the persistent challenge in CLIL is to find ways of creating and specifying an *integrated pedagogy* and to convince content-trained CLIL teachers that overt attention to language serves the purposes of the content subject in very direct ways. For this to work, a more specific understanding of the "language to be learned" needs to be applied in CLIL contexts, moving the goalposts from general communicative competence in the L2 to subject-specific language and language for academic purposes, which connects CLIL and CBI to ESP and EAP (see chapters by Brinton and Frodesen, this volume). The ESL/CBI field has produced high quality work in this respect, especially with regard to classroom reading and writing and has served as an inspiration to CLIL educators (Schleppegrell & O'Hallaron, 2011). The problem with any direct transfer of materials and activities is that with CLIL being a worldwide phenomenon, a wide range of contexts with different educational traditions and curricula needs to be taken into account. In order to convince subject educators that attending to language is in their own best interest, it is necessary to identify content-learning goals in their local curricula that directly implicate language. CLIL subject teachers' regular attention to subject-specific vocabulary is evidence of their readiness to do it where they are aware of it. Beyond the level of the lexicon, several notions that have recently been examined as potential zones of overlap for integrated CLIL pedagogy are *genre* and *cognitive discourse functions*. For example, learning to produce subject-specific genres or text types like the biographical account in history plays a constitutive role in leading learners towards an understanding of historical agency (Llinares & Morton, 2010; Llinares, Morton, & Whittaker, 2012). Cognitive discourse functions, on the other hand, verbalize content-oriented thought processes (such as classifying, evaluating, or hypothesizing) in order to make them accessible to those present in the classroom—that is, other learners or teachers (Dalton-Puffer, 2013). Research shows that L2-speaking CLIL teachers are perfectly able to realize the genres and cognitive discourse functions pertaining to their subject and required for working on a particular topic. They frequently perform them while working with their students, but practically never direct learners' attention to them or provide them with specific phrases and discourse structures that would enable the students to competently demonstrate content-relevant knowledge and skills. In sum then, two fundamental dilemmas need to be addressed by all CLIL programs:

> **Dilemma 1:** CLIL is conceived as a non-elitist way of involving all types of learners in additive bilingual education, while actual CLIL programs often attract learners who are either academically more gifted or whose parents show high levels of interest in education and additive multilingualism.

> **Dilemma 2:** CLIL is conceived as a language education measure motivated by the intention to enhance foreign or L2 learning, but it is institutionally tied to content education and predominantly taught by content teachers, thereby making balanced or integrated pedagogy hard to achieve without intervention.

Observations and Underlying Principles |||

Table 11.1 illustrates key observations and summarizes the underlying principles of CLIL as discussed in this chapter.

Research Agenda |||

A positive side effect of the dominance of English as a CLIL language has been that it gives researchers access to educational contexts that would otherwise remain closed to them because they do not know the local majority language. International research collaboration has decidedly been enabled by this circumstance. Discourse analytic research on the use of the L2 for learning has produced a wealth of evidence on how the micro-system of the CLIL classroom works as part of the overall ecology of institutional L2 learning. This has given us a non-idealized picture of language practices in numerous CLIL contexts (see Nikula, Dalton-Puffer, & Llinares, 2013 for an overview), but it has become evident that educational and pedagogical research perspectives (including those of subject educators) must be pursued more intensively in the future.

Table 11.1: Underlying Principles of CLIL

Observations	Underlying Principles
1. Learners and teachers in CLIL classrooms do not use the L2 100 percent of the time, but do use the majority language for a variety of purposes.	CLIL is a multilingual space where participants can and do draw on their full linguistic repertoire beyond the CLIL language. Monolingual immersion ideologies, though still officially embraced by many stakeholders, do not do justice to CLIL (Lin, 2015).
2. CLIL learners report that after a certain amount of CLIL exposure, they experience a marked drop in language anxiety and feel at ease using the L2 actively in and out of class.	Content-driven situations help steer learners' attention away from language forms to things accomplished and meanings conveyed through language. This may be particularly relevant for English due to its role as the dominant worldwide lingua franca.
3. In situations where both parties are L2 speakers of the CLIL language, subtle adjustments in learner and teacher roles lead to a more egalitarian relationship between CLIL learners and their content teachers.	This observation can be made particularly in contexts where the CLIL language is a high-status major lingua franca (i.e., mostly English outside North America). Such a language is known well enough by non-language specialist content teachers to be able to teach in it. The let-it-pass principle (*it* being linguistic problems) typical of lingua franca communication can similarly take hold in the content-driven CLIL classroom.
4. Language scaffolding by teachers and peers is a regular feature in CLIL classrooms.	Classroom interaction per se offers numerous routines for scaffolding understanding, such as fine-tuned questioning techniques, co-construction sequences, multimedia support, etc. Some of these routines involve the use of the L1.
5. There is next to no proactive language pedagogy in CLIL lessons.	Content-trained teachers lack training in language pedagogy and mostly subscribe to "maximal input is all that's needed" views of language learning. Reliable production of formally and stylistically appropriate subject-specific language does need conscious pedagogical attention. CLIL-specific pre-service and in-service teacher preparation is therefore a great desideratum.

For instance, CLIL research needs a wider empirical basis regarding the pedagogical designs of lessons, comparing them with other types of lessons in the same education system and across education systems. Such comparisons need to involve CLIL, content lessons in the L1, examples of language-sensitive content teaching to linguistically vulnerable (e.g., immigrant) populations, and foreign language lessons. When CLIL is contrasted with foreign language teaching, this is usually done as if there was only one type of language lesson, namely that with a form-and-accuracy focus. Especially with learners at more advanced levels of foreign language competence, however, the "carrier content" can be quite elaborate. Because the selection of that content is frequently incidental, it is then often experienced as shallow and boring by learners. More research into the linkage between foreign language lesson content and CLIL content is definitely necessary. Also of interest is an empirical check on how balanced CLIL lessons actually are in relation to the occurrence of the four language skills (listening, speaking, reading, and writing) and how the findings of such research could feed back into the planning of foreign language programs that run parallel to CLIL provision. Another topic at the juncture of CLIL and language teaching is the teaching and learning of English for specific and academic purposes. Which aspects of "general EAP" could English lessons take over for instance, and which should best be left with the CLIL subject itself?

Another area where clear needs exist with regard to CLIL is collaborative research for pedagogical development. Whether framed as Action Research or Lesson Study,[3] the crucial factor is the cooperation of educational linguists with subject educators and CLIL teachers. The aim for such research and development teams will be to explore how insights from CLIL stakeholder surveys and classroom-based research can be translated into classroom practice in a principled fashion. Core concerns in this respect would be language-aware content teaching (for instance, with regard to genres and cognitive discourse functions), learning designs that combine inquiry-oriented content pedagogies with sufficient opportunities for learner verbalization (both oral and written), and the calibration and adaptation of learning materials. For Type B-CLIL (content-driven foreign language teaching), research is needed to explore how language-trained teachers can identify and define worthwhile and well-founded content-learning goals that find acceptance with learners and so foster their engagement.

As we look into the future of CLIL, it would be desirable to ascertain how far the real and assumed benefits of a CLIL education are discernible over a longer time span and in hindsight. The fact that growing cohorts of students leave school with a CLIL experience will make this a feasible and worthwhile undertaking in the near future.

APPLYING WHAT YOU LEARNED
Questions and Tasks

1. In its conception, CLIL is an *integrated* educational approach merging content and language. The author describes several structural obstacles toward achieving integrated pedagogies.

   a. What are the main obstacles? Do you see any further ones?

   b. How do you think they could be overcome?

   c. How does this compare with a CBI context that you are familiar with?

2. CLIL has many similarities with one-way foreign language immersion. If you know such a program, compare it with what you have learned about CLIL.

   a. What, for you, seem to be the main similarities?

   b. What, for you, seem to be the main differences?

3. What could be advantages of judiciously employing learners' L1 during CLIL/CBI lessons? For what purposes would you or do you use it?

Acknowledgments

I would like to thank the UAM CLIL Research Group and especially Tom Morton for permission to reproduce these extracts here.

ENDNOTES

1. The Netherlands and some regions of Germany and Spain are exceptions in this respect.
2. Exceptions are in evidence in some autonomous regions of Spain.
3. Both are classroom-based research strategies that involve teachers in researching specific aspects of their own practice with a view to changing them. See D. Reynolds (this volume) for more detail on the Lesson Study paradigm.

REFERENCES

Bentley, K. (2010). *The TKT course: CLIL module.* Cambridge, England: Cambridge University Press.

Bundesministerium für Bildung und Frauen (BMBF). (2011). Austrian Ministry of Education and Women's Affairs. Retrieved from http://www.htl.at/htlat/schwerpunktportale/clil-content-and-language-integrated-learning.html

Cenoz, J. (2015). Content-based instruction and content and language integrated learning: The same or different? *Language, Culture and Curriculum, 28,* 8–24. doi: 10.1080/07908318.2014.1000922

Coyle, D. (2007). Content and language integrated learning: Towards a connected research agenda for CLIL pedagogies. *International Journal of Bilingual Education and Bilingualism, 10,* 543–562. doi:10.2167/BEB459.0

Coyle, D., Hood, P., & Marsh, D. (2010). *CLIL—Content and language integrated learning.* Cambridge, England: Cambridge University Press.

Dalton-Puffer, C. (2007). *Discourse in content and language integrated learning (CLIL) classrooms.* Amsterdam, The Netherlands: Benjamins.

Dalton-Puffer, C. (2011). Content and language integrated learning—From practice to principles? *Annual Review of Applied Linguistics, 31,* 182–204. doi:10.1017/S0267190511000092

Dalton-Puffer, C. (2013). A construct of cognitive discourse functions for conceptualising content-language integration in CLIL and multilingual education. *European Journal of Applied Linguistics, 1,* 216–253. doi:10.1515/eujal-2013-0011

Dalton-Puffer, C., Hüttner, J., Schindelegger, V., & Smit, U. (2009). Technology geeks speak out: What students think about vocational CLIL. *International CLIL Research Journal, 1*(2), 17–25. Retrieved from http://www.icrj.eu/12-741

Dalton-Puffer, C., & Smit, U. (2013). Content and language integrated learning: A research agenda. *Language Teaching, 46,* 545–559. doi:10.1017/S0261444813000256

European Council. (2008). *Resolution 2008/C320/01: A European strategy for multilingualism.* Retrieved from http://eur-lex.europa.eu/legal-content/EN/TXT/?uri=celex:32008G1216(01

Gierlinger, E. (2015). "You can speak German, sir": On the complexity of teachers' L1 use in CLIL. *Language and Education, 29,* 347–368. doi:10.1080/09500782.2015.1023733

Hüttner, J., Dalton-Puffer, C., & Smit, U. (2013). The power of beliefs: Lay theories and their influence on the implementation of CLIL programmes. *International Journal of Bilingualism and Bilingual Education, 16,* 267–284. doi:10.1080/13670050.2013.777385

Kong, S. (2009). Content-based instruction: What can we learn from content-trained teachers' and language-trained teachers' pedagogies? *Canadian Modern Language Review, 66,* 233–267. doi:10.3138/cmlr.66.2.233b

Lin, A. (2015). Conceptualising the potential role of L1 in CLIL. *Language, Culture and Curriculum, 28,* 74–89. doi:10.1080/07908318.2014.1000926

Llinares, A., & Dalton-Puffer, C. (2015). The role of different tasks in CLIL students' use of evaluative language. *System, 54,* 69–79. doi:10.1016/j.system.2015.05.001

Llinares, A., & Morton, T. (2010). Historical explanations as situated practice in content and language integrated learning. *Classroom Discourse, 1*(1), 46–65. doi:10.1080/19463011003750681

Llinares, A., Morton, T., & Whittaker, R. (2012). *The roles of language in CLIL.* Cambridge, England: Cambridge University Press.

Lyster, R. (2007). *Learning and teaching languages through content: A counterbalanced approach.* Amsterdam, The Netherlands: Benjamins.

Maillat, D. (2010). The pragmatics of L2 in CLIL. In C. Dalton-Puffer, T. Nikula, & U. Smit (Eds.), *Language use and language learning in CLIL classrooms* (pp. 39–58). Amsterdam, The Netherlands: Benjamins.

Massler, U., Stotz, D., & Queisser, C. (2014). Assessment instruments for primary CLIL: The conceptualisation and evaluation of test tasks. *The Language Learning Journal, 42,* 137–150. doi:10.1080/09571736.2014.891371

Ministerio dell'Istruzione, dell'Universitá e della Ricerca (MIUR). (2016). Italian Ministry of Education, Universities and Research. Retrieved from http://hubmiur.pubblica.istruzione.it/web/istruzione/dg-ordinamenti/clil

Nikula, T., Dalton-Puffer, C., & Llinares, A. (2013). European research on CLIL classroom discourse. *International Journal of Immersion and Content Based Language Education, 1,* 70–100. doi:10.1075/jicb.1.1.04nik

Norris, J., & Ortega, L. (2000). Effectiveness of L2 instruction: A research synthesis and quantitative meta-analysis. *Language Learning, 50*(3), 417–528. doi:10.1111/0023-8333.00136

Paulsrud, B.-A. (2016). English-medium instruction in Sweden: Perspectives and practices in two upper secondary schools. *Journal of Immersion and Content-Based Education, 4*(1), 108–128.

Rumlich, D. (2013). Students' general English proficiency prior to CLIL: Empirical evidence for substantial differences between prospective CLIL and non-CLIL students in Germany. In S. Breidbach & B. Viebrock (Eds.), *Content and language integrated learning (CLIL) in Europe. Research perspectives on policy and practice* (pp. 181–201). Frankfurt, Germany: Lang.

Schleppegrell, M., & O'Hallaron, C. L. (2011). Teaching academic language in L2 secondary settings. *Annual Review of Applied Linguistics, 31,* 3–18. doi:10.1017/S0267190511000067

Seikkula-Leino, J. (2007). CLIL learning: Achievement levels and affective factors. *Language and Education, 21*(4), 328–341. doi:10.2167/le635.0

Tedick, D., & Wesely, P. (2015). A review of research on content-based foreign/second language education in US K–12 contexts. *Language, Culture and Curriculum, 28,* 25–40. doi:10.1080/07908318.2014.1000923

Verspoor, M., de Bot, K., & Xu, X. (2015). The effects of English bilingual education in the Netherlands. *Journal of Immersion and Content-Based Language Education, 3,* 4–27. doi:10.1075/jicb.3.1.01ver

Chapter 12

Helping Content Teachers Move beyond Language: Translanguaging in Lesson Study Groups

Dudley W. Reynolds

A Glimpse into a Translingual Classroom

The boys in teacher Mostafa's seventh grade science class at a Qatari middle school are having an unusually good time today because the lesson is different. Generally, Mostafa begins class by asking them about the textbook pages they were supposed to read for homework. Since most do not read the homework, Mostafa ends up talking for 10–15 minutes, summarizing the textbook and demonstrating a concept or showing a video about the topic. They then work in groups to write definitions for key terms or answer questions from the textbook. Although students used to use English in their science classes, for the past two years their textbook has been in Arabic, and they only use Arabic in class. Many of the scientific terms in Arabic were new to them at first, but with time they have become more accustomed to the way terms are constructed and concepts explained. Because many of the resources on the internet are in English, however, now they have problems with some of the videos that Mostafa finds and also when they need to research a topic on their own. Since Mostafa is a science teacher, he never really thought about what students understood when they read in Arabic or English, and the only time he talks about what might be considered language learning is when he assigns vocabulary terms for the students to memorize.

In the last class, Mostafa put the boys in groups to work on projects for an upcoming science fair hosted by the Education Ministry. He also told them that in the next class he would help them research their projects. What the boys do not know is that Mostafa, along with two other science teachers and three English teachers from the school, have been participating in a Lesson Study group (Dudley, 2012; Fernandez & Yoshida, 2004; Lewis, 2002), exploring ways to help students read better in both Arabic and English. With support from a university professor specializing in second language literacy development, the science and English teachers have been learning that for students to improve the effectiveness of their reading processes, they have to do more than simply practice reading or learn vocabulary: They need to learn about reading strategies and how to apply them while reading. One of the teaching activities the professor suggested was to model effective reading by performing a "think-aloud" for students.

Today Mostafa surprises the boys by showing them what happens when he reads a text in English about moon rocks from a museum website. Mostafa studied English in secondary school and at university and uses it a lot for everyday communication in Qatar, but he does not consider himself a fluent reader of English. Mostafa begins the think-aloud by asking himself in Arabic, "Why am I reading this?" and answering that he wants to find information that might be helpful for his science fair project. He then elaborates that he has a general idea to compare rocks in Qatar with moon rocks, and he brainstorms some categories of information that might be useful to find out about. Next he focuses on the title of the webpage. He sounds it out in English the best he can, identifies one word that he does not know the meaning of, and comments that he will need to figure it out while reading. He is using more English than Arabic at this point. After working with the title, he models for students how he would scan the text as a whole. He says in Arabic that the presence of subtitles suggests that the text is divided into four sections. He reads each subtitle in English and makes a prediction in Arabic concerning what the section will be about. He notes that one of the sections specifically focuses on similarities between moon rocks and rocks on Earth and announces that this is where he is going to start reading. As he reads, he begins taking notes in Arabic and drawing pictures on the board that he labels with English terms. The boys are giggling while Mostafa does all of this because they are not used to a teacher admitting that he does not completely understand something. After Mostafa finishes, he asks the boys to fill in a chart, putting the characteristics of moon rocks on one side and the characteristics of Earth rocks on the other side. He tells them that they can write in Arabic or English on the chart because the purpose of the chart is to help them remember what they learned.

Mostafa's think-aloud lesson represented a number of big changes for him and for his students. First, he had to shift his use of class time from presenting knowledge to focusing on how knowledge is learned. Second, instead of focusing exclusively on the knowledge of science, he was also trying to help students build language skills that will support science learning. What may not be clear from the scenario is that Mostafa had to expand his own concept of language from being sets of rules and vocabulary that could be memorized to utilizing routines and practices that enable comprehension and development. Finally, he was breaking a taboo in many classrooms around the world dictating that instruction should be in only one language at a time. In response to the need of the moment, he was going back and forth between Arabic and English in front of his students following a pedagogical approach known as *translanguaging* (Canagarajah, 2013; Garcia & Wei, 2013). In this chapter we will focus on the approach to teacher development that encouraged Mostafa to consider making these changes—Lesson Study—and how it can support teachers' abilities to address both content and language goals with their students.

In-Service Teacher Development for CBI |||

Teacher development programs seek to impact what teachers know as a foundation as to how teachers put that knowledge into practice. In the education literature, what teachers know and believe is often referred to as *teacher cognition* (Borg, 2003, 2006) or *teacher knowledge* (Freeman, 2002). Reviews of the influences on teacher cognition, such as those by Borg and Freeman, suggest that what teachers know is shaped by their prior experience as learners and teachers. This presents a problem for teacher education programs that are trying to introduce new ideas and practices. Too often teachers learn to "talk the talk" of educational reform efforts but then fall back on the way they have always done things when it comes time to teach a class (cf. Basturkmen, Loewen, & Ellis, 2004). Borg (2003) concludes therefore that "although professional preparation does shape trainees' cognitions, programmes which ignore trainee teachers' prior beliefs may be less effective at influencing these" (p. 81). Teacher development programs that hope to make an impact must engage teachers in active reflection about both their beliefs and data from their classroom experiences, ideally in a learning community of peers, and not just engage outside experts to tell teachers what they should be doing (Wei, Darling-Hammond, Andree, Richardson, & Orphanos, 2009).

One conceptual challenge that many teachers face—whether they are science teachers or English teachers—is their understanding of what needs to be learned. Too often teachers see themselves as simply imparting *knowledge of something* rather than developing *knowledge about how to think and learn*. The problem with the former is that it prioritizes memorization at the expense of students' being able to use knowledge to develop more knowledge. Thelen (1984) writes: "All too often, the science teacher has never been aware of how to teach content *and* process at the same time. . . . One of the recommendations by the National Commission on Excellence in Education was to include as goals in science education the teaching of concepts, laws, and processes of the physical and biological sciences. Yet science classes today are still overwhelmingly fact oriented" (p. 49). With respect to language learning, Swain (2006) makes a similar distinction between teaching students to construct output (the language they produce) based on memorized input (i.e., vocabulary and grammar rules) and teaching them to "[language] about language . . . [to operate] on linguistic data and [come] to an understanding of previously less well understood material" (p. 98). Referencing Derewianka (2001), Mohan and Slater (2005) describe this as the difference between traditional and functional views of language. The traditional view is "concerned with the form and structure of language" (p. 155) while the functional view emphasizes the text or discourse as a whole in relation to its context, and recognizes that lexis and grammar vary with text and context. This view sees language as a resource for making meaning and provides tools to investigate and critique how language is involved in the construction of meaning.

When science and English teachers view what they are teaching not merely as factual information but also as ways of interacting with and building on previous knowledge, then many possibilities for cross-disciplinary collaboration are opened up. Greenleaf et al. (2011) write: "Science provides a setting in which students may be intellectually obligated to set purposes, ask questions, clarify ambiguities, draw inferences from incomplete evidence, and make evidence-based arguments—the very dispositions required as good readers and writers" (p. 649).

This emphasis on using previous knowledge as a resource for engaging with and learning from new experiences and exposures is one which also undergirds the pedagogical approach of translanguaging (Canagarajah, 2013; Creese & Blackledge, 2010; Garcia & Wei, 2013). Translanguaging views all of the linguistic knowledge that participants bring to an interaction as resources for building meaning. It makes no attempt, therefore, to designate what languages should be used for particular functions, a precept that goes against standard practice in many places (Creese & Blackledge, 2010). In the case of Qatar, for example, educational policy makers beginning in 2002 specified that newly created government schools should teach science in English. Faced with widespread criticism that teaching science in English was causing students to underperform both in science and Arabic, they then switched science instruction to Arabic in 2012 and created a separate course where students would learn scientific vocabulary in English. In 2014, this second course was dropped from the curriculum because of a popular perception that focusing solely on vocabulary held little value for students.

The policies adopted in Qatar assumed that instruction must be in one language or the other. The problem with this perspective is that it ignores the reality of how language is used outside the classroom in Qatar, where approximately 88 percent of the population is expatriates and at least 70 percent are from countries where Arabic is not a native language (Snoj, 2014). To truly prepare students for the ways in which they will use language outside the classroom in day-to-day interactions as well as when searching for information in an online environment that is still dominated by English (ICT Qatar, 2014), instruction needs to build students' capacity to engage strategically with language. As Canagarajah (2009) puts it:

What we need is a paradigm shift in language teaching. Pedagogy should be refashioned to accommodate the modes of communication and acquisition seen outside the classroom . . . Rather than focusing on a single language or dialect as the target of learning, teachers have to develop in students a readiness to engage with a repertoire of codes in transnational contact situations. While joining a new speech community was the objective of traditional pedagogy, now we have to train students to shuttle between communities by negotiating the relevant codes. To this end, we have to focus more on communicative strategies rather than on form. (p. 20)

Content, Language, and Teacher Agency in Lesson Study Groups |||

The Lesson Study group that Mostafa was participating in when he demonstrated a think-aloud for his students was formed as part of a research project aimed at improving the abilities of Qatari middle school students to read scientific material. The impetus for the project was the fact that Qatar had been scoring near the bottom on international standardized science achievement tests, namely the Programme for International Student Assessment (PISA) and the Trends in International Mathematics and Science Study (TIMSS). Because students were also scoring low on two international reading tests—the PISA and Progress in

International Reading Literacy Study (PIRLS)—it was hypothesized that students' reading ability might be impacting their performance on the content area tests.[1] Although particularly important for Qatar, the need to improve students' first and second language literacy abilities with respect to science has been widely documented for other contexts as well (e.g., Greenleaf et al., 2011; Lee, 2005).

Lesson Study is a method of school-based, cyclical, peer learning originally developed with mathematics teachers in Japan (Fernandez & Yoshida, 2004); the method later spread to the U.S. (Fernandez & Chokshi, 2002; Lewis & Takahashi, 2006) and the U.K. (Dudley, 2012). As illustrated in Figure 12.1, Lesson Study begins with the formation of a group of in-service teachers who agree on a topic to study, generally a goal they have for student improvement. The group then embarks on a series of Lesson Study cycles during which they collaboratively: (1) study an aspect of the topic, (2) plan a lesson that is influenced by what they studied, (3) engage one member of the group to teach the lesson while the others observe, and then (4) reconvene to reflect on the success of the lesson for promoting student learning and to discuss possible modifications.

Key to the success of the approach is that what the teachers are studying is the lessons they design, not each other. They take joint responsibility for the lesson by planning it together. When they observe it being taught, the Lesson Study participant teaching the lesson assigns high-, average-, and low-performing students for the others to watch and evaluate students' learning. Then during the reflection period, discussion focuses not on the teacher's performance but rather on how the lesson impacted each of these groups of students and how the lesson could be improved. In an ideal situation, one of the other Lesson Study participants may then teach the modified lesson, but this is not always practical. At the very least, a different participant should serve as the teacher of the lesson for each new cycle to ensure that the focus is on the design features of the lesson rather than the performance of any individual teacher.

Fernandez and Chokshi (2002) advocate involving the participating teachers in the selection and formulation of the group's learning goals, possibly through an action research

Figure 12.1: Lesson Study Cycle

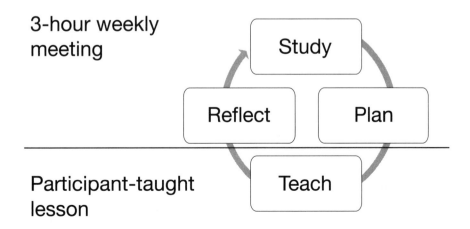

project. As implemented in Qatar, however, the goal was identified by the research team independently of the participating teachers since the research team identified a need to help teachers understand: (1) reading as a process with particular reference to science texts, and (2) ways to incorporate reading strategy instruction into their teaching.[2] The Qatar program was run over two successive years. In the first year, the research team led Lesson Study groups in two schools. In the second year, the researchers trained teachers who then led groups in their individual schools.

As indicated in Figure 12.1, a Lesson Study group meeting has three phases: reflection on the previous lesson, studying for the new lesson, and planning the new lesson. In the Qatar project, teacher reflection was scaffolded with the following questions:

1. What were students supposed to learn from the lesson?
2. What was done to promote these objectives?
3. How well did different students learn the objectives? How do you know?
4. Which activities were most effective for students? Why?
5. What would you suggest doing differently?
6. What did you learn about designing a lesson to teach strategic reading?

The study phase of the training sessions each year focused on increasing the participants' awareness and understanding of functions for reading within a curriculum, more and less effective reading processes, and specific activities that could be used in their classes. Content for the learning phase was developed during the initial year and then revised and enhanced in the second year. Appendix 12A presents an overview of the objectives that specifically related to reading knowledge and instruction for the six cycles in the second year as well as a brief description of the activities used to scaffold the objectives.

The final phase of the training sessions dealt with planning. One early finding of the research team during the first year was that the teachers tended to plan lessons around what students would do (i.e., activities) rather than around learning outcomes. Since it was important for the team to be able to evaluate the lessons based on student learning, a series of templates was developed to scaffold lesson planning, observation, and reflection in the second year. The templates, which are presented in Appendix 12B, attempt to foreground student learning.

With respect to the use of languages during the session, three of the four members of the research team were bilingual in Arabic and English, although to varying degrees of competency, and all of the participating teachers except for one English teacher in the first year were bilingual, again to varying degrees of competency. At the initial session in both years, participants were told that speakers could use whatever language they wanted and if someone did not understand, they should ask someone else to translate. In addition, handouts and sample texts for activities distributed during the sessions were sometimes in English, sometimes in Arabic, and sometimes in English with Arabic glosses.

As pedagogical approaches, both translanguaging and Lesson Study privilege negotiation; it is the key discursive practice that leads to learning. When translanguaging is allowed and encouraged in classroom interactions, a speaker may use Language A but another speaker will then respond in Language B. Written texts and diagrams may be presented with some sections in one language and other items in another language. It is accepted that everyone will not understand everything that is said or written, and participants are encouraged to question and problem solve to figure out and make meaning. The questioning and problem solving may relate to language forms, language uses, or the content that the language represents. With Lesson Study, there are no lectures or content to be mastered. Instead, content knowledge accrues as participants cycle through the phases of studying, planning, teaching, and reflecting. The group leader facilitates the cycle, but responsibility for learning is clearly in the hands of the participants and results from the interactions between the participants.

When Mostafa modeled his reading process for his students, he showed them what it means to negotiate meaning. He did not perform the text; that is, he did not read it aloud as if its language and content were obvious. Instead, he modeled integrated problem solving with respect to both language and content. He showed students a process where he made hypotheses about the text's meaning using all of his linguistic knowledge; he tried out his hypotheses by continuing to read; and he reflected on his understanding, which sometimes led him to change his hypotheses. In short, he modeled the mode of learning for both translanguaging and Lesson Study.

Underlying Principles |||

As reflected in Table 12.1, the design and implementation of the Qatar Lesson Study groups exemplify a number of underlying principles for effective professional development that enable schools to address in a more comprehensive manner the needs of all students for both *content* and *languaging* opportunities, that is, the use of all one's language resources to talk about and work through new opportunities for making meaning.

Research Agenda |||

Much of the literature on teacher development for CBI studies language and content teachers working with either study-abroad or migrant students (e.g., Celic & Seltzer, 2011; Greenleaf et al., 2011; Hamann, 2008; Lee, 2005; Polat & Mahalingappa, 2013). Very little attention has been directed towards contexts such as Qatar where students may be studying a content subject like science in a second language, and those studies that do exist tend to focus on the language teachers but not the content teachers (cf. Borg, 2003). There is great need for more research investigating the knowledge and beliefs that content teachers in such contexts bring to their teaching, the interaction between their cognition and practice, and the ways in which they are influenced by contextual factors such as prescribed syllabi or language-use policies (cf. Williams, 2015).

With respect to the practice of using translanguaging in content classrooms, more research is needed into the difference between language as resource and language as target. One of the traditional arguments against language mixing in classrooms has been that it inhibits the development of fluency in any language. The argument here has been that languaging encourages learners to be more strategic and hence effective in their communication prac-

Table 12.1: Principles of Effective Professional Development Modeled in Qatar Lesson Study Groups

Observations	Underlying Principles
1. The learning phase of the training sessions typically began with an experiential activity (see Appendix 12A), such as choosing readings for an exercise with a specified purpose and comparing the selections to texts chosen by another group for an exercise with a different purpose. This was followed by a discussion of the relation between reading purpose and informational needs. Teachers were then asked to construct an activity that would teach the principles they had just abstracted and how they would know what the students had learned about the impact of purpose on what and how we read.	Effective professional development encourages teachers to formulate concepts and principles based upon concrete experiences and data. It then gives them an opportunity to practice what they have learned and prepares them to assess. This same sequence of *model, explain, practice,* and *evaluate* can be applied to the design of effective student learning as well.
2. Teachers initially wanted to convince the researchers that lack of vocabulary was why students had difficulty with reading and that they were already equipped with routines such as K-W-L (What do I Know, What do I Want to Know, What did I Learn) for teaching reading. With time, they began to acknowledge that they had not thought about some of the topics we were discussing before, and at the end of the program they talked enthusiastically about what they had learned.	Effective professional development acknowledges that learning takes time. The cyclical structure of Lesson Study emphasizes the developmental aspects of learning over concept mastery and provides opportunities for participants to build knowledge by making connections with experiences in previous cycles.
3. When asked at the end of the project how students' reading could be supported, one teacher said: "They should know why they are reading this … what's their purpose. I think they should know how to skim and scan a text … how to get new vocabulary words, acquire and understand them through context clues, understanding the main idea, understanding some reading strategies, how to be able to understand the reading through these strategies …. I think that it's like a process, you have to know the process and the strategy so that at the end they will get the text."	In order for teachers to support students' language development, they must make the mental work that goes into processing, storing, and formulating language a conscious process for students. They cannot expect that students will learn this by being asked to read a passage and answer comprehension questions. Nor can content teachers assume that the work done in language classes will transfer.
4. One teacher praising a model lesson in which a science and English teacher had collaboratively taught students about the food pyramid by giving them a diagram with the pyramid in English and then a text about the pyramid in Arabic said: "[The students] enjoyed it because they know they can ... those who don't understand any English words they can read in Arabic to understand the English... and they can share their ideas in English."	Translanguaging in the classroom encourages students to use what they already know to negotiate new meaning-making opportunities. Professional development programs must model the benefits of translanguaging because many teachers come with an assumption that instruction must be in one language or another.
5. During the reflection discussions in the training sessions, the most difficult questions for the teachers to answer related to what the students learned and how they knew. They wanted to report on what the students had done instead. Similarly, in the planning of new lessons, they would frequently begin with the activities they would use rather than what students needed to learn. Getting them to talk more explicitly about conceptual knowledge and processes frequently required a series of probing questions and requests for examples.	As noted by Freeman (2002) and Borg (2003), teacher cognitions underlie classroom practices, and they are difficult for professional development programs to impact. Effective programs will tackle this by directing teachers towards sustained reflection about real experiences. For effective CBI, the reflection should be about both the content and the language used to embody the content.

tices. Once "learned," however, there is a need for learners to be able to express the content-oriented concepts and understandings that they have developed, often in a monolingual form. More ecologically based research (van Lier, 2004) into the use of translanguaging in different types of classrooms as well as psycholinguistic research into the mental processes and strategies used by translanguagers is needed. For example, when multiple languages are used in a classroom setting, what factors seem to influence both students' and teachers' language choices? Similarly, in classrooms where translanguaging is the norm, what might think-aloud protocol research reveal about how students read or write a monolingual text? Are the processes different for students who study in schools where content subjects are taught in the dominant language and English is used only in the foreign language class?

Finally, with respect to Lesson Study as a method for teacher development, more research is needed into how to promote it as a type of teacher-directed, self-regulated learning (Zimmerman & Schunk, 2011). The project described here was initiated and scaffolded by a team of researchers working to help improve instruction for Qatari students. One question that remains is the degree to which teachers in different contexts can take ownership of the Lesson Study process as Fernandez and Chokshi (2002) suggest is possible. In cases such as Qatar, where Lesson Study is used to address system-wide development, more work is needed on how to take Lesson Study to scale across a large number of schools at one time.

APPLYING WHAT YOU LEARNED
Questions and Tasks

1. Lesson Study as described here was used to develop science and English teachers' awareness of strategic reading processes as well as their ability to design activities that promote improved student reading. List three to four other topics that might be appropriate for a Lesson Study group to focus on and explain why with reference to the Underlying Principles section in Table 12.1.

2. The use of translanguaging described here involved the mixing of Arabic and English in contexts where the majority of participants had some degree of proficiency in both languages. How might you incorporate elements of translanguaging into a professional development context: (a) where the majority of participating teachers were monolingual English speakers and (b) where the participating teachers' classrooms had students with many different home languages, many of which the teachers do not know?

3. Activities such as think-alouds, reading guides (Thelen, 1984), and concept maps (Novak, 2010) were suggested as ways of focusing student (and teacher) attention on how individuals make meaning when reading. What activities might you model as part of professional development for teachers interested in helping students with languaging for academic listening or speaking?

Acknowledgments

The author gratefully thanks the other members of this project's research team: Andrew Cohen, JoAnn Crandall, Nancy Allen, Samah Al-Sabbagh, Maha Ellili Cherif, Zohreh Eslami, and Katherine Wright for their help in collecting the data and discussing the analysis presented here. This article was made possible by NPRP grant # 4-1172-5-172 from the Qatar National Research Fund (a member of Qatar Foundation). The statements made herein are solely the responsibility of the author.

ENDNOTES

1. For information on TIMMS and PIRLS, visit http://timssandpirls.bc.edu/. For information on PISA, visit www.oecd.org/pisa/.
2. Dudley (2012) describes a similar use of Lesson Study in the U.K. to increase the use of formative assessment in schools.

REFERENCES

Basturkmen, H., Loewen, S., & Ellis, R. (2004). Teachers' stated beliefs about incidental focus on form and their classroom practices. *Applied Linguistics, 25*(2), 243–272.

Borg, S. (2003). Teacher cognition in language teaching: A review of research on what language teachers think, know, believe, and do. *Language Teaching, 36*(2), 81–109.

Borg, S. (2006). *Teacher cognition and language education: Research and practice*. London, England: Continuum.

Canagarajah, A. S. (2009). The plurilingual tradition and the English language in South Asia. *AILA Review, 22*(1), 5–22. doi: 10.1075/aila.22.02can

Canagarajah, A. S. (2013). *Literacy as translingual practice: Between communities and classrooms*. New York, NY: Routledge.

Celic, C., & Seltzer, K. (2011). *Translanguaging: A CUNY-NYSIEB guide for educators* (Vol. 20). New York, NY: CUNY-NYSIEB, The Graduate Center, The City University of New York. Retrieved from http://gn009.k12.sd.us/ELL%20Resources/Translanguaging%20Guide.pdf

Creese, A., & Blackledge, A. (2010). Translanguaging in the bilingual classroom: A pedagogy for learning and teaching? *The Modern Language Journal, 94*(1), 103–115.

Derewianka, B. (2001). Pedagogical grammars: Their role in English language teaching. In A. Burns & C. Coffin (Eds.), *Analysing English in a global context: A reader* (pp. 240–269). London, England: Routledge.

Dudley, P. (2012). Lesson Study development in England: From school networks to national policy. *International Journal for Lesson and Learning Studies, 1*(1), 85–100. doi: 10.1108/20468251211179722

Fernandez, C., & Chokshi, S. (2002). A practical guide to translating lesson study for a U.S. setting. *Phi Delta Kappan, 84*(2), 128–134.

Fernandez, C., & Yoshida, M. (2004). *Lesson study: A Japanese approach to improving mathematics teaching and learning*. Mahwah, NJ: Erlbaum.

Freeman, D. (2002). The hidden side of the work: Teacher knowledge and learning to teach. *Language Teaching, 35*(01), 1–13.

Garcia, O., & Wei, L. (2013). *Translanguaging: Language, bilingualism and education*. New York, NY: Palgrave Pivot.

Greenleaf, C. L., Litman, C., Hanson, T. L., Rosen, R., Boscardin, C. K., Herman, J., … Jones, B. (2011). Integrating literacy and science in biology: Teaching and learning impacts of reading apprenticeship professional development. *American Educational Research Journal, 48*(3), 647–717.

Hamann, E. T. (2008). Meeting the needs of ELLs: Acknowledging the schism between ESL/bilingual and mainstream teachers and illustrating that problem's remedy. Lincoln, NE: University of Nebraska, Department of Teaching, Learning and Teacher Education. Retrieved from http://digitalcommons.unl.edu/cgi/viewcontent.cgi?article=1072&context=teachlearnfacpub

Hidi, S. (2001). Interest, reading, and learning: Theoretical and practical considerations. *Educational Psychology Review, 13*(3), 191–209.

ICT Qatar. (2014). *Qatar's ICT Landscape 2014: Households and Individuals* (Text). Doha, Qatar: Supreme Council of Information & Communication Technology. Retrieved from http://www.ictqatar.qa/en/documents/document/qatars-ict-landscape-2014-households-and-individuals

Lee, O. (2005). Science education with English language learners: Synthesis and research agenda. *Review of Educational Research, 75*(4), 491–530.

Lewis, C. (2002). *Lesson study: A handbook of teacher-led instructional change.* Philadelphia, PA: Research for Better Schools.

Lewis, C., & Takahashi, A. (Eds.). (2006). *Learning across boundaries: U.S.-Japan collaboration in mathematics, science and technology education.* Oakland, CA: Mills College of Education. Retrieved from www.lessonresearch.net/LOB1.pdf

Mohan, B., & Slater, T. (2005). A functional perspective on the critical "theory/practice" relation in teaching language and science. *Linguistics and Education, 16*(2), 151–172. doi: 10.1016/j.linged.2006.01.008

Novak, J. D. (2010). Learning, creating, and using knowledge: Concept maps as facilitative tools in schools and corporations. *Journal of E-Learning and Knowledge Society, 6*(3), 21–30.

Polat, N., & Mahalingappa, L. (2013). Pre- and in-service teachers' beliefs about ELLs in content area classes: A case for inclusion, responsibility, and instructional support. *Teaching Education, 24*(1), 58–83. doi: 10.1080/10476210.2012.713930

Snoj, J. (2014, December 7). Qatar's population—by nationality. *bq magazine.* Retrieved from http://www.bqdoha.com/2013/12/population-qatar

Swain, M. (2006). Languaging, agency and collaboration in advanced second language proficiency. In H. Byrnes (Ed.), *Advanced language learning: The contribution of Halliday and Vygotsky* (pp. 95–108). New York, NY: Continuum.

Thelen, J. N. (1984). *Improving reading in science* (2nd ed.). Newark, DE: International Reading Association. Retrieved from http://eric.ed.gov/?id=ED250675

van Lier, L. (2004). *The ecology and semiotics of language learning.* Dordrecht, The Netherlands: Kluwer.

Wei, R. C., Darling-Hammond, L., Andree, A., Richardson, N., & Orphanos, S. (2009). *Professional learning in the learning profession: A status report on teacher development in the U.S. and abroad* (Technical Report). Dallas, TX: National Staff Development Council. Retrieved from http://www.learningforward.org/news/NSDCstudytechnicalreport2009.pdf

Williams, D. G. (2015). *A systematic review of English medium instruction (EMI) and implications for the South Korean higher education context.* Retrieved from https://blog.nus.edu.sg/eltwo/files/2015/04/EMI-in-South-Korea_editforpdf-1gmsyy5.pdf

Zimmerman, B. J., & Schunk, D. H. (2011). *Handbook of self-regulation of learning and performance.* New York, NY: Taylor & Francis.

APPENDIX 12A
Content Objectives and Activities for Qatar Lesson Study Focused on Strategic Reading for Science

Cycle	Content Objectives (*Participants will be able to . . .*)	Activities
1	Reading Interest 1. Describe how interest contributes to learning from reading.	■ Compare two reading interest inventories. ■ Given three science readings in Arabic, discuss which one is the most interesting and how a less interesting reading could be made more interesting. ■ Review handout summarizing work on individual and situational interest by (Hidi, 2001).
2	Reading Purposes 1. List examples of different purposes for reading in a science or English class. 2. Provide examples of classroom reading tasks that involve selecting texts, reading texts, and communicating knowledge from texts and explain how the task purpose affects each of these stages.	■ Brainstorm list of reading purposes related to current course activities. ■ Divide into groups and give each group the same packet of 10 Arabic and English readings. Assign each group a task (e.g., science fair project, class presentation, extracurricular enrichment) for which they must (1) select readings and (2) describe how the task would impact reading.
3	Reading Process 1. Compare and contrast learning a reading strategy and reading strategically. 2. List and discuss four steps in teaching reading strategies to students (model, explain, practice, evaluate).	■ Given a list of reading strategies, note when they hear one demonstrated in a recording of an English-speaking research team member performing a think-aloud with an Arabic text.
4	Text Analysis 1. Analyze a reading for challenges and opportunities for comprehension. 2. Identify strategies that could help with comprehension of a reading.	■ In groups, analyze Arabic science reading and identify: (1) what information is important to understand, (2) what might be difficult to understand, and (3) opportunities to demonstrate a strategy. ■ Design a Level 1 reading guide (Thelen, 1984) to direct students' reading of the text.
5	Comprehensive Lesson Design 1. Analyze a reading for literal knowledge to be comprehended, interpretations that can be inferred, and opportunities for the extension or application of knowledge. 2. Identify strategies that could be used for constructing knowledge while reading a specific text. 3. Construct an activity that helps students practice strategies for comprehension, inference, and extension.	■ Given one Arabic and one English reading on a related topic: (1) design an activity that would require students to read both texts; (2) analyze readings for information to be comprehended, inferred, and extended; (3) identify strategies that would support understanding at each level; and (4) design activities that would support student use of strategies: two and three level reading guides (Thelen, 1984); concept maps (Novak, 2010).
6	Review 1. Articulate an approach for incorporating strategic reading into their instructional practices. 2. Apply principles for developing strategic reading competency to the design of a lesson.	■ Discuss how topics for Cycles 1–5 fit together in the context of designing a single lesson: (1) develop interest; (2) articulate purpose for reading; (3) select and analyze texts for comprehension/inference/and extension; (4) identify strategies that will support understanding relative to purpose; and (5) plan activities that support learning, practice, and evaluation of strategies. ■ Apply understanding to designing a lesson based on a textbook chapter.

APPENDIX 12B
Templates for Lesson Planning, Lesson Observation, and Lesson Reflection

<u>Lesson Planning</u>

    Objectives: What should students learn?

        Students will learn/be able to

        Students will learn/be able to

        Students will learn/be able to

    Materials: What do we need to prepare before class?

    Activity Outline: What will students do to learn objectives? How long will each step take?

    Assessment: How will we know if objectives were met?

<u>Lesson Observation</u>

1. This week I am observing ":   Weaker student   Average student   Stronger student
2. At what points in the lesson does the student seem to be "getting it?" What student behaviors give me that impression?
3. Overall, to what extent did I think the student achieved the objectives? What student behaviors gave me that impression?
4. Based on my observations, what was the best (most effective) activity in the lesson?
5. Based on my observations, what should we consider changing in our lesson design? Why?

<u>Lesson Reflection</u>

1. What were students supposed to learn from lesson?
2. What was done to promote these objectives?
3. How well did different students learn objectives? How do we know?
4. What activities were most effective for students? Why?
5. What would we suggest doing differently?
6. What did we learn about taking advantage of student interests or making activities more interesting for students?

Chapter **13**

Content-Based Instruction as a Means of Addressing Linguistic Diversity in Higher Education: A South African Example

Arlys L. van Wyk

||| A Glimpse into the Adjunct Model Classroom

Jamie Williams teaches at the University of the Free State (UFS) in Bloemfontein, South Africa, where the Faculty of Humanities offers first-year students who come from diverse linguistic backgrounds (such as isiXhosa, Sesotho, isiZulu, Setswana, Afrikaans, and isiNdebele) a unique content-based program consisting of a language tutorial paired with a content course to help ease their transition into the university. All of these students are registered for an extended degree program (a three-year degree program that has been extended to four years for students who do not meet the regular access requirements). For all the students in Jamie's class, English is a second or additional language, and due to their prior educational experiences (such as underresourced schools where there are no libraries to support literacy acquisition and where classroom methodologies focus on rote memorization, copying from the blackboard, choral answers, and repetition of what the teacher says), many students lack the essential literacy skills that are required for success in university study.

This is Jamie's second year teaching the language tutorial component. She is aware that her goal is to help students acquire the linguistic skills that will allow them access to the content areas and enable them to successfully engage in the active reading of academic texts and completion of written academic assignments. Many of the students registered for her course come from primary and secondary schools that have not prepared them for reading and writing tasks; as a result, her students experience great difficulty reading their academic texts and writing their assignments and essays. Thus, Jamie's approach in her contact sessions with students is to assist them in engaging with their assigned texts in the content areas and also to facilitate the process of their "learning to write" and "writing to learn" in their content areas.

Students attend Jamie's two-hour contact session every week; there, she links literacy skills with the first-year criminology course in which students are concurrently enrolled. The contact sessions are carefully structured to focus on literacy skills identified by Refiloe Motsai (the content specialist) and Jessica du Toit (the language specialist) collaboratively.

Today's contact session topic is "victimization of the elderly"—the topic being covered by Refiloe in criminology this week. In an attempt to provide a structured reading experience, Jamie has designed a worksheet (see Appendix 13A) in collaboration with Jessica to guide students through the relevant chapter from their criminology textbook. The worksheet represents a series of steps to scaffold students' reading comprehension. They are required to survey the text, do a pre-reading activity, focus on while-reading, and make connections within the text that assist in meaning making. Jamie has also built in opportunities for students to infer meaning from the text and to use graphic organizers to tabulate information. Jamie's worksheet concludes with a post-reading activity that requires students to use a graphic organizer to scaffold the writing of a compare/contrast paragraph. She is optimistic that the worksheet will help to prepare students for a compare/contrast assignment that they will be required to complete for Criminology later in the semester.

The Adjunct Model of CBI |||

At the University of the Free State (UFS), 70 percent of students study in English, their second or additional language. After the demise of Apartheid and the first South African democratic elections of 1994, admissions to higher education increased considerably. This inflow of first-generation multilingual students resulted in the creation of several alternative admission programs intended to address the educational needs of students from very diverse prior-learning backgrounds. Many of these students come from primary and secondary schools that have not prepared them linguistically for the tasks required to achieve success in higher education. Further, the fact that South African education policy espouses an early exit model (i.e., requiring that learners switch to English from their mother tongues at age nine before their cognitive academic literacy skills have been fully attained) leaves many first-year students unable to meet the demands of the cognitive-communicative tasks required in higher education (Heugh, 2009). The situation is exacerbated by the under-resourcing of schools and the fact that many teachers who instruct learners in primary and secondary schools are themselves not proficient in English (Nel & Müller, 2010). Collectively, these dynamics negatively affect the trajectory of learners' schooling and their subsequent higher education achievements. While physical access has greatly improved country-wide, providing epistemological access (i.e., access to content knowledge through the active reading of academic texts and writing of academic assignments) and finding ways to support incoming students is an ongoing concern (Scott, 2013). One solution being implemented to address the influx of underprepared students to the UFS is the adjunct model of CBI, which offers the opportunity of facilitating students' access to authentic, academic content while simultaneously building and extending their critical language skills.

A key feature of an adjunct model is that students are concurrently registered for linked content and language courses that are taught by specialists in these respective fields (see Brinton and Snow, this volume). Students are given the safe opportunity, in the language component of the model, to work with the discourse of the content disciplines (Brinton, Snow, & Wesche, 2003). This presents the immediate, hands-on epistemological access that motivates students, who perceive the purpose and relevance of the language learning experience. Assisting students studying in a language that is not their mother tongue is a key attribute of the adjunct model.

As a result of a high student attrition rate in the UFS Faculty of Humanities, a special program was developed to assist underprepared students to gain access. This intervention was created along the lines of a hybrid, adjunct model. This "twist" on the adjunct model entails students enrolled in two concurrent courses (a content area class and a language tutorial class); however, the tutorial class is not taught by a language practitioner. Instead, the language practitioner trains the tutors, in this manner guiding the students' acquisition of academic literacy skills. The aim of the tutorial classes is to assist students to integrate language skills in the content areas.

Tutors for this program are carefully selected based on their English proficiency and possession of a post-graduate qualification in the content area in which they are tutoring. The language practitioner schedules regular training sessions with tutors during which the tutors are guided to create the language-related activities needed for the teaching. Thus, the features of this hybrid adjunct model deviate somewhat from the traditional adjunct model in that these tutors are not themselves language practitioners, but rather are trained by a language practitioner. As a rationale for this model, it should be mentioned that there is a dire shortage of trained L2 practitioners at the UFS and, indeed, country-wide throughout South Africa. The UFS hybrid approach described in this chapter evolved as a means of addressing this constraint. Other hybrid versions of the adjunct model have been described in the literature (e.g., Snow & Kamhi-Stein, 2002; Srole, 1997) in which peer study group leaders were employed along with language specialists.

Perspectives on Adjunct Instruction |||

Since 1996, research in academic literacy has been driven, in the South African higher education context, by vast social transformation. This social transformation has resulted in a significant increase in participation rates in higher education. Many higher education institutions were obliged to find ways and means of addressing the linguistic diversity evident in higher education enrollments (Lillis & Scott, 2007). Much of the early discourse around developing students' academic literacy was framed in deficit terminology, focusing on what students *could not* bring to the academic situation rather than what they *could* bring. It also focused on possible detrimental outcomes for the academy, such as falling standards. In light of a changing South African reality from monolingual higher education to a diverse, multilingual reality, ideological perspectives shifted to enable this transformation—that is, with many educational institutions committed to finding ways of accommodating literacy development and enabling transformation. In search of a pedagogy that would enable a transformative approach, the UFS chose to embark on a CBI approach to literacy development. This course of action finds its rationale in this quote from Lillis and Scott (2007):

> Confronted by deficit framings and unconvinced by public and official discourses, many teacher-researchers in higher education with a responsibility or interest in language-based pedagogy—in the U.K. and elsewhere—have sought out and engaged in research and theorizations of language use which take account of the complex contexts in which they work. (p. 8)

At the UFS, we view the competencies of academic reading and writing as socially situated, not as discrete entities that can be transmitted from one context to another. Academic reading and writing are shaped by the social context, in this case higher education, in which they are practiced (Gee, 1990). In light of this philosophical stance, we see the development of literacy as the responsibility of the educational institution to ensure that appropriate provision is made for the acquisition of literacy skills in context. Thus, the pedagogical approach chosen to provide L2 learners with contextual, linguistic support becomes a crucial choice. CBI offers a means of assisting L2 learners with access into their chosen content areas and, simultaneously, providing linguistic support.

Furthermore, this view of literacy as socially situated allows us to embrace and acknowledge learners' diversity and to reject a deficit view of students' competencies (van Wyk, 2014). We also recognize the different ways in which our students are socialized by their prior learning. Many of our students have been socialized in ways that work against any real constructive engagement in their learning—that is, they were taught in primary and secondary schools by way of rote learning and copied notes that were reproduced verbatim when tested. Consequently, students view knowledge as a commodity to be obtained where they produce what they are given in order to receive a passing grade. In local studies on school-based literacy teaching and how this influences the transition to university, the findings are discouraging. Kapp (2004) finds that literacy practices in many South African schools are based on an instrumental model. Her study reveals that little critical literacy engagement occurs in schools and assessment focuses on literal interpretations presented in summary form or one-word answers. The focus of the writing program is on what is termed "real-life" writing of instrumental documents such as agendas, letters, and brochures. The crucial point here is that L2 learners often memorize and reproduce these verbatim for examination purposes and thus little, if any, real learning occurs.

The challenge then is to find ways to interrogate literacy practices in higher education so that students' literacy needs are effectively addressed. Much research has been done (e.g., Cummins, 1996) to identify meaningful ways that L2 students can be assisted in acquiring academic language proficiency through the provision of effective support, or scaffolding. Cummins and Early (2015) describe scaffolding as "a central component in promoting academic success for English language learners" (p. 60). They further note that certain, well-researched instructional approaches address factors that are responsible for low academic achievement. These approaches are:

- teaching academic language explicitly across the curriculum
- scaffolding students' comprehension and production of language across the curriculum
- maximizing literacy engagement
- connecting instruction to students' lives
- affirming students' identities in the context of academic work.

Therefore, from a pedagogical perspective, we can provide the linguistic and contextual support our students need to complete the tasks of the academy through the literacy delivery choices that we make. We need to facilitate academic language proficiency within a curricular approach that provides for:

- the delivery of language across the curriculum.
- smaller classes where students are given the opportunity to relate to the content and experience increased literacy-related activities.
- educational contexts where the linguistic tasks of the academy are systematically and incrementally taught through content that is authentic.

CBI affords us the means to provide cross-curricular support as it both heightens students' understanding of the interface between language and content and facilitates language use within disciplinary content (Crandall & Kaufman, 2002). There is an added advantage of the adjunct model in that content specialists gain an understanding of how language influences student learning; this, in turn, counteracts the view that many academics hold that language is the field of the language practitioner only. The UFS instructional shift to include authentic, academic literacy content and collaboration with content-area faculty stemmed from the conceptual framework outlined previously and inspired the hybrid adjunct model described here. In the section that follows, details of the CBI program as applied in the Faculty of Humanities are outlined.

The Adjunct Model

In the Faculty of Humanities, the adjunct model hinges on a close collaboration between the tutors, the language practitioner, and the content specialists. The group meets every term to outline content, language focus, activities, and classroom pedagogy. Content specialists identify the content themes, materials, and assessment tasks to be covered for each term. The language practitioner assists the tutors and content specialists to pinpoint the most important academic reading and writing skills needed to accomplish the assessment tasks. In a separate meeting and in collaboration with the language practitioner, the tutors are assisted with designing activities for the tutorial sessions that scaffold the tasks identified

Figure 13.1: The UFS Hybrid Adjunct Model

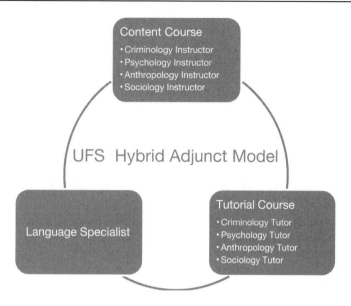

in the group. The tutorial classes are not credit-bearing but are compulsory for all students on the extended program; these sessions are relatively small, with only 30 students per group. These tutorial sessions are organized according to the different disciplines, in this case anthropology, criminology, psychology, and sociology (see Figure 13.1).

The materials and content for the sessions are developed through close collaboration between the language practitioner and content specialist. The content specialists share their content goals and identify where their students need help linguistically. Through this process of collaboration, materials are developed that focus on achieving the required language goals needed to access the content. For example, the content specialist informs the language practitioner that his/her students have not been completing the required readings from their textbooks and have difficulty comprehending the text. The language practitioner then helps the tutor to create scaffolding activities to assist students with reading strategies based on the assigned textbook reading for that particular week. Other issues are also addressed in this way, such as plagiarism, which is a coping mechanism for many students who have not acquired the academic literacy skills of paraphrasing or summarizing. Accordingly, the techniques of paraphrasing and summarizing are taught in the tutorial classes using sections from students' assigned texts.

In addition to the hybrid course described, all students in the extended program are enrolled in a one-year, mandatory academic literacy course that is run through the UFS Centre for Teaching and Learning. These courses are department based, so that students are exposed to the literacy skills required by their degree programs. The literacy courses are taught by language facilitators who are trained by well-qualified language practitioners in the Centre for Teaching and Learning. The contents of the literacy course are shared with the tutors in the adjunct program, who are encouraged to replicate activities and scaffolding approaches in their tutorial classes using the target content of their content areas. One such example is evident in the compare/contrast essay presented in this chapter. Students have been taught how to write a compare/contrast response to an academic prompt in the mandatory literacy courses. Tutors of the adjunct CBI sessions therefore align their teaching with the scaffolded approach used in the general literacy classes. Thus, another opportunity is created to reinforce literacy instruction for this at-risk group.

Underlying Principles |||

Table 13.1 presents the classroom activities used with a cohort of students who have great difficulty reading their assigned texts and then applying what they have read in written format. The focus is on providing students with the strategies to deal with their academic reading and the particular discourse types and assisting students to use the tools at their disposal to improve their writing skills.

Research Agenda |||

In a country that has recently undergone significant educational transformation and social turmoil, the research agenda has had to shift from researching the reasons for low-literacy proficiency to how this problem should be effectively addressed in this context. The high attrition rate in higher education bears testimony to our inability to effectively facilitate epistemological access. Scott (2013) confirms: "The overall graduation rate after five years is only 35 percent. If allowance is made for students taking longer than five years or re-entering at a later stage, the graduation rate is still only about 45 percent" (p. 17). Thus, any research on evidence-based instructional practices that further epistemological access in higher education would provide valuable guidelines to higher education institutions.

Reading ability is central to success at university. Thus, research related to how CBI, in particular the adjunct model, could effectively provide entry-level students with a useful reading intervention to help them access their academic texts would make a significant contribution. As Harley (2012) maintains: "Without academic literacy instruction and support, learners will continue to struggle to read and write in the academy's preferred reading and writing genres. . . ." (p. 345). Such research could contribute toward assisting higher education to address the articulation gap between secondary school and higher education.

Another important research direction for action research practitioners is how CBI can contribute toward effectively embedding literacy skills across the curriculum. Many institutions now realize that literacy transfer occurs best within content that is authentic and meaningful to students. As Nomdo (2013) notes: "Furthermore the decontextualized and generic nature of the content of these EAP courses made it difficult for students to integrate the knowledge they gained from them into the discourses of the respective disciplines they were studying" (p. 102). Models where literacy is taught generically, using decontextualized content, rarely provide for the successful transfer of skills in this context, yet there is little local research in this area.

Table 13.1: Classroom Activities and Underlying Principles in the UFS Adjunct Model Program

Classroom Activities	Underlying Principles
1. Students survey the text so that they have an idea of how the information in the chapter "Victimisation of the Elderly" is organized and what content is covered by the text. They work in pairs to create an outline of the text. They then activate their background knowledge by answering three questions relating to the introductory section of the content lecture. These questions refer to the general state of elder abuse in South Africa as presented by the content lecturer in the introductory lecture: a. What are some of the findings of the Helpline for Elder Abuse? b. In what settings does elder abuse take place most frequently in S.A.? Why? c. What kind of abuse is reported most in S.A.?	These collaborative activities enable students to draw on their prior knowledge and relate the content of the chapter to the introductory lecture on the topic. The fact that they work in pairs enables them to clarify what they do not understand with their peers and helps focus attention on the key concepts of the text. We encourage the use of their mother tongue (where possible) in this process of meaning-making. Students do, however, give their feedback in English.
2. Students identify cause and effect relationships in the text.	The text is characterized by cause and effect constructs. Students' attention is focused on this rhetorical feature; they are guided to write their own cause and effect constructs on the worksheet. They work collaboratively so that the process is scaffolded in a non-threatening manner.
3. Students complete a graphic organizer where they identify and list the key differences and similarities between elder abuse and elder neglect, which are the key issues in the reading. This is done with a partner.	Collaboratively, students transfer this information into the graphic organizer. The shared responsibility for this task enables them to clarify ideas and negotiate concepts. This visual means of organizing the information serves as a scaffold for the writing process that follows.
4. Students write a comparative summary on elder abuse and elder neglect.	Students are referred to their academic literacy textbook for information on how to write a comparative text, thus aligning with the scaffolded approach taken in the mandatory literacy classes. They have already organized and selected the information in the graphic organizer that guides their writing of the paragraph.

APPLYING WHAT YOU LEARNED
Questions and Tasks

1. This chapter focuses on the needs of students from a learning background that has not equipped them to deal with the reading and writing demands of higher education. The problem is exacerbated by the fact that they are studying in English, which is their second language.

   a. How is CBI, particularly the adjunct model, a useful approach for students who need to improve their cognitive academic language proficiency in a second language?

   b. What possible advantages does the UFS hybrid adjunct model offer over the traditional adjunct model? Are there any possible disadvantages?

2. Think of a setting or settings that you are familiar with where students enter the university without adequate academic literacy skills.

   a. How do these context(s) compare to that of the UFS?

   b. Are there any shared challenges?

   c. What are the unique challenges faced at the UFS?

3. Assume you are the language practitioner preparing for your first meeting with the tutors you will be working with.

   a. What challenges do you expect to encounter?

   b. Which issues would you prioritize for your initial meeting?

4. The Worksheet: Reading Guide for "Victimisation of the Elderly" (see Appendix 13A) provides a set of activities used at UFS to teach the language skills needed by the targeted students. After reading through the various activities, design additional activities that might be used with the content reading:

   a. an additional pre-reading activity

   b. an additional post-reading activity

   c. an additional writing assignment

REFERENCES

Brinton, D. M., Snow, M. A., & Wesche, M. (2003). *Content-based second language instruction* (Classics ed.). Ann Arbor, MI: University of Michigan Press.

Crandall, J., & Kaufman, D. (2002). *Content-based instruction in higher education settings.* Alexandria, VA: TESOL.

Cummins, J. (1996). *Negotiating identities: Education for empowerment in a diverse society.* Ontario, CA: California Association for Bilingual Education.

Cummins, J., & Early, M. (2015). *Big ideas for expanding minds: Teaching English language learners across the curriculum.* Ottawa, Canada: Pearson Canada.

Gee, J. (1990). *Social linguistics and literacies ideology in discourses.* London, England: Falmer Press.

Harley, D. (2012). *Doing a school literacy information project in a South African context* (Unpublished doctoral dissertation). Indiana University of Pennsylvania, Indiana, PA.

Heugh, K. (2009). Literacy and bi/multilingual education in Africa: Recovering collective memory and expertise. In T. Skutnabb-Kangas, R. Phillipson, A. K. Mohanty, & M. P. Panda (Eds.), *Social justice through multilingual education* (pp. 103–124). Bristol, England: Multilingual Matters.

Kapp, R. (2004). "Reading on the line": An analysis of literacy practices in ESL classes in a South African township school. *Language and Education, 18*(3), 246–263.

Lillis,T., & Scott, M. (2007). Defining academic literacies research: Issues of epistemology, ideology and strategy. *Journal of Applied Linguistics, 4*(1), 5–32.

Nel, N., & Müller, H. (2010). The impact of teachers' limited English proficiency on English second language learners in South African schools. *Journal of Education, 41,* 1–24.

Nomdo, G. (2013). Collaborating by design: Language embedded in an economics course. In J. Pym & M. Paxton (Eds.), *Surfacing possibilities: What it might mean to work with first-generation higher education students* (pp. 100–122). Champaign, IL: Common Ground.

Scott, I. (2013). Paving the way for systemic change: Curriculum change for development and equity. In J. Pym & M. Paxton (Eds.), *Surfacing possibilities: What it might mean to work with first-generation higher education students* (pp. 14–25). Champaign, IL: Common Ground.

Snow, M. A., & Kamhi-Stein, L. D. (2002). Teaching and learning academic literacy through Project LEAP. In J. Crandall & D. Kaufman (Eds), *Content-based instruction in higher education settings* (pp. 169–181). Alexandria, VA: TESOL.

Srole, C. (1997). Pedagogical responses from content faculty: Teaching content and language in history. In M. A. Snow & D. M. Brinton (Eds.), *The content-based classroom: Perspectives on integrating language and content* (pp. 104–116). White Plains, NY: Longman.

van Wyk, A. (2014). English-medium education in a multilingual setting: A case in South Africa. *International Review of Applied Linguistics in Language Teaching, 52*(2), 205–220.

APPENDIX 13A
Worksheet: Reading Guide for "Victimisation of the Elderly"

This worksheet was developed for first-year students at the University of the Free State registered for criminology. The worksheet is based on the following content reading:

Delport, R. (2013). Victimisation of the elderly. In R. Peacock (Ed), *Victimology in South Africa* (2nd ed., pp. 161–169). Pretoria, South Africa: Van Schaik.

STEP 1: Survey

Surveying the entire text before you read will make it easier to understand. Look at the headings to get a clear idea of what the text is about and how it is organised. You should not read every word. If necessary, create an outline of the text to help you. Look at the headings and sub-headings.

STEP 2: Pre-Reading

After reading the title, discuss with a partner what you already know about *victimisation* and the *elderly*. Make short notes.

_____

_____

_____

STEP 3: While-Reading

1. Read Paragraph 1. The word *violence* has been emphasised. Think about what this word means to you and discuss the concept with your partner. Thereafter, find two words from Paragraph 1 that the author relates to the word *violence*. Write these words down below.

_____

_____

2. Read Paragraph 2. Find seven reasons why the victimisation of the elderly is gaining increasing awareness. Write these below. Discuss with your partner after completing the list.

1.	
2.	
3.	
4.	
5.	
6.	
7.	

3. Read Paragraphs 3 and 4. Complete the following cause-effect diagram based on the problems identified in these paragraphs. Look at the causes given and predict the possible effects of the phenomenon. Compare your answers with your partner.

Cause		**Effect**
Para. 3. A dramatic increase in the world's population as a result of aging is predicted.	⇨	Para. 3
Para. 4. Africa has the largest population growth as a result of aging.	⇨	Para. 4

4. Read Paragraph 5. What seems to be the implication of these problems? Find one sentence in Paragraph 5 that supports your opinion.

_____

_____

_____

5. Before you read the next section, what do you expect to learn in the rest of the chapter?

_____

_____

_____

_____

6. Based on your understanding thus far, complete the following definition.

Victimisation	**is**		**that**	

7. Read Paragraphs 7 and 8. Write four words that you don't know. Share and discuss your words with a partner. Thereafter, guess the meaning of the words from the context.

_____

_____

_____

_____

8. Underline the main idea in Paragraphs 9 and 10. Rewrite the main ideas using your own words in the space below. Share your answer with your partner.

_____

_____

_____

_____

STEP 4: Post-Reading

9. Read Paragraphs 9–11. Complete the Venn diagram below where you outline the similarities and differences of elder abuse and elder neglect as discussed in Paragraphs 9–11. Complete this with your partner.

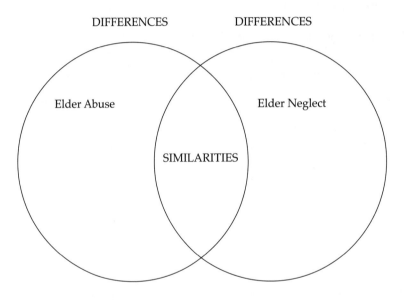

DIFFERENCES   DIFFERENCES

Elder Abuse   Elder Neglect

SIMILARITIES

10. Using your Venn diagram from the previous question, write a summary in which you compare and contrast elder abuse with elder neglect. Read the guidelines for writing a compare/contrast text before completing this task.

_____

_____

_____

_____

_____

Chapter 14

Teaching Content and Language in Art: Onsite and Online Approaches

Lisa Chou & Sherise Lee

||| A Glimpse into the CBI Art Classroom

Scenario A: Eunmin, an undergraduate Architecture major at the Academy of Art University in San Francisco, California, listens intently as her instructor explains that students should base their design on their site analysis and how the space will be used. The teacher continues, "It's not enough to say you chose a design just because you like it . . . you need to articulate your decisions based on your investigations." For any beginning Architecture student this is hard enough, but for Eunmin, the challenge is even greater as a second language learner. Her English for Art Purposes course anticipates the demand of her major classes and scaffolds the necessary critical-thinking skills utilized in the design process while also maintaining the language learning objectives defined by the English for Art Purposes program.

Scenario B: Hiroki rolls out of bed and logs into his Academy of Art University online class to see his assignments that are due this week. As an ESL student, he finds the content on Art History both linguistically and culturally challenging. Thankfully, he is enrolled in a section that not only has a content instructor who teaches the subject matter but also has an Online Language Support (OLS) instructor who provides content-based language and writing support for L2 learners. If Hiroki has difficulty understanding the course readings or assignment directions, he can click on the "Language & Writing Support" discussion thread that is embedded within the online discussion board to ask questions and access the OLS instructor's timely explanations of the course content.

CBI Models ||

CBI is now widely regarded with little dispute as a positive approach to language teaching, even as issues remain as to its implementation (Snow, 2005). Responding to the various demands of learning for college ESL students, the use of CBI has the potential to promote linguistic proficiency, expose students to academic discourse, and facilitate critical thinking (Kasper, 2000a). Three models are prominent: *theme-based*, *sheltered*, and *adjunct* (Brinton, Snow, Wesche, 2003). Based on these models are a number of variations that have been appropriated in different educational settings and populations as "CBI is an approach with an increasing number of programmatic models or options" (Crandall & Kaufman, 2002, p. 2). As these models have evolved, Snow (2014) asserts that "different features have been borrowed, blurring many of the key distinctions" (p. 442). The models nevertheless have provided a helpful basis for subsequent variations and also have certain shared features, including "dual learning objectives, enhanced motives for L2 learning, adaptation of language input, orientation into a new discourse community, centrality of expository discourse, and focus on developing academic language proficiency" (Wesche, 2010, pp. 278–279).

The *theme-based*, *sheltered*, and *adjunct* models are distinguished by the amount of attention focused on language versus content. Met (1999) places content and language integration on a continuum that spans a spectrum from content-driven on the one end to language-driven on the other. The relationship between language and content can further be understood as an interdependent relationship in which content can be used to serve language, and language can also be adapted for content (Nordmeyer, 2010). In a content-driven course, students are held accountable to content, and in a language-driven course, content is used to facilitate learning language objectives. With these distinctions, a *theme-based* course would be more language driven with instruction depending on relevant themes to provide context for language learning. Stoller and Grabe (1997) further propose a Six Ts Approach to the theme-based model that details curricular design criteria for implementing CBI (see Stoller & Grabe, this volume, for an update on the "Six Ts"). The *adjunct* model straddles the middle of the continuum as instructors work together to ensure both language and content objectives are met. Language and content courses are paired together and tightly aligned in their outcomes, syllabi, and assignments. Finally, the *sheltered* course would be the furthest on the continuum toward being content-driven—that is, where content teachers are trained in working with language learning students in a course separate from native speakers. (See Snow, 2014, p. 439, for a graphic depiction of the continuum.)

Added to the mix of language and content in CBI is the opportunity to teach critical-thinking skills and strategic competence. Critical thinking continues to be in demand for students, yet "translating the skills associated with it into a manageable, flexible, and usable framework or sequence" (Beaumont, 2010, p. 2) remains an area for further discussion. Bloom's (1956) taxonomy was one of the initial attempts to articulate a framework for the ordering of higher-level thinking skills. Students need proper scaffolding for academic success in their coursework, and CBI is a ripe method for both critical thinking and strategy instruction. CBI instructors can assist by breaking down tasks for students to assemble academic information. In addition, "the content component of a content-based classroom provides the extended coherent material into which strategy instruction can be integrated and recycled on a daily basis" (Grabe & Stoller, 1997, p. 9).

CBI is further complicated in an increasingly digital age, which has led to "new kinds of CBI delivery to language learners" (Wesche, 2010, p. 286). Emerging technology has offered opportunities for new means of design and implementation of CBI, but instructors must also take into consideration the independence gained by students and the increased responsibility placed on students in their own learning process (Kasper, 2000b). The growth of online education is one such recent trend that offers students greater independence and flexibility in their learning and mediates new types of interactions between students and teachers. As noted by Warschauer (2001), compared to in-person interactions, online communication facilitates greater participation of reticent students and increases the amount of student versus teacher discourse.

Perspectives on CBI in the Art Classroom ||

Arriving at the best solution to prepare second language students for success in the college and university setting is much like the analogy of a group of blind men touching an elephant, with each man concluding differently about the animal according to the part he touches. With the many facets of CBI, the resulting implementation within even one university setting can be diverse. At the Academy of Art University, we have implemented various approaches to the integration of content and language based on factors such as language level, major, class type, and administrative considerations. Stoller (2002) contends that the "success of CBI depends on the details of its implementation" (p. 3). These details are what we aim to describe here for both an onsite and online course at the university.

The first example concerns a high-intermediate English for Art Purposes class offered onsite. The English for Art Purposes courses at the Academy of Art University are taken simultaneously with other major coursework. The English for Art Purposes course targeting the undergraduate Architecture, Interior Architecture and Design, and Landscape Architecture majors (designated as EAP4 ARH) developed out of the need for greater content-driven language learning over the more generalized approach to art content present in the other English for Art Purposes sections, where a mix of different Art majors are enrolled together.

As a four-skills course in speaking, listening, writing, and reading, the language objectives remained in place with the design of EAP4 ARH. Because the course is offered within the English for Art Purposes Department and not within a major department, "content learning may be considered a gratuitous but welcome by-product, but neither students nor their teachers are held accountable for ensuring that students learn it" (Met, 1999, p. 6). The course utilizes the theme-based approach as its model and follows the Six Ts Approach of Stoller and Grabe (1997; see also Stoller & Grabe, this volume) in which the design of a language and content course implements themes, topics, threads, transitions, texts, and tasks. The fact that theme-based instruction is the most flexible of the approaches allowed for the course to take on desired content without making significant administrative changes to the existing course. Given the student demographic, the central theme for the 15-week semester is the design process, with the first topic in the course focused on acknowledging the idea of beliefs behind design and the second topic unpacking how these beliefs are applied to design. Threads and transitions create the necessary links between the topics and relate back to the overall theme of the design process and establish curricular coherence (Stoller, 2002). The threads and transitions in the course use Bloom's (1956) taxonomy as a means of ordering and reflecting the critical-thinking skills required by these majors (see Table 14.1), as expressed by content instructors when a needs analysis was conducted.

Texts encompass the content materials used to support the selected theme(s) of the course. They include: *instructor-compiled* (e.g., texts from industry websites, articles from journals or books, interviews, and video footage from TED.com and YouTube), *instructor-generated* (e.g., PowerPoints, handouts, vocabulary lists), *task-generated* (e.g., essays, presentations, sketches), and *external resources* (guest department speakers, field trips). In EAP4 ARH, instructor-compiled and external resources are acquired with help from the content departments and have accumulated over the semesters the course has run. These texts derive from authentic sources that must then be appropriated to the needs of the students. Instructor- and task-generated content result from working with these authentic sources.

The tasks include the actual activities that happen within a given course. They make use of the various texts that have been compiled and generated to create the course content. These tasks reflect desired language outcomes and also embody activities that can both pair well with the content and are accessible enough for students to comprehend. The sequencing follows the thread of building critical-thinking skills by scaffolding the type of thinking required by the students to complete a particular task (while also mirroring the sequence employed in the design process). Table 14.2 illustrates an example of a sequence of tasks compiled to help students succeed at their first major assignment, a two- to three-page essay in which they describe and analyze their belief in design. Included in the chart are underlying principles and desired language outcomes for each activity.

A second example of CBI at the university comes from the OLS program. Since there is little precedent for CBI in online courses, our approach was to modify the existing onsite language support program for the specific needs of L2 learners in an online environment. The online nature of the OLS program is conducive to a modified version of the adjunct model, with ESL-trained faculty allocated to online content courses needing language support, thus obviating the need for the concurrent language course typically found in the adjunct model. While the traditional and modified adjunct model[1] are both content-based

Table 14.1: Theme, Topics, Transitions, Threads in EAP4 ARH

Theme	Design process
Topics	Belief and practice
Transitions	Students move from exploring their own beliefs to examining other architects' and designers' beliefs and how they apply their beliefs to concept and design
Threads	Identifying, summarizing, applying, and analyzing how designers think and practice

Table 14.2: Tasks in EAP4 ARH

Tasks	Language Outcomes	Underlying Principles
1. Note-Taking Exercise— Designer Interviews Students listen to and take notes on interviews of designers describing a variety of design beliefs and are then tasked to paraphrase these beliefs.	Retain and paraphrase main points and content words of a short listening exercise through the use of guided note-taking.	Authentic content material related to design motivates students and activates schemata to introduce the topic of beliefs. This lays the foundation for the necessary critical thinking skills needed for students to later analyze their own beliefs. The use of content material also allows the teaching of integrated skills, which for this activity are listening and note-taking.
2. Discussion—Where Do Beliefs Come From? Students discuss as a class using the think-pair-share technique (first writing down individual answers, comparing with a partner, and then sharing with the whole class) on the question of where beliefs come from.	Combine and articulate personal beliefs with the ideas and information from others, both experts and classmates.	Students continue to develop a frame of reference for their design beliefs by brainstorming sources of beliefs. This reinforces the idea that beliefs have a starting place. Students review content material from the previous activity while merging their own ideas.
3. Personal Timeline Students create a visual timeline of the specific influences in the area of design that have led them to make it their field of study.		The task sequence builds with students using their newly gained knowledge about sources of beliefs to make meaningful application and relate it to their own lives. The timeline also serves as a visual brainstorm for the essay assignment.
4. Partner Interviews Students examine their personal timelines in pairs and relate specific events and influences that have shaped them.	Express opinions with persuasive, credible support and respond to questions or comments with answers that accurately provide the information requested.	Having students engage in collaborative talk assists them in developing higher-level thinking skills of analysis and evaluation; simultaneously, their comprehension of the material is assessed by having them restate and articulate to classmates their past experiences and influences.
5. Design Belief Essay Students describe and analyze their own beliefs about design in an academic essay, where they work through the processes of pre-writing, drafting, revising, editing, and submitting a final draft.	Construct well-developed, multi-paragraph narrative and expository essays with a clear main idea and supporting details. Produce and proofread multi-clausal sentences (including subject-fronted relative clauses), present and past verb tenses, common suffixes and active and passive voice structures.	The final culminating activity involves applying written skills to the topic of beliefs. The previous tasks help ease the cognitive demand of producing a clear piece of writing that fully examines the students' beliefs. This formal written assignment demonstrates students' knowledge of the structure of an academic essay and emphasizes both fluency and accuracy. See Appendix 14A for the assignment directions.

Figure 14.1: Adjunct vs. Modified Adjunct Model at Academy of Art University

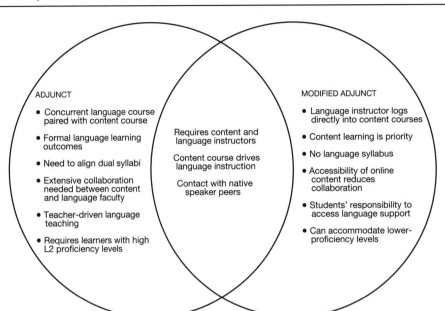

approaches facilitated by content and language instructors with opportunities to interact with native speaker peers, the unique nature of online language support leads to evolving roles of content faculty, language faculty, and students. Figure 14.1 summarizes the similarities and differences between the traditional versus modified adjunct model developed at the Academy of Art University.

Wesche (2010) notes, "Adjunct courses are not common because of the complex cross-departmental collaboration and high L2 learner proficiency levels they require" (p. 283). However, by combining content and language instruction into one mainstream course, the modified adjunct model lessens the administrative challenge of content faculty working intimately with language faculty, as in the adjunct model. In the online platform, the immediate visibility of course content for OLS instructors saves content instructors time in communicating the course objectives. Not requiring a concurrent language course with its own syllabus removes the need for dual syllabi alignment. Fulfilling content outcomes is primary to this approach, rather than meeting the formal language learning outcomes of a separate language course. Relying on the expertise of ESL instructors relieves content instructors of the daunting task of modifying their curriculum and teaching methods to suit the linguistic needs of L2 learners. At the same time, content faculty and OLS instructors can still collaborate closely via email or other forms of communication to ensure struggling students are receiving the language support they need to succeed in the content course.

Once an online course is designed, the content remains relatively fixed between semesters. Due to online content being more uniform and regulated across different course sections and instructors, online language support can be more systematic. OLS instructors can anticipate the language support that is needed by students, so instructors can be assigned to more courses than in a traditional onsite CBI environment. OLS instructors log into classes just as students do, but OLS faculty have full access to the course, including seeing the grading feedback from content instructors on all the work submitted by each student. This allows OLS instructors to pinpoint the learning gaps and exact types of improvement the students need to make. Each online course with an OLS instructor has a separate thread within a discussion board, where students can easily access the support materials provided by the OLS instructor.

In accordance with Snow's (2014) observation that content-based instruction be student centered, taking into account learners' proficiency levels, academic or career objectives, and needs, the OLS program engages in an ongoing needs analysis to determine which types of language support are most beneficial for students. The majority of students find that OLS instructors' simplified explanations of assignments and discussion topics are the most helpful, followed closely by explanations of key concepts and vocabulary. Appendix 14B shows an example of vocabulary assistance OLS instructors provide, which falls into the categories of what Snow, Met, and Genesee (1989) call "content-obligatory language" (language that is necessary for understanding content material) and "content-compatible language" (language elicited by the content material, such as a difficult grammar point) (p. 201).

The asynchronous nature of online classes at the university lends itself to a student-centered environment, in which students access the course content at their own convenience, with the only requirement being that they submit their work within given deadlines. Participating in asynchronous online class discussions also gives students more time to reflect without the pressures of a face-to-face environment. Lower-proficiency students can benefit from reviewing difficult material as often as needed and can easily look up definitions at their leisure. This context is in opposition to the traditional adjunct model, which typically targets L2 learners with higher-proficiency levels and relies on a more teacher-driven form of language teaching. In the OLS modified adjunct model, students are empowered to navigate the support materials most pertinent to their specific needs. This means students need to take a more active role in utilizing resources to achieve academic success, which points to what Kasper (2000b) calls the self-directedness of learners in the online setting. To mediate this process, OLS instructors prompt students via email to access support resources and to apply strategies that enable them to acquire the language needed to successfully complete the coursework. To illustrate, *Art History through the 19th Century* is a preparatory course many undergraduate students take to gain familiarity with the artistic traditions of the past. The learning outcomes require that students apply historical art terminology to identify, analyze, compare, and contrast major artistic period styles, artworks, and artists from the High Renaissance to Impressionism to evaluate how an artwork's stylistic and cultural characteristics exemplify its period and culture. For each week's module, students must read a significant amount of text, participate in class discussion boards related to the reading, and complete assignments that usually include research and writing tasks. The final assignment in the course is a compare and contrast research paper that investigates how two works of art from different periods represent a particular theme in art. The OLS instructor's role is to scaffold each step of this major project in order to help students achieve the content objectives. Table 14.3 sums up the underlying principles for the types of online language support designed to help students reach the outcomes of this assignment.

Research Agenda |||

Because the success of CBI is so closely connected to how it is implemented within a particular setting, we agree that considerable reflection by educators and administrators is necessary. Stoller (2002) contends that there is the tendency to use content as "simply a shell for language teaching" (p. 3). To arrive at CBI as a true framework for language and content learning takes intention and thought, but it sometimes feels as if we grope blindly along in the dark (much like the analogy of the blind men and the elephant) rather than making clear assessments about our teaching and/or programs. Kaufman (1997) asserts, "Few preservice teacher education programs include models for interdisciplinary collaboration which provide mainstream teacher candidates with alternative approaches to educating linguistically diverse populations or immerse TESOL teacher candidates in exploration across the content areas" (pp. 175–176). CBI teacher education continues to need a more substantive body of research, as per Brinton's (2000) call for teacher educators to "fill the gap" (p. 64). At the post-secondary level, a greater problem is that "university instructors usually do not focus on pedagogy in their graduate education and do not necessarily participate in professional development in this area" (Crandall, 2012, p. 154). Given these factors, what role can pre-service and in-service teacher education take to help this? How can pre-service teachers be adequately prepped to manage both language and content learning outcomes? For in-service teachers, what institutional changes can positively facilitate collaboration between language and content faculty, knowing that these changes require a "cultural change of a kind which is often difficult to bring about within educational institutions" (Graddol, 2006, p. 86)? Horn (2011) also notes that "in schools that sincerely want to undertake a CBI approach, the view should be that teaching language and teaching content are a shared responsibility" (p. 7).

Another area for research given the changing landscape of technology in education is how to thoughtfully incorporate CBI in the digital age. To be effective in a time when technology changes are constant, there need to be clear objectives attached to the use of various technologies as they develop. For universities that regularly offer content courses online, the burden of self-directed learning increases, and students need to learn how to effectively navigate the wealth of information that exists online and apply it to their studies. Kasper (2000b) notes that "technology benefits content-based ESL instruction only insofar as it is used to afford students increased opportunities and support for self-directed learning and to build communicative competence along with linguistic accuracy" (p. 209). In this self-directed learning environment, what are the best ways for students to assess their language use and development? Also, beyond the modified adjunct model described in this chapter, how can other models of CBI be incorporated online? Do certain CBI models yield more

Table 14.3: Types of Online Language Support in an Art History Modified Adjunct Class

Online Language Support	Course Outcomes	Underlying Principles
1. Language Strategies OLS instructors create multimedia tutorials on reading comprehension strategies and effective discussion participation in online classes.	Raise clear and precise questions; use abstract ideas to interpret information and reach supported conclusions.	Teaching strategic competence for reading comprehension and discussion participation aids the development of academic language proficiency.
2. Vocabulary Definitions & Cultural Knowledge The vocabulary focus is on the elements of art and cultural information for key artworks. Adding further explanations, pictures, websites, videos, and suggested learning apps can reinforce key definitions and concepts.	Analyze and discuss course topics using discipline-specific terminology.	Various modes of language and content instruction appeal to students' different learning modalities and lead to better depth of processing of essential art and academic vocabulary, relevant idioms, cultural concepts, and historical events that may be unfamiliar to L2 learners.
3. Assisted Explanations of Assignments OLS faculty can paraphrase assignment directions and list the necessary assignment steps to assist students at lower-proficiency levels.	Identify and compare the similarities and differences between various artists and period styles and recognize how they influence each other.	Simplified assignment instructions can lead to increased comprehension of what is expected of students, who also need help distinguishing the critical-thinking skills of comparison, description, and analysis in this assignment.
4. Writing Tips OLS instructors scaffold the writing task with step-by-step tutorial guidelines, walking students through pre-writing, thesis development, outlining, and drafting a compare-and-contrast essay. Personalized feedback can be given on drafts.	Identify artwork from various periods and styles. Analyze the ways art can affect and/or reflect cultural, political, and humanistic issues.	Breaking the research paper into smaller tasks makes the assignment more feasible for students. Familiarizing students with the expository discourse structure of a compare-and-contrast research paper helps students to organize and develop their ideas.
5. Research Skills OLS instructors post online resources and provide individualized feedback, teaching students how to evaluate the reliability of sources, cite properly, and synthesize information.	Gather, identify, and apply relevant information and reference material in coursework.	Teaching proper research and citation skills with authentic texts is a crucial part of developing academic language since L2 learners are not always clear what constitutes plagiarism, and it is especially easy to improperly appropriate information found online.
6. Grammar Essentials OLS faculty provide sentence frames and a multimedia tutorial for effectively using compare and contrast logical connectors. Proofreading strategies also equip students to find and correct their most prevalent grammar mistakes.	Write with conciseness and clarity and apply the conventions of standard written English to communicate effectively in a variety of contexts.	Form-focused instruction leads to greater student accuracy and supports their content learning with an explicit focus on contextually appropriate language forms.

positive outcomes online? It seems that for CBI to continue to be relevant for the future, such considerations should continually be proposed and their success rates assessed.

This chapter describes one university's approach to make CBI work for onsite and online settings, underscoring the fact that appropriate models need to be adapted according to a variety of factors, ranging from pedagogical to administrative. Crandall and Kaufman (2002) note that "the evolution of the various programs and the bases for making decisions and changes demonstrate the importance of flexibility and responsiveness in CBI program development" (p. 7). Such is the mindset in adopting a model of CBI that fits within the instructional, institutional, and student needs of a population (Kasper, 2000a).

APPLYING WHAT YOU LEARNED
Questions and Tasks

1. The onsite and online courses described in the chapter represent two different approaches to CBI. Describe the approaches and where they fit on the continuum (Met, 1999) between content- and language-driven.

2. Compare and contrast the roles of the content faculty and language faculty in the two approaches mentioned in this chapter. Consider the pros and cons of these roles.

3. "Ultimately, future CBI teachers won't necessarily have to be taught about specific technologies….as much as they will need to be taught how technology can be effectively incorporated into content and language teaching" (Horn, 2011, p. 7). On a scale of 1 to 5 (1 = strongly disagree, 5 = strongly agree), identify the degree to which you agree with this statement and explain your answer.

4. How do the tasks and types of support presented meet the respective objectives for each of the courses in this chapter?

ENDNOTE

1. For an alternate example of a modified adjunct model co-taught by a language instructor and a peer group leader, see Snow and Kamhi-Stein (2002).

REFERENCES

Beaumont, J. (2010). A sequence of critical thinking tasks. *TESOL Journal, 1*(4), 1–22.
Bloom, B. S. (1956). *Taxonomy of educational objectives, Handbook I: The cognitive domain.* New York, NY: McKay.
Brinton, D. M. (2000). Out of the mouth of babes: Novice teacher insights into content-based instruction. In L. F. Kasper (Ed.), *Content-based college ESL instruction* (pp. 48–70). Mahwah, NJ: Erlbaum.
Brinton, D. M., Snow, M. A., & Wesche, M. B. (2003). *Content-based second language instruction* (Classics ed.). Ann Arbor, MI: University of Michigan Press.

Crandall, J. (2012). Content-based instruction and content and language integrated learning. In A. Burns & J. C. Richards (Eds.), *Cambridge guide to pedagogy and practice in second language teaching* (pp. 149–160). New York, NY: Cambridge University Press.

Crandall, J., & Kaufman, D. (2002). Content-based instruction in higher education settings: Evolving models for diverse contexts. In J. Crandall & D. Kaufman (Eds.), *Content-based instruction in higher education settings* (pp. 1–9). Alexandria, VA: TESOL.

Grabe, W., & Stoller, F. (1997). Content-based instruction: Research foundations. In M. A. Snow & D. M. Brinton (Eds.), *Content-based classroom: Perspectives on integrating language and content* (pp. 5–21). White Plains, NY: Longman.

Graddol, D. (2006). *English next: Why global English may mean the end of English as a foreign language.* London, England: British Council.

Horn, B. (2011). The future is now: Preparing a new generation of CBI teachers. *English Teaching Forum, 49*(3), 2–9.

Kasper, L. F. (2000a). Content-based college ESL instruction: Theoretical foundations and pedagogical applications. In L. F. Kasper (Ed.), *Content-based college ESL instruction* (pp. 3–25). Mahwah, NJ: Lawrence Erlbaum.

Kasper, L. F. (2000b). The role of information technology in the future of content-based ESL instruction. In L. F. Kasper (Ed.), *Content-based college ESL instruction* (pp. 48–70). Mahwah, NJ: Lawrence Erlbaum.

Kaufman, D. (1997). Collaborative approaches in preparing teachers for content-based and language-enhanced settings. In M. A. Snow & D. M. Brinton (Eds.), *Content-based classroom: Perspectives on integrating language and content* (pp. 175–186). White Plains, NY: Longman.

Met, M. (1999, January). Content-based instruction: Defining terms, making decisions. *NFLC Reports.* Washington, DC: The National Foreign Language Center. Retrieved from http://carla.umn.edu/cobaltt/modules/principles/decisions.html

Nordmeyer, J. (2010). At the intersection of language and content. In J. Nordmeyer & S. Barduhn (Eds.), *Integrating language and content* (pp. 1–13). Alexandria, VA: TESOL.

Snow, M. A. (2005). A model of academic literacy for integrated language and content instruction. In E. Hinkel (Ed.), *Handbook of research in second language learning and teaching* (pp. 693–715). Mahwah, NJ: Erlbaum.

Snow, M. A. (2014). Content-based and immersion models of second/foreign language teaching. In M. Celce-Murcia, D. M. Brinton, & M. A. Snow (Eds.), *Teaching English as a second or foreign language* (4th ed., pp. 438–454). Boston, MA: National Geographic Learning/Heinle Cengage Learning.

Snow, M. A., & Kamhi-Stein, L. D. (2002). Teaching and learning academic literacy through Project LEAP: Learning-English-for-Academic-Purposes. In J. Crandall & D. Kaufman (Eds.), *Content-based instruction in higher education settings* (pp. 169–181). Alexandria, VA: TESOL.

Snow, M. A., Met, M., & Genesee, F. (1989). A conceptual framework for the integration of language and content in second/foreign language programs. *TESOL Quarterly, 23*(2), 201–217.

Stoller, F. (2002). *Content-based instruction: A shell for language teaching or a framework for strategic language and content learning?* Retrieved from http://www.carla.umn.edu/cobaltt/modules/strategies/Stoller2002/stoller.pdf

Stoller, F., & Grabe, W. (1997). A six-T's approach to content-based instruction. In M. A. Snow & D. M. Brinton (Eds.), *The content-based classroom: Perspectives on integrating language and content* (pp. 78–94). White Plains, NY: Longman.

Warschauer, M. (2001). Online communication. In R. Carter & D. Nunan (Eds.), *The Cambridge guide to teaching English to speakers of other languages* (pp. 207–212). Cambridge, England: Cambridge University Press.

Wesche, M. A. (2010). Content-based second language instruction. In R. Kaplan (Ed.), *Oxford handbook of applied linguistics* (pp. 275–293). New York, NY: Oxford University Press.

APPENDIX 14A
EAP4 ARH: Design Belief Essay

Write a 2- to 3-page essay, typed, size 12-point font, double-spaced, describing and analyzing your own belief about design.

Step 1: Think of Your Main Idea or Belief Statement
Start with a brainstorm and/or mind map based on your personal timeline. Reflect on those important moments or experiences that helped you choose your field of study. Think about what these moments have taught you about design.

Step 2: Organize Your Essay
After you develop a clear belief, think about how you can support your belief in your body paragraphs. Ideas for your body paragraphs are:

(1) *Tell a story or experience:* Think of your own experiences, background, work, family, culture, etc., and describe the things that helped you develop your belief.

(2) *Use other sources or examples that have shaped yo*u. Use examples from other sources (e.g., books) or people of influence (e.g., designers) to help support your ideas and develop your belief.

Where do your beliefs come from?

- Experiences (positive   • Books
  and negative)   • History
- Life Lessons   • Media
- Parents and Family   • Culture
- Friends   • Religion
- Teachers and Mentors   • Personality
- School and Education

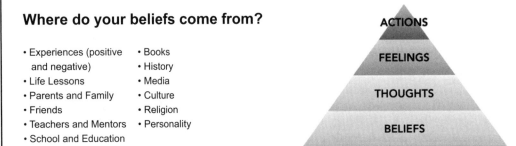

APPENDIX 14B
Sample Language Tips in the Online Course

KEY LANGUAGE for COMPARE and CONTRAST

When you are writing your comparison and contrast, here are some sentences that may help you.

"X is similar to Y"
Notice that with the word *similar* you use the word *to*.

OR

"X is different from Y"
Notice that with the word *different* you use the word *from*.

For example:

"Artwork X is different from Artwork Y because Artwork X focused on the religious ideas of the time, while Artwork Y was more interested in politics."

Here are some more:

"The similarity between X and Y is . . ."
"The difference between X and Y is . . ."
Notice that with *similarity* and *difference* you use *between*.

For example:

One stylistic difference between Artwork X and Artwork Y is in the use of shadow. We can see this by looking at . . .

Examples from art history readings:

- "**Like Gauguin, Van Gogh was interested in** using color in an expressive and more symbolic way than the Impressionists. **However,** his work tends to be more personal than Gauguin's."

- "**Whereas** *The Night Cafe* pushes the viewer into an enclosed and agitated space and forcibly makes us experience the desperation of the people in the scene, **in his** *Starry Night,* Van Gogh seems to have zoomed out, away from the town and put that human experience into perspective."

- "**Unlike Realist painters** who believed art should deal with contemporary issues and the artist's response to the visible world, **Symbolists wanted** to explore the world of dreams, fantasy, and imagination in their work."

- "*The Scream* and *Evening on Karl Johan Street* **are both excellent examples of** the theme of alienation that we will see again and again in the work of 20th century artists."

You can click on this **link** for an Online Language Support tutorial that summarizes how to use appropriate compare & contrast language.

Also, you can visit this **link** to see how to organize a sample Compare & Contrast essay.

Chapter **15**

"Bringing the Outside In": Content-Based Instruction and English Language Adult Continuing Education

Anne Burns & Susan Ollerhead

A Glimpse into the Adult Continuing Education Classroom

Scenario 1: The College of Lake County, a Community College in Grayslake, Illinois, in the U.S., offers a Vocational English as a Second Language (VESL) program. It provides co-enrollment for learners with low levels of English into vocational programs taught in English and into ESL courses with curricula "customized to support those programs" (Chisman & Crandall, 2007, p. 67). The aim is to assist learners to transition to occupational training and ultimately to improve their employment prospects in areas such as medical and health professions or landscape gardening. In contrast to diagnosing their weaknesses, the program builds on learners' existing strengths (which may be unevenly developed) in language, general education, and work experience. The focus of the content is on authentic materials drawn from the kind of vocational tasks learners will need to be able to perform. Teachers in the vocational programs and the ESL program collaborate to develop the content, and ESL teachers undertake considerable preparation to provide appropriate supportive instruction, even to the extent of taking the vocational courses themselves in order to understand the content. The program content includes intensive vocabulary development for medical and health professions, measurement terminology and conversion formulas, authentic non-adapted medical material for reading, communication with patients and co-workers, study skills, critical thinking skills for objective testing, and preparation of a portfolio documenting eligibility for state registration (including relevant background checks). The students must make an oral presentation and prepare a written report on a medical topic that reflects a similar task in the vocational course.

Scenario 2: At the Institute of Technical and Further Education (TAFE) in Tasmania, Australia, many of the ESL students, whose ages may range from the 20s to 70s, come from refugee backgrounds and have low levels of literacy (Williams & Chapman, 2008). The learners are characterized by:

- little experience of formal learning in classrooms
- low or no literacy skills (sometimes disproportionate with their oral skills)
- a lack of knowledge of learning strategies
- a need to learn through experiential, concrete tasks and informal learning approaches
- a need for a slow-paced approach to learning.

Three of the teachers initiated a project that identified topics of direct relevance to their students' lives. They focused on safety in the home, because learners, their families, and community groups working with refugees reported that they were sustaining minor injuries through lack of familiarity with household equipment (such as heating appliances or hair dryers). Owing to a lack of ready resources for this type of learner, the teachers decided to create their own content-based readers with classroom activities based on the readers. Using colored photographs collected from photo shoots in private homes, the readers they produced incorporate images learners can relate to. Minimal text appears on each page, and color and symbols are used to show safe (green ticks/checks) and unsafe (red crosses) safety practices. In order to get the learners to engage actively with the content, flashcards and picture cards supplement the readers, so that teachers can use them in various ways. Manual dexterity activities, such as using realia, matching cards and content, cutting and pasting pictures, and sequencing sentences, are placed on CDs and shared on the intranet for other teachers to use or adapt. The learners also have opportunities for hands-on experiential learning by participating in physical activities involving equipment in the kitchens used for other TAFE courses. The learners have made considerable gains in language and literacy development, as well as increasing their confidence in using equipment safely and recognizing the relevance of their learning to their personal lives.

In both of these examples, CBI enabled teachers and learners by "bringing the outside into the classroom" (Baynham, 2006, p. 6). Bringing the outside in means recognizing that English language adult continuing education (ACE) classrooms in many countries are a "globalized social learning space" containing learners whose reasons for being there often have to do with migration or displacement, as well as with goals, aspirations, and visions for the future for themselves and their families (Burns & Roberts, 2010, p. 411). Adult learners' attendance in such classes involves considerable commitment of time, personal investment, and agency (i.e., the ability to make choices and act upon them meaningfully) (Cooke, 2006; Norton, 2000) and is usually entangled with other work, family, and personal demands on their time. What adults are seeking in ACE classes, therefore, is learning through content that can enhance their lives in the communities in which they wish to become participants.

Adult Continuing Education |||

English language ACE essentially focuses on learners in post-compulsory educational environments. The scope of instructional programs within adult English education is broad and complex, incorporating both ESL and Adult Basic Education (ABE) literacy classes and EFL instructional systems. ESL—or ESOL as it is known in some countries—usually comprises adult sectors in English-dominant countries (Australia, Canada, Ireland, New Zealand, the United States, and the United Kingdom) that provide programs for adult immigrants and refugee-background learners (who may be recent arrivals or more long-term residents) and for asylum seekers wishing to settle in those countries.

These kinds of programs encompass general English classes at basic, intermediate, and sometimes advanced levels, and may also provide specialized or focused instruction in areas such as pronunciation, literacy, workplace, or vocationally oriented skills. Some are nationally funded language programs, with common curricula frameworks, such as in the Australian Adult Migrant English Program (AMEP) or the Language Instruction for Newcomers to Canada (LINC) Program, while others are more fragmented, often with limited funding, and locally delivered programs, such as in the United States (Murray, 2005; Schaetzel & Young, 2007) or in New Zealand (Roach & Roskvist, 2007; Roach, personal communication, September 2, 2015). An overarching trend in recent years is that government policies in these countries have oriented increasingly toward vocational and work-related goals to overcome the challenges posed by unemployment and the high costs of social welfare programs (see the collection of articles in Burns & de Silva Joyce, 2007, and in Burns & Roberts, 2010). They have also become subject to greater bureaucratization with its pressures for accountability and transparency, and a "tightening of the relationship between language, immigration, citizenship and national security, seen most clearly in the rise of language and citizenship testing" (Cooke & Simpson, 2008, p. 4).

ESL programs also frequently overlap or are conflated with adult literacy programs. These ABE classes, as they are frequently referred to, cater to post-compulsory education learners seeking to strengthen their literacy and numeracy skills, usually for the purposes of enhancing their life skills, study, or employment goals. Students in ABE classes may be first language speakers of English who have failed to develop adequate literacy skills during compulsory schooling or those who may have limited ability because English is not their L1. ABE classes in English-dominant immigrant/refugee-receiving countries typically comprise learners with limitations in first and/or second language literacy.

Adult EFL continuing education programs based in non–English dominant countries, on the other hand, are more likely to include adults, whether locally born or from other language backgrounds with more advanced educational qualifications, or more stable and/or "white collar" employment histories. Many of these programs are run by private schools that offer courses in general English, conversation classes, intensive study-oriented courses, or training for international tests such as the International English Language Testing System (IELTS)[1] and TOEFL®[2]; they may also provide business-related English classes for companies, or for sectors such as hospitality or tourism (generally held at the workplace).

Orem (2012) emphasizes that those who work with ACE learners should take into account two key dimensions: (1) knowledge of the characteristics of adult learners (e.g., their backgrounds, learning histories, and goals); and (2) knowledge of the instructional parameters within which instruction takes place (e.g., national policies and standards, familiarity with teaching approaches and strategies that meet the needs and characteristics of adult learners). Teachers working in such programs need to be cognizant of how adult learning differs from the learning of children or adolescents. Knowles (1984) constrasts the notion of *pedagogy* (with its origins in the Greek, "to lead the child") used in mainstream education with the particular learner characteristics, learning needs, and teaching principles important in adult learning. He employs the term *andragogy* to foreground the methods and practices relevant to the teaching and learning of adults.

Knowles argues that as people mature, their learning becomes more self-directed and autonomous; it is linked with their previous life experiences and related to their social goals for learning. They seek learning that is readily applicable and enables them to solve problems; their motivation to learn is internally, rather than externally, directed. Brookfield (2000), building on the work of Knowles and others, argues that the cognitive dimensions of adult learning encompass embedded logic (using contextually based reasoning), dialectic thinking (moving between particularistic and abstract ways of thinking), epistemic cognition (self-conscious awareness of how we learn), transformative learning (reframing thinking about discrimination and inclusion), and critical reflection (scrutinizing information for assumptions of power and hegemony).

It follows from these principles that content-based approaches in ACE classes need to focus on learning experiences that are highly relevant to the lives and aspirations of the learners (Auerbach, 1996; Ollerhead & Burns, 2016). Instruction should be problem-oriented, allowing learners to use their life experiences as a basis for learning, with appropriate learning-oriented feedback that helps them to develop further. Adult learners value involvement in the planning and evaluation of the content, so that it can build on their needs and goals. In this chapter, while our focus is mainly on ESL and ABE programs for immigrants and refugee-background learners, some of the learning and teaching principles that we outline would also be pertinent in EFL classes.

CBI in English Language Adult Continuing Education Programs ||

CBI focuses learning on "meaningful content or subject matter" Crandall (2012, p. 149), without neglecting an appropriate emphasis at various times on language development (grammar, vocabulary, skills, language strategies, and so on) (Snow, 2014). It utilizes "a group of approaches to language teaching in which language is contextualized in an area of knowledge that is of significance to learners" (Williams, 2004, p. 1). Many adult ESL and ABE classes incorporate learners who have an immediate need to "survive" in their new country; therefore, content for these programs should naturally lend itself to topics relevant to their lives outside the classroom such as accessing health care, children's schooling, housing, social services, and employment assistance (McKay & Tom, 1999; Parrish, 2004; Snow &

Kamhi-Stein, 2006). Interestingly, although CBI has been widely recognized in the literature in relation to school-based ESL or ESP programs (see Brinton, this volume), it is less often connected to discussions of ESL and ABE program design (Williams & Chapman, 2008). Moreover, in ESP, learners may already have considerable knowledge of the content (e.g., Marketing, Aviation, Nursing) but lack the requisite skills in the language they are learning. In ACE, learners are likely to lack both the content knowledge and the language required. The role of the teacher in working closely with learners is to identify their challenges and needs outside the classroom, and the content and language central to meeting these needs is therefore vital.

Brinton, Snow, and Wesche (2003) propose three ways of conceptualizing content that may be applicable in ACE: (1) topic- or theme-based courses drawing on learners' needs and interests; (2) sheltered programs, where the content of the subject matter is primary but is taught with language support; and (3) adjunct programs, where learners are located in content classes with ESL and subject teachers working in teams to support students' language learning needs. In practice, many ACE programs are theme- or topic-based, although some programs such as citizenship courses (see Griswold, 2010) could be considered as a form of sheltered CBI. Snow (2014) suggests that CBI models differ in the degree to which they place emphasis on either content or language. Following Met (1999), she places these various models on a continuum ranging from total immersion and partial immersion through to sheltered, adjunct, theme-based, and language classes that incorporate frequent use of content for language practice. (See also Brinton & Snow, this volume.)

An early manifestation of CBI in the Australian context was work by Cleland and Evans (1985). Working with newly arrived immigrants, they adopted a topic approach, first identifying rather specific areas of interest (e.g., *The life of the Buddha*) and then developing broader themes, such as *families*, which would lend themselves to different topics and were closer to learners' resettlement interests (see Williams, 2004). Their four-stage framework focused on integrating the four skills and building learners' knowledge of the topic:

1. **Using a visual presentation:** Using visuals, learners explored their knowledge of the topic, practicing speaking and learning new vocabulary. Learners then generated written sentences to illustrate their understanding of the topic.

2. **Building a reading passage:** Using true/false statements and then sequencing them, learners were guided to build a text that resembled authentic texts on the topic.

3. **Analyzing and extending a reading passage:** Learners' attention was focused on linguistic features of the text (e.g., cohesion, verb patterns, adverbials of time). They then completed tasks to practice their fluency and accuracy in using these features. Other texts on the topic could be introduced for comparison.

4. **Creating a passage:** The learners created another text on any related aspect of the topic, drawing on the passage they had analyzed. The text could be either written or spoken.

This structured approach could be used either for fairly straightforward topics such as purchasing an item in a shop or for more complex or contentious issues such as understanding consumer rights or discrimination. With its focus on topics of interest to the learner and its linking of content and texts, this approach was an early illustration of the concept of the learner-centered curriculum (Nunan, 1988). The Certificates in Spoken and Written English, now used in the AMEP, are also examples of a genre-based curriculum and assessment framework (NSW AMES, 2015).

From a U.S. perspective, Stoller and Grabe (1997; see also Stoller & Grabe, this volume) offer a Six Ts structure for a theme-oriented CBI approach based on six elements. In this outline, the examples show what teachers could include for the theme of health.

1. **Themes:** The central concept organizing the syllabus (e.g., health).
2. **Topics:** The sub-components of the content that relate to the theme (e.g., making an appointment with the doctor, attending a consultation, reading a prescription).
3. **Texts:** The spoken and written resources that link with the topic (e.g., health brochures, talks by visiting health professionals, visits to local health centers, a recording of someone making an appointment).
4. **Threads:** Linkages creating coherence across the syllabus (e.g., local health provision facilities, challenges in access, learners' own experiences).
5. **Tasks:** The instructional activities included in the syllabus (e.g., role-plays, speaking and writing activities related to the genres of health care).
6. **Transitions:** Links made between different topics and tasks in the syllabus (e.g., comparing health care in the learners' countries of origin and in the new country).

In Scenario 2 (at the beginning of the chapter), where learners were taught language on safe practices with household appliances, the components of the two CBI approaches just outlined are illustrated. In consultation with the learners, the program identified an important (and potentially life-threatening) issue affecting the settlement of recent refugees. It considered their life and educational experiences and their existing L2 proficiency. The materials that were developed provided learners with a resource they could use beyond the classroom. Learning activities were fine-tuned to their pace of learning and their learning styles through topic recycling and experiential and hands-on instruction. This scenario is an example of a theme-based course, but it could also be said to have elements of a total immersion model as learners in this multilingual, multicultural class were being taught exclusively in the language they were learning. This combination of CBI models is typical of many English language ACE programs in English-dominant countries.

The vocational program described in Scenario 1, on the other hand, can be seen as an adjunct model (see Brinton & Snow, this volume). Adjunct models aim to provide a two-way integration of language and disciplinary areas. In one sense, they are comparable to ESP programs; however, in adjunct programs, learners may have little knowledge of the content area or profession they are studying, and therefore the students' acquisition of the content area becomes the primary driver for the language class. Unlike ESP classes, adjunct courses must also prepare students for the knowledge and skills they need for future professional or disciplinary participation. Total immersion may also permeate adjunct models, especially when learners are enrolled in programs where use of the L2 is not feasible because of the wide range of learner L1 backgrounds, as happens in most English-dominant countries.

In Scenario 1, the needs of the students were identified within a framework of legislated requirements for professional registration. Therefore, subject and language teachers worked together to inform themselves of content and specialized language and to pool their expertise. The learners' more differentiated needs were taken into account by analyzing their existing strengths and weaknesses, which were seen as a positive source for identifying the nature of the support they would require in the course. The authentic materials provided direction for pinpointing the terminology and texts and the procedures and measurements the learners would need to be able to master in health-related occupations.

While these kinds of approaches frequently result in considerable success in English language ACE programs, there are also many challenges. Cooke and Roberts (2009), for example, ask "What counts as authenticity in the ESOL classroom?" and point to the "anodyne" content and "invented or oversimplified materials" (p. 620) that characterize many adult classrooms, particularly at a time of often stringent and reductionist bureaucratic accountability and prescriptive curriculum content. They argue that the authentic voices and experiences of learners may be overlooked or screened out of classroom interactions, tasks, and resources and propose that content authenticity should include materials that draw on learner narratives and research-based naturalistic sources of communication (see also Burns, Gollin, & Joyce, 1997).

Teachers may also be reluctant to touch on sensitive or taboo topics, such as gender discrimination, racism, or sexuality (e.g., Nelson, 2010) or may feel ill-equipped to deal with content that touches on trauma experienced by refugees (cf. McPherson, 1997). Teachers may have difficulty in differentiating between "content" and "language" (Williams, 2004), focusing unduly on language, while being oblivious to real and pressing concerns and challenges facing their learners. In vocational courses, there may be unrealistic expectations, both of the amount of time it takes to learn a language and of the outcomes that can be expected from the course. In these courses, content teachers may be reluctant to focus on language, fail to understand the need to do so, or have little awareness of the links between content and language (Burt & Mathews-Aydinli, 2007).

Underlying Principles | | |

Snow emphasizes that "[c]ontent-based instruction is a student-centered approach" (2014, p. 452). We have also made a case in this chapter for the critical importance in English language ACE programs of "bringing the outside in." In considering what key principles should operate in effective CBI for adult ESL learners, we draw out features from Scenario 2 from the beginning of this chapter (see Table 15.1).

Table 15.1: Observations and Underlying Principles in a CBI Course for Adult ESL Learners

Observations	Underlying Principles
1. Teachers carefully analyze the backgrounds, characteristics, and current and previous learning experiences of their learners. In doing so, they gain knowledge of the likely factors they need to take into account in preparing content.	Taking into account learners' previous life and learning experiences is a central tenet of adult learning. In English language ACE classes, it is also important to consider the cultural and linguistic factors that may affect learning, as well as the kind of teaching approaches that will be appropriate, especially when learners have limited literacy.
2. Teachers consult the learners, as well as family and community members, about issues that are of concern to learners.	Issues that directly affect the lives of the learners are central in ESL and ABE contexts. Curriculum content should be closely aligned to real-life needs and/or interests both inside and outside the classroom.
3. The materials in the form of readers are developed by teachers experienced in teaching immigrants and refugee-background learners, who draw the content directly from learner and community needs and challenges.	Materials should assist learners to adopt a problem-solving approach to their lives outside the classroom and to build transferable skills. Also, materials should be motivating and enable learners to apply the literacy skills they gain in real-life contexts.
4. The activities developed from the course reader are varied and use different learning modalities, drawing on the learners' visual, manual, kinaesthetic, and oral skills. In addition, the activities are shared with other teachers, enabling staff to pool their resources and to continue to relate learner activities to real-life issues.	Classroom activities should aim to help learners acquire skills that align with their learning styles and strategies. In addition, activities should increase learners' cognitive ability to move between concrete concepts (e.g., photos of equipment) and more abstract representations relating to those concepts (e.g., green and red ticks and crosses reflecting more universal symbols).
5. The teachers also take advantage of facilities and resources at their workplace, such as the kitchens used for other courses, where they can provide safety demonstrations and opportunities for the learners to practice new skills that mirror real-life situations outside the classroom.	Experiential learning is important for adults. Hands-on activities allow learners not only to experience and practice new skills, but they also to introduce them to the language related to these skills. In this way, learners' confidence in both the content and language increase simultaneously. In addition, they can receive immediate feedback on their learning progress through contextually and conceptually relevant practice.

Research Agenda |||

In general, English language ACE is a highly underresearched area, and even more so in relation to research that makes connections with CBI theory. As Burns and Roberts (2010) argue: "Research on adult learners' global movements and their settlement into and experiences of living and learning in a new (pluri)linguist environment is scarce indeed" (p. 416). They argue that, among other areas, much more research is needed to illuminate "the creation and implementation of curricula that speak to [learners'] realities, rather than close them off or drive them into narrowly focused channels" (p. 416). Within such a research orientation, at least three areas linking to CBI suggest themselves.

One important area of research centers around links between effective learning outcomes and the pedagogy and content used in ACE classrooms. More studies are needed to identify what works in relation to effective language and literacy instruction. Condelli, Wrigley, and Yoon (2009) studied 38 classrooms, with a total of 495 students in 13 English language ACE programs in seven U.S. states (Arizona, California, Illinois, Minnesota, New York, Texas, and Washington), and took into account attendance patterns and factors related to attendance in these classrooms. In terms of content, they identified that where teachers made connections to the "outside" or real world, learners showed more growth in their development of basic reading skills development. Faster growth also occurred when learners' L1 was used for clarification (to explain concepts, provide instructions), and when teachers employed varied instructional modalities and encouraged learner interaction. Other studies that have also begun to document actual practices within classrooms and, among other aspects, to highlight key issues in selecting appropriate pedagogical content, include Morgan (1998), Roberts et al. (2004), Warriner (2007), Burns and de Silva Joyce (2008), and Yates (2010). Although case studies of classroom practices such as these are increasing, they are still too few in number to provide clear guidance for English language ACE CBI.

As Cooke and Roberts (2009) suggest, another area that needs to be researched much more extensively is the question of which materials should be used in content-based ACE classes. Many of the materials used in English language ACE courses are invented or idealized versions of life outside the classroom, with their predictable, uniform, and standard varieties of English and equally distributed interactional roles. These materials are inappropriate, given that immigrant and refugee-background learners often find themselves in contexts where they have less powerful cultural, institutional, and social status. Learners need more exposure to naturally occurring talk and should be provided with scaffolding that assists them to deal with unpredictability, cultural differences, and gate-keeping power structures. More research needs to be undertaken in this area in a variety of community contexts, with a view to producing materials and texts relevant to ACE classrooms. Data such as those reported in Holmes, Stubbe, and Vine (1999) collected from workplaces in New Zealand provide valuable resources for teachers preparing learners in vocational courses, for example.

From a SLA perspective, many more studies are needed to understand the impact of lack of literacy on language processing and learning more generally. Tarone (2010) points out that "almost all research on oral SLA has focused on educated, highly literate learners" (p.

75). She questions the basic assumption that the findings of this research hold true for learners with little or no alphabetic literacy, who make up increasingly large numbers of adult learners in ESL and ABE classes worldwide. Reviewing research in cognitive and experimental psychology, she concludes that "grapheme-phoneme correspondence—the ability to associate a phoneme and a visual symbol—changes the way oral language is processed" (p. 82). Such research has significant implications for what kind of content is selected in ACE classrooms, how it is presented, and what kind of instructional strategies and processes accompany the selected materials and resources.

APPLYING WHAT YOU LEARNED
Questions and Tasks

1. Prepare a case for and against the use of CBI for English language ACE learners. What are the advantages? What are the potential disadvantages?

2. Consider the three key types of CBI (theme-based, sheltered, and adjunct). Discuss some of the different teaching strategies that could be used by ACE teachers in each approach. Which approach is most suitable for this teaching context?

3. Examine some materials currently being used with ACE students in your context. In what ways could they be supplemented or improved to create a unit of work that utilizes CBI?

4. What kinds of challenges do ACE learners in your context face in their lives outside the classroom? How could these challenges become the basis for CBI in local ACE classes? How could teachers develop activities that would allow for discussion of these issues among the students, and, if necessary, enable them to act upon them?

ENDNOTES

1. See www.ielts.org/ for more information.
2. See www.ets.org/toefl for more information.

REFERENCES

Auerbach, E. (1996). Adult ESL/literacy from the community—to the community: A guidebook for participatory literacy training. Mahwah, NJ: Erlbaum.

Baynham, M. (2006). Agency and contingency in the language learning of refugees and asylum seekers. *Linguistics and Education, 17*(1), 24–39.

Brookfield, S. (2000). Adult cognition as a dimension of lifelong learning. In J. Field & M. Leicester (Eds.), *Lifelong learning: Education across the lifespan* (pp. 89–101). Philadelphia, PA: Falmer Press.

Brinton, D. M., Snow, M. A., & Wesche, M. (2003). *Content-based second language instruction* (Classics ed.). Ann Arbor, MI: University of Michigan Press.

Burns, A., & de Silva Joyce, H. (Eds.). (2007). Policy, practice and research in adult ESOL programs: An international perspective [Special issue]. *Prospect: An Australian Journal of TESOL, 22*(3). Retrieved from http://www.ameprc.mq.edu.au/resources/prospect/volume_22_number_3,_2007

Burns, A., & de Silva Joyce, H. (2008). *Clearly teaching: Explicit ESL pedagogy in action.* Sydney, Australia: Adult Migrant English Program Research Centre. Retrieved from http://www.ameprc.mq.edu.au/docs/research_reports/Clearly_teaching_FA.pdf

Burns, A., Gollin, S., & Joyce, H. (1997). Authentic spoken texts in the language classroom. *Prospect, 12*(2), 72–86.

Burns, A., & Roberts, C. (2010). Migration and adult language learning: Global flows and local transpositions. Introduction to special issue on migration and adult language learning. *TESOL Quarterly, 22*(3), 409–419.

Burt, M., & Mathews-Aydinli, J. (2007). Workplace instruction and workforce preparation of adult immigrant. *CAELA Brief.* Washington, DC: Center for Applied Linguistics. Retrieved from http://www.cal.org/caela/esl_resources/briefs/WorkplacePrep.pdf

Chisman, F. P., & Crandall, J. (2007). *Passing the torch: Strategies for innovation in community college ESL.* New York, NY: Center for Advancement of Adult Literacy. Retrieved from http://www.caalusa.org/eslpassingtorch226.pdf

Cleland, B., & Evans, R. (1985). *Learning English through topics about Australia.* Melbourne, Australia: Longman Cheshire.

Condelli, L., Wrigley, H., & Yoon, K. S. (2009). "What works" for adult literacy students of English as a second language. In S. Reder & J. Bynner (Eds.), *Tracking adult literacy and numeracy skills: Findings from longitudinal research* (pp. 132–159). New York, NY: Routledge.

Cooke, M. (2006). "When I wake up I dream of electricity": The lives, aspirations and "needs" of adult ESOL learners. *Linguistics and Education, 17*(1), 56–73.

Cooke, M., & Roberts, C. (2009). Authenticity in the adult ESOL classroom and beyond. *TESOL Quarterly, 43*(4), 620–642.

Cooke, M., & Simpson, J. (2008). *ESOL: A critical guide.* Oxford, England: Oxford University Press.

Crandall, J. (2012). Content-based instruction and content and language integrated learning. In A. Burns & J. Richards (Eds.), *The Cambridge guide to pedagogy and practice in second language teaching* (pp. 149–160). New York, NY: Cambridge University Press.

Griswold, O. (2010). Narrating America: Socializing adult ESL learners into idealized views of the United States during citizen preparation classes. *TESOL Quarterly, 44*(3), 488–516.

Holmes, J., Stubbe, M., & Vine, B. (1999). Analysing New Zealand English in the workplace. *New Zealand English Journal, 13,* 8–22.

Knowles, M. S. (1984). *Andragogy in action: Applying modern principles of adult learning.* San Francisco, CA: Jossey-Bass.

McKay, H., & Tom, A. (1999). *Teaching adult second language learners.* New York, NY: Cambridge University Press.

McPherson, P. (1997). *Investigating outcomes for clients with special needs in the Adult Migrant English Program.* Sydney, Australia: National Centre for English Language Teaching and Research. Retrieved from http://www.ameprc.mq.edu.au/docs/research_reports/research_report_series/BOOK_9_Special_needs.pdf

Met, M. (1999, January). Content-based instruction: Defining some terms, making decisions. *NFLC Reports.* Washington, DC: The National Foreign Language Center. Retrieved from http://carla.umn.edu/cobaltt/modules/principles/decisions.html

Morgan, B. (1998). *The ESL classroom: Teaching, critical practice and community development.* Toronto, Canada: University of Toronto Press.

Murray, D. (2005). ESL in adult education. In E. Hinkel (Ed.), *Handbook of research in second language teaching and learning* (Vol. 1, pp. 65–84). New York, NY: Routledge.

Nelson, C. (2010). A gay immigrant student's perspective: Unspeakable acts in the language classroom. *TESOL Quarterly, 44*(3), 441–464.

Norton, B. (2000). *Identity and language learning: Gender, ethnicity and educational change.* Harlow, England: Longman Pearson Education.

NSW AMES. (2015). *Curriculum licenses.* Haymarket, NSW, Australia: Author. Retrieved from http://ames.edu.au/curriculum-licences

Nunan, D. (1988). *The learner-centred curriculum.* Cambridge, England: Cambridge University Press.

Ollerhead, S., & Burns, A. (2016). Creativity as resistance: Implications for language teaching and teacher education. In R. H. Jones & J. C. Richards (Eds.), *Creativity in language learning: Perspectives from research and practice* (pp. 227–240). New York, NY: Routledge.

Orem, R. (2012). Teaching adults. In A. Burns & J. C. Richards (Eds.), *The Cambridge guide to pedagogy and practice in second language teaching* (pp. 120–127). New York, NY: Cambridge University Press.

Parrish, B. (2004). *Teaching adult ESL: A practical introduction.* New York, NY: McGraw Hill.

Roach, K., & Roskvist, A. (2007). ESOL provision for adult immigrants and refugees in New Zealand: Policy, practice and research. *Prospect, 22*(3), 44–63. Retrieved from http://www.ameprc.mq.edu.au/resources/prospect/volume_22_number_3,_2007

Roberts, C., Baynham, M., Shrubshall, P., Barton, D., Chopra, P., Cooke, M., …Whitfield, S. (2004). *English for speakers of other languages (ESOL)—Case studies of provision, learners' needs and resources.* London, England: National Research and Development Centre for Adult Literacy and Numeracy.

Schaetzel, K., & Young, S. (2007). Content standards for teaching adult English language learners. *Prospect, 22*(3), 64–78. Retrieved from http://www.ameprc.mq.edu.au/resources/prospect/volume_22_number_3,_2007

Snow, M. A. (2014). Content-based and immersion models of second/foreign language teaching. In M. Celce-Murcia, D. M. Brinton, & M. A. Snow (Eds.), *Teaching English as a second or foreign language* (4th ed., pp. 438–454). Boston, MA: National Geographic Learning/Heinle Cengage Learning.

Snow, M. A., & Kamhi-Stein, L. (Eds.). (2006). *Developing a new course for adult learners.* Alexandria, VA: TESOL.

Stoller, F., & Grabe, W. (1997). A six-Ts approach to content-based instruction. In M. A. Snow & D. M. Brinton (Eds.), *The content-based classroom: Perspectives on integrating language and content* (pp. 78–94). White Plains, NY: Longman.

Tarone, E. (2010). Second language acquisition by low-literate learners: An under-studied population. *Language Teaching, 43*(1), 75–83.

Warriner, D. S. (2007). Language learning and the politics of belonging: Sudanese women refugees becoming and being "American." *Anthropology and Education Quarterly, 38*(4), 343–359.

Williams, A. (2004). *Fact sheet—Enhancing language teaching with content.* Sydney, Australia: Adult Migrant English Program Research Centre. Retrieved from http://www.ameprc.mq.edu.au/docs/fact_sheets/03TeachingIssues.pdf

Williams, A., & Chapman, L. (2008). Meeting diverse needs: Content-based language teaching and settlement needs for low literacy adult ESL immigrants. In M. Young-Sholten (Ed.), *Low-educated second language and literacy acquisition. Proceedings of the Third Annual Forum* (pp. 125–136). Durham, England: Roundtuit Publishing.

Yates, L. (2010). *Language training and settlement success: Are they related?* Sydney, Australia: Adult Migrant English Program Research Centre. Retrieved from http://www.ameprc.mq.edu.au/docs/LanguageTrainingSettlement_.pdf

Chapter **16**

English-Medium Instruction and the International Classroom

Joyce Kling

||| A Glimpse into the English-Medium Classroom

Scenario 1: Drug Discovery and Development, a course offered in English in the Master's of Science (MSc) degree program in Pharmaceutical Sciences at the University of Copenhagen (UCPH), enrolls students from a broad variety of national, language, and disciplinary backgrounds. The lecturer for this course is Swedish and has been in Denmark for approximately two years. In this first semester cross-disciplinary course, students work on topics on a variety of applied science backgrounds in pharmacology and medicinal chemistry.

The aim of this course is to introduce graduate students to the various phases involved in drug discovery and development, as well as to give them an overview and a solid understanding of the dynamics and interdisciplinary nature of the development process. The small class sessions provide a venue for students to discuss topics of special interest or problem areas in drug development with scientists from the university or the pharmaceutical industry as well as other students. In addition, given the diversity of the students' academic backgrounds, the lessons provide an opportunity for the students to improve their ability to communicate in an interdisciplinary environment. To complete their assignments, students are expected to work in small groups to conduct literature searches and write reports in English related to the elements of drug discovery and the development of a registered drug. One specified learning outcome for this interactive, project-based course is that students are expected to display an understanding and ability to use the basic technical terms used in drug discovery and development that they have acquired from their studies.

Scenario 2: With the aim of addressing the goal of internationalization[1] at the university, the Departments of Obstetrics/Gynecology and Pediatrics at the School of Medicine at two UCPH teaching hospitals initiated an innovative training scheme employing English-medium instruction. Seeking to move beyond mobility statistics and outbound student exchange,[2] in particular, and focus more on international learning outcomes and workplace expectations/

requirements, the program offers a clinical training program in English for medical students in their final semester of graduate study that provides local students opportunities to gain international experience without going abroad.

The courses enroll cohorts of ten students, five international and five local, who study and work together for ten weeks in the hospitals to complete their training. All coursework, lectures, and exams are conducted in English. However, in this scenario, Danish doctors and senior medical students from diverse linguistic and cultural backgrounds also move beyond the classroom and engage in authentic clinical activities, interacting with both patients and hospital staff. Because the setting is a Danish hospital, only a very small percentage of the patients seen by these students are English-speaking and accept treatment conducted in English by medical students. Thus, although the courses, morning meetings, and clinical training are taught in English, the majority of clinical situations are conducted in Danish. Under the guidance of appointed lecturers/doctors, the medical students rotate between outpatient clinics and other specialized clinics on each ward, with local students serving as interpreters for guest students who do not speak Danish, allowing both groups of students to develop their medical English proficiency. Within the departments, the doctors have collaborated to develop glossaries of terminology to assist both the students and their colleagues in working in this environment.

These two scenarios illustrate how EMI has been implemented at the UCPH in Denmark to address goals of (1) internationalization and student/staff mobility and (2) internationalization of the curriculum.[3] More specifically, they show how the university has developed (1) curricular content and education goals that aid students in developing a global perspective and (2) Internationalization at Home (IaH),[4] which entails providing opportunities for all students, both local and mobile, to benefit from international higher education. Both courses use English as the lingua franca (ELF) or language of wider communication (Jenkins, 2013) for teaching and learning but typically do not address explicit foreign language (FL) development or "the integration of particular content with language-teaching aims" (Brinton, Snow, & Wesche, 2003, p. 2). In this chapter, I will consider the definition of EMI, look at some of the issues behind its implementation in higher education in non-Anglophone countries, and describe initiatives that address some of the challenges of undertaking EMI.

English-Medium Instruction ||

EMI, the practice of using English as the language for learning and teaching of academic content, is a policy agenda or strategy employed for teaching and learning in countries where English is not the dominant language. Although EMI is sometimes utilized in primary and secondary education, much of the current EMI research focuses on activities taking place in tertiary education, where it is being extensively utilized to address challenges in non-Anglophone countries related to globalization, internationalization, and mobility (Hultgren, Gregersen, & Thøgersen, 2014). (See also Stillwell, this volume.)

Non-Anglophone countries around the world have witnessed a rapid increase in the number of English-taught programs at universities. Typically, existing courses running in a national language are simply replaced by EMI courses, with little change other than the translation of teaching materials. Europe alone has seen a rise of almost 1,000 percent in the number of Bachelor's and Master's degree programs conducted in English since the turn of the century (Wächter & Maiworm, 2014). There appears to be agreement that the rapid expansion of EMI in higher education throughout Europe has its roots in several established motivations. Although not part of the initial agenda, the implementation of the Bologna Declaration (Wächter, 2008) and the increase of international exchange programs—for example, Erasmus[5]—set off a chain of events across Europe with universities vying to attract more international academic staff and students. More recently, with an eye on globalization, countries in east Asia have followed suit (Brown & Iyobe, 2013; Chapple, 2015; Dearden, 2014). In these countries, where English is not the dominant language, arguments for this type of curricular programming include the desire to prepare local researchers, lecturers, and students to become successful global players in international universities and in their professional lives. Increasingly, across all disciplines, global networking, collaboration, and knowledge sharing for research and education drive educational initiatives. However, another key motivation for globalization is income generation. Universities are being viewed as corporations governed by market forces (Coleman, 2006), with recruitment of international students on the agenda as universities compete for enrollments and tuition money (Byun et al., 2011; Wächter & Maiworm, 2014) as well as global ranking. To compete both nationally and internationally, under the guise of EMI, an increasing number of university faculties are being encouraged by university management teams and national governmental agencies to recruit overseas fee-paying students who are required to pay much higher tuition than local students. Unfortunately, this increased focus in the economic gain through EMI can cast a shadow on intended academic and cultural gains (Doiz, Lasagabaster, & Sierra, 2013). The desire for globalization then often overrides development of internationalization in regard to curricular development, learning outcomes, and/or foreign language learning support.

While EMI may be implemented in homogeneous language and cultural educational settings, such as elite universities in Korea and Taiwan, EMI lends itself to the use of English as an *academic lingua franca*, through which content specialists can teach increasingly heterogeneous groups of students who themselves come with a range of L1s. The current research literature utilizes a broad range of terminology besides EMI for this rising phenomenon, including *English-taught programs* (Wächter & Maiworm, 2014) and *English-medium teaching* (Coleman, 2006). Since the players in teaching and learning in the university settings, namely the content specialist(s) as well as the students, are typically non-native speakers of English and use a FL for teaching and learning, EMI often gets categorized together under the broad umbrella of CBI (Brinton & Snow, this volume), and, more recently, CLIL (Coyle, Hood, & Marsh, 2010) and Integrating Content and Language in Higher Education (ICLHE) (Dafouz, 2014; Wilkinson & Walsh, 2015). However, as Smit and Dafouz (2012) clarify, it is vital to emphasize distinctions between the pedagogical language learning goals of the models. Whereas CBI and ICLHE have explicit integrated content and language learning aims, EMI generally does not.

Issues in EMI |||

Full degree EMI programs are currently being taught at all levels of instruction at universities around the world, though with considerable variation between disciplines at graduate and post-graduate level (Hultgren, 2013). Though this change of medium provides increased academic opportunities for all university stakeholders, the use of English typically by non-native speakers for teaching and learning in non-Anglosphere countries necessitates consideration of the ramifications of EMI.

There tends to be agreement that both teachers and students alike need to have a threshold level of English language proficiency for EMI to be successful in terms of teaching and learning. This minimum proficiency level, however, has been debated. Previous research suggests that lecturers should have a minimum level of proficiency of C1 on the Common European Framework of Reference (CEFR)[6] or a comparable score of 110–120 on the *TOEFL iBT*,[®7] while students should have a minimum of B2 on the CEFR or 87–109 on the *TOEFL iBT®* (Klaassen & Bos, 2010). However, this level has not been verified in this changing EMI context and is a topic for further investigation. It is also vital to emphasize that both teachers and students require not only general and academic language proficiency but also domain specific language and literacy knowledge. Consequently, in addition to student admissions requirements, universities have increasingly begun to implement quality assurance measures in the form of language proficiency testing and language assessment tools for experienced lecturers who teach their subjects in English (Dimova & Kling, 2015; Haines, Meima, & Faber, 2012; Klaassen & Bos, 2010). More recently, the EMI research community has begun to discuss the issue of academic disciplinary literacy, in particular bilingual discipline literacy (Airey & Linder, 2008; Kling, 2016), and the related needs of both teachers and students. Experience from Europe has also highlighted an increased focus on the need for intercultural competence development for both students and teaching staff to address the constantly changing diversity of the EMI setting (Carroll, 2015; Lauridsen & Lillemose, 2015; Tange, 2010).

The composition of EMI course populations can vary greatly. In the EMI classroom, the student population may be fairly homogeneous, for example, at universities in countries such as Japan (Brown & Iyobe, 2013). Here, the students and the lecturers share a common culture and L1, typically the national language, and the course is conducted in everyone's foreign language, English. But as student and staff mobility increases, it is often more likely that the population consists of a diverse heterogeneous international mix of students representing different languages and cultural backgrounds. Regardless of their background, the students are taking EMI credit-bearing courses for both full degree or elective credits. In this respect, the goals of the EMI courses parallel what we can call *traditional L1 content instruction* (e.g., the learning outcome is a transfer of content knowledge, etc.). However, there are notable differences that must be considered. To clarify some of the differences between traditional L1 content instruction and EMI, I consider the comparative model in Figure 16.1. The model illustrates some differences between the lecturer's language of instruction, the makeup of the student populations, as well as some goals for instruction in these two teaching contexts. In this model, Danish is used as the content specialist lecturer's L1, but any language could be substituted here for Danish.

Figure 16.1: Comparison of Traditional L1 Content Course and EMI Content Course

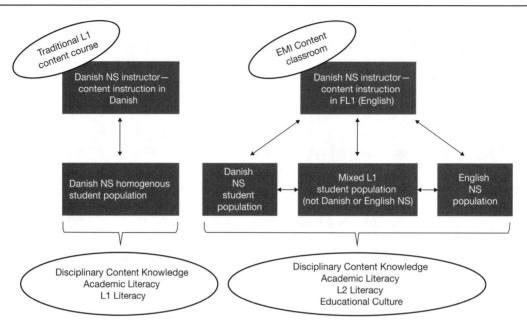

Considering first the model on the left in Figure 16.1, we see a traditional L1 content course structure: a classroom setting where the teacher and the students share a common L1 (typically the national language) and culture. The content course is delivered in this language to a fairly homogeneous group of students who share a familiarity with the nationally defined educational system. (In the traditional L1 content classroom, students using the national language as a second language may also be enrolled. For example, in Denmark, it is not uncommon for students from Greenland, Iceland, other Scandinavian countries, as well as members of established immigrant communities in Denmark for whom Danish is an L2, to enroll in Danish universities and take Danish-medium courses.) In a small country like Denmark, this translates into a great deal of common, tacit knowledge. Lecturers and students tend to share similar understandings of language, history, culture, and academic norms—that is, as regards academic literacy for a particular educational system. Thus, the goals, and perhaps challenges, for teachers in this setting are the transmission of new disciplinary content knowledge and academic literacy—for example, the fluent control and mastery of discipline specific norms (Jacobs, 2004) and the general academic training of the students as independent thinkers in a specific field of study.

In contrast to the model on the left, the EMI classroom model on the right illustrates a multilingual, multicultural learning environment, where the teacher and the students may or may not share an L1 and/or culture, or in other words, an ELF setting. In the Danish context, the lecturer is often the same person as in the traditional content classroom—that is, a Danish L1 lecturer—but the overall situation is quite different. To begin with, the Danish L1 lecturer now teaches the course using her L2 (English) to a multilingual, multicultural student population. Compared to the previous population that shares an L1 and academic culture, this population may now consist of: (1) speakers of Danish[8] who are non-native speakers of English, (2) "other" non-native speakers of English (who do not speak Danish), and sometimes (3) native speakers of world Englishes (e.g., native speakers of global varieties of English such as American English, British English, Nigerian English, or Singaporean English). In this heterogeneous mix, the teacher may now only have shared background about the general knowledge of academic norms and expectations with a portion of the student population (the Danish-speaking students). However, even this shared background can become muddled since teachers no longer use Danish (their L1) as the medium of instruction (in a Danish university) but work through a common FL, namely English, with students at different levels of proficiency. Naturally, the same challenges noted for the traditional content classroom still exist in the EMI situation—that is, the demands for disciplinary content and academic literacy training. However, additional challenges in relation to language and educational culture are added to the mix. Although the lecturers still share a tacit understanding of the academic and social culture with the Danish L1 students, many aspects of the didactics in the classroom must be negotiated in respect to the inclusion of the other students. All these factors can contribute to communication breakdowns and loss of content knowledge dissemination and comprehension. Content teachers can find themselves at a loss as to how best to teach in English (also their FL) to groups of students with a diverse range of English language proficiency, academic skills, and often academic cultural backgrounds.

Given the range of challenges associated with EMI, what is the motivation for implementing broad-scale EMI in university degree programs? One argument from university management teams and national governmental agencies has been the promotion of language learning as an outcome of this type of programming, though as mentioned earlier, this learning outcome is usually not explicitly built into the curriculum. Instead, the context and learning environment is assumed to provide sufficient exposure so as to "advance their [the students'] language competence by developing receptive and productive skills though in an unplanned, unsystematic way" (Dueñas, 2004, p. 7). Universities offering EMI courses and degree programs have typically expected students who are non-native speakers to complete their studies in their FL under the same conditions as if the courses were offered in their L1, treating language as a "non-issue" (Hultgren et al., 2014). This implied belief that the use of English as a medium of instruction will boost language proficiency skills for those involved is now under investigation by both language policy and EMI researchers. Awareness of the need to address and accommodate for the range of language proficiency of both the students and lecturers is on the rise.

The two scenarios described at the start of this chapter exemplify different styles of EMI. In neither case are specific foreign language learning outcomes officially listed. Still, in both scenarios, the content teachers involved in the teaching recognize the need for focused development of domain-specific English in their content areas. In the first scenario, for example, the lecturer includes linguistic focus in her approach to disciplinary literacy and explicitly includes this element in her desired learning outcomes and her instruction. Drawing on process writing and continuous written and oral feedback, she works to support the development of her students' disciplinary language in English. In the second scenario, where EMI is used to increase international exposure for local students who have limited opportunities to go on an exchange, the medical teaching staff at a Danish hospital work directly with guest students (who do not speak Danish) by embedding linguistic awareness-raising sessions into clinical medical training courses through internal initiatives such as the development of support materials provided in English (e.g., internal medical English glossaries) and the extension of the use of English beyond the classroom in morning staff meetings.

Thus, while EMI is typically defined as teaching that goes on in English where the *content* is a substantive academic course without explicit language instruction, there is increasing awareness of the teaching and learning challenges associated with a shift in language of instruction. As a result, at the request of content lecturers, some universities have started ad hoc interventions that are based on models that utilize ESP or EAP principles—where disciplinary content is used as a means to enhance language instruction and learning. To address the challenges that students and lecturers are facing, adjunct model workshops and courses (see Brinton & Snow, this volume) derived from CLIL and CBI approaches are being implemented. The courses aim to provide specially designed ESP/EAP instruction to students studying in particular courses or programs. While these adjunct model interventions advocate cooperation between language instructors and content instructors to develop specially designed instruction to support the students' academic and disciplinary language as well as subject matter acquisition, experiencing UCPH is also a positive by-product of these courses. At the same time as the students receive instruction to aid in their language and content acquisition, the lecturers are benefitting from in-service training and developing their skills to be able to autonomously support their L2 learners.

By cooperating with language teachers, content teachers are adopting pedagogical tools to support their students' progress in the content areas and success on exams (written and oral) and to give appropriate feedback to L2 writers (Ball & Lindsay, 2013). For example, after realizing a considerable increase in the dropout rate in a newly developed EMI program in the Department of Human Nutrition at UCPH, competence development workshops for teaching and studying in EMI programs were established for new graduate students at the start of their degree program. The goal of these adjunct workshops is to raise awareness of both students and content teachers. In the student sessions, the students are introduced to strategies and tools to meet the linguistic challenges of graduate education in an L2. In addition, they receive instruction on how to recognize the strengths and weaknesses of their individual language proficiency. Concurrently, EMI teachers from the same degree program receive instruction on pedagogical support strategies for teaching through their L2 in a multilingual, multicultural classroom. They are also invited to observe the student sessions. In this manner, both the teachers and students are on the same page and prepared to face the challenges of this particular EMI program (Swerts & Westbrook, 2013).

Observations and Underlying Principles ||

As outlined in this chapter, as a model, EMI does not serve as a foreign language teaching methodology. Unless explicit foreign language instruction is integrated into content programming, EMI is exactly what the name describes, namely, *instruction* that takes place through the *medium of English*, in an L2 setting. Without integrated FL instruction, the onus to support students in need of increased FL proficiency for success in their university courses and future careers often falls on the content teachers. Their attention to the development of genre and academic disciplinary knowledge in students' L2 can assist students with the building blocks for success. For example, the goal of the lecturer in Scenario 1, a Swedish associate professor working at a Danish research university, is to deliver a substantive academic content course on drug discovery and development. Although she is not explicitly teaching English for academic purposes, she does support the development of transferable academic literacy skills through content-related in-class activities and course assignments, such as oral presentations and written projects, and the development of disciplinary literacy, just as she would do if the medium of instruction was Swedish. Table 16.1 summarizes the principles underlying the practices of an EMI course in this context.

Table 16.1: Observations and Underlying Principles in an EMI Class

Observations	Underlying Principles
1. Students and teachers interact using English as an academic lingua franca.	For EMI to function successfully, both students and teaching faculty must have a threshold proficiency level of English.
2. Assignments are designed to activate use of English as a lingua franca among students from diverse linguistic and academic backgrounds.	Students should receive both peer and teacher feedback on their English usage in written papers and reports, as well as oral performance.
3. There is an acknowledgment that there are challenges associated with students' learning through an L2.	Students' development of general, academic, and disciplinary language needs to be supported through both ad hoc and established CLIL/CBI training–both pre-sessional (with a language expert) and throughout regular courses (with a content and/or language expert).
4. The multilingual, multicultural EMI classroom provides opportunities for intercultural dialogue.	In the EMI classroom, teachers can use the diversity of the student population, as well as the FL course material, as a teaching and learning resource for the understanding of the development of the target educational culture and cross-cultural competence.
5. Content teachers are aware of challenges of teaching EMI courses.	Content teachers are trained to use explicit pedagogical strategies for the multilingual, multicultural learning space of the EMI classroom, taking into account the linguistic diversity and English proficiency of their students.

Research Agenda |||

A great deal of research over the past two decades has focused on attitudes and policy considerations, particularly at the national level, related to initial implementation of EMI for academic degree programs (Dimova, Hultgren, & Jensen, 2015). While these studies have provided insight into the sociopolitical dimension of such curricular decision-making, we need to have more empirical data regarding the outcomes of this expansive development. As a strategy for internationalization, universities may often adopt EMI initiatives to accommodate the recruitment of international staff and students. More research into the linguistic and intercultural communicative preparedness of both these content teachers and students for participation in the multilingual, multicultural learning space is needed. Are users of English as an academic lingua franca able to handle the rigors of higher education in their L2? Is there content loss or are the students and teachers able to perform at expected academic standards? Further research is also necessary to determine how language experts can contribute to EMI curricular innovations and provide language support for those who do not meet minimum proficiency requirements.

Another issue related to EMI that deserves attention is the role of L1 educational experience and teaching experience. As EMI becomes more prevalent at all levels of instruction at universities around the world, more and more lecturers will find themselves teaching only in their L2. An additional twist to the scenario is that less experienced teachers entering the academic workforce may themselves be graduating directly from EMI programs. With the increase in EMI at post-graduate levels, novice lecturers may find fewer opportunities to study or hone their teaching skills in their L1. Thus, we must continue to investigate the ramifications of English-medium programming in institutions of higher education around the globe. In an era of market-driven higher education, continued research is needed into domain loss and the cost of the elimination of national language-medium instruction for the sake of EMI. EMI course designers and administrators need to investigate what the trade-offs are and to document the benefits.

APPLYING WHAT YOU LEARNED
Questions and Tasks

1. Why is EMI on the rise at universities in countries where English is not the official language? Is this increase sustainable? In your opinion, why or why not?

2. At several universities in Europe, all post-graduate courses are taught through EMI, with some faculties/colleges teaching 100 percent in English.

   a. Should state/national universities in non-Anglophone countries be obligated to provide students with the option to study in their L1?

  b. Will students completing degrees in other languages other than English find themselves at a disadvantage?

  c. What about domain loss in the national language(s) if all higher education is conducted in English?

3. Are there specific academic disciplines that lend themselves to EMI? Are there specific language-related challenges associated with particular disciplines?

4. Given the demand for EMI at the tertiary level, what are the implications for EFL training in secondary education/high school in non-Anglophone countries?

ENDNOTES

1. In higher education, *internationalization* tends to be used synonymously with *globalization*. For the purpose of this chapter, *internationalization* refers to the integration of an international dimension to teaching and research. *Globalization* then refers to the adaptation of policy, processes, and systems to meet the needs of the global market.

2. Statistics reporting academic mobility cover the number of degree students who complete their full degrees abroad, as well as exchange students who may only study abroad at one of their university's partners for a semester or two. Mobility can include both long- and short-term study visits, practical training, and work placements.

3. "Internationalisation of the curriculum is the incorporation of international, intercultural and global dimensions into the content of the curriculum as well as the learning outcomes, assessment tasks, teaching methods and support services of a program of study" (Leask, 2009, p. 209). It is focused on the assurance of international/intercultural learning outcomes, it involves and includes all students, and it can drive curriculum change, innovation, and rejuvenation (Leask, 2015).

4. "Internationalisation at Home is the purposeful integration of international and intercultural dimensions into the formal and informal curriculum for all students, within domestic learning environments" (Beelen & Jones, 2015).

5. See http://ec.europa.eu/programmes/erasmus-plus/index_en.htm for more information.

6. See www.coe.int/t/dg4/linguistic/cadre1_en.asp for more information.

7. See www.ets.org/toefl/ibt/about for more information.

8. This population may include those previously described as Danish L2 speakers who have participated in Danish-medium instruction.

REFERENCES

Airey, J., & Linder, C. (2008). Bilingual scientific literacy? The use of English in Swedish university science courses. *Nordic Journal of English Studies, 7*(3), 145–161.

Ball, P., & Lindsay, D. (2013). Language demands and support for English-medium instruction in tertiary education: Learning from a specific context. In A. Doiz, D. Lasagabaster, & J. M. Sierra (Eds.), *English-medium instruction at universities: Global challenges* (pp. 44–64). Bristol, England: Multilingual Matters.

Beelen, J., & Jones, E. (2015). Redefining Internationalization at Home. In A. Curaj, L. Matei, R. Pricopie, J. Salmi, & P. Scott (Eds.), *The European higher education area: Between critical reflections and future policies* (pp. 59–72). Cham, Switzerland: Springer International. doi: 10.1007/978-3-319-20877-0_5

Brinton, D. M., Snow, M. A., & Wesche, M. (2003). *Content-based second language instruction* (Classics ed.). Ann Arbor, MI: University of Michigan Press.

Brown, H., & Iyobe, B. (2013). *The growth of English-medium instruction in Japan.* Retrieved from https://www.academia.edu/8003031/The_growth_of_English-medium_instruction_in_Japan

Byun, K., Chu, H., Kim, M., Park, I., Kim, S., & Jung, J. (2011). English-medium teaching in Korean higher education: Policy debates and reality. *Higher Education, 62*(4), 431–449.

Carroll, J. (2015). *Tools for teaching in an educationally mobile world.* London, England: Routledge.

Chapple, J. (2015). Teaching in English is not necessarily the teaching of English. *International Education Studies, 8*(3). Retrieved from http://www.ccsenet.org/journal/index.php/ies/article/view/37071/24735

Coleman, J. A. (2006). English-medium teaching in European higher education. *Language Teaching, 39*(01), 1–14.

Coyle, D., Hood, P., & Marsh, D. (2010). *CLIL: Content and language integrated learning.* New York, NY: Cambridge University Press.

Dafouz, E. (2014). Integrating content and language in European higher education: An overview of recurrent research concerns and pending issues. In A. Psaltou-Joycey, M. Mattheoudakis, & E. Agathopoulou (Eds.), *Cross-curricular approaches to language education* (pp. 289–304). Newcastle upon Tyne, England: Cambridge Scholar.

Dearden, J. (2014). *English as a medium of instruction—A growing global phenomenon.* Oxford, England: British Council.

Dimova, S., Hultgren, A. K., & Jensen, C. (2015). English-medium instruction in European higher education: Review and future research. In S. Dimova, A. K. Hultgren, & C. Jensen (Eds.), *English-medium instruction in European higher education: English in Europe* (Vol. 3). Berlin, Germany: De Gruyter Mouton.

Dimova, S., & Kling, J. (2015). Lecturers' English proficiency and university language policies for quality assurance. In R. Wilkinson & M. L. Walsh (Eds.), *Integrating content and language in higher education: From theory to practice—Selected papers from the 2013 ICLHE Conference* (pp. 50–65). Frankfurt, Germany: Lang.

Doiz, A., Lasagabaster, D., & Sierra, J. M. (2013). Future challenges in English medium instruction at the tertiary level. In A. Doiz, D. Lasagabaster, & J. M. Sierra (Eds.) *English-medium instruction at universities: Global challenges.* Bristol, England: Multilingual Matters.

Dueñas, M. (2004). A description of prototype models for content-based instruction in higher education. *BELLS: Barcelona English Language and Literature Studies, 12.* Retrieved from http://www.publicacions.ub.es/revistes/bells12/PDF/art04.pdf

Haines, K., Meima, E., & Faber, M. (2012). Formative assessment and the support of lecturers in the international university. In D. Tsagari (Ed.), *Selected papers in memory of Dr. Pavlos Pavlou–dfouzklaasen. Language testing and assessment round the globe: Achievements and experiences.* Frankfurt, Germany: Lang.

Hultgren, A. K. (2013). *Parallelsproglihed på danske universiteter: En status rapport 2013* (Vol. C5) [Parallelingualism in Danish universities: A status report 2013]. Copenhagen, Denmark: University of Copenhagen, Faculty of Humanities.

Hultgren, A. K., Gregersen, F., & Thøgersen, J. (2014). English at Nordic universities: Ideologies and practices. In A. K. Hultgren, F. Gregersen, & J. Thøgersen (Eds.), *English in Nordic Universities: Ideologies and practices* (pp. 1–26). Amsterdam, The Netherlands: Benjamins.

Jacobs, C. (2004). The integration of academic literacies into the tertiary curriculum: Creating discursive space. In R. Wilkinson (Ed.), *Integrating content and language: Meeting the challenge of a multilingual higher education* (pp. 162–177). Maastricht, The Netherlands: Universitaire Pers Maastricht.

Jenkins, J. (2013). *English as a lingua franca in the international university: The politics of academic English language policy*. New York, NY: Routledge.

Klaassen, R. G., & Bos, M. (2010). English language screening for scientific staff at Delft University of Technology. *Hermes—Journal of Language and Communication Studies, 45*, 61–75.

Kling, J. (2016). Content teachers engaged in English medium instruction in Denmark. In J. Crandall & M. Christison (Eds.), *Teacher education and professional development in TESOL: Global perspectives* (pp. 224–239). New York, NY: Routledge.

Lauridsen, K. M., & Lillemose, M. K. (Eds.). (2015). *Opportunities and challenges of the multilingual and multicultural learning space: Final document of the IntlUni Erasmus Academic Network project 2012–15*. Retrieved from http://cip.ku.dk/forskning/netvaerk/intluni-erasmus/The_opportunities_and_challenges_of_the_MMLS_Final_report_sept_2015.pdf

Leask, B. (2009). Using formal and informal curricula to improve interactions between home and international students. *Journal of Studies in International Education, 13*(2), 205–221.

Leask, B. (2015). *Internationalizing the curriculum*. London, England: Routledge.

Smit, U., & Dafouz, E. (2012). Integrating content and language in higher education: An introduction to English-medium policies, conceptual issues and research practices across Europe. *AILA Review, 25*(1), 1–12.

Swerts, S., & Westbrook, P. (2013). Preparing students and lecturers for English medium instruction at the University of Copenhagen. *Sprogforum, 56*, 71–78.

Tange, H. (2010). Caught in the Tower of Babel: University lecturers' experiences with internationalisation. *Language and Intercultural Communication, 10*(2), 137–149.

Wächter, B. (2008). *Internationalisation and the European higher education area*. Brussels, Belgium: Academic Cooperation Association.

Wächter, B., & Maiworm, F. (Eds.). (2014). *English-taught programmes in European higher education: The state of play in 2014*. Bonn, Germany: Lemmens Medien.

Wilkinson, R., & Walsh, M. L. (Eds.). (2015). *Integrating content and language in higher education: From theory to practice*. Frankfurt, Germany: Lang.

Chapter 17

Supporting Lecturers and Learners in the Use of English-Medium Instruction

Christopher Stillwell

‖ A Glimpse into Professional Development for EMI Lecturers

Scenario 1: To allow for the principled adaptation of courses to EMI, university leaders in Taiwan and Japan arrange for lecturers to attend one- to three-week *EMI at UCI* programs at the University of California–Irvine (UCI) Division of Continuing Education. This division offers custom-designed programs for professionals who wish to further develop their expertise, with an arm dedicated to international programs. The reason for universities to take such an interest in the quality of their EMI courses is because of the capacity for EMI courses to aid their universities and nations in the move toward increased internationalization, which brings a range of benefits. In the programs, participants learn about the challenges that EMI courses typically bring to teachers and students alike, exchange ideas about how to adapt lessons accordingly, and learn techniques for supporting students and creating conditions for content learning. The program is bookended by two cycles of demonstration lessons in which participants perform sample lessons from their own courses, reflect and receive feedback, and make instructional improvements. In addition, participants observe university courses in order to experience authentic content instruction via English and learn about current approaches to higher education. Following the completion of the program, the lecturers maintain contact with one another and program specialists via an informal social media and email support network (Fenton-Smith, Stillwell, & Dupuy, 2017).

Scenario 2: Teams of discipline faculty, language specialists, and study group leaders at the California State University–Los Angeles (CSULA) Project LEAP (Learning English for Academic Purposes) worked together to modify syllabi and instructional techniques for conceptually and/or linguistically challenging undergraduate general education courses. Their goal was to make the courses more accessible for language-minority students while simultaneously increasing the courses' academic rigor. Participants first attended a ten-week training seminar on issues related to the integration of language and content, discussing the distinct demands of content instruction, reading key literature from the field of CBI, and designing instructional strategies for addressing both language and content goals. They also discussed the characteristics and the specific academic needs of the language-minority students on campus, primarily multilingual or Generation 1.5 (immigrants who arrived to the U.S. as adolescents) students who comprised the bulk of the targeted students in Project LEAP. Teams developed "language enhanced" versions of the courses that adhered to the professors' standards while increasing accessibility of the content for language-minority students. Faculty trialed modified versions of their courses in the subsequent term, with further student support provided by a supplemental study group led by peers who were typically senior or graduate students majoring in the discipline and who had performed well in their own coursework. Teams made revisions to the courses as necessary, ultimately formatting innovations into training manuals (Snow, 1997).

EMI: Teaching Content via an Additional Language |||

A seemingly simple change is coming to colleges and universities around the world, in places where English is not the local language, but where the ability to speak English is thought to open the doors of opportunity (see also Kling, this volume). Lecturers in various content areas, from nursing to business to engineering, are being asked to change their instruction from teaching in the local language to teaching in English. They are asked to do so despite the fact that, typically, neither the lecturer nor the students speak English as their L1. Where lecturers and students both speak the local language, the local language may be used to support communication and comprehension. However, in many contexts, such recourse is unavailable, as EMI drives the enrollment of international students and the hiring of international faculty who speak the local language with varying degrees of confidence and proficiency (and further challenges may arise from their unfamiliarity with the local culture and environment).

Challenges related to medium of instruction are not limited to non-Anglophone settings. As Scenario 2 demonstrated, lecturers in Anglophone countries who are adept speakers of English face challenges as well, for their classrooms increasingly include students with a range of cultural backgrounds and language abilities that require support in order to ensure that the conditions for learning are created. Although the project depicted in the second scenario shows many features of EAP, it also deals with many of the challenges and issues of faculty development in EMI concepts. (See Brinton & Snow, this volume, for further discussion of the characteristics of EMI, EAP, and ESP.)

In the EMI abroad context (exemplified by the lecturers from Scenario 1), both lecturers and students may struggle to comprehend and communicate via a language that is not a shared L1. The primary challenge identified for the EMI lecturers is quite simply that they generally lack preparation to teach in English (Coleman, 2006). Dearden's (2014, 2015) survey of 55 countries around the world found that 83 percent lacked lecturers who were qualified to teach using EMI. In many cases, selection for the job often came down to those who have been abroad, who speak well, or who volunteer, Dearden reported. Furthermore, lecturers' awareness of the implications of EMI may be extremely limited, with many failing to appreciate that EMI amounts to more than "simply a matter of translating course material and slides from L1 to L2" (Dearden, 2014, p. 6).

Lack of resources and guidance can be a compounding issue faced by these EMI lecturers. Dearden's (2014) report elaborates on the fact that textbooks, learning materials, and exams tailored to EMI learners are often hard to come by, and guidance from home departments or the administration is typically unavailable. Further, 60 percent of the countries surveyed have no national guidelines on how to teach through EMI. Where guidelines and policies are articulated, they may be driven by curriculum planners' need to put forth ambitious goals (Marsh, 1991), and lecturers may either be unaware of their existence or they may encounter policies that are overly vague or unrealistically demanding. In such circumstances, other reports have found that lecturers are left to become de facto policymakers, interpreting and carrying out the policy as best they can (Hamid, Nguyen, & Baldauf, 2013; MacDonald, 2009) while the program on the whole languishes in indirection. On the other hand, when reasonable policies are clearly communicated, lecturers have the capacity to make sure that classroom practices are aligned accordingly (McKay, 2014). For instance, if the primary aim of a program is to help local students access professional literature and publish, then English literacy should be a prime focus, but it may not be necessary or even desirable to compel the use of English for lectures and all other aspects of a class (Shohamy, 2012).

A university's decision to transition from the local language as medium of instruction to EMI can have a dramatic impact on the livelihood of its lecturers. Some lecturers may benefit, as the challenges force them to improve both instructional and language skills. Improved language skills can, in turn, yield rewards in the domains of various professional responsibilities, including increased opportunities for collaborative international research, publications, and presentations. Naturally, all of these factors may be crucial to administrators' decisions regarding promotion, and lecturers adept at EMI may find more work opportunities elsewhere, as such professionals are increasingly in demand. However, those lecturers who cannot meet the challenge of transitioning to EMI may be in jeopardy of losing prestige, or worse. For instance, Dearden (2014) reported that EMI may become an excessive burden for older lecturers who are not able or willing to adapt their teaching to English. Jensen and Thøgersen's (2011) finding of a relationship between age/experience and comfort with EMI seems to correspond.

We might conjecture that EMI should be significantly easier for visiting lecturers who are expert speakers of English working in universities in non-Anglophone countries, yet such lecturers face considerable challenges as well. These lecturers may be unable to employ locally relevant examples to make their content accessible (Flowerdew, Miller, & Li, 2000), and in contexts where other regional English varieties or English as a lingua franca (English as a language of wider communication) are held in higher regard, these lecturers may find that their variety of English itself is not esteemed (Macaro, 2015). In addition, these "outsiders" may be unpopular due to perceptions that they are usurpers of local lecturers' jobs or even representatives of globalizing forces that threaten to exterminate the local culture (Gallix, 2013; Smith, 2004).

Regardless of whether EMI content courses take place in EMI contexts abroad or in English as L1 contexts, it must be remembered that a lecturer's facility with the language does not inherently bestow the skills necessary to teach non-expert speakers through English. In fact, lecturers who have spoken English all of their lives may have great difficulty empathizing with their students and appreciating their needs because they cannot draw upon the shared experience of struggling to learn English or because they are unaware of the language demands of content instruction.

Common Issues in Making English Content Lectures Accessible to Speakers of English as an Additional Language |||

Whereas differences in lecturers' teaching contexts and English language abilities can create great distinctions in the nature of the problems posed by the use of English to teach content, we find greater uniformity when we frame the challenges of teaching disciplinary subject matter through English in terms of the drive to meet the needs of students who are learning content via a second/additional language (either in EMI contexts abroad or, in cases of language-minority students, in English as L1 university contexts). From this perspective, the key issues amount to (1) the need for lecturers to see how the provision of language support is a necessary prerequisite to students' successful learning of content and (2) the importance of ensuring that lecturers have the skills, knowledge, and support to be able to create the conditions for all students to learn.

Lecturer Perspectives on Providing Language Support

Many content lecturers do not feel that language learning outcomes fit within their responsibilities. With regard to EMI contexts abroad, Dearden (2014) reports that teachers "firmly believed that teaching English was not their job.... They did not see themselves as language teachers in any way.... *I'm not interested in their English. I'm interested in their comprehension of micro-biogenetics,'*" (p. 6) said one respondent. Such a stance should perhaps be unsurprising given that "foreign language learning in itself is NOT the reason why institutions adopt English-medium teaching" (Coleman, 2006, p. 4, emphasis in original). As Unterberger and Wilhelmer (2011) explain, this perspective is typical in EMI, where "the central focus is on students' content mastery and no language aims are specified.... the emphasis is almost exclusively on the transmission of subject-specific knowledge" (p. 96). In the same vein, Taguchi (2014) notes that "English is viewed as a tool for academic study, not as a subject itself" (p. 89).

One reason that many lecturers are reluctant to accommodate the needs of less proficient speakers of English in their content classrooms is because the lecturers feel hard-pressed to "cover" all of the content material and meet all the goals that their syllabi require. Lecturers in EMI contexts abroad frequently express that English exacerbates the challenge of meeting all curricular objectives within the allotted time (Hamid et al., 2013). When English is not the lecturer's L1, EMI can negatively impact both the quality and the quantity of classroom communication (Tange, 2010), partly because lecturers often feel it necessary to water their content down as they struggle to convey their material in a foreign language to students who similarly struggle to comprehend (Huang, 2012). Even the simple act of slowing a lecture down can create numerous complications, as Flowerdew et al.'s (2000) lecturers in Hong Kong found because: (a) they were unable to cover as much material as was necessary; (b) most students still thought the lecture was too fast; and, (c) the more proficient students found the slower lectures boring. In addition, many students resisted lecturers' use of English in class altogether because they knew the lecturers were able to speak Chinese.

Snow (1997) found some of these issues and sentiments echoed in the U.S., as faculty members were reluctant to take responsibility for supporting language-minority students, saying, "I'm an Economics professor. You can't expect me to become an English teacher, and anyway, I don't have the time" (p. 290). Srole (1997) observed similar sentiments from university history faculty:

> Neither trained nor interested in teaching remedial skills, faculty . . . lament [their] own lack of suitable training, [and] shun "handholding" . . . Ultimately, university professors fear that confronting the educational demands of these new student populations sacrifices course content and lowers university standards. (p. 105)

Naturally, curtailing curricular territory to a strict content focus limits students' language learning opportunities. Dearden (2014) notes that

> we may ask how students are supposed to understand lectures and classes if the EMI teacher does not help with their knowledge of English by paraphrasing, by teaching subject-specific vocabulary and technical terms . . . If subject teachers do not consider it their job to improve the students' English, whose job is it? (p. 6)

To attain faculty buy-in on attending to language-minority students' needs, Snow (1997) astutely suggests "framing discussion about language as a vehicle for improving *content mastery*" [emphasis in original] rather than "discussion about improving students' reading and writing skills" (p. 301).

Student Comprehension Issues

For lecturers to effectively address EMI and language-minority students' needs, they must take an interest in much more than simply transmitting content. They must be adept at communicating in a clear fashion, in English, and giving students the opportunity to explore ideas and confirm their own understanding. In essence, a large part of the difficulty of accommodating EMI and language-minority students' needs is that it places heavy additional burdens on lecturers whose existing teaching capacities may be limited or who already carry heavy teaching loads. As Unterberger and Wilhelmer (2011) observe, "didactical competence and methodological skills are often neglected in higher education and certainly do not get as much attention as on the secondary level" (p. 97).

In EMI contexts, "changing the lecturing language merely accentuates communication problems that are already present in first-language lectures" (Airey, 2009, p. 84). Jochems (1991) reports that planning and executing EMI lessons significantly increases lecturers' workload and simultaneously diminishes the quality of instruction. Klaassen and de Graaff

(2001) catalog a number of negative outcomes that can result from EMI. It can cause lecturers to have: less clarity, less flexibility, less redundancy, and less expressiveness; problems with pronunciation, accent, fluency, and intonation; and a reduction of non-verbal behavior (which can be essential to supporting communication). All of these outcomes result in lengthy monologues and a lack of classroom rapport, humor, and interaction. EMI can also inject an air of artificiality to the classroom, as lecturers find it unnatural to keep using English when many students would clearly understand better in the L1 (MacDonald, 2009). Lecturers in English as L1 contexts may similarly find it difficult to cater to the needs of language-minority students without detracting from the experience of the English-speaking majority or the more academically prepared students.

Supporting Lecturers

Clearly, addressing the needs of language-minority and EMI learners requires lecturers to have a breadth of teaching skills sufficient to make accommodations while still addressing all intended content within the allotted time. Relevant skills may include those specific to language instruction, such as formulating clear language learning goals and determining how and when to focus on form (i.e., taking time away from a content focus to specifically explore such language issues as grammar and pronunciation), as well as more specific strategies for moderating classroom discourse in order to facilitate student understanding (Huang, 2012), such as introducing, defining, emphasizing, and eliciting (Tsai & Tsou, 2015). Furthermore, because there is much evidence to support the idea that students' L1s should be used as a resource, "the monolingual mindset that has traditionally been preeminent needs to be replaced by a multilingual mindset" (Doiz, Lasagabaster, & Sierra, 2012, p. 218). For instance, lecturers may allow students opportunities to discuss English reading material in their native languages with classmates (MacDonald, 2009).

For lecturers who lack the adequate skills and strategies to address students' language needs, professional development workshops can provide a start, but it must be recognized that such capacities cannot be developed overnight. Effective professional development programs require meaningful and sustained support (Hawley & Valli, 1999). Extended initiatives such as EMI at UCI and Project LEAP described in the scenarios at the start of the chapter offer ideal means for lecturers to learn to adapt their courses in order to support language learners while maintaining academic rigor. Hallmarks of these programs are that they merge the expertise of language specialists with that of content experts through discussion, observation, and hands-on experimentation. Along similar lines, Dearden (2014) has identified language centers within universities and *grandes écoles* in France and Spain that provide such useful services as helping lecturers improve their instruction in English.

Unfortunately, such collaboration between content and language educators is rare, as language specialists are often marginalized from all aspects of EMI (Marsh & Laitinen, 2005). (See also Goldstein, this volume). Universities can address this issue by placing a premium on particular collaborative practices and by making evidence thereof a precondition for professional advancement; they can also structure working relationships in a principled fashion so as to promote collaboration. For instance, content and language lecturers can be scheduled to teach courses in teams, guided by published accounts of other successful team-teaching endeavors in similar contexts (see, for instance, Stewart, Sagliano, & Sagliano, 2002) as well as by such aids as Airey's (2011) discussion matrix, which provides a basis for content and language teachers to share expertise and learn from one another as they pursue shared aims of facilitating students' acquisition of language and content. And in the absence of institutional support, lecturers may independently seek to tap the expertise of fellow professionals who face similar challenges in similar contexts, from within the same institution or at parallel sites. For example, Gee (1997), a language instructor, found that starting small with a collegial social science professor was key to the development of a successful collaboration. Attendance at discipline-specific conferences and participation in professional organizations can provide useful means of striking up such relationships. Whatever the institutional or individual circumstances may be, it is crucial that lecturers not struggle alone, deprived of that valuable resource in their midst: other teachers.

Techniques and Underlying Principles | | |

Lecturers who engage in extended professional development to enhance their capacity to make English content courses accessible to all students will likely learn about many of the strategies described earlier, as well as simple policies such as firmly requiring students to read content before class (Airey, 2009). They may also focus on pedagogical basics that are typically given greater attention in the education of primary and secondary teachers. Table 17.1 identifies extended techniques for supporting English speakers of all proficiency levels in content classes.

Research Agenda | | |

EMI courses abroad and content courses in Anglophone contexts attended by language-minority learners hold the potential to aid students as they seek to develop both their content knowledge and their language skills. Because content objectives typically take precedence over language development aims in these courses, research that identifies the best ways of incorporating language support without compromising content instruction would be of great value. Yet specific studies on precisely what aspects of content learning may be compromised by language issues, and how these compromises might be mitigated, are lacking. Further research is necessary to ascertain which disciplines are best suited to the simultaneous learning of content and language, and how various discipline-specific approaches to education affect the implementation of teaching practices intended to support the development of language proficiency.

Another area of research interest is the differential place EMI may hold in various contexts, particularly in relation to the differing place that English itself holds. Whereas a push for EMI as a means of promoting opportunity and internationalization may be reasonable in some contexts, in other places the historical role that English has played in colonization and cultural domination makes the embrace of EMI more problematic. Studies may seek to determine the broader cultural impact of EMI on a society, as well as the extent to which cultural backgrounds in relation to the English language impact students' and teachers' perceptions and motivations with regard to EMI.

Table 17.1: Techniques for Supporting Students of Mixed Language Abilities in Content Classes

Techniques	Underlying Principles
1. Flip the classroom, so that students' initial exposure to content comes via readings, videotaped lectures, and other materials that students can access on their own time and revisit as often as they like while making reference to supplementary support materials.	The shift of content exposure to the students' out-of-class time makes it possible for lecture periods to be dedicated to discussion, support, and the application of new learning to novel situations.
2. Use cooperative learning techniques, such as assigning students particular roles for group work.	Asking students to take such roles as note-taker, leader, and comprehension checker naturally builds support into lessons and makes students responsible for one another's learning.
3. Routinely begin classes with small-group discussions of different questions about the previous lecture and then ask groups to present their responses to the class.	When students know they will be held accountable, they come to class prepared, and when they collaboratively review key material, they put it into their own words and make it their own (Snow, 1997).
4. Provide explicit guidance in how to be effective students. Offer guidelines on topics such as how to take notes and strategies for textbook reading.	Students do not learn content simply by being exposed to it; they need direction to keep from getting lost in dense material. Explicit instruction in the structures that govern and guide academic English reading, listening, and writing can help (Srole, 1997). Because students may vary in their degrees of academic preparedness, it should not be assumed that students will automatically know what is required of them in order to complete major assignments. Various forms of support can make goals and requirements transparent (e.g., detailed assignment guidelines and grading rubrics), thus making success attainable for all students.
5. Scaffold and support students' completion of major writing assignments by breaking them into multi-step exercises that teach the skills required for the assignment (see Appendix 17A).	Professors model sections of the assignments, provide sample papers (excellent as well as poor examples with teacher annotations), and give students opportunities for peer and teacher feedback in class (Snow, 1997).
6. Require students to attend office hours.	This requirement fosters active participation in the class, allowing lecturers to better understand students' needs and abilities and giving students who lack confidence to speak up in front of the whole class a chance to ask questions in a less intimidating, more comfortable setting (Snow, 1997).
7. Pair and group students in a fashion that mixes students of differing backgrounds (e.g., local and international students) and different levels of English proficiency.	Deliberate assignment of students to particular groups can begin to actualize the potential of EMI classrooms to be international learning communities, fostering intercultural dialogue and the development of support networks.
8. Make strategic use of students' L1 as a resource.	Principled approaches to the incorporation of students' L1 can provide valuable support without undermining the goals of EMI. Lecturers may allow students to read in English but use their native language in class (or vice versa) (MacDonald, 2009), or lecturers may set aside time before the end of class for students to ask questions in their L1 (Airey, 2009). Naturally, this inclusion of students' L1 should not be limited to the local language; international students may, for instance, be invited to work with partners who share the same language or to draw upon other resources in their own native language.

This chapter has suggested that providing support for lecturers must begin by helping them: (1) to appreciate their responsibility to assist students in dealing with language challenges and (2) to recognize that assistance with language skills might actually enhance students' ability to learn the targeted discipline content. Accordingly, lecturers must be given the opportunity to develop the pedagogical skills needed to provide appropriate learner support. Most studies are light on the details of professional development programs and light on evidence for what topics and approaches in particular seem to work and why. In addition, though there is much reason to imagine that initiatives that promote lecturers' capacity to support language learners may have a positive carryover effect on these lecturers' teaching in general, evidence to support this contention is lacking.

APPLYING WHAT YOU LEARNED
Questions and Tasks

1. How can lecturers and students mitigate the extra challenges that learning in an additional language can bring? And what can lecturers and students do to facilitate the simultaneous development of language skills and the acquisition of content knowledge?

2. What is the role of context and cultural background in learning via an additional language? What adaptations need to be made to instruction and policy in relation to various contexts of instruction as well as in relation to students' (and lecturers') varying cultural backgrounds?

3. Think of a content course that you might teach in which the students may not be fully proficient in English, and think of a major assignment you might give. What steps would the students need to know about in order to complete the assignment correctly? How might the assignment itself be divided into subcomponents to further support students as they learn the necessary procedures? (See Appendix 17A for an example of a writing assignment.)

4. Appendix 17B provides a professional development questionnaire on beliefs regarding the teaching of content via an unfamiliar language. What might be ideal responses to the questions? How could you support your views in response to others who might hold contrary opinions?

5. What makes EMI appealing to institutions of higher education abroad? And why might Anglophone institutions of higher education embrace opportunities to include language-minority students? How can these institutions best reap the benefits of diverse learning contexts while avoiding potential pitfalls?

REFERENCES

Airey, J. (2009). *Science, language, and literacy: Case studies of learning in Swedish university physics.* Uppsala, Sweden: Acta Universitatis Upsaliensis.

Airey, J. (2011). The disciplinary literacy discussion matrix: A heuristic tool for initiating collaboration in higher education. *Across the Disciplines, 8*(3). Retrieved from http://wac.colostate.edu/atd/clil/airey.cfm

Coleman, J. A. (2006). English-medium teaching in European higher education. *Language Teaching, 39*(1), 1–14.

Dearden, J. (2014). *English as a medium of instruction–A growing global phenomenon: Phase 1—Interim report.* London, England: British Council. Retrieved from https://www.britishcouncil.org/sites/default/files/english_as_a_medium_of_instruction.pdf

Dearden, J. (2015). *English as a medium of instruction—A growing global phenomenon.* London, England: British Council. Retrieved from www.britishcouncil.org/education/ihe/knowledge-centre/english-language-higher-education/report-english-medium-instruction

Doiz, A., Lasagabaster, D., & Sierra, J. M. (2012). Future challenges for English-medium instruction at the tertiary level. In A. Doiz, D. Lasagabaster, & J. M. Sierra (Eds.), *English-medium instruction at universities: Global challenges* (pp. 213–221). Bristol, England: Multilingual Matters.

Fenton-Smith, B., Stillwell, C., & Dupuy, R. (2017). Professional development for EMI: Exploring Taiwanese lecturers' needs. In B. Fenton-Smith, P. Humphreys, & I. Walkinshaw (Eds.), *English medium instruction in higher education in Asia-Pacific: From policy to pedagogy.* Dordrecht, Germany: Springer.

Flowerdew, J., Miller, L., & Li, D. C. S. (2000). Chinese lecturers' perceptions, problems and strategies in lecturing in English to Chinese-speaking students. *RELC Journal, 31*(1), 116–138.

Gallix, A. (2013, May 23). The French protect their language like the British protect their currency. *The Guardian.* Retrieved from http://www.theguardian.com/commentisfree/2013/may/23/language-french-identity

Gee, Y. (1997). ESL and content teachers: Working effectively in adjunct courses. In M. A. Snow & D. M. Brinton (Eds.), *The content-based classroom: Perspectives on integrating language and content* (pp. 324–330). White Plains, NY: Longman.

Hamid, M. O., Nguyen, H. T. M., & Baldauf, R. B., Jr. (2013). Medium of instruction in Asia: Context, processes and outcomes. *Current Issues in Language Planning, 14*(1), 1–15.

Hawley, W. D., & Valli, L. (1999). The essentials of effective professional development: A new consensus. In L. Darling Hammond & G. Sykes (Eds.), *Teaching as the learning profession: Handbook of policy and practice* (pp. 127–150). San Francisco, CA: Jossey-Bass.

Huang, Y.-P. (2012). Design and implementation of English-medium courses in higher education in Taiwan: A qualitative case study. *English Teaching and Learning, 36*(1), 1–51.

Jensen, C., & Thøgersen, J. (2011). Danish university lecturers' attitudes towards English as the medium of instruction. *Ibérica, 22*, 13–34.

Jochems, W. (1991). Effects of learning and teaching in a foreign language. *European Journal of Engineering Education, 4*(4), 309–316.

Klaassen, R. G., & de Graaff, E. (2001). Facing innovation: Preparing lecturers for English-medium instruction in a non-native context. *European Journal of Engineering Education, 26*(3), 281–289.

Koch, N., Krilowicz, B., Srole, C., Galanti, G., Kamhi-Stein, L. D., & Snow, M. A. (1997). The multistep writing assignment. In D. M. Brinton & P. Master (Eds.), *New ways in content-based instruction* (pp. 243–257). Alexandria, VA: TESOL.

Macaro, E. (2015). *Going global 2015: English medium instruction—Seven key points of controversy* [ppt document]. Retrieved from http://www.slideshare.net/British_Council/going-global-2015-48709789?related=1

MacDonald, K. (2009, October). Korean higher education striving for international competitiveness: The role of English-medium instruction and micro-level policy makers. *TESOL Review*, 51–76.

Marsh, C. (1991) Implementation. In C. Marsh & P. Morris (Eds.), *Curriculum development in East Asia* (pp. 22–36). London, England: The Falmer Press.

Marsh, D., & Laitinen, J. (2005). *Medium of instruction in European higher education: Summary of research outcomes of European Network for language learning amongst undergraduates (ENLU) Task Group 4.* Jyvaskyla, Finland: Uni COM, University of Jyvaskyla.

McKay, S. L. (2014). Commentary: English-medium education in the global society—Findings and implications. *International Review of Applied Linguistics in Language Teaching, 52*(2), 221–228.

Shohamy, E. (2012). A critical perspective on the use of English as a medium of instruction at universities. In A. Doiz, D. Lasagabaster, & J. M. Sierra (Eds.), *English-medium instruction at universities: Global challenges* (pp. 196–210). Bristol, England: Multilingual Matters.

Smith, K. (2004). Studying in an additional language: What is gained, what is lost and what is assessed. In R. Wilkinson (Ed.), *Integrating content and language: Meeting the challenge of a multilingual higher education* (pp. 78–93). Maastricht, The Netherlands: Universitaire Pers Maastricht.

Snow, M. A. (1997). Teaching academic literacy skills: Discipline faculty take responsibility. In M. A. Snow & D. M. Brinton (Eds.), *The content-based classroom: Perspectives on integrating language and content* (pp. 290–304). White Plains, NY: Longman.

Srole, C. (1997). Pedagogical responses from content faculty: Teaching content and language in history. In M. A. Snow & D. M. Brinton (Eds.), *The content-based classroom: Perspectives on integrating language and content* (pp. 104–116). White Plains, NY: Longman.

Stewart, T., Sagliano, M., & Sagliano, J. (2002). Merging expertise: Developing partnerships between language and content specialists. In J. Crandall & D. Kaufman (Eds.), *Content-based instruction in higher education settings* (pp. 29–44). Alexandria, VA: TESOL.

Taguchi, N. (2014). English-medium education in the global society. *International Review of Applied Linguistics in Language Teaching, 52*(2), 89–98.

Tange, H. (2010). Caught in the tower of Babel: University lecturers' experiences with internationalisation. *Language and Intercultural Communication, 10*(2), 137–149.

Tsai, Y.-R., & Tsou, W. (2015). Accommodation strategies employed by non-native English-mediated instruction (EMI) teachers. *Asia-Pacific Education Researcher, 24*(2), 399–407.

Unterberger, B., & Wilhelmer, N. (2011). English-medium education in economics and business studies: Capturing the status quo at Austrian universities. *International Journal of Applied Linguistics, 161*, 90–110.

APPENDIX 17A
Multi-Step Writing Assignment

Large writing assignments may overwhelm any students who lack familiarity or prior experience with the steps necessary to get from a blank page to a satisfactory draft, including those students who may also be challenged to learn content that is taught in English. To support these students, lecturers can break the assignment into a "multi-step writing assignment," so that it does not constitute a single, monolithic, unsupported task, but rather a series of highly scaffolded steps. For instance, in Koch et al.'s (1997) example of a multi-step writing assignment from a course in animal biology, the components are assigned one by one, thus implicitly and explicitly teaching the skills required for the assignment. Lecturers can provide additional support by providing annotated sample papers to show exemplary or unacceptable work, as well as by giving students opportunities for peer and teacher feedback in class (Snow, 1997).

Topic: Chronobiology: The Study of Biological Rhythms

Phases

The scientific paper will be written in different phases:

Phase 1. Data collection: Personal chronobiology and library exercise. DUE ON _____

Phase 2. First draft of Materials and Methods. DUE ON _____

Phase 3. First draft of Results and Literature Cited. DUE ON _____

Phase 4. First draft of Introduction. DUE ON _____

Phase 5. First draft of Discussion. DUE ON _____

Phase 6. Final version of the complete paper. DUE ON _____

Selecting the Sources

The journal articles cited in your paper should be selected from the following sources: *Scientific American, Science News, Science* (News and Comment section). *Nature* (News and Comment section), *Psychology Today,* and *Discover.*

Writing the Introduction

1. The Introduction should comprise two to three paragraphs maximum.
2. The Introduction should provide a scientific perspective. How does your topic fit into the context of biology?
3. The Introduction should familiarize the reader with your topic. Tell the reader what the literature has to say about your topic. For this purpose, you need to cite two or three references that contain information pertaining to your topic.
4. The Introduction should resemble a "book report." This means that when you cite the literature, you have to be objective.
5. In the last sentence of the Introduction, you should state your hypothesis or the purpose of the study.

Writing the Materials and Methods Section

1. The Materials and Methods section should detail exactly what you did to collect your data. The detail should be such that, with only your report to follow, a fellow scientist could repeat the experiment.
2. In completing the chronobiology paper, tell the reader that the data, consisting of your pulse measurement, eye-hand coordination, and adding speed, were collected at the time you woke up and went to bed, and at other time points during the 24-hour day. In addition, describe the procedures you followed in measuring your pulse and eye-hand coordination and your adding speed.

Writing the Results Section

The Results section of a scientific paper describes the data collected. The Results section should include:

■ A description of the data collected, and

■ A visual presentation of the data collected in the form of tables or figures. The same data should not be presented more than once, and your tables and figures should:

  ▪ Be self-explanatory. This means that the reader has to understand the results by looking at the tables or figures only.
  ▪ Have a number and a title. If your tables or figures include symbols, you need to explain what they mean.
  ▪ Be referred to by name (e.g., *see Fig. 1*) in the text.

Writing the Discussion Section

1. The Discussion section should explain what your results mean.
2. Interpret your results in terms of previous experiments published in the scientific literature. For this purpose, you need to cite five or six journal articles (from the journals listed earlier) on the topic of chronobiology. Decide whether or not your findings support the literature on the topic you are investigating.
3. In one paragraph, explain any errors you may have made in the data collection process. Explain how the experiment could be improved.
4. The last paragraph in the Discussion section should include a general conclusion.

Writing the Literature Cited Section

1. Abumrad, N. N., D. Rabin, M. P. Diamond, and W. W. Lacy. Use of a heated superficial hand vein as an alternative site for the measurement of amino acid concentrations and for the study of glucose and alanine kinetics in man. *Metab. Clin. Exp.* 30:936-940, 1981.

2. Bergstrom, J., P. Furst, L. O. Noree, and E. Vinnars. Intracellular free amino acid concentration in human muscle tissue. *J. Appl. Physiol.* 36:693-697, 1974.

Below is an explanation of how you should arrange your references.

1. Number the references (as in the examples above).
2. List the references in alphabetical order. Start with the first author's last name and initials (e.g., Abumrad, N. N.). Continue with the second author's initials and last name (e.g., D. Rabin).
3. Include the title of the article in lowercase. (Use of a heated superficial hand vein as an alternative site for the measurement of amino acid concentrations and for the study of glucose and alanine kinetics in man.)
4. Include the title of the journal in italics or underlined, capitalizing the first letter in each word (*Metab. Clin. Exp.*). Include the volume number (30:), page numbers (936–940), and year of publication (1981).

From "Appendix B: The Multistep Writing Assignment in Animal Biology" (Koch et al., 1997). Reprinted with permission from *New Ways in Content-Based Instruction*, copyright 1997 by TESOL International Association. All rights reserved.

APPENDIX 17B
Lecturer Opinion Questionnaire

Professional development workshops for EMI lecturers and lecturers who teach language-minority learners can begin with an assessment of participants' opinions regarding the needs of their students and the responsibility to provide support. In EMI at UCI, participants are given this Likert scale questionnaire. Responses are analyzed as a part of needs assessment to identify beliefs that may need to be challenged in order for lecturers to improve their effectiveness with language learners as well as beliefs that can be highlighted and built upon. In a subsequent workshop session, direct discussion of questionnaire responses allows for robust debate, as the facilitator calls attention to areas of consensus or disagreement and invites commentary.

Lecturer Opinion Questionnaire

Opinions about Teaching Content Through English					
Please circle the best choice.					
1. It is a lecturer's responsibility to help students who have trouble with English.	Strongly disagree	Disagree	Neutral	Agree	Strongly agree
2. Regardless of any language issues, it is the students' responsibility to figure out the requirements of a class.	Strongly disagree	Disagree	Neutral	Agree	Strongly agree
3. Supporting language learners requires class content to be watered down and made less rigorous.	Strongly disagree	Disagree	Neutral	Agree	Strongly agree
4. If a student does not understand something in class, it is his/her responsibility to ask a question.	Strongly disagree	Disagree	Neutral	Agree	Strongly agree
5. It is the lecturer's responsibility to check to see if students understand a lesson.	Strongly disagree	Disagree	Neutral	Agree	Strongly agree
6. In classes taught through English, some students will have greater advantages than others.	Strongly disagree	Disagree	Neutral	Agree	Strongly agree
7. Classes that include English language learners/ language-minority learners require more preparation from lecturers than other classes do.	Strongly disagree	Disagree	Neutral	Agree	Strongly agree
8. In class, an English-only policy is best. Students should be discouraged from using their L1.	Strongly disagree	Disagree	Neutral	Agree	Strongly agree
9. When students struggle with assignments because of language issues, there are places in the university they can go to for help.	Strongly disagree	Disagree	Neutral	Agree	Strongly agree
10. It is often difficult to cover all the material on the syllabus in a class that caters to non-native speakers of English.	Strongly disagree	Disagree	Neutral	Agree	Strongly agree
11. Lecturers should try to help non-native English speaking students get the support they need.	Strongly disagree	Disagree	Neutral	Agree	Strongly agree
12. It is important to give non-native English-speaking students opportunities to discuss course content with classmates.	Strongly disagree	Disagree	Neutral	Agree	Strongly agree

Part IV

Content-Based Instruction and Related Approaches: Shared Connections

Chapter 18

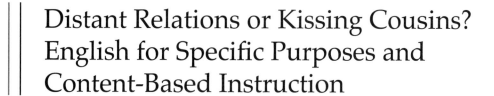

Distant Relations or Kissing Cousins? English for Specific Purposes and Content-Based Instruction

Donna M. Brinton

||| A Glimpse into the ESP Classroom

Scenario 1: At Unitec Institute of Technology in Auckland, New Zealand, the Department of Accounting offers first-year courses to a wide range of students, including both immigrant and international students for whom English is a second or additional language (Basturkmen & Shackleford, 2015). These same courses are also offered in English at an affiliated university in China, where all students are second language users of English. The primary goal of these courses is to examine the role that accounting plays in business decision-making. According to research conducted by the authors, the content lecturers provided incidental language support through a variety of means. These language-related episodes,[1] most commonly initiated by the lecturers, occurred with relative frequency and centered on the elucidation of accounting-related vocabulary. In an apparent effort to socialize students into the discourse of the accounting community, lecturers also focused attention on the articulation of core ideas. In rarer instances, the language-related episodes involved recasts by the lecturer of student language, ostensibly to provide a more target-like utterance. Overall, through multiple language-related episodes that occurred in the lectures examined, the content-area lecturers were shown to make systematic efforts to support their students' field-specific language development.

Scenario 2: Hong Kong University is one of several English medium–only universities in the region, with the vast majority of students attending the university being L1 Chinese. In an effort to prepare its first-year student population to write in the legal genre of the problem-question-answer (PQA), the university's law faculty, dissatisfied with the language training they had been able to provide, asked for assistance from its EAP unit (Bruce, 2002). To better assess student needs, the EAP lecturers decided to shadow the law faculty's Torts class. This, in turn, led to a close collaboration between the content and language faculty, requiring both faculties to dovetail their instructional objectives. At the center of the language course were the actual assignments that students needed to complete for their Torts class. These were approached from a genre perspective, with the EAP instructors clarifying for students the rhetorical moves typically involved in the PQA.

As we shall see shortly, both of these scenarios entail a narrowing of the language syllabus such that the instructors and students involved can focus their energies on the language that is most critical to their ability to function within their chosen disciplines. This approach to second or foreign language (SFL) teaching is known as ESP. The two scenarios also entail the use of a CBI syllabus as an organizing principle for the course. We'll come back to this issue later, as we discuss the symbiotic relationship between ESP and CBI.

English for Specific Purposes |||

As defined in the seminal work on ESP by Hutchinson and Waters (1987), ESP constitutes one of two branches of SFL teaching—the other being English for general purposes (EGP). What distinguishes these two branches of language teaching is the underlying purpose behind the learners' need and desire to learn the language. In EGP, especially in its most typical application of school language learning, there is no specified need for the language. Rather, the language is being acquired for its own sake, often with the goal of the learner's becoming a more broadly informed or educated individual. In ESP, on the other hand, the focus is narrowed to the language and discourse features that are most needed for the learners' occupational or vocational needs.

The territory of specialized language needs that ESP covers is broad. Attempts to "map" this territory are numerous, most notably the attempts by Strevens (1977) and Hutchinson and Waters (1987), whose "tree" of language teaching depicts the two main branches (ESP and EGP) dividing off into their respective sub-branches. In the case of ESP, the three sub-branches are English for Science and Technology (EST), English for Business and Economics (EBE), and English for Social Science (ESS).

This division into three main sub-branches (EST, EBE, and ESS), however, fails to mention English for Occupational Purposes (EOP) and English for Vocational Purposes (EVP), which are traditionally included under the umbrella of ESP (see, for example, Johns & Price, 2014). Joining the ranks of the ESP courses that traditionally fell under the rubric of ESP (such as English for Marketing, Business English, Aviation English, English for Medical Purposes, Legal English) are hosts of other courses aimed at the language needs of specific groups of academic or occupational/vocational learners. In fact, a look at the table of contents of several recent volumes dedicated to ESP reveals the vast diversity of ESP courses that comprise the field today. Here are a few: Problem-Solving for Nursing Students, ESP for Critical Citizenship (Belcher, 2009); ESP for Shipbuilders, ESP for Brewers, ESP for Home Cleaning Services (Orr, 2002); English for Thesis and Dissertation Writing, and English for Research Publication Purposes (Paltridge & Starfield, 2013).

Belcher (2009) observes that what particularly distinguishes ESP is its commitment to learners' target needs. Taking these needs into account, in turn, results in the development or adaptation of field-specific materials and methods. At the heart of the ESP course designers' responsibility is the needs analysis (NA) process, during which text samples are collected and analyzed and insiders to the specific discourse community are consulted. Belcher stresses that NA is not a one-time (pre-course) process but rather ongoing. The results of the

NA feed into the design of course tasks and materials, which in Belcher's terms are "needs responsive" (p. 7).

In agreement with Belcher on the central position that NA plays, Hyland (2007) adds that other defining features of ESP include its eclectic theoretical foundation, its commitment to ethnography and research-based teaching, and its awareness of the importance of critical perspectives. As for the long-term impact of ESP on the field, he cites its focus on communication as the end goal of instruction, its employment of collaborative pedagogical practices, its emphasis on discourse variation, and its awareness of the political implications of the teaching act. According to Hyland (2007), "Together these features of ESP practice emphasize a situated view of literacy and underline the applied nature of the field" (p. 391).

CBI in the ESP Classroom |||

As intimated in the title of this chapter, a great deal of discussion has been generated around the issue of the relation between CBI and ESP. Are they distant relatives? Or, rather, are they kissing cousins? Preliminary analyses of the relation between the two (Brinton, 1993; Johns, 1992, 1997) noted certain similarities, such as their dissatisfaction with abstraction of language in traditional language teaching approaches, their use of authentic language and field-specific discourse to prepare students for the real world, and their end goal of having students transfer the skills and content knowledge that they learn to real-life contexts. These analyses, however, tended to focus more on the differences between CBI and ESP than their similarities, noting the different populations served (a broad population for CBI but restricted to adult learners in the case of ESP), the skills covered (all skills for CBI but typically a single skill for ESP), and the differing research traditions (pedagogically based for CBI and linguistically and text-based for ESP).[2] In essence, then, these analyses tended to compare ESP and CBI as differing approaches to language teaching—that is, perhaps as close or not-too-distant relatives.

Deeper insight was shed on the relation between ESP and CBI by Eskey (1997) and Master (1997), both of whom analyzed ESP as one of two basic approaches to language teaching (EGP vs. ESP) and CBI as a syllabus type or organizing principle. Applying Wilkins' (1976) distinction between synthetic and analytical syllabi, Master characterized CBI as belonging to the category of the analytic syllabus. In this distinction, synthetic syllabi are seen as those in which discrete language items are presented step by step, with learners gradually combining (or synthesizing) these items to form a whole; the learner's task, then, is to re-synthesize the discrete language items to produce utterances. Analytic syllabi, on the other hand, entail presenting language to learners holistically (i.e., in context) and providing structured ways for learners to focus on and analyze the distinct features of the language. In this case, greater linguistic variety is permitted from the outset, and the learner's task is to produce utterances that approximate the global language samples being presented. As shown in Figure 18.1, one example of the synthetic syllabus is the grammatical syllabus, while examples of the analytical syllabus are the notional/functional, content-based, and task-based syllabi.

According to Master (1997), rather than looking for differences *between* ESP and CBI, we should instead be examining the role that CBI can play *in* ESP courses. According to him,

Figure 18.1: Analytic and Synthetic Syllabi

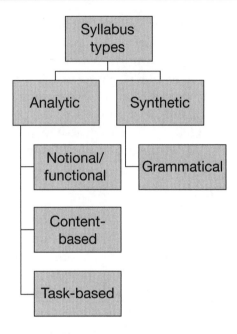

the fallacy behind attempting to compare and contrast ESP and CBI lies in the fact that "the two are basically not comparable as they operate at different levels in the ELT hierarchy. ESP is simply a domain of ELT that makes substantial use of the CBI syllabus" (p. 10). In a similar vein, Eskey (1997) pointed out that

> the content-based syllabus is best viewed as an even newer attempt to extend and develop our conception of what a syllabus for a second-language course should comprise, including a concern with language form and language function, as well as a crucial third dimension—the factual and conceptual content of such courses. (p. 135)

Thus, according to Eskey, the content-based syllabus, by combining a focus on linguistic form, linguistic function, and conceptual content, presents an attractive alternative to other syllabus types (such as the grammatical or notional/functional syllabus) for the organization of either a general or specific purposes course (see Figure 18.2).

Finally, in her review of the role played by CBI in ESP courses, Brinton (2013) sides with both Master and Eskey in analyzing CBI as a syllabus type that is frequently, and effectively, implemented in ESP. As she notes: ". . . CBI can not only be a highly effective way of delivering EGP courses but can serve as an equally efficient organizing principle for EAP and ESP courses." Citing Basturkmen (2006), she agrees that there can be definite advantages to the CBI syllabus when applied to the design of an ESP course. These include the fact that as a holistic approach, the CBI syllabus integrates all skills and exposes students to multiple sources from which they are required to synthesize and extrapolate information. A second advantage lies in CBI's use of authentic "specific purposes" texts that are embedded within

Figure 18.2: CBI as a Syllabus Option in EGP and ESP Courses

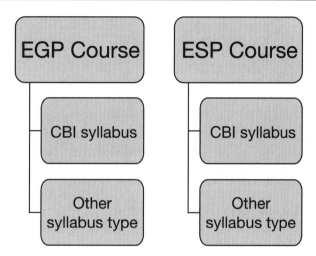

the content area. This practice helps to avoid the pitfall of other syllabus types (especially synthetic syllabi), which tend to extract texts from their natural contexts for the purpose of grammatical or lexical analysis.

To understand how a content-based syllabus can be applied to an ESP course, let us return to the two scenarios at the outset of this chapter. In Scenario 1, lecturers from the university's accounting faculty are delivering a first-year course through the medium of English to a range of students for whom English is a second language. This scenario depicts one possible application of the content-based syllabus to a specific purposes course, namely EMI. In this case, the responsibility for both content and language instruction falls to the content-area instructors. In the scenario, the content instructors address their responsibility for language support—in what the researchers term *language-related episodes*—by focusing primarily on accounting-related vocabulary and the articulation of core ideas. They also, though less frequently, correct students' non–target like language use by repeating students' utterances using correct target forms (i.e., by recasting the students' utterances). This incidental attention to language form by the content instructor is part of the theoretical construct of EMI and/or sheltered instruction (see Brinton & Snow, this volume).

In the second scenario at Hong Kong University, members of the university's EAP unit are asked by the law faculty to assess students' language needs in the first-year torts class and respond to these needs by creating a class specifically designed with these needs in mind. As a preface to designing the course, the EAP lecturers shadow their law counterparts, conducting a thorough analysis of the students' language-related needs in the torts class. Next, in the course design phase, the two faculties collaborate in the planning process, carefully dovetailing their instructional objectives. The model of content-based syllabus that emerges from this planning process is a classic adjunct model (see Brinton & Snow, this volume), with two linked but separate courses being offered, each with its distinct aims and objectives. In this model, the EAP lecturers assume the primary responsibility for specific purposes language instruction while the law instructors assume the primary responsibility for the Tort content.

What we see in both of these scenarios is the direct application of a content-based syllabus to an ESP course, with the academic subject matter domain (accounting and law, respectively) providing the content around which all other aspects of the course revolve. As noted by Master and Brinton (1998):

> [CBI] joins the other types of syllabi recognized in the field, namely, the grammatical, the notional-functional, the rhetorical, and the task-based syllabus. The organizing principle is the content or subject matter on which any implementation of CBI (i.e., adjunct, sheltered, and thematic courses) is based. (p. vii)

Observations and Underlying Principles |||

To examine the underlying principles of a CBI syllabus as it is applied to an ESP course, let us return to Scenario 2 at the outset of this chapter. In this scenario, the EAP faculty members at Hong Kong University collaborate closely with their law faculty colleagues to help prepare the L2 student population enrolled in a first-year torts class for the specific English language demands of the course. As their primary goal, the EAP lecturers determine the needs of the Torts students vis-à-vis their mastery of the legal genre of the PQA. Table 18.1 summarizes the principles underlying the instructional practices in this adjunct model course.

Research Agenda |||

The juncture of CBI and ESP is an area ripe for research: "As professionals accustomed to doing research in their own local contexts . . . , ESP practitioners should be able to look to, and ideally, contribute to, published research as a resource that will facilitate their praxis" (Belcher, 2013, p. 536). Several research directions suggest themselves: (1) research into the pedagogy of ESP, (2) research on the discourse of the content- and language-integrated ESP classroom, and (3) research on collaboration between language and content faculty.

Regarding the first research direction, a key area of investigation involves research into the efficacy of a CBI syllabus for different types of ESP courses (both EAP and EVP/EOP). This question is all the more pertinent since, as we have seen, a CBI syllabus is only one of several options when designing an ESP course. As Brinton (2013) maintains, "While early debates focused on delineating the boundaries between [CBI and ESP], later works more accurately analyze their symbiotic nature, stressing the role that a CBI syllabus plays in ESP course design" (p. 904). To date, research on this topic is scant if not non-existent.

A second direction that is ripe for research centers around classroom discourse. The research study reported in Scenario 1 at the outset of this chapter (Basturkmen & Shackleford, 2015) is an excellent example of this type of research. As the authors note in their conclusions: "Further studies, drawing on the methodology used in this study, could be conducted to determine if content classes in other settings and disciplines would involve

Table 18.1: Observations and Underlying Principles in an ESP Adjunct Model Class

Observations	Underlying Principles
1. The EAP faculty, when approached about designing a language support course, ask to shadow the law faculty as they teach the torts class. By so doing, EAP faculty are able to better assess the needs of the law student enrolled in the course.	Needs analysis (NA) is a central tenet of ESP curriculum design. In NA, the skills and tasks that learners require in order to function most efficiently in their discipline or area of interest are determined. Based on the NA, the curricular objectives of the course are narrowed down to reflect these skills and tasks. These objectives form the backbone of the curriculum, allowing for the integration of key vocabulary, grammar, and skill-based instruction.
2. The law and EAP instructors select a paired or adjunct course model for the delivery of the course.	In adjunct instruction, students are enrolled in linked content and language classes. In this "two for one" model, students gain increased language proficiency and content knowledge. This model is especially appropriate for advanced-level learners in EAP courses.
3. The law and EAP faculty collaborate closely, dovetailing their instructional objectives.	The goals of the adjunct language support course are typically driven by those of the content course, which provides a point of departure for all language- and skill-based instruction. For this to be achieved, close collaboration of the two faculties and a shared instructional philosophy is required.
4. The EAP course uses the actual disciplinary assignment of the legal PQA, which requires students to demonstrate their legal reasoning skills and their ability to apply tort law to practical legal problems.	A standard practice in adjunct instruction is the joint paper assignment. Typically, the evaluation of the paper by the content faculty is heavily weighted toward accuracy of the content material while evaluation by the language faculty focuses primarily on the quality of writing itself (including organization and language). Evaluation practices vary. Language and content faculty may assign one joint grade (having previously agreed upon their evaluation criteria); alternatively, they may assign separate grades (reflecting differing evaluation criteria that have been communicated to students).
5. The EAP lecturers adopt a genre perspective to teach the PQA.	A common practice in ESP involves taking a functional approach to analyzing a discipline-specific genre (in this case, the PQA). The instructional focus is on identifying the structure of legal reasoning and the accompanying rhetorical functions and structures that are used to express this reasoning.[3] The EAP lecturers apply their own rhetorical expertise and the insights about rhetorical-legal reasoning and argumentative skills that they have gained from the NA procedure to scaffold students' mastery of the genre. In this way, a bridge is formed between students' experiences in the language class and the linguistic demands of the content curriculum.

a similar frequency of language-related episodes and thus interest in language collaboration between language and content faculty" (p. 95). Other existing research on this topic is found in Arkoudis (2005), who investigated the long-term planning conversations of an ESL teacher and a science teacher collaborating on a Year 10 science class, and Dalton-Puffer and Nikula (2006), who examined the pragmatics of teacher and student directives in CBI subject matter classrooms.

A final suggested area of potential research into the juncture of CBI and ESP entails the often problematic collaboration of language and content faculty. Here, existing research includes Airey's (2012) investigation of the attitudes toward language teaching of Swedish physics lecturers and Tan's (2011) study of Malaysian mathematics and science teachers in the EMI classroom, specifically vis-à-vis how these teachers viewed their expanded responsibility for teaching language as well as content (see Pawan & Greene and Goldstein, this volume). Both of these studies document the reluctance of content faculty to recognize their responsibility for language instruction along with their assumption that language does not play a large role within their disciplines. The Tan study also documents the lack of systematic collaboration between the language and the content teachers.

This chapter has examined the symbiotic nature of CBI and ESP, concluding that CBI is a highly flexible syllabus type that is frequently applied in the design of ESP courses. It has also examined the issue of EMI in content courses offered at international universities (i.e., where the traditional language of instruction is not English) and the pivotal role that CBI can play in ESP language support courses.

APPLYING WHAT YOU LEARNED
Questions and Tasks

1. According to Hutchinson and Waters, there are only two main approaches to SFL teaching: ESP and EGP. List as many ways as you can in which these two approaches differ.

2. Do you agree or disagree with the following statements about ESP courses? Why or why not?

    a. ESP should not be taught before the intermediate level of English language proficiency.

    b. ESP curriculum designers should have specialized content knowledge.

    c. The ESP instructor should be familiar with the dominant written (and spoken) genres of the discourse communities to which the (future) professions of the ESP students belong.

    d. ESP instructors should teach the means to learning and not the content itself.

    e. A specific purpose approach to curriculum design is more efficient than a general purpose approach.

3. The two scenarios at the outset of this chapter represent quite different applications of the content-based syllabus to ESP course design. Comment on the differences, taking into account the following factors:

   a. the student population

   b. the faculty

   c. the content area of the course

   d. the degree and type of language support available

   e. the primary goal(s) of the course

4. As Bruce (2002) comments in his discussion of the EAP/law torts adjunct, "The balance between language and content in such a course is a delicate one" (p. 340). Which factors do you believe contribute to this delicate balance?

ENDNOTES

1. The term *language-related episode* was first used by Swain and Lapkin (1998) to designate instances where interlocutors "talk about the language they are producing, question their language use, or correct themselves or others" (p. 326). Here, the term is more broadly defined to mean "transitory shifts of the topic of the discourse from content to language" (p. 87).
2. For a more thorough discussion of this literature, see Brinton (2013).
3. The two most common rhetorical functions used in the PQA were *concession* and *condition*. As examples of rhetorical structures used, the author cites "although X can show Y, s/he may still need to show Z" (concession) and "if X had done Y, she would not have been liable" (condition) (Bruce, 2002, p. 327).

REFERENCES

Airey, J. (2012). "I don't teach language." The linguistic attitudes of physics lecturers in Sweden. *AILA Review, 25,* 64–79.

Arkoudis, S. (2005). Fusing pedagogic horizons: Language and content teaching in the mainstream. *Linguistics and Education, 16,* 173–187.

Basturkmen, H. (2006). *Ideas and options in English for specific purposes.* Mahwah, NJ: Erlbaum.

Basturkmen, H., & Shackleford, N. (2015). How content lecturers help students with language: An observational study of language-related episodes in interaction in first year accounting classrooms. *English for Specific Purposes, 37,* 87–97.

Belcher, D. (Ed.). (2009). *English for specific purposes in theory and practice.* Ann Arbor, MI: University of Michigan Press.

Belcher, D. (2013). The future of ESP research: Resources for access and choice. In B. Paltridge & S. Starfield, (Eds.), *The handbook of English for specific purposes* (pp. 535–551). Malden, MA: Wiley Blackwell.

Brinton, D. (1993, August/September). Content-based instruction and English for specific purposes: Same, or different? *TESOL Matters, 3–4,* 9.

Brinton, D. M. (2013). Content-based instruction in English for specific purposes. In C. Chapelle (Ed.), *The encyclopedia of applied linguistics* (pp. 897–906). New York, NY: Blackwell.

Bruce, N. (2002). Dovetailing language and content: Teaching balanced argument in legal problem answer writing. *English for Specific Purposes, 21*, 321–345.

Dalton-Puffer, C., & Nikula, T. (2006). Pragmatics of content-based instruction: Teacher and student directives in Finnish and Austrian classrooms. *Applied Linguistics, 27*(2), 241–267.

Eskey, D. (1997). Syllabus design in content-based instruction. In M. A. Snow & D. M. Brinton (Eds.), *The content-based classroom: Perspectives on integrating language and content* (pp. 132–141). White Plains, NY: Longman.

Hutchison, T., & Waters, A. (1987). *English for specific purposes: A learning-centred approach.* Cambridge, England: Cambridge University Press.

Hyland, K. (2007). English for specific purposes: Some influences and impacts. In J. Cummins & C. Davison (Eds.), *The international handbook of English language education* (Vol. 1, pp. 391–402). New York, NY: Springer.

Johns, A. M. (1992). What is the relationship between English for specific purposes and content-based instruction? *CATESOL Journal, 5*(1), 71–76.

Johns, A. M. (1997). English for specific purposes and content-based instruction: What is the relationship? In M. A. Snow & D. M. Brinton (Eds.), *The content-based classroom: Perspectives on integrating language and content* (pp. 363–367). White Plains, NY: Longman.

Johns, A. M., & Price, D. (2014). *English for specific purposes: International in scope, specific in purpose.* In M. Celce-Murcia, D. M. Brinton, & M. A. Snow (Eds.), Teaching English as a second or foreign language (4th ed., pp. 471–487). Boston, MA: National Geographic Learning/Heinle Cengage Learning.

Master, P. (1997, December). Content-based instruction vs. ESP. *TESOL Matters,* 10.

Master, P., & Brinton, D. M. (1998). *New ways in English for specific purposes.* Alexandria, VA: TESOL.

Orr, T. (Ed.). (2002). *English for specific purposes.* Alexandria, VA: TESOL.

Paltridge, B., & Starfield, S. (Eds.). (2013). *The handbook of English for specific purposes.* Malden, MA: Wiley Blackwell.

Strevens, P. (1977). Special-purpose language learning. *Language Teaching and Linguistics Abstracts, 10*(3), 145–163.

Swain, M., & Lapkin, S. (1998). Interaction and second language learning: Two adolescent French immersion students working together. *The Modern Language Journal, 82*(3), 320–337.

Tan, M. (2011). Mathematics and science teachers' beliefs and practices regarding the teaching of language in content learning. *Language Teaching Research, 15*(3), 325–342.

Wilkins, D. A. (1976). *Notional syllabuses.* Oxford, England: Oxford University Press.

Chapter 19

English for Academic Purposes through Content-Based Instruction

Jan Frodesen

||| A Glimpse into the EAP Classroom

Scenario 1: In a six-week unit on the theme of sustainability, titled "The Earth Needs Us," small groups of students, mostly international, interviewed other students belonging to campus organizations devoted to environmental concerns such as recycling, organic/community farming, and saving energy. Students used their recorded interviews and information from a variety of readings and class discussions and then drew on the language and rhetorical skills developed in class activities to write papers on their assigned topic. The groups also gave oral presentations on the results of their project to their classmates. Some students submitted essays written for this project that were ultimately selected for inclusion in a refereed anthology of first-year writing, *Starting Lines*, published annually by the campus's writing program (Gough, 2014). The course described took place in the English for Multilingual Students Program at the University of California, Santa Barbara.[1] The program offers four levels of Academic English, all of which confer degree credit and are preparatory to a required freshmen writing course. The theme-based courses focus primarily on developing students' academic reading and writing proficiency; however, with the growing population of international students entering as freshmen from their home countries, the courses also integrate needed academic speaking and listening skill development. While some instructors have developed a single theme across an entire ten-week quarter (e.g., issues in civility within different social contexts such as campus life and sports), most courses feature two themes varying from four to six weeks. Increasingly, these courses offer opportunities for students to interact with the campus community.

Scenario 2: At Kingsborough Community College of the City University of New York, a content-based EAP program offered full-time ESL students, primarily recent immigrants, the opportunity to enroll in an interdisciplinary program that linked an ESL course; a speech course; student development courses; and a content course in either psychology, sociology, history, or health and physical education. The students in the content-linked courses also worked with tutors in the Reading and Writing Center. A study of the effects of the CBI program, which compared students enrolled in the program over a period of five years with those who received ESL instruction that was not content linked, found that students in the content-based program performed better in subsequent ESL and developmental English courses. The study also indicated that the students in the content-linked program achieved better long-term academic success than did the ESL students not in the content-linked courses, as measured by overall grade point average, English proficiency tests, and retention and graduation rates (Song, 2006).

These two scenarios illustrate two of the most common applications of CBI in higher education contexts: the theme-based model and the adjunct or linked-course model. The first scenario, involving a theme-based content course, is an especially common organizing principle for EAP courses in both college preparatory programs, such as those offered by intensive English programs (IEPs) and community colleges, and college/university programs for matriculated students who are simultaneously taking courses across the disciplines. However, as this chapter will discuss, EAP and CBI are by no means synonymous, even in courses that use a theme-based approach.

CBI and EAP ||

In the inaugural issue of the *Journal of English for Academic Purposes (JEAP)* in 2002, Ken Hyland and Liz Hamp-Lyons cited the growing population worldwide of students needing to gain proficiency in English language academic discourses that has led to "a new field in the teaching of English as a Second/Foreign Language," developed over several decades: that of EAP (p. 1). Originally construed as a branch of English for Specific Purposes (ESP) (Master & Brinton, 1998), EAP has gained recognition as a field in and of itself, responding to rising demands for academic English instruction in countries where English is a first language, serving large immigrant populations; in former colonial territories, where English remains a second language and often the medium of instruction in secondary and post-secondary education; and in other countries throughout the world where scholars require knowledge of English to contribute to research in their disciplines (Flowerdew & Peacock, 2001). In recent years, both the dramatic increase in international students pursuing higher education in English-speaking countries and the growth of newly developed English-medium institutions in other countries reflect an even greater demand for EAP instruction (de Chazal, 2014).

Overviews of EAP generally define it in terms of its goals of helping learners to study or conduct research in English (Flowerdew & Peacock, 2001) and its scope in covering all areas of academic communication, including lectures, writing assignments, and various types of classroom interaction (Hyland, 2006). In their introduction to the first issue of *JEAP*, Hyland and Hamp-Lyons (2002) elaborate the primary goals of EAP as seeking "to provide insights into meanings of academic texts, into the demands placed by academic contexts on communicative behaviors, and into the pedagogic practices by which these behaviors can be developed" (p. 3). These goals reflect a more specific range of issues related to the learning and teaching of English than those with which many teachers of general English, including those in post-secondary education, have been concerned. Published articles in *JEAP* during the last decade reveal much attention to analyses of language and rhetorical structure of specific discourses within disciplines as well as EAP's close connections with a number of research fields in applied linguistics such as text analysis, genre analysis, and corpus linguistics.

The influences on EAP of a number of approaches, methods, and perspectives on the teaching of ESL, as well as of applied linguistics research areas, are discussed by de Chazal (2014). Noting that the significance of these influences varies depending on the EAP context, de Chazal highlights such early influences as general English language teaching—reminding us that many EAP teachers started out in general English language teaching—register analysis (especially language differences between scientific English and general English as noted elsewhere by Harwood and Petrić, 2014), and study skills. Later influences, extending from the 1990s and beyond, include genre analysis, systemic functional linguistics, U.S. L2 composition, and critical EAP. In this chapter, our consideration of such influences will, of course, be focused on their relevance to EAP classrooms, materials development, and teacher preparation concerned with CBI.

A final important distinction preliminary to the next section exploring CBI in EAP is that between "general" EAP (EGAP) and "specific" EAP (ESAP). Comparing content and coverage in these major branches of EAP, de Chazal (2014) identifies "subject-specific language" (p. 18) as the main feature that separates EGAP and ESAP, with its inclusion only in ESAP. In his discussion of EGAP, ESAP, and other ESP contexts, de Chazal mentions CLIL, stating that it differs from both EGAP and ESAP in its assessment of students' subject knowledge. In contrast to CBI, CLIL, as described by de Chazal, appears to apply primarily to courses in which acquiring content knowledge is the central focus, with language instruction used to teach content, as in the applications of Systemic Functional Linguistics to school genres in elementary and secondary schools (Schleppegrell, 2004; Schleppegrell & de Oliveira, 2006). (For further discussion of CLIL as a type of CBI, see Dalton-Puffer, this volume.)

CBI in the EAP Classroom |||

As previously discussed, CLIL has been distinguished from EAP due to its focus on learning content through language rather than academic language learning through content. Other models of CBI (see Brinton & Snow, this volume) have long played a role in both college preparatory programs and college/university ESL curricula. For example, theme-based units, as discussed at the beginning of this chapter, may be informed by CBI principles when the content is sustained to some extent, when development of more than one of the skill areas—reading, writing, listening, speaking—is targeted, and when a good part of the language (grammar, vocabulary, and lexico-grammatical patterns focused on in instruction) derives from language features in the content. Some commercially produced content-based materials for EAP offer a wide range of academic strategies, vocabulary, and grammar derived solely from content, including readings and authentic videotaped lectures, and provide students ample opportunities for practice in all skill areas (reading, writing, speaking, listening). However, such comprehensive treatment is not necessary for developing an EAP course informed by CBI. As with all pedagogically sound curriculum development, students' needs and contexts will determine which areas should receive the most focus. For example, during the last decade or so, the tremendous increase in international students entering first-year writing programs in the U.S. has caused administrators and instructors to shift the balance of skill areas to include more explicit and varied types of academic listening and speaking tasks in courses that had been primarily developed as writing classes. Unlike many multilingual immigrant students, whose primary academic English needs involve reading and writing, international freshmen often require multi-skills academic English support to adapt successfully to their studies across the curriculum in English-medium institutions.

Brinton (this volume) has clarified the relationship between ESP and CBI as not one of different approaches to be compared but rather, citing Master (1997), as occupying different levels in the hierarchy of ELT, with CBI serving as an effective type of syllabus for ESP courses. As a branch of ESP, EAP also makes frequent use of content-based materials; indeed, the theme-based model in particular has been effectively used in many reading, composition, and multi-skills programs in higher education (Basturkmen, 2010). Thus, in considering the "evolving architecture of CBI," as Brinton and Snow (this volume) put it, the questions we might raise in regard to EAP is how some recent approaches to EAP influenced by research and pedagogy in applied linguistics and composition can inform the development of CBI course materials, syllabi, and teacher preparation.

Genre-Based EAP and CBI

In *Genre and Second Language Writing,* Hyland (2004) defines *genre* as "a term for grouping texts together, representing how writers typically use language to respond to recurring situations" (p. 4). Since the early 1990s, genre has occupied a central role in the research and teaching of academic writing, with authentic academic content as a primary source of study. Hyon (1996) cites genre's diverse applications to the fields of rhetoric, composition studies, and ESP, among others, and notes not only the rapid growth of genre scholarship but its ever-changing nature; these ongoing changes in the concept of *genre* have, according to Hyon, resulted in challenges for scholars and teachers to understand its meaning. Hyon examines three approaches to genre and their applications to language teaching: ESP analyses, New Rhetoric studies, and Australian genre theories. Of the three approaches, she states that EAP instruction has been primarily influenced by ESP genre researchers in applied linguistics and linguistics (e.g., Bhatia, 1993; Dudley-Evans, 1994; Flowerdew, 1993; Swales, 1990, among many others), who focused on identifying the dominant organizational patterns, or *structural moves*, of academic and professional writing. With the development of corpus linguistics analysis, EAP genre studies have investigated form-function relationships of lexico-grammatical features in genres and text-types within and across disciplines (Flowerdew, 2004; Hyland, 2005). ESP genre studies have been distinguished from the New Rhetoric approach by their focus on linguistic and structural features in contrast to the macro-level approach of rhetoric-composition studies, which investigates genres as "sites of typified social action" (Aull, 2015). Despite their focus on textual features, ESP researchers have also described genres in terms of communicative events and the expectations of discourse communities. For example, Swales (2004), found significant differences in the structure of the PhD dissertation's *prospectus* or *proposal*, part of what he calls a "chain of genres" serially ordered as stages in the dissertation. He observed that in some cases, the required prospectus might be a lengthy document of perhaps 100 pages, sometimes with rigid guidelines dictated by a funding agency. In other cases, the expectations for the prospectus could be simply an introduction followed by a literature review. Some might include a timetable detailing what has been completed and what is to be done, and others not. In short, neither written nor spoken genres can be described simply in terms of structural templates but rather as types of communicative events situated in and defined by contexts involving readers, writers, and purposes.

Clearly, for advanced students studying academic English in specific disciplines, authentic content-based materials would constitute a significant part of their studies. Instructors can guide students in analyzing and discussing language features, organizational structures, audiences, and purposes of written texts representing instances of genres in their disciplines, such as the research article, conference abstract, thesis, or dissertation. In addition, the language and structures of academic spoken genres such as lectures and conference presentations can be examined, as well as the structure and content of supporting visual materials such as PowerPoint slides. In classes with students from a variety of academic fields, students can identify shared features of these genres as well as those features that may differ across the disciplines.

To date, much of the focus on genre analysis in applied linguistics research has concerned graduate and professional written genres. Johns (2009), however, argues that "genre awareness should be the principal goal of novice undergraduate EAP courses" (p. 49). She distinguishes *genre awareness* (involving active exploration by students of academic tasks and texts across the curriculum) from *genre acquisition*, with its focus on learning templates such as the five-paragraph essay or other text artifacts that do not reflect authentic writing. Based on findings from a study of undergraduate writing tasks (McLish & Johns, 2006), Johns asserts that, rather than focusing solely on the formulaic academic essay, students in EAP classes should be reading, discussing, and responding to a variety of texts for multiple purposes. Response tasks might include summarizing, analyzing, synthesizing, or identifying an argument, all of which could involve selecting and citing source materials. Such a goal is certainly compatible with a CBI syllabus. For example, in Brinton, Frodesen, Holten, Jensen, and Repath-Martos (1997), a content-based biology unit on the proximate and ultimate causes of animal behavior included a scientific report on dispersion of ground squirrels, an academic text passage on behavioral ecology, and a personal observation of insect life by naturalist Annie Dillard, as well as an essay on altruism by sociobiologist Lewis Thomas. Pre-writing tasks included summarizing research hypotheses from the science report and analyzing the costs and benefits of behaviors. After watching authentic videotaped excerpts of lectures from the course on which the unit was based, students analyzed types of discourse markers that signaled key information.

The five-paragraph essay, often referred to as a "school genre" not representative of authentic texts, has certainly not disappeared from American first-year composition instruction at the post-secondary level (a review of current textbooks intended for second language writers attests to its prominence); increasingly, instructors trained in EAP approaches and compositionists are sensitive to the variety of written and spoken genres that undergraduate students encounter across the disciplines. A content-based approach allows instructors to select a range of text types connected by a theme for undergraduate or graduate students or students in college preparatory programs, not only to provide content for writing tasks but to explore structure and language, guided by awareness of audience and purpose. Texts for both reading and writing could include science reports, textbook excerpts, fiction, poetry, and journal reflections. Even the email message as a form of academic and professional as well as personal communication may be the focus of instruction. For example, in the sustainability unit described at the beginning of this chapter, students reviewed principles and polite expressions for making requests in email messages as the groups composed messages to ask for interviews with students in campus environmental organizations.

While teachers should introduce a variety of genres and text types in CBI-based EAP instruction, the essay remains one of the genre families found most frequently across major disciplinary areas at the undergraduate level (Nesi & Gardner, 2012). Thus, it is still an important genre family for reading and writing focus in preparatory and undergraduate EAP. Nesi and Gardner's (2012) taxonomy of six different essay types and their structures offers EAP instructors a useful framework to engage students in analysis of authentic readings across the curriculum and for scaffolding appropriate writing assignments.

In adjunct courses for undergraduate students who have declared specific majors (ESAP), much of the content may depend on a linked course, which typically offers some variety of written genres for students to analyze. But even when a linked course includes only a few discipline-based genres for the assigned reading, teachers can draw on course textbooks as sources for analysis of forms related to functional and rhetorical purposes. Frodesen (2015) describes an upper-division writing course activity in which international students majoring in economics explored examples of interactional register constructions in their microeconomics textbook, such as the use of frequent rhetorical questions to introduce topics, of exclamatory sentences to emphasize points, and of second-person pronouns to directly address the student reader—features that seldom, if ever, would be found in published research articles in their field and would be inappropriate in research-based writing assignments (but which seem to be increasingly common in textbooks for undergraduate students). PowerPoint lectures and other materials posted on course websites, while not considered genres, can, of course, also serve as sources of analysis and discussion for EAP courses linked to content courses.

Corpus-Based Approaches and Content-Based EAP

As discussed, in applied linguistics research, academic genre studies and corpus analyses are closely interrelated, with many investigations of specific genres utilizing corpus linguistics to identify recurring language patterns and functional systems (such as interactional grammar employed to engage readers). These scholarly research findings, combined with the access that EAP instructors, materials developers, and students now have to online and paper corpus-based resources, have greatly helped to inform language instruction in EAP content-based courses and to encourage students to be investigators of language use and autonomous learners. (See Cortes, this volume, for further discussion of the role of corpus linguistics in CBI.)

A critical need for many EAP students developing advanced academic language proficiency is to improve their receptive knowledge and productive use of vocabulary. According to Folse (2004), many students list academic vocabulary as their number one obstacle to improvement. Recent research in vocabulary acquisition emphasizes the multiple characteristics that learners need to know about a word, including such features as its different meanings, its register, its relative frequency, the words with which it commonly occurs (collocations), its word forms, and its grammatical environments (Nation, 2011; Zimmerman & Schmitt, 2005). Frodesen and Wald (2016) explicitly demonstrate for students and teachers how readily available corpus-based resources can help students explore all of these characteristics and, as a result, select vocabulary that will be most valuable in their repertoire of linguistic resources or that will best fit their immediate contexts when engaged in academic writing tasks.

For example, students can consult a learner's dictionary to discover through corpus-based examples whether a noun is count or non-count or both, whether a verb is used in a transitive or intransitive context or both, and which prepositions typically follow specific verbs in intransitive contexts (e.g., *contribute to, prohibit from*). They can learn whether a word is formal or informal register (e.g., formal register *abundant* as contrasted to informal *tons of* to describe a large amount). By consulting corpus-based collocations dictionaries (such as *Ozdic.com* and the *Oxford Collocations Dictionary for Students of English*), which show words that tend to appear together in academic texts (e.g., adjective + noun combinations), students not only expand their vocabulary but can also select appropriate modifiers for specific words. For example, as shown in Figure 19.1, the word *evidence* in the *Oxford Collocations Dictionary* offers the same adjective collocations with a variety of meanings.

Figure 19.1. Adjective + *evidence* as shown in *Exploring Options* (Frodesen & Wald, University of Michigan Press, 2016, p. 14); data from *Oxford Collocations Dictionary*

ADJ.
abundant, ample, considerable, extensive, plentiful, substantial, widespread | growing | clear, compelling, conclusive, irrefutable, overwhelming, persuasive, positive, powerful, solid, striking, strong, unambiguous, unequivocal | insufficient, scant | concrete, direct, firm, first-hand, objective, tangible
- convincing, decisive, good, hard, incontrovertible, adequate | flimsy, inadequate
The figures provide concrete evidence of the bank's claim to provide the best service.

As this entry shows, while some of the adjectives might collocate with many other nouns, others, such as *scant,* are more limited. And quite a few of the options shown (e.g., *irrefutable, striking*) are likely to be ones that student writers, even native English speakers, rarely use. It goes without saying, perhaps, that EAP instructors can play an important role in helping students learn how to use these valuable resources for work in their content courses as well as in their English courses.

As shown in Figure 19.2, using a concordancer such as COCA (Davies, 2008), students can investigate text samples of word use to check grammatical environments, another important characteristic of word knowledge. For example, given this sentence with a verb error *The high cost of living dwindled the student's savings*, students can notice from COCA concordance examples of the word in context that *dwindled* cannot be used with a noun object following it and that further, it is often followed by the preposition *to*.

In addition to using corpus-based resources for investigating features of word use, EAP instructors and their students can use these resources to explore contexts of use for functional vocabulary such as cohesive devices, reporting verbs in referencing sources, or words and phrases for expressing causation or change of state. As one example, students in one of the author's graduate writing classes were discussing logical connector prepositions such

Figure 19.2: Excerpt from Table 1.8, Context Results for *dwindled*, as shown in *Exploring Options* (Frodesen & Wald, University of Michigan Press, 2016, p. 21); data from COCA

MAG	MotherJones	64 percent of newborn American males were cut. By 2006, that number had **dwindled** to 56 percent. Immigration trends may be partially responsible for the drop-off: Worldwide
MAG	Redbook	've been married for 18 years, and my connection to my husband has slowly **dwindled** down to nothing. I'd always been hopeful that things could get better,
MAG	Astronomy	majority of the houses there feature personal observatories. As the available land at ASV **dwindled**, Turner began acquiring land across the state line in New Mexico. His second
MAG	CountryLiving	the final nail into Sharon Springs' coffin. By 1960, the population had **dwindled** to about 350 residents. Cut to 2008, when Brent Ridge, a physician-turned-brand
MAG	MilitaryHistory	the disaster of the Battle of the Masts and as their holdings in western Europe **dwindled**, they chiefly concentrated on defending the Aegean. In 904, Leo of Tripoli
MAG	ScienceNews	today a densely forested, frigid swath of northern Europe. Forest plants and animals **dwindled** during ancient winters, the scientists say. Crucially, though, geological analyses indicate
NEWS	Houston	during the same period totaling $107 billion, records show. U.S. Coast Guard spending **dwindled** from $7 million in 1992 to just $600,000 last year. # Two other agencies
NEWS	Denver	for Rockies spring games in Tucson has been unimpressive for 18 years, and crowds **dwindled** even as the Rockies became a World Series participant. The numbers were down 6
NEWS	SanFranChron	the San Francisco police drug lab was in crisis. # Its overwhelmed staff had **dwindled** to two technicians, down from six just a few months before - and one
NEWS	NYTimes	over 1.7 billion yen in debt. The attractions fell into disrepair. Tourist numbers **dwindled**. # Now, the town of 7,000 is desperate to attract new visitors.
NEWS	Denver	symptomatic sabbatical issue - this nationally constituted system is one in which public funds have **dwindled**. # In short, it's not the big bad English professor who cheats
NEWS	Denver	private insurance products once covered religious nonmedical health care institutions, but the number has **dwindled** to a handful, Boettiger said. # " What we want, " Jones
NEWS	Denver	to protect the environment in the face of virulent industry opposition that now has largely **dwindled**. # He engineered many incentives for solar- and wind-energy development, and successfully pushed
ACAD	Bioscience	from very recent times. In 2000, the San Miguel population of island fox **dwindled** to only 15 animals, and all of them were removed from the wild and
ACAD	Bioscience	(a species absent from San Miguel) boomed as the local population of foxes **dwindled**. All this demonstrates the fox's powerful role in structuring island ecosystems. Other

as *due to, on account of, given,* and *in light of* for creating cohesion across sentences in combination with reference forms and classifier nouns (e.g., *given the conclusions of the panel, in light of the proposed solutions*). They asked for more information about the connector *in light of,* which none of them had ever used. By consulting COCA's academic register, the class found multiple text examples of this connector (e.g., *in light of the circumstances, in light of this objection, in light of these considerations*), prompting further discussion of what kinds of reference forms (*the, this, these*) and classifier nouns[2] co-occurred with this connector and other features of the contexts. Clearly, this activity created greater understanding of this connector in use as well as its value in creating cohesion, in contrast to the typical listings of single word or phrase result connectors (e.g., *therefore, consequently*) in most grammar books.

In summary, whether used for pre-course materials development or spontaneous in-class investigations (assuming internet access), corpus-based resources offer numerous ways of helping students notice language in authentic content and develop expanded lexico-grammatical knowledge of academic English in content-based materials.

Critical EAP and CBI

With ever increasing globalization and the spread of English as a lingua franca, researchers and practitioners have recognized the need for critical approaches to ESP, and, by extension, EAP, giving attention not only to preparation for higher education and the workplace but, as Master (1998) urges, to individual self-betterment.

"Common to all critical approaches," as Benesch (2001) explains, "is interrogating assumptions on which theory and practice are based" (p. xvii). In the case of EAP, critical theorists have interrogated the complex sociopolitical contexts of teaching and learning in English for academic purposes, in particular the power relationships between institutional purposes and students' educational goals. More specifically, Benesch (2009) describes the role of critical EAP, or CEAP, as exploring academic genres and classroom activities "in relation to EAP students' and teachers' complex and overlapping social identities: class, race, gender, ethnicity, age, and so on" (p. 81).

Needs analysis has long been an essential principle of EAP curriculum design, traditionally concerned with identifying learners' future needs in academic settings (skills and assignments) and assessing their current proficiencies related to these needs prior to creating objectives and instructional activities (Charles & Pecorari, 2016). Such analyses typically precede actual implementation of a course or curriculum. Benesch (2001) points out some of the problems of generalizing pre-course needs analyses to EAP courses linked to content courses, citing Johns' (1990) recommendation that EAP courses need to be sensitive to the ongoing contexts of the specific content classes to which they are linked. In short, the needs of students in any given class and context cannot be predetermined in their entirety but rather must be refined and negotiated as an ongoing process.

To give students a more participatory role as active members of the academic communities they have joined, Benesch has proposed that needs analysis be accompanied by *rights analysis,* in which students are invited to question institutional policies and instructional requirements within their local contexts and given the opportunity to negotiate change: "Needs analysis is used to study the linguistic and cognitive challenges EAP students face, yet the findings are interrogated rather than unconditionally accepted" (p. 62). Likewise, the instructors of linked courses adopting a CEAP approach do not merely carry out requirements of a content course to which they are connected but, when appropriate, modify the structure of the EAP course to address content or structure issues. Benesch emphasizes that *rights* in CEAP, as a supplement to needs analysis, represent neither a set of demands nor entitlement to rights but rather a conceptual framework for raising questions about power relationships, a framework that assumes each local situation is unique in its possibilities for effecting change.

CBI is prominent in many examples of CEAP put into practice. As an EAP instructor for a course linked to a psychology course, Benesch (1996, 2001) discusses her implementation of a reading/writing unit on anorexia, a topic briefly mentioned in the content course textbook, in order to counter what she felt was a lack of attention to women's psychology. Acknowledging that this assignment was teacher-imposed and not student-selected, Benesch describes the opportunities students were given through journal writing to express their resistance to the topic (by male students). She notes that the accessibility of the novel she assigned on the topic helped some less proficient students better connect to the course content; other students were able to relate the more in-depth treatment of the topic to their educational goals and personal challenges in their lives. In another EAP course linked to a social science class, Benesch instructed students to select their own topics for a research paper. Two topics in particular, domestic violence and crime in dating violence, led to extended debate and discussion among students regarding their beliefs and values on these issues. Reflecting on both courses, Benesch compares the advantages and disadvantages of teacher-generated and student-selected themes in realizing CEAP principles and considers how, in retrospect, she might have re-conceived her introduction and treatment of the anorexia topic to allow students greater participation in ongoing syllabus design.

Another example of the intersection of CEAP and CBI is discussed by Chun (2009). In this case, dialogic interrogation of the topic of a reading unit during an EAP class in a university IEP was triggered by what the instructor observed as an uncharacteristic lack of engagement among a group of international students. In attempting to lead the class in a discussion of the unit's theme, the importance of emotional intelligence in workplace success, Chun observed that his "normally talkative, enthusiastic class quickly ran out of things to say or even stayed sullenly silent" (p. 118). One student commented that the notion of emotional intelligence in the workplace was not relevant in the culture of her home country. After considering the resistance of his students to the textbook's unqualified acceptance of emotional intelligence (as expressed by the questions asking how people could improve this trait, and how employers could teach the "skills" related to emotional intelligence), Chun returned to the classroom with a plan to elicit alternative positions, starting with students' analysis of a cartoon in the textbook featuring a brilliant but emotionally inept male scientist and his friendly, supposedly emotionally intelligent female colleague to spark discussion. Through this activity, students were invited to challenge assumptions and framing of the concepts of the unit, after which they collaborated in creating a list of negative elements and consequences of emotional intelligence, which presumably they could then compare to positive ones presented in the textbook unit.

As these examples suggest, it is hard to imagine CEAP apart from content of one kind or another, whether in an English course linked to a content course or in a theme-based course. Other examples of CEAP intersecting with content could involve negotiating the content delivery in a linked course, such as incorporating more opportunities for interaction in the structure of a large lecture class (as described in Benesch, 2001) or perhaps negotiating writing requirements in either a language or content course. Obviously, CBI would also be relevant to CEAP courses whose syllabi are genre-based. The examples here indicate that critical approaches to content in EAP courses may be implemented at various stages in a syllabus and may arise spontaneously in response to student resistance to assumed values underlying course content.

Underlying Principles ‖

The first scenario in this chapter described a theme-based first-year composition course on the theme of sustainability designed for multilingual writers. Theme-based courses are a very common model of CBI in EGAP classes in IEPs and freshmen courses. A look at the development of this course and its materials and activities reveal underlying principles central to CBI in EAP, as illustrated in Table 19.1.

Research Agenda ‖

Given that EAP is often viewed as falling under the more general category of ESP, some of the areas of research suggested by Brinton in this volume are relevant to EAP courses/ curricula that embrace CBI, especially those involving courses linked with content courses. Specifically, the effectiveness of a CBI syllabus in EAP courses remains an area for investigation. In the second scenario at the beginning of this chapter, Song's (2006) five-year study found improved performance in subsequent English courses and greater academic success over the long term among students in an ESL program with courses linked to content courses as compared to ESL students not enrolled in the linked courses. Further research on the effectiveness of ESAP linked-course contexts is needed as well as ways in which these types of courses may better address students' goals through greater student participation and agency in the ongoing development of their course assignments and through fostering meaningful communication channels between multilingual students and faculty of content courses, as suggested by Benesch (2001).

As this chapter has discussed, scholars in linguistics and applied linguistics in the past several decades have produced a rich body of research identifying the linguistic features and discourse patterns that characterize genres and text types within and across disciplines. This continues to be a significant area for future research, aided by growing and diverse corpora for analyses, especially online corpora, with obvious applications to EAP course and curriculum development utilizing CBI principles. Of course, as the sociopolitical contexts and the members of academic institutions and disciplines change and evolve (especially with increasing internationalization), so do the texts produced within and for them.

With the shifting populations in EAP/first-year composition programs designed for undergraduate students in English-speaking countries, another research direction could

Table 19.1: Underlying Principles in a Theme-Based EGAP Course

Observations	Underlying Principles
1. The instructor submits a proposal and receives funding from the university Academic Senate and the Chancellor's Academic Sustainability Workgroup to develop a content-based course that infuses concepts on sustainability.	As described by the university funding sponsors, the theme of sustainability "offers a vision of progress that integrates immediate and longer-term needs, local and global needs, and regards social, economic and environmental needs as inseparable and interdependent components of human progress" (Academic Sustainability Workgroup, 2015). This theme thus speaks to authentic, significant issues on both local and global levels.
2. In introducing the "Sustainability Project," the instructor informs students that the purpose is to give them the opportunity to find out about campus student organizations devoted to environmental and sustainability concerns.	Authentic tasks should form the core of the EAP curriculum. In this case, a central task in which students will be engaged is primary research via campus interviews with students who belong to campus environmental organizations. Developing knowledge and skills in primary research is an important university-level activity.
3. Students engage in reading assignments concerning environmental issues, ranging from specific topics such as "the high price of cheap food" to broader ones, such as Jared Diamond's (2003) claims about the collapse of societies that have disregarded environmental problems. Prior to discussions, they complete guides that include critical reading responses, academic vocabulary development, and grammar-noticing tasks. In the reading guides, students are asked to focus on both general and topic-specific key vocabulary, to research additional information on the internet, to use reporting verbs and summary words to cite sources, and to use explanatory sentences to follow quotations. Noticing tasks ask students to identify cohesion devices such as reference words and logical connectors.	EAP tasks should provide students with tools for reading critically and should incorporate sequenced steps in building the language skills needed to successfully complete major assignments. (See Appendix 17A in Stillwell, this volume, for an example of a multi-step writing assignment.)
4. Students in small groups arrange to meet with students in campus organizations involved in sustainability projects such as recycling and creating a greenhouse/garden. In preparation for the interviews, the instructor provides groups questions to consider asking and has them add their own questions or modify the ones suggested. Students are instructed to record the interview with permission, to summarize responses to the questions, and to submit a written document. Each group later gives a brief presentation of their interview findings to the class.	In addition to helping students develop the important academic skill of primary research, the interview activity offers international students an opportunity to connect with others in their campus community and to learn more about campus organizations. This objective addresses an institutional goal of better integrating its growing population of undergraduate international students into campus life. The interviews as well as the groups' subsequent oral presentations in class provide authentic, meaningful speaking and listening practice. The write-up of the interviews gives students practice in a written genre other than the academic essay.

Table 19.1 (*continued*)

Observations	Underlying Principles
5. As a culminating assignment, students write individual papers on a sustainability issue, drawing on relevant assigned readings, supplemental readings, internet research, and their interview reports. They are asked to summarize, describe, and evaluate information. Students are encouraged to submit their papers for possible publication in *Starting Lines*, an annual anthology of writing by students in first-year composition classes published by the campus Writing Program. During each of the two years the instructor has taught this unit, several sustainability essays have been accepted for publication.	In their final papers for the project, students synthesize information from multiple sources, including written and spoken texts. They are expected to incorporate the language and rhetorical skills and strategies they have practiced through the prior reading and writing assignments as well as class discussions. Students' submissions of their papers to the campus *Starting Lines* publication offers an opportunity for an expanded audience for their work, especially that of their peers. Each year, multiple sections of first-year composition classes use *Starting Lines* as part of course materials for reading and analysis.

involve exploring the ways in which thematic models of CBI can be adapted to address the language learning needs of international students as well as multilingual immigrant students. As noted in this chapter, many university-level EAP programs, especially those at research universities, have focused for decades largely on reading and writing development, with academic speaking and listening typically considered skill areas for emphasis in pre-university intensive programs or in non-credit coursework in two-year colleges. More recently, many entering international freshmen enrolled concurrently in content classes need not only intensive writing instruction but also specialized English instruction in academic speaking and listening in order to participate effectively in classroom and campus life. In addition, content-based themes drawing on authentic readings and other materials produced in English-speaking countries may need adaptations or supplementary materials that allow international students to draw on their knowledge and backgrounds in ways that contribute global perspectives—that is, materials, assignments, and classroom activities that transcend the often simplistic "compare your home country and the country where you are studying" topics common in many ESL textbooks.

Another area for further research concerns the important and persistent challenge for instructors in EAP classes using a CBI syllabus of how to balance language and content emphases and what the sources of CBI grammar and vocabulary instruction should be. Brinton and Holten's (2001) survey of EAP instructors attempting to achieve this balance raised a number of issues still quite relevant today. Primary among these issues is the extent to which language topics should—and can—be "mined" from course content (i.e., in contrast to providing students supplementary instruction not directly tied to content). This issue is clearly tied to the significant time and effort needed to develop language materials from course content. This seems an excellent area for collaborative action research among instructors working together in EAP programs. With current internet repositories for sharing information, including university-owned cloud storage, instructors might investigate how best to develop, organize, and maintain a bank of content-based grammar and vocabulary activities.

Finally, future research could further investigate methods and effectiveness of integrating online resources into content-based EAP language instruction, including corpus-based learner dictionaries, collocation dictionaries, and concordancers.

APPLYING WHAT YOU LEARNED
Questions and Tasks

1. De Chazal (2014) cites a number of influences on the development of English for academic purposes. Of those noted in this chapter, which do you think are most relevant to instructional materials for content-based EAP?

2. Are you familiar with any commercially produced content-based EAP materials? What proficiency level(s) were these texts produced for? How is content used in these materials? What are the advantages and disadvantages of using commercially produced EAP materials?

3. Many college-preparatory and college-level EAP content-based writing courses in the U.S. focus on the essay and rhetorical modes for developing it (e.g., narration, comparison/contrast, cause/effect, argument) for both reading and writing instruction. After reading this chapter, critique this approach. How would you decide what other types of reading and writing assignments to add?

4. What makes CEAP especially relevant to EAP courses that are content-based? Do you agree with Sarah Benesch that students' rights are an important part of any EAP course? What are the potentially positive outcomes? What factors might create challenges or difficulties for an EAP instructor?

5. Consider topics that could be the focus of a theme-based EAP unit. What considerations guided your choices? Choose a piece of extended writing from a textbook, an anthology, or a media source such as a magazine or newspaper article that you think could be part of the theme-based EAP unit. What genres or text types does the extended writing lend itself to? Identify and discuss vocabulary and grammatical features you see that could be focused on for either noticing activities in the reading, production exercises, or both.

6. Choose two to three words or expressions that serve a similar function such as logical connectors for cohesion, phrases to introduce topics (e.g., *as regards…, as for…*), or reporting verbs used to reference sources (e.g., *reports, states, suggests*). Investigate their frequency and grammatical environments in one or more registers (e.g., spoken, journalism, academic writing) using COCA or a concordance system of your choice.

Acknowledgments

I am grateful to my colleague Judy Gough for sharing with me her course development process, activities, and materials for the content-based sustainability unit described in this chapter. I also thank the editors of this volume for their many thoughtful comments and suggestions on earlier chapter versions.

ENDNOTES

1. The term *multilingual* describes speakers who use two or more languages, with at least one of them being the first language learned during early childhood. The term has been widely used in the fields of applied linguistics, rhetoric and composition, TESOL, and education, especially (though not exclusively) in reference to students who have been educated from a young age in a language other than their first language. In the United States, these students have been referred to as Generation 1.5 learners (Harklau, Losey, & Siegal, 1999).
2. Classifier nouns, also called summary words (Swales & Feak, 2012), and signaling nouns (Flowerdew, 2010) are frequently used in academic writing and speaking to summarize prior information. Some examples are *approach, concept, development, issue, possibility, result,* and *trend.* For a comprehensive list of classifier nouns, see Frodesen and Wald (2016).

REFERENCES

Academic Sustainability Workgroup. (2015). *Turning over a new leaf: Greening your course.* Santa Barbara, CA: Author. Retrieved from http://grants.id.ucsb.edu/sites/default/files/NewLeafGrant_CallforProposals_2.pdf

Aull, L. (2015, Spring). Linguistic attention in rhetorical genre studies and first year writing. *Composition Forum, 31.* Retrieved from http://compositionforum.com/issue/31/linguistic-attention.php

Basturkmen, H. (2010). *Developing courses in English for specific purposes.* New York, NY: Palgrave Macmillan.

Benesch, S. (1996). Needs analysis and curriculum development in EAP: An example of a critical approach. *TESOL Quarterly, 30,* 723–738.

Benesch, S. (2001). *Critical English for academic purposes: Theory, politics, and practice.* Mahwah, NJ: Erlbaum.

Benesch, S. (2009). Theorizing and practicing critical English for academic purposes. *Journal of English for Academic Purposes, 8,* 81–85.

Bhatia, V. K. (1993). *Analysing genre: Language in professional settings.* London, England: Longman.

Biber, D., Johannson, G., Leech, S., Conrad, S., & Finegan, E. (1999). *The Longman grammar of spoken and written English.* London, England: Longman.

Brinton, D. M., & Holten, C. (2001). Does the emperor have no clothes? A re-examination of grammar in content-based instruction. In J. Flowerdew & M. Peacock (Eds.), *Research perspectives on English for academic purposes* (pp. 239–251). Cambridge, England: Cambridge University Press.

Brinton, D., Frodesen, J., Holten, C., Jensen, L., & Repath-Martos, L. (1997). *Insights 2: A content-based approach to academic preparation.* White Plains, NY: Longman.

Charles, M., & Pecorari, D. (2016). *Introducing English for academic purposes.* New York, NY: Routledge.

Chun, C. W. (2009). Contesting neoliberal discourses in EAP: Critical praxis in an EAP classroom. *Journal of English for Academic Purposes, 8,* 111–120.

Davies, M. (2008). *The corpus of contemporary American English: 450 million words,* 1990–present. Retrieved from http://corpus.byu.edu/coca

de Chazal, E. (2014). *English for academic purposes*. Oxford, England: Oxford University Press.

Dudley-Evans, T. (1994). Variations in the discourse patterns favoured by different disciplines and their pedagogical implications. In J. Flowerdew (Ed.), *Academic listening: Research perspectives* (pp. 146–158). Cambridge, England: Cambridge University Press.

Diamond, J. (2003, June). The last Americans: Environmental collapse and the end of civilization. *Harper's Magazine*, 43–51.

Flowerdew, J. (1993). An educational, or process, approach to the teaching of professional genres. *ELT Journal, 47*, 305–316.

Flowerdew, J. (2010). Use of signaling nouns across L1 and L2 writer corpora. *International Journal of Corpus Linguistics 15.1*, 36–55. doi:10:1075/ijcl.15.1.02flo

Flowerdew, J., & Peacock M. (2001). Issues in EAP: A preliminary perspective. In J. Flowerdew & M. Peacock (Eds.), *Research perspectives on English for academic purposes* (pp. 8–24). Cambridge, England: Cambridge University Press.

Flowerdew, L. (2004). The argument for using English specialized corpora to understand academic and professional language. In U. Connor & T. Upton (Eds.), *Discourse in the professions: Perspectives from corpus linguistics* (pp. 11–33). Amsterdam, The Netherlands: Benjamins.

Folse, K. (2004). Myth 1: Teaching vocabulary is not the writing teacher's job. In J. Reid (Ed.), *Writing myths: Applying second language research to classroom teaching* (pp. 1–18). Ann Arbor, MI: University of Michigan Press.

Frodesen, J. (2015). Beyond first-year composition: Academic English instructional support for international transfer students. *CATESOL Journal, 27*(2), 33–54.

Frodesen, J., & Wald, M. (2016). *Exploring options in academic writing: Effective vocabulary and grammar use*. Ann Arbor, MI: University of Michigan Press.

Gough, J. (2014, October). *Building bridges to the campus community through writing classes*. Paper presented at the UC Writing Programs Conference, San Diego, CA.

Harklau, L., Losey, K., & Siegal, M. (Eds.). (1999). *Generation 1.5 meets college composition: Issues in the teaching of writing to U.S.-educated learners of ESL*. Mahwah, NJ: Erlbaum.

Harwood, H., & Petrić, B. (2013). English for academic purposes. In J. Simpson (Ed.), *The Routledge handbook of applied linguistics* (pp. 243–258). New York, NY: Routledge.

Hyland, K. (2004). *Genre and second language writing*. Ann Arbor, MI: University of Michigan Press.

Hyland, K. (2005). *Metadiscourse*. London, England: Continuum.

Hyland, K. (2006). *English for academic purposes: An advanced resource book*. New York, NY: Routledge.

Hyland, K., & Hamp-Lyons, L. (2002). EAP: Issues and directions. *Journal of English for Academic Purposes, 1*, 1–12.

Hyon, S. (1996). Genre in three traditions: Implications for ESL. *TESOL Quarterly, 30*, 683–722.

Johns, A. M. (1990). Coherence as a cultural phenomenon: Employing ethnographic principles in the academic milieu. In U. Connor & A. M. Johns (Eds.), *Coherence in writing: Research and pedagogical perspectives* (pp. 209–226). Alexandria, VA: TESOL.

Johns, A. M. (2009). Tertiary undergraduate EAP: Problems and possibilities. In D. Belcher (Ed.), *English for specific purposes in theory and practice* (pp. 41–59). Ann Arbor, MI: University of Michigan Press.

Master, P. (1997, December). Content-based instruction vs. ESP. *TESOL Matters*, 10.

Master, P. (1998). Positive and negative aspects of the dominance of English. *TESOL Quarterly, 32*, 716–725.

Master, P., & Brinton, D. M. (1998). *New ways in English for specific purposes*. Alexandria, VA: TESOL.

McLish, G., & Johns, A. M. (2006, March 10). *College writing tasks across the curriculum*. Paper presented at the College for All Conference, San Diego, CA.

Nation, I. S. P. (2001). *Learning vocabulary in another language*. Cambridge, England: Cambridge University Press.

Nesi, H., & Gardner, S. (2012). *Genres across the disciplines: Student writing in higher education*. Cambridge, England: Cambridge University Press.

Schleppegrell, M. (2004). *The language of schooling: A functional linguistics perspective*. Mahwah, NJ: Erlbaum.

Schleppegrell, M., & de Oliveira, L. (2006). An integrated language and content approach for history teachers. *Journal of English for Academic Purposes*, 5, 254–268.

Song, B. (2006). Content-based ESL instruction: Long-term effects and outcomes. *English for Specific Purposes*, 25, 420–437.

Swales, J. M. (1990). *Genre analysis: English in academic and research settings*. Cambridge, England: Cambridge University Press.

Swales, J. M. (2004). *Research genres: Exploration and applications*. Cambridge, England: Cambridge University Press.

Swales, J. M., & Feak, C. B. (2012). *Academic writing for graduate students* (3rd ed.). Ann Arbor, MI: University of Michigan Press.

Zimmerman, C., & Schmitt, N. (2005). Lexical questions to guide the teaching and learning of words. *The CATESOL Journal, 17*(1), 164–170.

Chapter **20**

Academic Language across Educational Levels in Content-Based Instruction

Marguerite Ann Snow, Jennifer McCormick, & Anna Osipova

||| A Glimpse into the Content-Based Classroom

Scenario 1: Ms. Sanchez is presenting a lesson on the Mayan society in her Grade 5 class-room. The learners in her class include native speakers of English, English learners (ELs) with varying levels of proficiency, and mainstreamed students from the special education program. At the start of the lesson, Ms. Sanchez previews the focus vocabulary. The textbook suggests pre-teaching four words: *ahau*, *nobles*, *commoners*, and *artisans*. As Ms. Sanchez reflects on her students' needs, she adds three more words to the list: *pyramid*, *social*, and *analyze*. Before she begins her presentation, she reads the words to the class, provides definitions, and gives examples and non-examples of the focus words' usage. She asks the class to read the words chorally. She reads a slide that briefly describes the Mayan social structure and then projects a colorful diagram on the board. She decides to review what she just taught and check for understanding.

Marissa and Carlos are the two EL students with an advanced intermediate level of English proficiency. They understand and use conversational English without noticeable difficulties but struggle when it comes to academic language. Ms. Sanchez also knows that content-area instruction such as social studies is especially difficult for these two students and that they need a lot of scaffolding in academic reading and writing instruction. Therefore, her use of a visual representation of the social structure is strategic. She decides to check how well Marissa and Carlos comprehend the lesson.

Ms. Sanchez:	*[pointing to the graphic] Let's analyze this slide. Who is at the top of the Mayan social structure, Marissa?*
Marissa:	*The king?*
Ms. Sanchez:	*The king? What did the Mayans call their kings? [pointing to the preview vocabulary list on the word wall]. Let's read this word together:*

Students:	*Ahau!*
Ms. Sanchez:	*Yes, ahau! Marissa, I will begin the sentence, and you finish it for me: "At the very top of the Mayan social structure is…"*
Marissa:	*At the very top of the Mayan social structure is ahau, the king.*
Ms. Sanchez:	*Excellent! Then we have priests and nobles; notice the s at the end! It is a noun, and so we make it plural. Then, commoners and artisans. And then at the bottom we have the slaves and the servants. This is the Mayan social pyramid. Who recognizes the word pyramid?*
Carlos:	*Pyramid is like a triangle.*
Ms. Sanchez:	*Yes, it looks like a triangle and in math it means 3D triangle. But here in history it means a social structure that has very few people at the top. We're going to talk about the elite class. Elite means a very small special group. This was only 10 percent of the population. That's a very small percentage. This class has all the social, religious, and political power. Imagine 100 percent, and 10 percent are at the top and everybody else is at the bottom.*

Ms. Sanchez's choice of focus vocabulary is determined by several considerations. She does not want to limit her students to learning only content-area specific words suggested by the textbook (i.e., *ahau*, *nobles*), but rarely encountered across the curriculum. In addition, she wants to include some general academic words (e.g., *analyze*) that her students will come across in several curricular areas. She also knows that polysemous words (words with multiple meanings, such as *pyramid* in this lesson) present a challenge for students, so she contrasts the meaning of *pyramid* in math with the way the word is used in social studies. In her lesson, Ms. Sanchez supports her students' academic language development at the word, sentence, and discourse levels, which she hopes will lead to better reading comprehension and more sophisticated essays.

Scenario 2: In a sheltered high school social studies classroom, Ms. Rodriquez asks her students to write a speech that ends with a call to action. The students in her class have been in the U.S. for about one month to roughly two years. Ms. Rodriquez has been teaching social studies for two years and is bilingual in English and Spanish. She provides the students with models of speeches by Martin Luther King and Cesar Chavez and instructs her class to think about what features of the language make these speeches convincing.

One student writes with clear passion for the passage of the DREAM Act, legislation that grants students who came to the U.S. as children a chance to become citizens. His speech reflects an ability to articulate an idea and provide supporting evidence for that idea. The writing also reflects the use of complex vocabulary, which demonstrates that the student knows quite a bit about the topic because he reads articles about immigration policy. However, the writer still needs to revise his speech for organizational coherence and syntax. Several grammatical errors may stem from language transfer. While other students in the class revise their speeches with peers, the teacher confers with the writer. During their conference, she compares sentence structures in English and Spanish, noting that in Spanish, adjectives must correspond to the subject. If the subject is plural, the adjective should reflect plurality. She explicitly says, "This rule governs Spanish syntax, but does not hold true in English." By initiating a discussion about differences in syntax across the two languages, Ms. Rodriguez hopes to heighten her student's metalinguistic awareness of how he composes sentences in both his first language (L1) and English. She reasons that explicit structural distinctions will lead to a conscious manipulation of sentence structures in both Spanish and English. She also believes that her student is more likely to internalize these distinctions in the context of revising ideas that he is motivated to convey to an audience.

Scenario 3: ESL teachers Annmarie Hehir and Pablo Garcia are team-teaching a thematic unit they designed on the First Amendment of the U.S. Bill of Rights for high-intermediate students in a community college credit-bearing ESL program in the Los Angeles metropolitan area. In this lesson, students are applying their knowledge about the First Amendment to the context of the Free Speech Movement by reading about the movement's historical significance and connection to contemporary free speech issues. In the previous class period, the students read an article entitled "The Free Speech Movement: Reflections on Berkeley in the 1960s," filled out a graphic organizer, prepared study cards for the boldfaced vocabulary in the text, and completed a timeline as a post-reading comprehension check. Today they are reading biographical texts written by three student activists, examining specific clue words indicating the speakers' stance and contrasting the speakers' tones in the first-person narratives. The culminating group project in the unit requires the students to write an essay on a topic related to the First Amendment. Each group will make a presentation and will be graded on how well they defend their position, use persuasive arguments, and incorporate targeted language structures and vocabulary learned in the unit.[1]

The students depicted in the three scenarios, though at different ages and educational levels, are all learning academic English, the language of school. These students represent a range of language backgrounds. Some are ESL students who emigrated with their families to the U.S.; others are multilingual students who were born in the U.S. and educated in English (Weigle, 2014). All are learning the type of English they need to succeed academically in their language arts or English classes and in their content classes in the mainstream curriculum in elementary and secondary school, or in composition classes and content courses in postsecondary settings.

Most of the scholarly work in academic language has focused on a particular educational level: Snow and Katz (2010), for example, considered the kinds of academic language that elementary school students need in instructed English Language Development classes, and Dutro and Kinsella (2010) described the kinds of explicit academic language required for school success at the secondary level. Considerable work has also been reported in the EAP literature (cf. Charles & Pecorari, 2016; Johns & Price, 2014) in describing the academic language demands of university classes and, in particular, the challenges of academic reading and the genres of academic writing that students must master. The goal of this chapter is to take a broader view in understanding the notion of academic language and the needs that all students have in learning academic language across educational levels in CBI.

Academic Language: Various Conceptualizations |||

Starting with the seminal work of Cummins (1980, 2000), who made the distinction between the language of everyday conversation (basic interpersonal communication skills) and that used in learning subjects in school (cognitive academic language proficiency), there has been a growing interest over the past decades in understanding the kinds of language that students need to succeed in school. Chamot and O'Malley (1987) defined academic language as "the language that is used by teachers and students for the purpose of acquiring new knowledge...imparting new information, describing abstract ideas, and developing students' conceptual understanding" (p. 40). In 2004, Schleppegrell extended the discussion to the demands of textbooks, noting that "...school based-texts are difficult for many students precisely because they emerge from discourse contexts that require different ways of using language than students experience outside of school...[drawing] on a different constellation of linguistic resources from what is typical or expected of everyday conversation" (p. 9). Saunders and Goldenberg (2010) described academic language as including all aspects of language, including vocabulary, syntax, and discourse structures. It is also characterized as including specific language functions needed, for example, to classify, compare, hypothesize, and make claims (Snow, 2017). Anstrom, DiCerbo, Butler, Katz, Millet, & Rivera (2010), in their comprehensive review, refer to academic English as a ". . . variety of English, as a register, or a style . . . typically used within specific sociocultural academic settings (pp. iv–v). The scenarios presented in the beginning of this chapter provide three such examples of specific sociocultural academic settings.

Early conceptualizations of academic language tended to focus on reading and writing; however, Schleppegrell (2004) argues that interactional spoken language can also be complex and cognitively demanding and that cognitive demand lies in the relationship between the tasks and the learner and not necessarily within the text or the task itself. Similarly, Bailey (2007) warns against characterizing social language as less sophisticated or less cognitively demanding than academic language, noting that it is perhaps more accurate to speak of the differences between social and academic language as differences in the "relative frequency" of complex grammatical structures, specialized terminology, and certain language functions (p. 9). Zwiers (2008) suggests that speakers and writers need academic language to: (a) describe complexity in clear and concise ways; (b) convey higher order thinking (such as the complex thinking processes needed to solve problems and express ideas); and (c) present abstract ideas and relationships. Wong Fillmore and Fillmore (2012) analyzed the language of complex academic texts and have identified grammatical structures and discourse devices for framing ideas, indicating relationships, and developing strong arguments. More recently, Gottlieb and Ernst-Slavit (2014) delineate three dimensions of academic language: (a) the word/expression level, which covers general, specialized, and technical content words and colloquial expressions; (b) the sentence level, which involves types of sentences including simple, compound, complex, and compound-complex; and (c) the discourse level including text types, cohesion of text, and coherence of ideas.

Making the connection between academic language and content learning, Schleppegrell (2004) notes: "Students need to use language in particular ways in order to be successful in science, history, and other subjects; to develop interpretations, construct arguments, and critique theories" (p. 5). To Short and Fitzsimmons (2007), academic literacy includes reading, writing, and oral discourse that varies from subject to subject and requires knowledge of multiple genres of text, purposes for text use, and text media—all of which are influenced by students' personal, social, and cultural experiences. They have characterized the demands of learning language and content as "double the work," and, while all students face the challenge of mastering the requisite academic language skills they need to master subject matter, ELs and multilingual students deal with the even greater demand of undertaking this challenge concurrently.

From the pedagogical perspective, there has been a shift over time, as Snow (2017) notes, in attitudes about how to teach the language students need to succeed in CBI programs. In the early years of CBI, there was a somewhat *laissez-faire* approach—just teach the content and the language will come—to, at present, very careful deliberation about ways to create the most effective conditions for language and content integration (see, e.g., Lyster, this volume). This shift includes greater interest in the target language itself, such as the features of academic language described in this section, and the varieties found in all types of school-based discourse, from classroom management to the demands of specific topics and discipline subject matter and the text types and genres that students must read and produce in writing at all educational levels. Along with enhanced understanding of the target language and content demands comes the challenge of preparing teachers to take on a dual role in the interface of language and content, in all its complexities.

Perspectives on Academic Language Progressions | | |

The challenging task of providing EL students across educational levels with instruction in developing language skills and content knowledge can be facilitated by examining students' academic language learning progressions, which can be defined as a sequence of significant and noticeable developmental changes that occur within the interconnected planes of academic language and cognition (Bailey & Heritage, 2014). Understanding of learning progressions allows for: (a) more precise monitoring of the acquisition and development of students' academic language and content knowledge; (b) more effective support of language and content knowledge in reading, writing, listening, and speaking; and (c) more accurate formative assessment to guide instruction.

Bailey and Heritage (2014) propose that students' learning progressions can be evaluated in terms of six different dimensions: quantity, quality, repertoire expansion, accuracy, rate, and order. While following students' progress along these dimensions, the authors underscore that the change in the progressions occurs gradually; they therefore suggest the sequence of *not evident*, *emerging*, *developing*, and *controlled* for gauging academic language progressions. Although individual and contextual factors contribute to idiosyncratic differences among the learners, tracking students' development along the six dimensions uncovers the qualitative and quantitative shifts in students' academic language, content knowledge, and cognitive development.

In early elementary grades (Kindergarten–Grade 3), EL students are faced with a number of cognitive tasks such as sequencing, taking perspective, and making predictions (Common Core State Standards Initiative, 2010). Since these students are in pre-operational and concrete operational stages of cognitive development (McCormick, Loeb, & Schiefelbusch, 2003), they are expected to carry out these tasks based on concrete experiences and observations. Along with the cognitive tasks, learners are faced with academic language development tasks such as describing, explaining, and retelling. These tasks are characterized by the following academic language progressions—expansion of topic vocabulary, use of sequencing markers (e.g., *first*, *next*), use of modal verbs for perspective taking, mastery of simple sentences, and development of compound sentence clauses that reflect causal and sequential relationships as well as expository text comprehension and construction (Bailey & Heritage, 2014). To support young ELs with vocabulary acquisition, word walls with topic vocabulary, visual supports, and concrete examples of differentiating word meaning can be used (August, Carlo, Dressler, & Snow, 2005). Comparing and contrasting words, word parts, and sounds in students' native language and English provides support in developing phonology and morphology (Kieffer & Lesaux, 2007). Wall charts with sentence starters that support the academic language tasks can also be helpful (Carrier & Tatum, 2006).

ELs in upper elementary and early secondary grades (Grades 4–6; 6–8) are progressing through the stage of concrete operations and approaching the stage of formal operations (McCormick et al., 2003). They are expected to engage in increasingly complex and abstract thinking that may or may not be supported with easily observable evidence. Learners encounter a rapid increase in the difficulty and variety of academic texts (including a range of genres) and tasks (Bailey, 2007; Chall & Jacobs, 2003) across academic disciplines. In accordance with the six parameters identified by Bailey and Heritage (2014), we can identify the following academic language progressions at this level: acquiring not only a vast number of topic-specific terms but also polysemous words that have content area–specific meanings (e.g., *base* in chemistry and geometry) and general academic words that are used across curricular areas (e.g., *hypothesis*, *contradiction*). In this context, ELs need explicit instruction in word meanings across disciplinary areas (Ernst-Slavit & Mason, 2011). Teachers can present ELs with word groups/families to support their development of morphological and semantic skills and contrast vocabulary meaning nuances by providing examples and nonexamples of focus words in context (Klingner, Vaughn, & Boardman, 2015). Students at this stage continue to master causality and develop compare and contrast and synthesis skills. They also work on comprehension and construction of oral and written expository texts. In the domain of syntax, students continue to develop their use of compound sentences with discourse markers that interconnect sentences and paragraphs (e.g., *in addition*, *consequently*). Teachers can support EL learners at the syntax and discourse levels by providing word banks and word walls for expressing opinions and forming hypotheses. They also provide graphic organizers with built-in discourse markers and essay frames for different academic tasks and genres (Munro, Abbott, & Rossiter, 2013).

EL learners at secondary and post-secondary levels (Grades 9 and above) are either at or entering the stage of formal operations (McCormick et al., 2003) and are expected to think abstractly within and across disciplines. Academic tasks at this level include critical analysis, evaluation, synthesis, and production of novel ideas. Academic language tasks include critiquing and defending, arguing and/or supporting a position, as well as formulating and developing ideas and constructs (Common Core State Standards Initiative, 2010). Along with personal narrative and expository texts, the genre of persuasive writing is emphasized, and with it, rhetoric devices and logically coherent arguments (Kibler, Walqui, & Bunch, 2015). Students are also introduced to the differentiation of genre characteristics within specific content areas (e.g., persuasive devices in social studies vs. science). Students at this stage are given a great deal of autonomy with an expectation of vocabulary expansion and increased syntax and text complexity acquired from attending to multiple sources of information (i.e., lectures, readings, conducting research, etc.). The rate and order of the acquisition of academic language progressions are largely dependent on learning opportunities. Bailey and Heritage (2014) provide an example of older ELs (as well as EFL learners) who may master literacy skills earlier than effective oral communication skills. In order to support academic language progressions in ELs at this later stage, it is critical that teachers provide frequent and well-balanced opportunities for oral and written practice of academic language (Lee & Buxton, 2013).

A report representing the Academic Senates of three segments of California's higher education system found that only 36 percent of students in three systems can synthesize information from several sources and less than 33 percent can analyze information or arguments based on their reading (Intersegmental Committee of the Academic Senates, 2002). In response to these statistics, authors of the report note: "As analysis and synthesis engage students in the critical thinking that lies at the heart of the college experience, it is essential that high school teachers undertake these tasks" (p. 48). With the introduction of Common Core standards in the U.S., there is an even stronger focus on the reading/writing connection. The report further notes that for students to be successful academically, they must also possess intellectual habits of mind such as being able to engage in intellectual discussions, ask provocative questions, challenge their own beliefs, and read with awareness of self and others.

Underlying Principles and Practice of Academic Language |||

Table 20.1 presents selected classroom activities and the principles that underlie the teaching of academic language across educational levels as depicted in the three scenarios that began this chapter and in the subsequent discussion of academic language learning progres-

Table 20.1: Classroom Activities and Underlying Principles to Teach Academic Language

Classroom Activities	Underlying Principles
1. In the *elementary* class, the teacher pre-teaches selected vocabulary related to her lesson on Mayan society, provides a list of new vocabulary on a wall chart, and refers to the chart at different times during the lesson. She also takes a cross-disciplinary approach when teaching vocabulary, pointing out that the meanings of words (e.g., *pyramid*) vary depending on the content area. In the theme-based course on the First Amendment, *post-secondary* students complete an activity where they have to guess the meaning of the boldfaced words from context using features of the text such as logical, grammatical, and punctuation cues; they then prepare study cards for further review.	Concept enhancement strategies for vocabulary instruction (including wall charts, word banks, semantic/concept maps) are more effective for the acquisition of new words than traditional strategies such as looking up definitions and rote memorization (Kinsella, 1997; Klingner et al., 2015). Teachers need to develop a comprehensive approach to teaching academic vocabulary that includes a principled plan for deciding which words to teach, e.g., Tier 1, Tier 2, Tier 3 (Beck, McKeown, & Kucan, 2002). Other useful guidelines include: topic words ("Words to Know") and high-utility words ("Words to Go") as suggested by Kinsella (2014) and the Academic Word List (Coxhead, 2000, 2006). Finally, teachers can implement explicit vocabulary activities such as focusing on word learning strategies.
2. During a follow-up reading activity on Mayan social structure, *elementary* students fill out a graphic organizer that aids them in unpacking the difficult text. They add details to the organizer as they progress through the lesson (i.e., before, during, and after teacher-led instruction). Similarly, in the theme-based unit, *secondary* students develop a timeline on the history of the Free Speech Movement as a post-reading comprehension check.	Graphic organizers provide visual supports for assisting students to understand text structure (e.g., social structure pyramid or chronology of events). They are also a means of addressing the different learning styles of students (Brinton, 2014). Visual and graphic representations are helpful to ELs across all educational levels.
3. During a follow-up reading activity, the *elementary* students also engage in Collaborative Strategic Reading (CSR). In CSR, with the teacher's guidance, the class previews the text, activating background knowledge, making predictions, and examining visual cues. During reading, students use comprehension monitoring strategies, synthesize the material, and state the main idea. In the wrap-up stage, students review the main ideas, generate questions, and write a concise summary.	Multicomponent reading instruction (such as CSR) supports diverse learners through explicit strategy instruction, comprehension monitoring, and collaborative learning; this practice enhances oral academic language and supports literacy (Klingner et al., 2012) as students move through academic learning progressions. Students at all levels need to develop a repertoire of reading strategies and receive extensive conscious practice in meaningful combinations (Grabe & Stoller, 2014).

Table 20.1 (*continued*)

Classroom Activities	Underlying Principles
4. In the *secondary* social studies class, students identify the organizational patterns in King's "I Have a Dream Speech" (i.e., repetition, transitional phrasing), and then discuss how these patterns create a sense of urgency for the audience. Follow-up strategies for rereading the text include students mapping the idea structure and paraphrasing King's major points in both their L1 and L2.	Proficient readers use text patterns such as comparison and repetition to comprehend meaning. Research indicates a strong correlation between an awareness of structure and overall comprehension (Pearson & Fielding, 1991). By drawing on the L1, the focus shifts from what students cannot do to what they can do. Everyday language practices are valuable resources that can leverage academic language development (Martínez, Orellana, Pacheco, & Carbone, 2008).
5. In a follow-up activity in the social studies class, students note references to historical texts in King's speech and, in pairs, explain why these particular references might appeal to audiences.	Awareness of rhetorical constructs supports the analysis and interpretation of complex texts (McCormick, Hafner, & Saint-Germain, 2013).
6. The *elementary* and *secondary* teachers point out relevant grammatical features (e.g., in English, most nouns become plural by adding -*s* and adjectives do not agree with nouns in terms of gender or plurality). In the *secondary* class, students' L1 is used as a point of comparison. Both teachers seek to enhance their students' metalinguistic awareness about word-, sentence-, and discourse-level grammar constructions.	Teachers can help students "notice" features of language as part of instructed L2 acquisition (Ellis, 2014). Relevant grammatical structures should be targeted and taught in context (Zwiers, 2008) and can be modeled through instructional strategies such as sentence starters: ▪ *I do not agree with . . . because . . .* ▪ *This connects to my own experience in that . . .* ▪ *The facts show . . .*

sions. The activities and principles would, of course, require modification by teachers to be appropriate for learners' age levels and L2 proficiency, and to meet the objectives or learning outcomes set by the teacher or required by relevant standards or learning outcomes.

Research Agenda |||

The review of literature on academic language and literacy development across educational levels suggests many directions for further research. For one, the construct of academic language progressions has been closely examined by Bailey and Heritage (2014) within the population of young monolingual and multilingual learners. More studies are needed to extend this line of research focusing on students within and beyond K–12 settings, further documenting the development and sequence of academic language progressions at the word, sentence, and discourse levels. Additionally, while the content areas of science and math have been examined relatively closely (Alonzo & Gotwals, 2012; Wilson, Sztajn, Edgington, & Confrey, 2014), academic language and literacy development and progressions within other content areas await further investigation. More research is also needed on teacher training both in the areas of formative assessment (Bailey & Heritage, 2014) and instructional supports that teachers can implement to scaffold and foster academic language and literacy in diverse populations of learners across many types of CBI contexts (Osipova, 2014).

Research that examines literacy development at the secondary level ranges from a critical focus on the academic text to a view that literacy constitutes a continuity of practices across home, school, and community. The combination of both perspectives could address the gap between secondary and college coursework. In addition, teachers are not always cognizant of how students acquire and perfect complex language structures through out-of-school activities, and thus miss a chance to facilitate metalinguistic awareness. Heath (1998) and Soepp (2006) demonstrate the linguistic benefits of working in arts-based youth organizations. Drawing on a national data set, Heath (1998) showed how adolescents practice complex language functions, such as hypothetical reasoning and conjecture, while planning, hypothesizing, and critiquing works of art. Other researchers have connected the in-school/out-of-school divide to suggest how teachers might draw on everyday language practices in the classroom (Martinez et al., 2008; Schultz, 2002; Skilton-Sylvester, 2002). Orellana and Eksner (2006) and Orellana and Reynolds (2008), for example, document the translation experiences of bilingual youth and propose that teachers help students build an awareness of the skills they perfect while translating—skills such as paraphrasing, the use of new vocabulary, a heightened awareness of varied sentence structures, and a heightened awareness of audience. This work points to promising directions for some settings of CBI.

Once students understand how rhetorical constructs can be used as a basis for analyzing and interpreting complex texts, they become more capable of meeting the rigorous reading and writing demands of college (McCormick et al., 2013). Research that bridges the focus on academic language with students' ongoing literacy experiences can foster instructional conditions that lead to the metalinguistic awareness necessary to read and write rhetorically. By identifying what students can already do and by providing further scaffolding, teachers can improve students' self-efficacy and increase their motivation to read and respond to academic text.

APPLYING WHAT YOU LEARNED
Questions and Tasks

1. What usually comes to mind first in describing academic language is vocabulary. And indeed the students in the three scenarios that began this chapter had to learn and use academic vocabulary to complete the tasks described.

   a. Has your concept of academic language expanded as a result of reading this chapter? How is it a "variety of English, a register, or a style" (Anstrom et al., 2010)?

   b. From you own experiences as a first or second language speaker of English, would you add anything else?

2. As mentioned in the chapter, Short and Fitzsimmons (2007) claim that ELs have "double the work."

   a. In your own words, explain what is meant by this characterization.

   b. How does CBI in its various configurations require "double the work" on the part of students?

3. Bailey and Heritage (2014) use six dimensions to monitor students' academic language learning progressions in their studies. Considering the six dimensions—*quantity, quality, repertoire expansion, accuracy, rate, and order*—explain why you think each is important in understanding learners' L2 acquisition, and then give some specific examples from the activities presented in Table 20.1 that illustrate the dimensions.

4. What strategies can you think of that might help students connect reading to writing? For example, how can you help students select evidence to support and develop their ideas? What other strategies can you suggest?

5. If you are currently teaching, monitor your own interactions with your monolingual and/or multilingual students.

   a. What types of questions scaffold and support their use of academic language in the content area that you teach?

   b. What types of questions solicit student responses that are more nuanced and more complex in their syntactic structure and feature higher-order cognitive skills (e.g., synthesis or analysis)?

6. Teachers in many CBI programs are encouraged to develop language objectives, content objectives, and learning strategy objectives in their lesson planning.

   How would teachers and students benefit from such an approach to lesson planning based on what you read in this chapter? Find a content text from a textbook or magazine that is suitable for elementary, secondary, or post-secondary students; analyze it; and then develop language, content, and strategy objectives for a lesson plan using this text.

ENDNOTE

1. *The First Amendment Unit* was developed by Annmarie Hehir and Pablo Garcia for TESL 564: Teaching English for Academic Purposes at California State University, Los Angeles, in Spring 2015. Used with permission.

REFERENCES

Alonzo, A. C., & Gotwals, A. W. (Eds.). (2012). *Learning progressions in science: Current challenges and future directions.* New York, NY: Springer Science & Business Media.

Anstrom, K., DiCerbo, P., Butler, F., Katz, A., Millet, J., & Rivera, C. (2010). *A review of the literature on academic English: Implications for K–12 English language learners.* Arlington, VA: The George Washington University Center for Equity and Excellence in Education.

August, D., Carlo, M., Dressler, C., & Snow, C. (2005). The critical role of vocabulary development for English language learners. *Learning Disabilities Research & Practice, 20*(1), 50–57.

Bailey, A. L. (Ed.). (2007). *The language of school: Putting academic English to the test.* New Haven, CT: Yale University Press.

Bailey, A. L., & Heritage, M. (2014). The role of language learning progressions in improved instruction and assessment of English language learners. *TESOL Quarterly, 48*(3), 480–506.

Beck, I. L., McKeown, M. G., & Kucan, L. (2002). *Bringing words to life: Robust vocabulary instruction.* New York, NY: Guilford Press.

Brinton, D. M. (2014). Tools and techniques of effective second/foreign language teaching. In M. Celce-Murcia, D. M. Brinton, & M. A. Snow (Eds.), *Teaching English as a second or foreign language* (4th ed., pp. 340–361). Boston, MA: National Geographic Learning/Heinle Cengage Learning.

Carrier, K. A., & Tatum, A. W. (2006). Creating sentence walls to help English–language learners develop content literacy. *The Reading Teacher, 60*(3), 285–288.

Chall, J. S., & Jacobs, V. A. (2003). Poor children's fourth-grade slump. *American Educator, 27*(1), 14–17.

Chamot, A. U., & O'Malley, J. M. (1987). The cognitive academic language learning approach: A bridge to the mainstream. *TESOL Quarterly, 21*(2), 227–249.

Charles, M., & Pecorari, D. (2016). *Introducing English for academic purposes.* London, England: Routledge.

Common Core State Standards Initiative. (2010). *Common Core State Standards for English language arts and literacy in history/social studies, science, and technical subjects.* Retrieved from http://www.corestandards.org

Coxhead, A. (2000). A new academic word list. *TESOL Quarterly, 34*(2), 213–238.

Coxhead, A. (2006). *Essentials of teaching academic vocabulary.* Boston, MA: Houghton Mifflin.

Cummins, J. (1980). Psychological assessment of immigrant children: Logic or intuition? *Journal of Multilingual and Multicultural Development, 1,* 97–111.

Cummins, J. (2000). *Language, power and pedagogy: Bilingual children in the crossfire.* Clevedon, England: Multilingual Matters.

Dutro, S., & Kinsella, K. (2010). English language development: Issues and implementation at grades six through twelve. *Improving education for English learners: Research-based approaches* (pp. 151–207). Sacramento, CA: California Department of Education.

Ellis, R. (2014). Principles of instructed second language learning. In M. Celce-Murcia, D. M. Brinton, & M. A. Snow (Eds.), *Teaching English as a second or foreign language* (4th ed., pp. 31–45). Boston, MA: National Geographic Learning/Heinle Cengage Learning.

Ernst-Slavit, G., & Mason, M. R. (2011). "Words that hold us up": Teacher talk and academic language in five upper elementary classrooms. *Linguistics and Education, 22*(4), 430–440.

Gottlieb, M., & Ernst-Slavit, G. (2014). *Academic language in diverse classrooms: Definitions and contexts.* Thousand Oaks, CA: Corwin.

Grabe, W., & Stoller, F. L. (2014). Teaching reading for academic purposes. In M. Celce-Murcia, D. M. Brinton, & M. A. Snow (Eds.), *Teaching English as a second or foreign language* (4th ed., pp. 189–205). Boston, MA: National Geographic Learning/Heinle Cengage Learning.

Heath, S. B. (1998). Working through language. In S. M. Hoyle & C. T. Adger (Eds.), *Kids talk: Strategic language use in later childhood* (pp. 217–240). New York, NY: Oxford University Press.

Intersegmental Committee of the Academic Senates. (2002). *Academic literacy: A statement of competencies expected of students entering California's public colleges and universities.* Sacramento, CA: Author.

Johns, A., & Price, D. (2014). English for specific purposes: International in scope, specific in purpose. In M. Celce-Murcia, D. M. Brinton, & M. A. Snow (Eds.), *Teaching English as a second or foreign language* (4th ed., pp. 471–487). Boston, MA: National Geographic Learning/Heinle Cengage Learning.

Kibler, A. K., Walqui, A., & Bunch, G. C. (2015). Transformational opportunities: Language and literacy instruction for English language learners in the common core era in the United States. *TESOL Journal, 6*(1), 9–35.

Kieffer, M. J., & Lesaux, N. K. (2007). Breaking down words to build meaning: Morphology, vocabulary, and reading comprehension in the urban classroom. *The Reading Teacher, 61*(2), 134–144.

Kinsella, K. (1997). Moving from comprehensible input to "learning to learn" in content-based instruction. In M. A. Snow & D. M. Brinton (Eds.), *The content-based classroom: Perspectives on integrating language and content* (pp. 46–68). White Plains, NY: Longman.

Kinsella, K. (2014, April). Cutting to the common core: The benefits of narrow reading units. *Language Magazine,* 18–23. Retrieved from www.languagemagazine.com

Klingner, J. K., Boardman, A. G., Eppolito, A. M., & Schonewise, E. A. (2012). Supporting adolescent English language learners' reading in the content areas. *Learning Disabilities: A Contemporary Journal, 10*(1), 35–64.

Klingner, J. K., Vaughn, S., & Boardman, A. (2015). *Teaching reading comprehension to students with learning difficulties* (2nd ed.). New York, NY: Guilford Press.

Lee, O., & Buxton, C. A. (2013). Integrating science and English proficiency for English language learners. *Theory into Practice, 52*(1), 36–42.

Martínez, R., Orellana, M. F., Pacheco, M., & Carbone, P. M. (2008). Found in translation: Connecting translating experiences to academic writing. *Language Arts, 5*(6), 421–431.

McCormick, J., Hafner, A., & Saint-Germain, M. (2013). From high school to college: Teachers and students assess the impact of an expository reading and writing course on college readiness. *Journal of Educational Research and Practice, 3*(1), 30–49.

McCormick, L., Loeb, D., & Schiefelbusch, R. L. (2003). *Supporting children with communication difficulties in inclusive settings* (2nd ed.). Boston, MA: Allyn & Bacon.

Munro, J., Abbott, M., & Rossiter, M. (2013). Mentoring for success: Accommodation strategies for ELLs. *The Canadian Journal of Action Research, 14*(2), 22–38.

Osipova, A. V. (2014). *Academic language self-reflection and coaching training of pre-service special education teachers in the context of content area writing instruction* (Doctoral dissertation). Retrieved from http://search.proquest.com/docview/1655359874?accountid=10352. (Order No. 3681017).

Orellana, M. F., & Eksner, H. J. (2006). Power in cultural modeling: Building on the bilingual language practices of immigrant youth in Germany and the United States. In C. M. Fairbanks, J. Worthy, B. Maloch, J. V. Hoffman, & D. L. Schaller (Eds.), *National Reading Conference Yearbook* (Vol. 55, pp. 224–234). Austin, TX: University of Texas at Austin.

Orellana, M. F., & Reynolds, J. F. (2008). Cultural modeling: Leveraging bilingual skills for school paraphrasing tasks. *Reading Research Quarterly, 43*(1), 48–65.

Pearson, P. D., & Fielding, L. (1991). Comprehension instruction. In R. Barr, M. L. Kamil, P. Mosenthal, & P. D. Pearson (Eds.), *Handbook of reading research* (Vol. 11, pp. 815–860). White Plains, NY: Longman.

Saunders, W., & Goldenberg, C. (2010). Research to guide English language development instruction. In *Improving education for English learners: Research-based approaches* (pp. 21–81). Sacramento, CA: California Department of Education.

Schleppegrell, M. J. (2004). *The language of schooling: A functional linguistics perspective*. Mahwah, NJ: Erlbaum.

Schultz, K. (2002). Looking across space and time: Reconceptualizing literacy learning in and out of school. *Research in the Teaching of English, 36*(3), 356–390.

Short, D. J., & Fitzsimmons, S. (2007). *Double the work: Challenges and solutions to acquiring language and academic literacy for adolescent English language learners — A report to Carnegie Corporation of New York*. Washington, DC: Alliance for Excellent Education.

Skilton-Sylvester, E. (2002). Literate at home but not at school: A Cambodian girl's journey from playwright to struggling writer. In G. Hull & K. Schultz (Eds.), *School's out! Bridging out-of-school literacies and classroom practice* (pp. 61–90). New York, NY: Teachers College Press.

Snow, M. A. (2017). Content-based language teaching and academic language development. In E. Hinkel (Ed.), *Handbook of research in second language teaching and learning* (Vol. III, pp. 159–172). New York, NY: Routledge.

Snow, M. A., & Katz, A. (2010). English language development: Foundations and implementation in kindergarten through grade five. In *Improving education for English learners: Research-based approaches* (pp. 83–148). Sacramento, CA: California Department of Education.

Soepp, E. (2006). Critique: Assessment and the production of learning. *Teachers College Record, 108*(4), 748–777.

Weigle, S. (2014). Considerations for teaching second language writing. In M. Celce-Murcia, D. M. Brinton, & M. A. Snow (Eds.), *Teaching English as a second or foreign language* (4th ed., pp. 222–237). Boston, MA: National Geographic Learning/Heinle Cengage Learning.

Wilson, P. H., Sztajn, P., Edgington, C., & Confrey, J. (2014). Teachers' use of their mathematical knowledge for teaching in learning a mathematics learning trajectory. *Journal of Mathematics Teacher Education, 17*(2), 149–175.

Wong Fillmore, L., & Fillmore, C. (2012). *What does text complexity mean for English learners and language minority students?* Paper presented at the Understanding Language Conference, Palo Alto, CA. Retrieved from http://ell.stanford.edu/sites/default/files/pdf/academic-papers/06-LWF%20CJF%20Text%20Complexity%20FINAL_0.pdf

Zwiers, J. (2008). *Building academic language: Essential practices for content classrooms, grades 5–12*. San Francisco, CA: Jossey-Bass.

Chapter 21

Checking Our Linguistic Intuitions: Corpora and Corpus Tools in Content-Based Instruction

Viviana Cortes

||| A Glimpse at the Use of Corpora in the Content-Based Classroom

Scenario 1: At Northern Arizona University (NAU), Kate Donley and Randi Reppen designed and taught a sustained content language teaching (SCLT) unit on cultural anthropology (Donley & Reppen, 2001). SCLT courses are often designed to help students acquire and develop the academic skills they will need in their transition from language classes to regular university courses. This type of course tends to emphasize vocabulary that is central to particular disciplines. As part of the design process for this EAP course, they collected a corpus of cultural anthropology texts made up of college-level textbooks and an anthology of essays in this discipline. They used a concordancer, Monoconc Pro Version 2.0 (Barlow, 1999), which is a very popular computer program used to analyze corpora, and they created a list of the most frequent words in the cultural anthropology corpus in order to identify target academic vocabulary. Next they compared their list to the Academic Word List (AWL) (Coxhead, 2000), a list of the words that have been found to appear frequently in English academic texts (words such as *analyze, context, formulate, method, results,* and *summarize,* to mention just a few). They then chose words that occurred frequently in the anthropology corpus (and that also appeared in the AWL) to ensure that this target vocabulary was frequent not only in anthropology but also across several academic disciplines. The selected vocabulary items were used to design activities for vocabulary instruction. In this scenario, corpora were used to inform teaching, helping the materials designers base their vocabulary selection on empirically based findings rather their own intuition and as a resource to select vocabulary and examples for class activities in which students themselves explored the use of academic vocabulary (Donley & Reppen, 2001).

Scenario 2: Convinced that the use of literature in the ESL and EFL class is a valuable vehicle for a wide variety of linguistic expressions, Danielle Saba (2014) used corpus-based research tools to create a literature-based unit for ESL students who were taking an extensive reading class in a university intensive English program. For this particular unit, Saba chose to use

Jane Austen's *Pride and Prejudice* to teach her students how to manage different meanings of certain words and expressions. Instead of allowing curricular decisions such as vocabulary selection or the choice of examples for activities to be guided by her own intuition, she decided to use corpora to inform these choices. In the first stages, Saba considered Austen's novel as her linguistic corpus. Using a concordancer, AntConc (Anthony, 2012), she built a frequency list to help her in the selection of target vocabulary. In addition, she used the online Corpus of Historical American English (COHA) (Davies, 2010) to check how frequent the words Austen used in her novel were in the period in which the novel was written. Saba used her findings not only to guide course decisions on which vocabulary items and frequent expressions to teach and when to teach them, but also to create classroom materials and activities based on real examples that reflected the use of linguistic features of that era.

These two scenarios provide us with only a glimpse of the immense potential that the use of corpora brings to ESL/EFL course design in general, and to the CBI classroom in particular. As Stoller (2008) suggests, the contribution of corpora to CBI is definitely closely connected to the ability to analyze authentic texts from different disciplines and genres; however, more specifically corpora provide an invaluable tool for CBI teachers, curriculum developers, and materials designers for describing empirical tendencies in discipline specific and topic specific language.

Corpora in Language Teaching ||

A corpus (plural: corpora) is a large collection of machine-readable texts. The study of corpora contributes to the description of a language as a whole or, in the case of specialized corpora, of particular registers of language. This type of descriptive information can be directly transferred to the language classroom (Cortes, 2013). There are many available corpora that can be used by researchers and instructors for a variety of purposes: to check their linguistic knowledge; to get information on how a wide range of linguistic features is used in natural language; to obtain real examples for materials design; or to conduct their own investigations, to name only a few applications.

Due to the complex process of collecting spoken corpora, which need to be transcribed to be made machine-readable for analysis, the majority of the corpora available are made up of written texts that can be scanned or downloaded into a computer. Consequently, there are many more studies that analyze written corpora and, as a result of this limitation, there are more and more comprehensive descriptions of written registers than of their spoken counterparts. A few examples of spoken corpora available for consultation are the Michigan Corpus of Academic Spoken English (MICASE), a collection of spoken language from different university registers such as lectures and study groups (Simpson, Briggs, Ovens, & Swales, 2002), and the spoken section of the Corpus of Contemporary American English (COCA) (Davies, 2008). COCA comprises a collection of more than 400 million words of fiction, magazine, newspaper, and academic writing, and spoken data collected mainly from unscripted television and radio news-related shows. There are other language corpora that have been used for the creation of dictionaries and grammar books that may be commercially available, and there are also corpora that are not openly accessible (Biber, Johansson, Leech, Conrad, & Finegan, 1999; Carter & McCarthy, 2006; Sinclair, 2003).

There are two general approaches to the use of corpus-based materials and tools in the language classroom. In the first approach, instructors can use the results of corpus-based investigations from the extant literature to check their linguistic intuitions or to create, evaluate, or adapt classroom materials and activities. Instructors can also collect corpora and analyze these language collections themselves and then use their findings in the design of curricula and materials for their classes. As the field of corpus-based research is a rather new area and is constantly evolving, the number of topic-specific corpora available for analysis is, in many cases, still under development. Several studies have collected and analyzed specialized corpora (a collection of texts that represents a sample of a particular field in a language) that have been used for the creation of vocabulary lists that can be applied to materials design and evaluation. These specialized academic corpora cover fields such as business (Hsu, 2011), agriculture (Martinez, Beck, & Panza, 2009), engineering (Liu & Han, 2015), and nursing (Yang, 2015). There are also a number of documented examples of the use of corpora in ESP courses such as English for the police (Basturkmen, 2010) and the Corpus of International Business Writing (CIBW) teaching project (Connor, Davis, De Rycker, Phillips, & Verckers, 1997). In the case of CBI and ESP/EAP scenarios, teachers could collect corpora of specific topics to identify tendencies in the language used in those texts that could inform their classroom materials and activities. A second approach is for teachers to introduce corpora into the classroom, training students to analyze corpora and corpus-based findings and to use corpus tools. Students' use of corpora in the classroom is connected to data-driven learning techniques (Johns, 1991), which confront learners with data and allow them to become language analysts, learning to discover patterns in language through exploration activities.

Whether corpora are used for linguistic analysis or applied to the classroom, several computer programs facilitate the analysis. Undoubtedly, the most popular corpus tool is the concordancer. Concordancers may be either commercially available or freely downloadable from the internet, depending on the source. This type of software allows for the identification of keywords, keywords in context (KWICS), collocations, and different types of formulaic language. Keyword analysis helps "identify words which occur with an unusually high frequency in a text or corpus when that text or corpus is compared with another corpus" (Bowker & Pearson, 2002, p. 115). These words are called *key types,* and they better indicate what the texts in a corpus are about. This application could be very useful for CBI teachers and material writers to create specialized word lists that can be easily identified in a text or a corpus of specific texts.

Just as corpora and concordancers have become essential tools in the identification and analysis of language features for EAP and ESP courses, the same advantages can surely extend to CBI settings. In spite of the fact that corpora and corpus tools present great potential, their use has not yet been fully exploited in the CBI classroom, where students learn the target language by using it to process new content. Corpus-based CBI materials, thus, would be ideal in both ESL and EFL contexts as these materials could potentially help students access the target language while at the same time expose them to authentic materials, for example, in thematic units. In addition, examples taken from corpora could be used to illustrate the real tendencies of authentic language use as revealed by corpus findings. Most of the corpus-based analysis of specialized discourse and most of the applications of corpus-based findings, corpora, and corpus tools, however, have taken place, as mentioned, in the EAP class and in selected ESP situations (see the Brinton and Frodesen chapters, this volume).

Use of Corpora in the CBI Classroom |||

This section will present various examples of the use of corpora and corpus tools in CBI-related scenarios, particularly in literature-based classrooms and in courses that focus on the teaching of EAP. I chose these examples because they present examples that clearly illustrate different uses of corpora in the language classroom. In the first example, corpora have been used to make better curricular decisions in a content-based literature class. The second example focuses on the use of corpora in CBI materials design for the selection of examples and for the development of activities. Finally, in the third example, corpora are used by both instructors and students in an advanced academic writing class that focuses on data-driven learning and genre analysis.

Corpora in the Content-Based Literature Class: Making Informed Curricular Decisions

As illustrated in Scenario 2, Saba (2014) downloaded the electronic version of the novel from Project Gutenberg (www.gutenberg.org/) in order to create materials for a content-based literature unit based on Jane Austen's *Pride and Prejudice.* She saved the file as a text file and uploaded it into a concordancer, *AntConc* (Anthony, 2012), generating a word list to determine which words most frequently occurred in the novel. In addition, she used AntConc to identify the most frequent three-word expressions in the text. McCarten (2007) explains that vocabulary frequency lists extracted from a corpus can provide interesting information about the language and can "help make choices about what to teach and in what order" (p. 4). Saba's findings helped her make better-informed choices, preventing her from selecting vocabulary words that looked like interesting choices but that rarely occurred in the text. Instead, she concentrated on the most frequent words yielded by the concordance.

After analyzing her findings, Saba decided to leave behind words that her students may have already encountered in their language learning and concentrate instead on the special uses of the words *manner* and *subject*, which were very frequently used in the novel, and on the expression *I dare say*, which was also very frequent in the text and which she knew would be new to her students. Figure 21.1 shows a screen shot of the list of three-word expressions yielded by AntConc (Anthony, 2012). The expression *I dare say* is in ninth place on the frequency list and was used 31 times in the text.

Saba did not use simple frequency as her only selection criteria. As mentioned, she also consulted the COHA, a collection of texts from various sources such as books, articles, magazines, and newspapers. This collection extends from the early 1800s to 2009. The benefit of using this corpus tool is that it allows educators to develop authentic materials based on

Figure 21.1: Most Frequent Three-Word Expressions (3-grams) in *Pride and Prejudice* (Anthony, 2012)

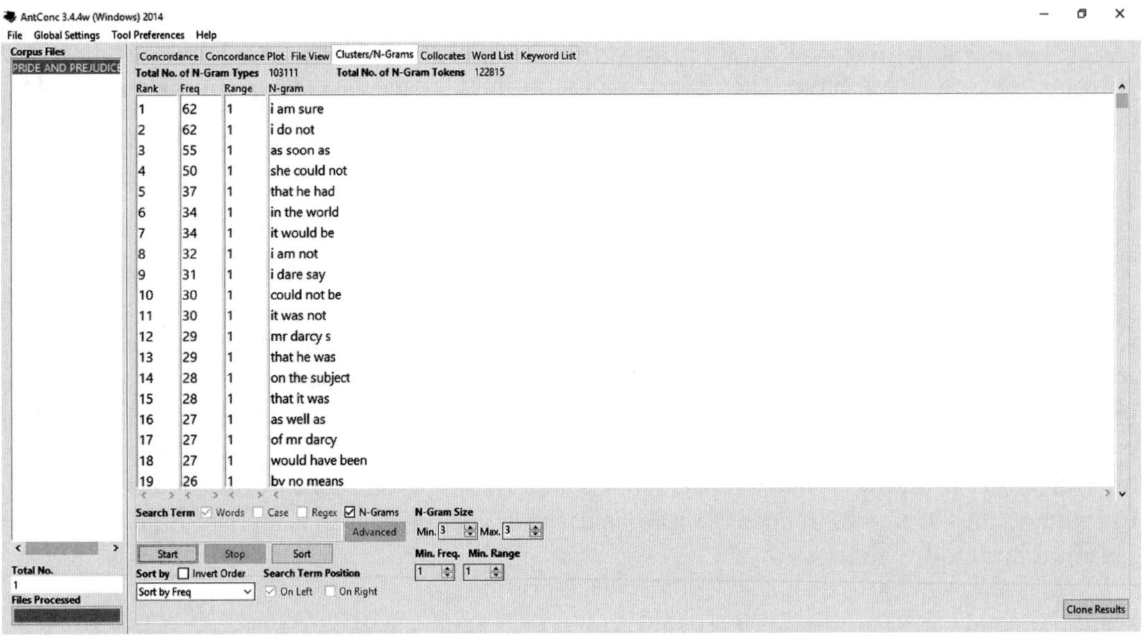

real language patterns. *Pride and Prejudice* was set in British society; COHA reflects similar trends in language use during this time period (Saba, 2014). Figure 21.2 shows how the frequency of *I dare say* was quite elevated until around 1890, where it suffered a marked decline in use. Drawing connections between natural language use and popular words or phrases raises the important notion of authenticity in CBI.

The results of her investigation of COHA showed that those vocabulary items (*manner* and *subject*) and that three-word expression (*I dare say*) were very frequent in the time period in which the novel was used. Saba could then be sure she was choosing expressions that were salient in the time period she had selected for her literature-based unit. She then used these words and expressions to create materials and activities for the vocabulary section of her literature unit.

Corpora in Materials Design: A Source of Real Examples and Text Samples

A corpus such as the one Saba developed is also a good source of examples for the use of corpora in materials design in a theme-based literature class. She used corpora to select examples from *Pride and Prejudice* to illustrate the use of the target expression *I dare say*. After reminding students of the idiomatic meaning of certain formulas in English, Saba provided students with a copy of some concordancing lines she extracted from the novel (see Figure 21.3) using Antconc (Anthony, 2012). She had students work in groups to discover the meaning of the phrase in context. Students were then asked to prepare some examples using *I dare say* reflecting situations similar to those in the contexts in the novel. Finally,

Figure 21.2: Frequency of the Phrase *I dare say* by Decade in COHA (Davies, 2010, p. 12)

SECTION	1810	1820	1830	1840	1850	1860	1870	1880	1890	1900	1910	1920	1930	1940	1950	1960	1970	1980	1990	2000
FREQ	14	129	209	220	242	260	299	390	186	134	160	121	85	55	35	30	12	9	3	10
PER MIL	11.85	18.62	15.17	13.71	14.69	15.24	16.11	19.20	9.03	6.06	7.05	4.72	3.45	2.26	1.43	1.25	0.50	0.36	0.11	0.34

SEE ALL
YEARS
AT ONCE

Figure 21.3: AntConc's Concordancing lines for *I dare say* in *Pride and Prejudice* (Anthony, 2012)

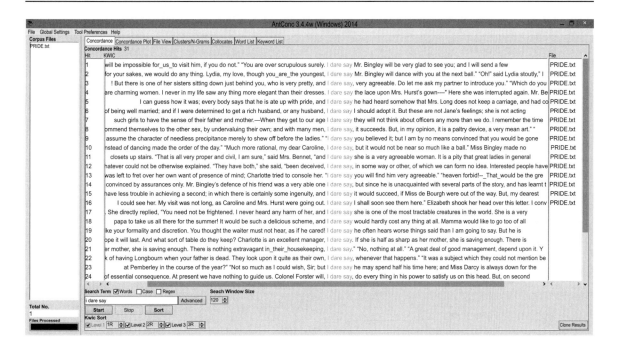

students were guided to locate passages in the book that contained the phrase, to answer questions about where in the text the phrase was used (dialogue or prose), and to identify which characters used the phrase more frequently.

Concordancing lines can be used to create materials to teach and practice specific uses of vocabulary items. Bullock (2014), for example, used concordancing lines to design an activity to teach her students the different meanings of the word *create*, a word that was included in the vocabulary list of the textbook she used for her extensive reading class. First she introduced her students to the different meanings of the word, helping them use the dictionary to identify different entries and senses. Some of the examples she extracted from the academic section of COCA that she used for a meaning identification activity are shown in Figure 21.4.

Figure 21.4: Meaning Identification Activity

Definitions for *create*

1. To bring into existence something new—*a plan to create new jobs*
2. To produce through imaginative skills—*create a painting*
3. To bring about by a course of action or behavior—*create a mess*
—Merriam Webster, n.d.

Read the examples of the word *create* and decide which definition matches the meaning of the word as it is used in the sentence. Write the definition below the sentence.

1. Programmers frequently solve programming problems by <u>creating</u> new tool programs.

   Appropriate definition: _____

2. The suffix –er can be affixed to many verbs to <u>create</u> new words (e.g., teacher, worker, and painter).

   Appropriate definition: _____

3. Collectively, these new businesses directly <u>create</u> millions of new jobs.

   Appropriate definition: _____

4. Most teachers attempt to <u>create</u> a positive learning environment in the classroom.

   Appropriate definition: _____

Adapted from Bullock, 2014, p. 36.

Using Corpus Tools in the EAP Class: Developing Student Autonomy

Providing students with concordancing lines is a very practical way of using corpus-based resources in the classroom; however, teaching students how to use a concordancer to analyze their own corpora or how to use a free online corpus extends beyond the classroom. It is a skill that students can continue using after the course is over. I designed an EAP writing class that was corpus- and genre-based (Cortes, 2007, 2011). The ESL students in her class were international graduate students who needed to polish their academic writing skills and whose main objective was writing for publication in journals in their disciplinary fields. I asked students to consult their advisors for good models of research articles and target journals; students then had to download the research articles from those journals to their computers. Finally, I instructed students in how to create their own corpus from the downloaded materials, showing them how to use a concordancer and how to analyze the writing in their respective corpora to discover linguistic conventions and organizational patterns in the published writing of their disciplines. Students read empirical findings from analyses of discourse that reflected general tendencies in the writing of research articles (Swales, 2004) and used these findings as a blueprint to evaluate and describe the writing of their specific fields. The content of this class focused on language description, and the course was designed around data-driven activities that helped students become language analysts, discovering tendencies in the writing of their disciplines that they could then apply to their own writing. I used this genre-based course to teach my students—researchers-in-training— to use corpora, corpus-based findings, and corpus tools to write for scholarly publication. After they finished analyzing the writing of their disciplinary corpora, students produced written reports showing their findings. The following is an example of a report written by a student in agronomy after analyzing the tendencies he discovered in the writing of research article introductions in his corpus (Cortes, 2007):

> The way the authors signal that they are about to start the summary of previous research of the introduction is pretty constant in my discipline, agronomy. In four out of five introductions (because the fifth didn't have Move 2) the authors used the word *research* or *studies* followed by a verb in present perfect tense (4 examples are below this paragraph). None of them used the word 'first' (I used the program Word Search) or the following verb in the past, but present perfect.
>
> We can see that all authors in my discipline (agronomy) referred to previous research following a subject orientation. All the verbs were in the present perfect. Some verbs were commonly used to report previous studies in my discipline such as: *identify, study, address,* and *conduct.* Therefore, two more verbs (*address* and *conduct*) can be added to the list of verbs mentioned by Swales: *suggest, propose, report, show, investigate, find, study, discuss, examine, develop, identify, refine, reveal, stress, summarize, support.* (p. 13)

Underlying Principles ||

The use of corpora, corpus-based research findings, and corpus tools in the language classroom cannot be viewed as a teaching approach but rather as resources that can be applied to language teaching in order to make better-informed curricular and materials development decisions—specifically about what to teach, what materials to provide students with, and when to teach certain aspects of the language. The use of these resources is closely connected to CBI because of the importance that CBI gives to the teaching of real language as a means to access content.

Let us go back to the previously described scenarios to illustrate the principles underpinning the use of these corpus-based activities and materials, as presented in Table 21.1.

Table 21.1: Observations and Principles in Using Corpus Tools in the Classroom

Observations	Underlying Principles
1. In Scenario 1, the teachers consulted anthropology professors to gather information about the types of texts they should collect for their corpus.	This stage reveals the collaborative nature of corpus-based research, which synchronizes well with the premise behind adjunct CBI courses, for example, in which content teachers and language teachers work together for curriculum decision-making and materials selection.
2. In Scenario 2, after choosing *Pride and Prejudice* as the content for her literature unit, the instructor decided to conduct her own investigation to select frequent and salient vocabulary and expressions in the text.	The use of corpora and corpus tools provided the instructor with an empirically based foundation for the selection of vocabulary and expressions to build her literature-based unit. One of the tenets of corpus-based research and its application to language teaching is to use empirically based findings to counteract linguistic intuitions that may be inaccurate or inappropriate.
3. Once target lexical items and expressions were identified in the novel, the instructor compared the frequencies in her one-text corpus to openly available online corpora.	This step supports another important principle in the investigation of corpora and corpus tools in the classroom: comparing findings across specialized corpora to determine tendencies and linguistic variation.
4. In both scenarios, teachers used corpora and corpus tools for materials design in order to create materials and activities that reflected actual language use.	CBI places a strong emphasis on the use of real language and authentic materials. Corpora offer innumerable samples of real texts and provide materials designers and teachers with an extensive number of samples of natural language to use in the design of classroom materials and activities.
5. In both scenarios, the corpus-based materials were used to familiarize students with analytical methods of studying language in search of structural and functional patterns and to discover special meanings of words and expressions in context.	These data-driven methodologies articulate with learner autonomy, another tenet of CBI. By acquiring these analytical skills, students feel empowered to continue investigating language outside the classroom, examining language use in a wide variety of contexts.

Research Agenda |||

The classroom applications of corpora presented in this chapter are only a small glimpse into the potential that the use of language corpora, corpus tools, and corpus-based findings offer to language instruction. Several areas related to the use of corpora in the classroom deserve further exploration. Among these areas are: (1) corpora and corpus-based materials availability, (2) the effectiveness of corpus-based instruction, and (3) teachers' engagement with and resistance to corpora.

Regarding corpora and corpus-based materials availability, there are, at this time, few free online corpora or corpus-based resources that are ready for teachers to use. In addition, there are a limited number of commercially available materials that are corpus-based or corpus-informed. With the exception of the series for the teaching of English for general purposes such as *Touchstone* (McCarthy, McCarten, & Sandiford, 2004), *Top Notch* (Saslow & Ascher, 2011), and *Grammar and Beyond* (Reppen, 2012), publishers have not yet taken full advantage of using corpora and corpus-based findings for the design of textbooks. The use of corpora for designing thematic units in specialized fields is in its initial stages of development. Small, specialized corpora collected for particular themes could be the core of a class or a module and would become very powerful tools in materials design. These materials could then be compared to more conventional materials used in the language classroom in order to determine whether corpus-based materials have positive effects on language learning.

Measuring the effects of the use of corpora, corpus tools, and corpus-based findings in language instruction needs to be studied in depth. Advancement in language learners' proficiency levels using corpus-based pedagogical methods or materials could be the key to more widespread use of corpora in language instruction. Staples (2009) analyzed a wide variety of studies that used corpora in the teaching of vocabulary, grammar, discourse level organization, and pragmatics in search of evidence of learning gains. The results of the studies were not conclusive. At times, the control group that did not use corpora outperformed the experimental group; at other times, there was no significant difference. Studies of this type, showing the impact of the use of corpora in language instruction, could provide more powerful evidence in favor of the use of corpora in curriculum design and in accelerated language development.

Finally, another area that needs further investigation is the relationship between teachers and corpora. Teachers often resist innovation, or only accept the parts of the innovation that align with their beliefs; other teachers may resist the innovation completely because they find it hard to accommodate within their existing orientation to teaching (Shi & Cummings, 1995). Teachers have shown varied reactions to corpus-based language instruction, from strongly embracing this innovation to strongly resisting it (Bunting, 2013). Corpus-based material development is perceived as time consuming and, realistically, it calls for the acquisition of many new skills (e.g., computer management, use of corpus tools, interpretation of corpus-based findings) that may cause negative reactions in some instructors. Further research in this area is essential to gather more evidence that could help convince those who still resist or doubt the usefulness of corpora in the language classroom.

This chapter introduced several applications of corpora and corpus tools in the classroom. The final section suggested three areas that need further investigation. Further studies in these areas could provide more information about the advantages and disadvantages of using corpora in the language classroom, in general, and in CBI and specialized language courses, in particular.

APPLYING WHAT YOU LEARNED
Questions and Tasks

1. In your opinion, how can corpora and corpus-based tools impact teachers' intuitions about the selection and sequencing of language in CBI courses?

2. Reflect on your own language learning or teaching experience. Do you see potential for corpus-related approaches to instruction and curriculum and materials design? More specifically, how might this apply to CBI contexts?

3. Visit COCA (http://corpus.byu.edu/coca/). Spend some time familiarizing yourself with the website. Go to "Where should I start?" and get information about the different options offered by the website (using the corpus to teach and learn English, a brief tour for non-linguists, etc.).

4. Think of a pair of words or expressions that your students frequently find problematic (e.g., *specially* vs. *especially*, *among* vs. *between*). Go to COCA and conduct simple searches looking for examples that could help your students distinguish between those words or expressions and that could be used to create definitions for the different uses of those terms.

REFERENCES

Anthony, L. (2012). *AntConc 3.2.3* [Computer software]. Tokyo, Japan: Waseda University. Available from http://www.laurenceanthony.net/

Barlow, M. (1999). *MonoConc Pro 2* [Computer software]. Houston, TX: Athelstan.

Basturkmen, H. (2010). *Developing courses in English for specific purposes.* New York, NY: Palgrave Macmillan.

Biber, D., Johansson, S., Leech, G., Conrad, S., & Finegan, E. (1999). *Longman grammar of spoken and written English.* London, England: Longman.

Bowker, L., & Pearson, J. (2002). *Working with specialized corpora: A practical guide to using corpora.* New York, NY: Routledge.

Bullock, M. (2014). *Using corpus-based materials to inform and enhance EAP vocabulary instruction.* Unpublished master's paper, Department of Applied Linguistics and ESL, Georgia State University, Atlanta, GA.

Bunting, J. (2013). *An investigation of language teachers' explorations of the use of corpus tools in the English for academic purposes (EAP) class* (Doctoral dissertation). Retrieved from http://scholarworks.gsu.edu/alesl_diss/26

Carter, R., & McCarthy, M. (2006). *Cambridge grammar of English.* Cambridge, England: Cambridge University Press.

Connor, U., Davis, K., De Rycker, T., Phillips, E., & Verckers, J. (1997). An international course in international business writing: Belgium, Finland, the United States. *Business and Professional Communication Quarterly, 60,* 63–74.

Cortes, V. (2007). Genre and corpora in the English for academic writing class. *The ORTESOL Journal, 25,* 9–16.

Cortes, V. (2011). Genre analysis in the academic writing class: With or without corpora? *Quaderns de Filología. Estudis Lingüístics, XVI,* 41–64.

Cortes, V. (2013). Corpora in the teaching of language for specific purposes. In C. A. Chapelle (Ed.), *The encyclopedia of applied linguistics.* New York, NY: Wiley Blackwell. doi:10.1002/9781405198431. wbeal0227

Coxhead, A. (2000). A new academic word list. *TESOL Quarterly, 34,* 213–238.

Davies, M. (2008). *The corpus of contemporary American English: 450 million words, 1990–present.* Retrieved from http://corpus.byu.edu/coca/

Davies, M. (2010). *The corpus of historical American English: 400 million words, 1810–2009.* Retrieved from http://corpus.byu.edu/coha/

Donley, K. M., & Reppen, R. (2001). Using corpus tools to highlight academic vocabulary in SCLT. *TESOL Journal, 10,* 7–12.

Hsu, W. (2011). A business wordlist for prospective EFL business postgraduates. *Asian ESP Journal, 7,* 63–99.

Johns, T. (1991). Should you be persuaded: Two examples of data-driven learning. *English Language Research Journal, 4,* 1–16.

Liu, J., & Han, L. (2015). A corpus-based environmental academic word list building and its validity test. *English for Specific Purposes, 39,* 1–11.

McCarten, J. (2007). *Teaching vocabulary: Lessons from the corpus, lessons for the classroom.* New York, NY: Cambridge University Press.

McCarthy, M., McCarten, J., & Sandiford, H. (2004). *Touchstone 1.* Cambridge, England: Cambridge University Press.

Martinez, I., Beck, S., & Panza, C. (2009). Academic vocabulary in agriculture research articles: A corpus-based study. *English for Specific Purposes, 28,* 183–198.

Reppen, R. (2012). *Grammar and beyond 1.* Cambridge, England: Cambridge University Press.

Saba, D. (2014). *Using corpus tools to teach vocabulary in a literature-oriented ESL/EFL class.* Unpublished master's paper, Department of Applied Linguistics and ESL, Georgia State University, Atlanta, GA.

Saslow, J., & Ascher, A. (2011). *Top notch* (2nd ed.). White Plains, NY: Pearson.

Shi, L., & Cummings, A. (1995). Teachers' conception of second language writing instruction: Five case studies. *Journal of Second Language Writing, 4,* 87–111.

Simpson, R. C., Briggs, S. L., Ovens, J., & Swales, J. M. (2002). *The Michigan corpus of academic spoken English.* Ann Arbor, MI: University of Michigan Press.

Sinclair, J. (2003). *Collins COBUILD advanced learner's English dictionary.* Glasgow, Scotland: HarperCollins.

Staples, S. (2009). *Using corpora in language instruction.* Unpublished manuscript. Department of English, Northern Arizona University, Flagstaff, AZ.

Stoller, F. (2008). Content-based instruction. In N. Van Deusen-Scholl & N. H. Hornberger (Eds.), *Encyclopedia of language and education* (pp. 59–70). New York, NY: Springer.

Swales, J. (2004). *Research genres.* Cambridge, England: Cambridge University Press.

Yang, M. (2015). A nursing academic word list. *English for Specific Purposes, 37,* 27–38.

Part V

Focus on Assessment and Research in Content-Based Instruction

Chapter 22

Fundamental Principles in Content-Based Assessment

Maureen Snow Andrade & Brent A. Green

||| A Glimpse into Assessment in the Adjunct Model Classroom

Jane teaches in an academic ESL program at a small, private four-year university with a large population of international students. The credit-bearing ESL program prepares matriculated students for future coursework, and many students are concurrently enrolled in ESL and other university-level courses. Most faculty at the university are familiar with, although not generally experts at, teaching ESL students. In the upcoming semester, Jane's ESL integrated skills course will be linked to an introductory level humanities course. Jane makes an appointment to speak with the humanities instructor, Professor Cory Smith, so that they can review the course requirements and their expectations for assessment. In preparation for the meeting, Jane reviews the syllabus for the humanities course and notes the objectives and related assignments: essay and short-answer exams; performance reviews of campus events in the areas of music, dance, drama, film, and art; and an online discussion forum. She also reviews the objectives for her own course in terms of targeted language skills: paragraph and essay structure, rhetorical patterns, grammatical accuracy, academic vocabulary development, lecture comprehension, note-taking, and presentation and discussion skills.

As Jane and Cory discuss the course, they identify the types of knowledge and skill development expected of students and particularly how each will evaluate assignments. Jane explains that her assessments will focus primarily on language tasks embedded in the humanities course assignments, and may also consist of unique assessments related to her course objectives, but which use the humanities course content. As an example of the former, she plans to develop a rubric for the performance reviews that focuses on content, organization, grammar, and mechanics; this will complement Cory's focus on students' ability to identify and critique various elements of fine arts performances and exhibitions (such as principles of design, creative expression, interpretation of artistic genres, technique, originality, communication of intent, and presentation as applicable to particular art forms). Jane will also have additional assignments for her course based on the humanities content but focused on the

ESL course objectives. This might include reading comprehension tests with readings related to the humanities textbook and lecture content. In this way, students will review and reinforce the content they are learning as they demonstrate their acquisition of reading comprehension and vocabulary skills.

In both classes, the instructors agree that the final exam will play a key role in whether or not students pass their courses. Cory recognizes that he is accountable for the decisions (e.g., grades) he makes at the end of the term. He has indicated that his final test will be worth 70 percent of the final grade. The test will be an indication of student achievement of the course outcomes identified in the syllabus. Jane views herself as accountable to the students and other stakeholders (i.e., future content teachers, ESL program administrators, fellow ESL teachers, university administrators, parents, etc.) for making the correct decisions about her students' academic language abilities. She understands that the decisions she has to make high-stakes decisions at the end of the semester. If she determines that students are not ready to move into introductory level coursework, these students must repeat the course and spend additional time developing their academic English skills. Although students in the ESL program are concurrently enrolled in ESL and other university courses, they must satisfactorily pass criterion-based English language exams to demonstrate their ability to succeed on their own in non-ESL coursework. They are then free to enroll in any course of their choosing without further ESL course support.

As such, Jane is determined to base her grades on students' demonstrated proficiency on academic language tasks rather than on effort such as attendance or participation (i.e., unless the latter is graded based on linguistic criteria). For example, she tells Cory that she will develop a rubric for students' participation in the online discussion board, which would be based on the ESL course objectives such as discussion skills as well as grammatical accuracy and organization. Cory indicates that he already has a rubric that Jane may want to adapt. Cory's focus is on number and length of posts, discussion board etiquette, and comprehension of content. Jane and Cory agree that although students will be getting credit for this assignment in both courses, the expectations, targeted objectives, and related grading will differ.

Assessment in the Adjunct Model |||

The adjunct model is a form of CBI that links a content course to an ESL course (see Snow & Brinton, this volume). The content course may be an introductory level university course while the ESL course typically focuses on integrated skills or emphasizes specific skills such as reading, listening/speaking, or writing. In some cases, more than one ESL course is linked to the content course, with each ESL course focused on different skill areas such as speaking, writing and grammar, reading, listening, and note-taking (Iancu, 1997). Rather than relying on published ESL textbooks, the ESL coursework is usually based on the readings, lectures, and related assignments of the linked content course.

An advantage of the adjunct model is student motivation. Students in the paired courses directly encounter the academic tasks typical of university courses and are better able to identify their linguistic strengths and weaknesses in terms of performing these tasks. Rather than ESL instructors telling their students about what to expect, the students experience authentic academic work for themselves with the support of an ESL instructor who facilitates their language learning. This authenticity provides an added incentive for both students and instructors.

CBI models can and should be adapted to specific contexts within institutions and even countries, depending on the size of the ESL population and the needs of students. For example, a type of CBI model proving to be effective in Australia, where more than 20 percent of post-secondary enrollments consist of international students (Institute of International Education, 2012), is discipline-specific English language support embedded in required coursework (Arkoudis, Baik, & Richardson, 2012). This model provides an alternative to "stand-alone" ESL courses that are not linked to a subject matter course (such as occurs in the adjunct model) but are instead traditional skill, integrated skill, or even theme-based courses taught by ESL professionals. In the discipline-specific model, language and content are integrated and the faculty member teaching the discipline courses, rather than an ESL professional, assumes responsibility for the development of both content and language (although ideally, the faculty member collaborates with ESL experts on approaches and materials development). Thus, faculty in various disciplines are gaining direct skill in teaching ESL students rather than this being the responsibility of an ESL instructor in a separate course, such as in the adjunct model.

While the adjunct model provides clear benefits, administrators and instructors must consider factors such as the time needed for the ESL instructor to identify learners' needs related to the content course, attend the course, create materials from the course textbook and lectures, and coordinate with the faculty member of the linked course. This is evident in the opening scenario where the two instructors meet to coordinate objectives and assignments. In some cases, ESL instructors are given additional workload credits to accommodate this additional effort (Andrade & Makaafi, 2001). Our experience indicates that content faculty members must be assured that there will be little extra work required and that they are expected to teach their course as they normally would. The primary accommodation on their part is having ESL students and an ESL instructor in the classroom. Some faculty members coordinate closely with the ESL instructor while others do not. Both approaches can be effective. Other logistics must also be considered, such as selecting appropriate courses and instructors, planning in-service training, delineating instructor roles, scheduling, registration, grading, and assessment (see Goldstein, this volume).

In our discussion of issues and principles for CBI assessment, we concentrate on the adjunct model. However, much of the discussion can be extended to variations of CBI, such as theme-based and sheltered approaches, and CLIL and EMI. Assessment of student learning in an adjunct course must take into consideration both language skills and content. However, in the model we are most familiar with, ESL instructors are encouraged to focus on language skills—lecture comprehension, vocabulary development, grammatical accuracy, organizational patterns, reading skills, presentations, and class participation, as well as cultural norms related to interacting in the academic context of an English-speaking university.

One of the major conundrums of language assessment in a content-based model is the issue that language and content are difficult to separate. In traditional language testing, the test developer's job is to ensure that test tasks allow test users to make correct inferences about a learner's language ability. In order to reduce variability, language testers try their best to strip the test of content in order to make tasks equitable for all learners, regardless of the previous knowledge they bring with them to the test. We can see that this can be an almost impossible task for the learner because learning and testing does not happen in a vacuum. It is extremely difficult to develop test tasks that hold background knowledge constant. Douglas (2013) captures the challenge for the tester:

> Practitioners have gradually come to the realization that language knowledge and background knowledge are very difficult to distinguish in practice and that, although specific purpose testers are not in the business of assessing professional, vocational, or academic competence in specific purpose fields, such competence is inextricably linked to language performance in those fields. (p. 369)

While Douglas' focus is on specific purpose tests, the same argument can be made for language teachers developing tests in CBI, especially in the adjunct model. In other words, language and content teachers must consider the complex interactions between language and content knowledge as they consider test content, tasks, and individual learner performance on such content and tasks (e.g., see Mislevy & Yin, 2009). The CBI test developer must find ways to situate and/or contextualize the test tasks and individual test items so that both content and language are considered a part of the construct being measured.

In the adjunct model of CBI, students learn content naturally as they develop proficiency through reading, writing, and discussion; however, the actual assessment of content is left to the instructor with expertise in that area. We support the view that "even though adjunct ... instructors feel that content cannot be disregarded, they will never understand the content to the same degree as the content instructor" unless they are trained in that discipline (Goldstein, Campbell, & Cummings, 1997, p. 336). The process of learning language and content simultaneously also holds true for other CBI models, such as theme-based instruction, which presents a similar situation to that of adjunct instruction in that the ESL instructor is not necessarily a content expert. The assessment in theme-based instruction, however, also involves an inextricable linking of learners' language ability and content knowledge.

A good starting place for any content or language teacher is an understanding of the purposes for which the tests will be designed. For a content teacher, this would more than likely include a demonstration of specific content knowledge. A language teacher would probably want to know if the student is able to handle the linguistic demands of specific content courses. Regardless, both content and language teachers are using test tasks to make inferences about what their learners know and can do with both language and content (Bachman & Palmer, 2010).

In an adjunct model, both teachers need to begin with a clear description of the language and content tasks required to successfully complete the course or particular aspects of the course. Generating test tasks is then a matter of sampling from the course content and academic language use domains. This gives both teachers the ability to make valid score interpretations and decisions about students' language and content abilities. Interpreting students' performance on test tasks and making decisions about that performance becomes a matter or establishing evidence about what students know and can do with both language and content.

This is analogous to a court of law where evidence is presented to support or rebut a legal decision. Bachman (2005), Bachman and Palmer (2010), and others (e.g., see Kane, 1992, 2006; Kane, Crooks, & Chohen, 1999; Mislevy, Steinberg & Almond, 2003) have suggested using an argument structure framework to justify the use of assessments in real-world and instructional settings. Providing justification requires a framework where claims about student ability on test scores are supported with warrants and backing while counterclaims are supported with rebuttal data. How one goes about justifying the decisions in a content-based instructional setting such as the adjunct model is described in the next section.

Perspectives on Assessment in the Adjunct Model |||

ESL instructors must determine their overall goals for assessment of student learning—what to measure, why, and how. In CBI models, assessment can be more meaningful than in more traditional language courses as the content and academic tasks are directly relevant to students. Instructors are presented with a number of assessment options, both formative and summative,[1] in a CBI course. As indicated in the opening scenario, course objectives provide the foundation for assessment decisions, and coordination with the content instructor is essential. We next present practical examples that identify some of the key issues faced by content and language instructors as they determine appropriate assessment strategies in the CBI model.

Building a Body of Evidence

Cory, the humanities instructor whom we met in the opening scenario, has administered two tests. One was an essay exam and the other a multiple choice test. As Cory reviewed the scores of the ESL students in the class, he found that they generally did much better on the multiple choice test than on the essay exam. He could not see the same pattern in the scores of his mainstream students. He wonders why the ESL students did better on the multiple choice test. Were English language skills an issue that interfered with the students' ability to express themselves effectively on the essay? Was it the content of the two exams—did students grasp the concepts tested by the multiple choice test better than they did the concepts examined by the essay exam? Had he taught the concepts differently? He wondered which of these exam types best fit what he wanted to accomplish in the course. What could he do differently to address the learning needs of the ESL students? He decided to meet with Jane to discuss the test results and get some insights.

What Cory needs to think about is how he can build a body of evidence based on his students' scores so that he can justify his test use (a determination of whether students are able to complete the performance-based goals he has set for them). Because he is getting differential results from his ESL students—that is, poor scores on constructed response items (such as the essay exam) and good scores on selected response items (such as the multiple choice test)—he is unsure whether the poor performance is due to inadequate learning, whether the writing task is too difficult for his leaners, or whether he is being overly harsh in his essay grading. Jane helps him to understand how to go about justifying his intended uses of the particular tests. She does this by first getting Cory to think about the purposes for his two tests, the multiple choice and essay. Cory explains that the multiple choice test is designed to check his students' understanding of course content while the essay is designed to help them apply the content to new situations. When asked about how he has prepared students for each test, Cory states that the multiple choice test corresponds to his lectures and textbook reading, but he admits that he has not really prepared students for the essay. In the past, Cory's students have not had trouble applying the principles to new situations and discussing how this works in writing. Based on this observation, Cory might consider integrating the key components of essay writing into his course. Better yet, Cory can share the essay results with Jane who will then work with students in the ESL course to help them improve on their essay skills. Since this corresponds with Jane' own course goals, this process works well for both instructors.

At this point it is important to discuss two important concepts in assessment that are pervasive in educational assessment literature and practice: validity and reliability. Reliability refers to consistency of measurement. In Cory's case, he needs to be certain that the test conditions (i.e., environment, test tasks, student preparation) remain consistent over subsequent administrations of the tests he gives during his class. If performance is not consistent, then he may need to look at the conditions that are impacting reliability. Validity refers to the "meaningfulness and appropriateness of the interpretations that we make on the basis of the test scores" (Bachman & Palmer, 1996, p. 21). Cory has to be concerned that the decisions he makes, such as assigning a grade or determining whether a student has met a particular learning outcome or all of the outcomes, must be based on tests that sample from the domain in which the outcomes were developed. It is evident in this case that Cory may have a problem with the interpretations of outcomes for the ESL students because their performance on the constructed response items and essay tests is mixed.

Two other approaches to challenges presented by Cory's tests are related to how he might modify or adjust his tests to address his concerns or perhaps those that might arise from his students, both mainstream and ESL. The first is to conduct a post-analysis on the constructed response (multiple choice) test, and the second is to determine the degree of rater difficulty on the essay by asking others to rate the essays and examining inter-rater reliability. By conducting a post-analysis of this multiple choice test, Cory may be able to determine if certain test items were too difficult or too easy. A common student complaint is that tests are too difficult. Our experience is that rarely do students complain about what they perceive to be easy test items. It is not difficult for Cory to analyze his tests to determine if this is the case and present that evidence to his students.

Cory can also gather evidence about his essay scores by asking Jane and other teachers to grade his students' essays based on the rubric Cory has developed for this test. If he finds that Jane and the other teachers are giving similar ratings, he has gathered evidence that his assessment rating practices are sufficient. If he finds that there is a significant mismatch between his scores and the other raters, he may need to modify his rating practices. While an explanation of the exact procedures for post-analysis and inter-rater reliability is beyond the scope of this chapter, this information can be readily found in most educational assessment texts (e.g., see Carr, 2011).

Using Assessment to Inform Pedagogical Practice

Jane attended the first few class sessions of the humanities course. She read the assigned textbook sections and took notes in the lectures. This gave her an idea of which tasks students needed to master in terms of academic language skills. Based on this, she began planning her lessons and how she would assess student learning. For example, she observed that Cory, the humanities instructor, used a lot of descriptive language to talk about paintings. She wondered if students were familiar with this type of language. She also noted that students would need to compare and contrast paintings that were representative of different periods of art. To do this, students had to synthesize, analyze, and support a position. Jane planned a lesson in which she introduced selected descriptive vocabulary from the context of her lecture notes. Students practiced this vocabulary as they responded orally in pairs to questions about the paintings and the time period. She introduced them to the comparison/contrast essay pattern. Students drafted and refined essays, focusing on the paintings they had studied. Jane scored the essays with a rubric she developed that accounted for linguistic features as well as content and organization.

For her part, Jane needs to identify how students' performance on the essays (based on their rubric scores) can inform her pedagogical practices. In addition, she needs to be certain that students who are not performing well can get the feedback and practice they need to improve. This might mean taking a formative approach to the assessment and allowing students to work on multiple drafts. In other words, students are given feedback based on the rubric grades and meet with Jane individually to discuss problem areas. Then students are given the chance to work through their problem areas by revising their work and resubmitting for a new score. The teacher can also use this evidence to see where to introduce new concepts or recycle previously covered content. The assessment and a careful analysis of the results provide the evidence needed for both students and teachers to change practices. While this is an important process where assessment is formative in nature, Jane must also think about the summative decisions she will need to make in terms of what students know and can do with academic language at the end of the term. She must determine whether students are ready to exit the ESL program and enter credit-bearing introductory level college coursework at the end of the semester. She must also keep in mind that she will more than likely be asked to justify the decisions she is making about her students.

Making Decisions Based on Assessment Evidence

One day, Jane was walking down the hallway where the ESL program instructors had their offices. She met up with Patrick, who was teaching another adjunct course—the one linked with American history. They started visiting, and Patrick explained how he had been focusing on helping students understand the content because they were lost due to not having the same background as their American classmates. He has been reviewing what the history instructor covered in each lecture, providing students with extra background readings, and then giving them a ten-question true/false quiz on the content. He expected that the history instructor would be testing students on this information. Jane reminded Patrick that students also needed to pass the summative ESL reading/writing exam, which required them to identify main ideas and supporting details, make inferences about the information, and express their analyses in written form. Scores would be based on students' abilities to complete these tasks and language proficiency would be emphasized. As Jane walked away, Patrick began to rethink his approach. Was what he was doing in class a good fit with what students were expected to achieve by the end of the course? Patrick recognized that he was addressing student needs for additional content background, but that he must integrate this more explicitly with language skill development for a balanced approach.

It is obvious that Patrick has not carefully thought out how his current assessment practices would help him determine the kinds of summative decisions he needs to make about his students at the end of the semester. Fortunately, there is still time for Patrick to change. Providing opportunities to access and acquire background knowledge will help students understand the content and is an important pedagogical practice in both adjunct instruction and in other models of CBI. However, this may be insufficient to determine if students can independently access content in other college-level courses. Coupled with this is the fact that a ten-item true/false test does not provide the necessary information needed to make a summative decision about Patrick's students. In other words, it would be hard for Patrick to justify to his students and colleagues that the decisions regarding whether students are ready to advance should be based on student scores on a series of ten-item true/false exams. Those summative decisions should focus on the degree to which course objectives are met in Patrick's class. By requiring students to demonstrate what they know and can do in terms of academic English skills, Patrick will be able to make good decisions about his learners.

We would recommend that Patrick rethink his practices and begin developing language test tasks embedded in the history content that closely resemble those that will be required of his students in college-level courses. Summative decisions at the end of each semester in ESL courses should be based on how well students are able to demonstrate that they can independently access college-level reading and writing in order to learn content.

Underlying Principles for CBI Assessment |||

As the information in the chapter has illustrated, these assessment principles must be considered in the adjunct model:

- Establish clear language and content learning outcomes.
- Create test tasks that sample from real-world or instructional domains.
- Determine how to assess in a formative and summative manner.
- Determine the kinds of interpretations being made about the language and content of the assessments.
- Be prepared to justify to key stakeholders the decisions being made about students based on the assessments.

Table 22.1 lists some observations from the scenarios and examples presented in the chapter and connects them to relevant assessment principles.

Table 22.1: Observations and Underlying Principles

Observations	Underlying Principles
1. The content and ESL instructors meet to discuss the syllabi and goals for each of their courses, collaborate on their approaches, and delineate their roles.	**Establishing Language and Content Learning Outcomes:** Pre-semester and ongoing planning is needed to determine learning goals and how to help students achieve them. Outcomes should reflect the learning goals of the content course and the ESL course with instructors focused on their own course goals and with the understanding that these reinforce each other.
2. The ESL instructor creates tasks directly related to observed student linguistic needs in the content course (e.g., verbal and written language practice with descriptive language, comparison/contrast patterns, discussion skills through the discussion board postings, etc.); she assesses students' progress using rubrics and criteria focused on the goals of the language class. The ESL instructor adapts a rubric from the content instructor so that it focuses on language learning outcomes.	**Creating Test Tasks:** In adjunct instruction, the roles of the content and ESL instructors must be clear in terms of pedagogical focus, design of activities, and assessments. Content and language are intertwined but the goal of the ESL instructor is to focus on language needs. Strategies for assessing learning may involve separate assessments for the two courses, single assessments emphasizing different grading criteria (e.g., content vs. language), or an integrated assessment approach. Test tasks in the ESL course reflect the actual academic tasks required in the content course.
3. Both instructors provide opportunities for students to demonstrate their progress on the established course learning outcomes. This includes using descriptive vocabulary activities, comparison/contrast writing assignments using organization patterns and new vocabulary, essay and multiple choice exams, and other measures.	**Determining Formative and Summative Measures:** A variety of formative and summative measures should be introduced to measure student learning on various academic tasks related to the content being learned. Instructors must stay focused on course goals and the decisions they will need to make at the end of the semester to determine students' ability to advance. The ESL instructor must be focused on intended language learning goals rather than helping students "pass" the content course by reviewing the content.
4. Different test types (multiple choice vs. essay) may produce different results, making it difficult to get a true understanding of students' content and language mastery. Student performance on formative and summative assessments must be analyzed to determine what is actually occurring in terms of learning.	**Interpreting Assessments:** Instructors must evaluate the effectiveness of the approaches, strategies, and instruments they use and compare learner performance. They must determine what needs to be retaught and also how to collaborate with each other to make sure student needs are being met. This involves analyzing test results, providing students with additional practice and assessment opportunities as needed, and considering how this information will assist with summative evaluations of students' mastery of the learning objectives.
5. In the adjunct model, ESL instructors may feel the need to provide additional content support and instruction rather than leaving this to the content instructor or collaborating with the content instructor related to this need.	**Justifying Decisions:** Decisions about student learning must be made on the basis of course learning objectives and results on the assessments instructors have administered to measure student achievement of these objectives. In this way, decisions about student progress can be justified to key stakeholders.

These principles are illustrated with examples from the adjunct model of CBI. However, they apply to all forms of CBI. The critical issue in the CBI approach is the relationship between content and language. Although the two are somewhat inseparable in terms of instruction and related assessment, test design (e.g., what is tested and how) and grading approaches (e.g., how points are assigned, and the use of rubrics with specific language-based categories and descriptors) can certainly help inform instructors and administrators of learners' linguistic abilities.

Research Agenda ||

Several important CBI assessment areas could benefit from additional study. The first is a deeper understanding of the interactions between the content, language, and background knowledge that learners bring to the assessment task and how these might impact the decisions teachers make about their learners. Douglas' (2000, 2001, 2013) work has helped us understand that content and language are difficult to isolate and assess. However, we also need to understand how background knowledge adds to or detracts from individual learner performance. Mislevy and Yin (2009) use an example from the German language: "What makes medical knowledge tasks in German difficult for German medical students is the medical knowledge, but what makes them difficult for American doctors studying German is the German language" (p. 260). The question is: How one can build an argument for assessment interpretations that accounts for individualized learner's prior knowledge? Research into this area could provide valuable insights into how we construct our arguments, make valid decisions, and justify those decisions to key stakeholders.

In order for us to unpack the kind of learner variation that occurs in assessment, we also need to examine how we might use more robust measurement models in the classroom. It has been our experience that very few ESL teachers use basic analysis tools with their class assessments. Some examples are rubrics and checklists for constructed type items and item analysis for selected response items to determine overall test performance and to gauge how well individual items are discriminating learner performance. Even those who know how to use such tools and recognize their value are unlikely to go a step further to consider how individual student variance is related to more than one factor or the interaction among a variety of factors. Multidimensional statistical modeling could be very helpful in giving us this information (e.g., see Brennan, 2001). The question is whether or not teachers can benefit from this knowledge and the application of such models in their classrooms. Another important question is whether they can be supported and educated to achieve this end goal.

Finally, it is important to better understand the use of argument structure in local classroom test settings. Since Bachman and Palmer's (2010) framework is relatively new, a deeper understanding of how effective it is in CBI classrooms and programs would be valuable. Bachman's (2005) own desire regarding the practical use of this framework is noted: "Hopefully, if language testers find this approach useful, experience with the approach will grow, and studies reporting on practical issues in actual test development settings will be forthcoming" (p. 29).

APPLYING WHAT YOU LEARNED
Questions and Tasks

1. Based on the discussion in this chapter, what do you consider to be the most challenging aspects of assessment regardless of the CBI model? If you were an ESL program administrator, how would you address these potential challenges with in-service training?

2. As an ESL instructor, what process would you use to determine appropriate assessments for your students in a CBI model? How would you ensure that these assessments help you justify the decisions you make about your students to key stakeholders?

3. Do you agree or disagree with the position taken by the authors that in the adjunct model, the content instructor should focus on assessing content and the language instructor should focus on assessing language? Can they be separated for assessment purposes? Explain.

4. Give an example of a formative and a summative assessment you would develop for the class described in this chapter. Provide justification for your approach using the assessment principles introduced. Then explain how you would use the results to inform your pedagogy.

ENDNOTES

1. Robert Stake is famously known for his definition of formal and summative assessment. He said, "When the cook tastes the soup, that's formative. When the guests taste the soup, that's summative" (Patton, 1997, p. 69). Tests given during instruction are often referred to as *formative* assessments. These are typically used to monitor progress, detect errors, and provide feedback for teachers and learners. Tests typically given at the end of a course are *summative* assessments. These are used to determine the degree to which learning outcomes and/or performance standards have been met. They are also used to certify accomplishments and assign grades (e.g., see Miller, Linn, & Gronlund, 2012).

REFERENCES

Andrade, M. S., & Makaafi, J. H. (2001). Guidelines for establishing adjunct courses at the university level. *TESOL Journal, 10*(2/3), 34–39.

Arkoudis, S., Baik, C., & Richardson, S. (2012). *English language standards in higher education: From entry to exit.* Camberwell, Australia: Australian Council for Educational Research.

Bachman, L. F. (2005). Building and supporting a case for test use. *Language Assessment Quarterly, 2*(1), 1–34.

Bachman, L. F., & Palmer, A. S. (1996). *Language testing in practice: Developing language assessments and justifying their use in the real world.* Oxford, England: Oxford University Press.

Bachman, L. F., & Palmer, A. S. (2010). *Language assessment in practice.* New York, NY: Oxford University Press.

Brennan, R. L. (2001). *Generalizability theory.* New York, NY: Springer.

Carr, N. T. (2011). *Designing and analyzing language tests.* Oxford, England: Oxford University Press.

Douglas, D. (2000). *Assessing language for specific purposes.* Cambridge, England: Cambridge University Press.

Douglas, D. (2001). Three problems in testing language for specific purposes: Authenticity, specificity and inseparability. In C. Elder et al. (Eds.), *Experimenting with uncertainty: Essays in honour of Alan Davies* (pp. 45–52). Cambridge, England: Cambridge University Press.

Douglas, D. (2013). ESP and assessment. In B. Paltridge & S. Starfield (Eds.), *The handbook of English for specific purposes* (pp. 367–383). Malden, MA: Wiley-Blackwell.

Goldstein, L., Campbell, C., & Cummings, M. C. (1997). Smiling through the turbulence: The flight attendant syndrome and writing instructor status in the adjunct model. In M. A. Snow & D. M. Brinton (Eds.), *The content-based classroom: Perspectives on integrating language and content* (pp. 331–339). White Plains, NY: Longman.

Iancu, M. (1997). Adopting the adjunct model: A case study. In M. A. Snow & D. M. Brinton (Eds.), *The content-based classroom: Perspectives on integrating language and content* (pp. 149–157). White Plains, NY: Longman.

Institute of International Education. (2012). *Project atlas.* New York, NY: Author. Retrieved from www.iie.org/Research-and-Publications/Project-Atlas

Kane, M. (1992). An argument-based approach to validity. *Psychological Bulletin, 112,* 527–535.

Kane, M. (2006). Validation. In R. L. Brennan (Ed.), *Educational measurement* (4th ed.). New York, NY: American Council on Education.

Kane, M., Crooks, T., & Chohen, A. (1999). Validating measures of performance. *Educational Measurement: Issues and Practice, 18*(2), 5–17.

Miller, M. D., Linn, R. L., & Gronlund, N. E. (2012). *Measurement and assessment in teaching* (11th ed.). Upper Saddle River, NJ: Prentice Hall.

Mislevy, R. J., Steinberg, L. S., & Almond, R. G. (2003). On the structure of educational assessments. *Measurement: Interdisciplinary Research and Perspectives, 1*(1), 3–62.

Mislevy, R. J., & Yin, C. (2009). If language is a complex adaptive system, what is language assessment? *Language Learning, 59*(1), 249–267.

Patton, M. Q. (1997). *Utilization-focused evaluation: The new century text* (3rd ed.). Thousand Oaks, CA: Sage.

Chapter 23

||| Conducting Research on
Content-Based Language
Instruction

Sandra Zappa-Hollman & Patricia A. Duff

||| A Glimpse into the Content-Based Classroom

At Vantage College, University of British Columbia (UBC), a group of several hundred international students have strong academic credentials but only borderline English language scores for university admission. These students are expected to benefit from very focused, content-based, academic English language instruction during the first year of their bachelor's degree and have therefore been admitted to a new one-year, custom-designed program with a dual focus on English academic discourse and content knowledge; that is, the program embeds academic English instruction across courses in their chosen disciplines in applied science, arts, management, or science through an adjunct-like model (e.g., Brinton, Snow & Wesche, 2003). With smaller size classes, a coordinated curriculum, and materials and instruction that view the learning of language and content as integrated, the students can develop their subject-area and language knowledge in tandem. Students attend weekly lectures in their disciplines together with a linked language-focused adjunct course. Content course instructors (e.g., in chemistry, geography, or math) and academic English instructors meet regularly to collaborate on different aspects of course and materials design and to exchange pedagogical strategies for teaching the same students. Because the program has just recently been launched, there is an institutional need—and desire—to examine and evaluate the implementation and results of the content-based (or perhaps more accurately, discipline-based) approach in order to improve the program and its outcomes going forward (if necessary). The administrators, course developers, instructors, and staff are considering what type of research should be carried out in this new program to better understand its effectiveness, students' and instructors' experiences, and learning outcomes.

Conducting Research in Content-Based Language Classrooms and Programs |||

An increasing number and type of content-based language programs or integrated programs are being offered worldwide from kindergarten through to graduate studies, both in countries where the language of instruction is also the language of the wider community and in countries where it is considered a foreign language. This growing demand for CBI representing a range of curricular models has provided opportunities for conducting research on the contexts, teaching and learning processes, and effectiveness of this pedagogy (e.g., in terms of linguistic and disciplinary learning outcomes and learner satisfaction). Much of the research to date has focused on program design and curriculum and materials development. Hence, there is a need for studies focusing on program evaluation and other kinds of research. A range of research approaches exist and are illustrated in the next section. They include, for example, quasi-experimental, quantitative studies and surveys as well as in-depth case studies of individual learners or ethnographic studies of classroom interaction. Also possible are micro-analytic studies examining the negotiation of language in relation to just one or a small number of oral or written language tasks or activities or written texts. Mixed-methods research designs, using both quantitative and qualitative methods, can also be used. Many existing resources provide guidelines for conducting classroom-based research in applied linguistics (e.g., Brown, 2014; Dörnyei, 2007; Duff, 2007; Lightbown, 2014; Mackey & Gass, 2016; McKay, 2006; Nunan & Bailey, 2009). Furthermore, recent empirical studies conducted in various parts of the world and representing a range of research traditions and questions can be found in such journals as the *Journal of Immersion and Content-Based Language Education, Annual Review of Applied Linguistics, TESOL Quarterly, Language Teaching Research, International Journal of Bilingual Education and Bilingualism*, and *Journal of English for Academic Purposes*.

Research Purposes, Approaches, and Questions |||

As several decades of research in the area of CBI or CLIL attest,[1] many kinds of research are possible in programs of the sort described in the scenario. The research questions and research design depend fundamentally on the issues of greatest importance or interest to the researcher and possibly to those sponsoring the research, for example, a school or university that seeks answers to urgent questions or concerns. Here, we outline five possible types of research, ranging from large, multi- or mixed-methods studies to smaller, more ethnographic case studies to more micro-level discourse analyses.

Program Evaluation

Institutionally designed research into the overall effectiveness of programs such as the one at UBC Vantage College described earlier usually involves a mixed-methods *program evaluation* (e.g., Lynch, 1996) seeking to document, measure, understand, and explain some of the most important processes and outcomes in programs, according to program stakeholders. This approach to research tends to be very broad, obtaining evidence of effectiveness through grades, test scores, retention data, and other quantitative measures, but also typically capturing the perspectives of program participants (e.g., students, instructors, administrators) as well regarding their reasons for selecting the program, their satisfaction with aspects of the program, their views on areas of curricular or instructional strength or weakness, issues of attrition, and so on. Thus, program evaluation involves obtaining both quantitative and qualitative data to provide a well-rounded understanding of the program with sufficient documentation to be useful to those in charge of the program and others (e.g., parents or prospective students) seeking evidence of its effectiveness. Case studies of individual students, instructors, or courses can also be included to provide concrete, vivid examples of experiences and outcomes, but these are often secondary to quantitative measures in program evaluation. More specifically, research design and methods for the purpose of program evaluation might include:

- Questionnaires (with students, instructors, administrators) about their backgrounds, goals, attitudes and motivation, and levels of satisfaction (Dörnyei, 2007)
- Semi-structured interviews (either one on one or in small groups known as focus groups) with participants and other stakeholders (see discussion in Talmy, 2010)
- Quantitative measures of student performance based on English assessments (e.g., pre-post tests or other ways of documenting progress) and content-course grades, perhaps in relation to a larger cohort (Lynch, 1996)
- Scheduled observations of courses, both adjunct-English (or other language of instruction, if not English) and content (McKay, 2006)
- Selection of cases to explore in somewhat more detail, likely selected on the basis of different types of ethnolinguistic or academic backgrounds and experiences (Duff, 2008)
- Observations of instructional planning meetings when issues and curriculum are discussed and revised
- An analysis of curriculum materials designed for the program involving both attention to language and content (Brown, 1995)
- Possible tracking of students beyond their year in the enriched CBI/CLIL program (i.e., into their second or remaining years of undergraduate study in a large multi-year study).

Classroom-Oriented Discourse and Feedback Processes

A second approach to research would be more focused, aiming to examine, for example, student writing or the discourse of CBI and oral interaction (see, e.g., Dalton-Puffer, 2007). Research questions might address the following themes, which have attracted considerable theoretical and practical discussion in recent years: What kind of feedback on a student's oral or written language is (or might be) most effective, and why? What functional models of language are espoused in the program; how, why, and to what effect? What is the role of metalanguage (e.g., *nominalization*) in scaffolding academic language development? Thus, the questions might address classroom interaction specifically and the nature and function of particular kinds of explicit language instruction and modeling, or feedback on language produced by students. The research might also document teachers' and students' changing practices and performance over time. For example, does a learner who appears to be reticent or who struggles to produce language earlier in the course become more able to participate in classroom discussion or activities over time, and if so, in what manner? How do novice teachers become more skilled at teaching in a CBI context with experience? How do their instructional practices, beliefs, professional identities (e.g., when working closely with content teachers), and language use change over time, and why?

Alternatively, the study might look closely at the processes, dynamics, and possibly power struggles underlying language instructors' and content instructors' collaborations to achieve an integrated curriculum (see Goldstein, and Pawan & Greene, this volume). These sorts of studies might be ethnographic or qualitative (and critical), involving very situated observations of interactions between subject and language experts over an extended period of time. The research would also elicit the insights and perspectives of the participants on their teaching and learning experiences, and not just the researchers' views (Duff, 2007; Nunan & Bailey, 2009). Studies looking at professional collaboration might also examine interactions between subject and language experts (e.g., when co-teaching) and students in the classroom setting or when engaged in discussions on course-related matters (e.g., negotiation of course outline content, the focus of courses, and even discourse features; or an analysis of how the adjunct course is characterized, if mentioned at all, in the content course outline). These kinds of analyses get at the heart of the relative value placed on content objectives versus language objectives in the program.

Instructional Tasks, Registers, and Genres

A third approach to research might examine the types of text, task design, and input that students receive in CBI/CLIL courses, the rationale behind such choices, and students' linguistic engagement with that textual and linguistic content. An analysis of tasks might examine the types of content and linguistic objectives they address; learning strategies that are promoted; linguistic structures that are emphasized within particular content domains (and why); or instructional materials that curriculum, lessons, activities, and tasks are based on. For instance, Llinares and Dalton-Puffer (2015) examined five commonly used tasks in European CLIL classrooms (i.e., whole-class discussion, group-work discussion, role-play, interview, and presentation) to identify the opportunities students are afforded to express *evaluative* meaning (e.g., the language to convey emotion, as in "I'm *sorry*" or judgment, as in "the *greatest* example"). The findings of their study show that some tasks are more conducive to stance- or perspective-taking than others. Therefore, the authors suggest the need to include a wide range of tasks in the CLIL classroom to support students' development of evaluative language.

Research questions in this third general approach might include the following: What do tasks that integrate language and content look like in different disciplines, and how well do they work? What kinds of language awareness, language use, and language development do they contribute to? Such questions might require a close examination of documents (the course outline, tasks, students' work) and student interaction data (if jointly engaged in tasks), types of input or instruction provided, and a detailed analysis of genre and register features of texts and task-related discourse (i.e., micro-linguistic analysis, text patterns). For example, Schleppegrell (2002), drawing on Systemic Functional Linguistics, offers a detailed analysis of linguistic features of school-based registers. Among other aspects, her work shows that the lexis (vocabulary) of school texts is highly technical and specific and that logical relations are explicitly stated through a more varied set of conjunctions than those used in spoken interaction. Furthermore, the language of schooling is also characterized by a high degree of structure and information packing (e.g., by means of nominalization: by converting verbs to nouns, as in *evaporate→evaporation*, and by the use of embedded clauses).

Gardner and Nesi (2013) provide a framework for classifying and analyzing genres typically found in higher education student writing. The authors created a corpus of university student work that included assignments across university years and disciplines and identified 13 genre families (e.g., case study and literature survey) according to their text purposes and staging patterns (i.e., text structure). This framework, the authors suggest, provides teachers with key information to guide instructional design and assessment decisions. It also serves students by providing them with an overview of typical text patterns and expectations across disciplines. Other research approaches with direct instructional significance might involve analytical tools from corpus linguistics (see Cortes, this volume).

Students' (or Teachers') Evolving Academic Identities, Self-Perceptions, "Voices," or Perspectives as Speakers and Users of Academic English in Content Areas

A fourth research approach would examine students' changing academic literacies in relation to their identities, (ideally) as capable multilingual students and subject majors or specialists able to participate meaningfully in a particular disciplinary community (e.g., Geography or Management). Comparable research could examine changes in teachers' identities (as either content teachers or language teachers, primarily, or perhaps both; cf. Moate, 2011; Pawan & Greene, this volume). What are teachers' and students' perceptions of CBI instruction, and what role do they see it playing in their academic/professional development and identities? How do they assess their own progress? What challenges do they encounter? This set of questions might require a longitudinal study (e.g., spanning at least a semester or term) of one or several students or teachers representing different disciplines and perhaps different initial levels of language proficiency on the part of students. For example, Urmeneta (2013) followed one student teacher who was learning to implement CLIL during a year-long study of her practical experience and reflections in a European classroom. And Coyle (2013) examined adolescent learners' "perceptions of 'successful learning'" longitudinally, in part to "encourage greater ownership [by the learners] of CLIL classroom events" (p. 244).

Data in research examining such issues could be elicited by means of:

■ individual or group (focus group) interviews or discussions, as in Moate's (2011) study of six teachers in European CLIL programs

■ surveys and questionnaires

■ structured and/or open reflections (e.g., using exit slips, in-class assignments, homework, personal reflective narratives or journals)

■ portfolios with samples of students' performance (oral, written, or multimodal) over time, such as oral presentations, drafts of written essays, corrected assignments with feedback, and the results of group work or team-based activities

■ audio or video excerpts or narratives of critical incidents (Farrell, 2008) illustrating how participants' understandings changed based on particular experiences, as in Coyle's (2013) study.

Language in Mainstream Content-Focused Classes and How It Differs from Language in Adjunct (or Sheltered CBI) Language-Focused Courses

A fifth approach to research might examine the contrast between course contexts to see how the adjunct language-focused courses enhance students' (and instructors') awareness of language use in the disciplines. Such attention to oral or written language use also increases the credibility and value ascribed by students (and subject instructors) to the adjunct (language-focused) courses. Research into classroom discourse might involve discourse analytical tools, examining language-related episodes (involving explicit talk *about* aspects of language, such as grammar or lexis) as a unit of analysis (as in Basturkmen & Shackleford, 2015). Additional questions might pursue effective means of scaffolding and developing linguistic, textual, or rhetorical awareness among students.

Underlying Principles |||

All of these approaches, and others, should be guided by the principles in Table 23.1.

Research Agenda ||

Possible topics and research agendas in relation to specific aspects of CBI are found in each of the chapters in this volume. For those interested in pursuing research on CBI, we recommend:

1. Include a greater range of the geographical, linguistic, and educational contexts for CBI/CLIL research; to date, elementary through secondary-level instruction involving European languages such as English or French in developed countries in Europe, North America, and Australia has received the most attention.

2. Widen the disciplinary contexts for research beyond humanities and social sciences subjects to include more science and applied science courses. Expanding the content areas studied will help researchers better understand the differing linguistic and discursive demands in particular content areas (e.g., Nikula, 2015). Aggregating research exemplifying diverse CBI/CLIL contexts will also help establish more general principles regarding effective program processes and outcomes (Cenoz et al., 2014).

3. Conduct more research on the usefulness or role of the students' L1 (or other languages) in L2 CBI, and on translanguaging practices (moving across languages for educational purposes), in keeping with current trends in applied linguistics (e.g., Lo, 2015). (See also D. Reynolds, this volume.)

4. Conduct more research on the training of teachers (pre-service and in-service) and aspects of preparation that prove most helpful among practitioners in CBI/CLIL (e.g., Lightbown, 2014; Schleppegrell, Achugar, & Oteíza, 2004; Snow & Kamhi-Stein, 2002).

5. Finally, promote a better balance among the following research approaches, paying attention to both macro- and micro-contextual dimensions:

   a. Quantitative or mixed-method research (as described earlier, in relation to program evaluation and other studies) to measure and explain educational processes or outcomes on a relatively large scale.

   b. Qualitative (interpretive) research that examines the inner workings and sometimes tensions, contradictions, and unpredictability of certain aspects of program design, instruction or learning, or of students' trajectories, given local contingencies. This approach to research may involve longitudinal (more extended) studies (e.g., Ortega & Byrnes, 2008) that take into account sociocultural aspects of identity, agency, and perceived transformation and social participation. Studies can also provide evidence of changes in participants' linguistic or academic abilities.

Table 23.1: Underlying Principles

Research Considerations	Underlying Principles
1. Contextualization: Descriptions of research setting (e.g., program, classroom, participants, purposes)	Include information about the course, program, educational institution; sociopolitical context; and participant details (language backgrounds and proficiency levels, motivation to be in the program, years of study in the program, etc.). This information provides researchers and readers clear and detailed descriptions of the research setting. Provide the reader with enough information to understand and draw inferences about the findings and their relevance to other contexts or populations. Since there is huge variation in demographics, levels, models, and types of CBI/CLIL programs (see Cenoz, Genesee, & Gorter, 2014, p. 257), this contextual information is important.
2. Theoretical framework and literature review	Identify the larger theoretical issues, debates, or questions that inform the study or that the study contributes to. Particular theoretical and pedagogical issues might include, for example, the role of the students' L1 in their L2 production; the role of collaboration in task performance (by students) or curriculum planning (by instructors or program designers); issues of identity or agency on the part of teachers or learners; or the effectiveness of certain kinds of instructional or corrective feedback. Since these themes have been explored by other researchers, it is important to know the current status of the issue or theory before embarking on a study on the same topic as it relates to CBI/CLIL.
3. Statement of research questions or problem(s) to be addressed	Include a clear statement of research purpose and, where applicable, identify the problems connected with CBI/CLIL to be addressed. This requires research questions that are clear and answerable within the scope of the study, together with the rationale for asking those particular questions. For each question, consider what data would help answer it and then how to collect and analyze the data.
4. Recruitment and selection/ sampling of participants; rationale	Consider how many participants (e.g., teachers or students), groups, classrooms, or schools/sites to include in the study in order to answer the research questions. If the study is exploratory or a small pilot study, perhaps just a few observations or interviews with students and teachers would suffice. If a larger program review is being conducted, it would be best to involve a greater number of participants and possibly a team of researchers.
5. Reliability or validity or their counterparts in qualitative research—for example, dependability, trustworthiness, credibility, transferability, thick description (i.e., detailed contextualized description)	Provide sufficient detail about these aspects of the study to increase confidence that the research has been conducted in a systematic and rigorous manner: that interviews, questionnaires, tests, or other research tools were carefully designed and consistently used; that data were examined thoroughly and systematically; and that all of the research tools and procedures were in fact directly relevant to answering the research questions.
6. Data collection, analysis, and reduction	Include sufficient details about which kinds of data were obtained and analyzed. Also, explain how the data were analyzed by providing a logical progression from the research questions to the analysis and findings. Statistics or other data reduction strategies (e.g., focusing on a small number of themes, critical incidents, or illustrative cases) may be appropriate, depending on the study.

Table 23.1 (*continued*)

Research Considerations	Underlying Principles
7. Interpretation of findings	Provide sufficient evidence or "warrants" for claims and findings that are made to account for counter-examples or unexpected findings. Consider what other explanations might account for the findings, including those that were not anticipated. Additionally, to demonstrate researcher "reflexivity," include explicit comments about how the researcher's own background or assumptions (or even presence at the research site) might have influenced the data or the findings.
8. Generalizability, transferability, and implications arising from the study	Acknowledge the limitations of the research as well as implications for program development, pedagogy, future research, or theory development. For instance, indicate how the findings or conclusions might be limited by the number and types of participants (or classes, courses, content areas, etc.) involved in the study, or by the very particular circumstances or setting of the study. Make suggestions for ways of refining such a study for future research based on this study. Lastly, suggest ways in which the findings might inform decisions by instructors/teachers, program administrators, parents, students, or other researchers in similar contexts.
9. Ethics	Obtain formal approval to conduct research if needed. Normally, approval is required by (and from) program directors, school boards, principals, and university research boards, as well as participants. Elaborate research ethics protocols established by universities and other institutions guide this process. Ensure that research participants or officials have enough information (in language that they can understand, which might be in their L1, if not English) to decide whether they agree to participate in the study or not by giving their written informed consent. Generally, it is required that the identities (names or other identifying features) of the program and participants be protected (e.g., using pseudonyms) in resulting publications. Therefore, research conducted at Vantage College (as described in the chapter-opening scenerio), would use a pseudonym and perhaps mask other ways of identifying the program in research to be published beyond the institution, unless an exemption from this ethical principle was obtained. As an ethical researcher, avoid harming participants (or their reputation and feelings) and, instead, maximize the possible benefits of participation in such research and contributing to new knowledge (e.g., De Costa, 2016; Duff, 2008; Duff & Abdi, 2016; Mackey & Gass, 2016).
10. Dissemination	After conducting the research, consider what lessons or insights have resulted from the study and how others interested in CBI/CLIL might benefit from that knowledge. Think about how to present and illustrate the findings to different groups—people at the research site itself, other researchers, policymakers, teacher educators, parents—in a way that would make sense to them.

c. Critical research that can question or critique the apparent benefits or outcomes of CBI instruction and learning (Cenoz et al., 2014) in light of a number of factors. Factors often associated with neoliberalism might include national, regional, and institutional pressures to market and generate revenue for schools, universities, and other institutions based on CBI/CLIL programs, putting economic interests ahead of educational ones. Also subject to critique is the widespread promotion of powerful global languages (such as English) in education that might undermine educational achievements in other local languages. Such pressures and policies—and not just "best pedagogical practices"—may drive many of the decisions related to program and research design, recruitment, and implementation. Furthermore, these factors may prioritize the enrollment of students from relatively elite educational and economic backgrounds (for whom this kind of program is another form of enrichment) at the expense of those from less well-resourced backgrounds (again, see Cenoz et al., 2014, who raise this issue in relation to interpreting research findings as well). Critical research might also consider power imbalances between language specialists and content specialists and how stratification based on perceived status (e.g., science specialist vs. language specialist; professor vs. instructor) is manifested in the curriculum or in other institutional discourses (e.g., Creese, 2002).

d. Action research, or practitioner-driven inquiry, examining how ongoing interventions in teaching based on issues encountered or identified by teachers themselves contribute to improved instruction, learning, and cooperation in a given context (Burns, 2011, 2015; Nunan & Bailey, 2009).

e. Multimodal research related to CBI and academic literacies, involving non-linguistic semiotic resources and learning (which may be discipline-specific), such as photographs, graphs, other images, and/or embodied or non-verbal aspects of learning (Early, Kendrick, & Potts, 2015; Lo & Lin, 2015).

APPLYING WHAT YOU LEARNED
Questions and Tasks

1. Returning to the scenario that opened the chapter, what would be the research questions of greatest interest to you as a (1) program administrator, (2) instructor/teacher, or (3) graduate student assisting in the university program? Why? Would you be most likely to select a quantitative, mixed, or qualitative design? How might you examine the site, the practices, and the ways people talk about the program from a critical (discourse) perspective? Compare your questions with the possible questions listed in Appendix 23A.

2. Why might program funders, ministries or boards of education, or administrators be less interested in very detailed, small-scale qualitative studies (or critical studies) than larger-scale quantitative or mixed-method studies? What are the strengths and weaknesses of each approach? Why might teachers prefer classroom-based studies that are smaller in scale with case studies of just a small number of learners' development over time?

3. Choose a recent CBI study presented in one of the journals listed earlier in the chapter. Using Table 23.1, consider the research and components of the study, as well as one or two major findings. What did you find most interesting about the study? Do you think the findings would apply to (or be relevant in) your educational context? Why or why not?

4. Consider the case of Garden High School (a pseudonym), in Vancouver, Canada. It is a mid-sized school with approximately 800 students. Over the last decade, the school has seen a dramatic increase in non-Anglophone international visa students and immigrant students, mostly from Chinese backgrounds. Many of these students have a strong foundation in mathematics and sciences, yet their academic English language proficiency may be quite limited, particularly in the case of recent arrivals. Placing the students immediately in mainstream English-medium content classes has not worked well and the curriculum has therefore been adapted to support their academic language learning, particularly in social studies, biology, and English. These subjects are taught ostensibly using CBI in separate sheltered classes (see Brinton & Snow, this volume) during students' first year at the school. However, not all of the content teachers have received training in sheltered instructional techniques.

   a. Design a small, manageable, and interesting research project that you could conduct in one course (classroom) in this context related to CBI and students' educational experiences. Assume that you have just six months to complete the study.

   b. What would you want to find out? Formulate one or two research questions.

   c. How might you gain access to this site (e.g., How would you aim to get to know the principal or teachers to introduce yourself and your study)?

   d. What kinds of tests, other instruments (e.g., questionnaires), or observation or interview protocols (procedures, equipment) would you use (if any), and why? What other kinds of data or evidence would you collect and analyze? Assuming that you select just a small number of students (and possibly just one teacher) as research participants, what might be your selection strategy?

e. How might you analyze data from, say, interviews or classroom observation transcripts? What larger issues about CBI would your findings help illuminate? Who might find your research significant and useful?

ENDNOTE

1. We use the terms CBI and CLIL somewhat interchangeably depending, in part, on how authors describe their own work.

REFERENCES

Basturkmen, H., & Shackleford, N. (2015). How content lecturers help students with language: An observational study of language-related episodes in interaction in first year accounting classrooms. *English for Specific Purposes, 37*, 87–97.

Brinton, D. M., Snow, M. A., & Wesche, M. (2003). *Content-based second language instruction* (Classics ed.). Ann Arbor, MI: University of Michigan Press.

Brown, J. D. (1995). *The elements of language curriculum: A systematic approach to program development.* Boston, MA: Heinle & Heinle.

Brown, J. D. (2014). *Mixed methods research for TESOL.* Edinburgh, Scotland: Edinburgh University Press.

Burns, A. (2011). Action research in the field of second language teaching and learning. In E. Hinkel (Ed.), *Handbook of research in second language teaching and learning* (Vol. II, pp. 237–253). New York, NY: Routledge.

Burns, A. (2015). Action research. In B. Paltridge & A. Phakiti (Eds.), *Research methods in applied linguistics* (pp. 187–204). London, England: Bloomsbury.

Cenoz, J., Genesee, F., & Gorter, D. (2014). Critical analysis of CLIL: Taking stock and looking forward. *Applied Linguistics, 35*(3), 243–262.

Coyle, D. (2013). Listening to learners: An investigation into "successful learning" across CLIL contexts. *International Journal of Bilingual Education and Bilingualism, 16*(3), 244–266. doi:10.1080/1367 0050.2013.777384

Creese, A. (2002). The discursive construction of power in teacher partnerships: Language and subject specialists in mainstream schools. *TESOL Quarterly, 36*(4), 597–616.

Dalton-Puffer, C. (2007). *Discourse in content and language integrated learning (CLIL) classrooms.* Amsterdam, The Netherlands: Benjamins.

De Costa, P. (2016). *Ethics in applied linguistics research: Language researcher narratives.* New York: Routledge.

Dörnyei, Z. (2007). *Research methods in applied linguistics: Quantitative, qualitative and mixed methodologies.* Oxford, England: Oxford University Press.

Duff, P. (2007). Qualitative approaches to second language classroom research. In J. Cummins & C. Davison (Eds.), *International handbook of English language teaching* (pp. 973–986). New York, NY: Springer.

Duff, P. (2008). *Case study research in applied linguistics*. New York, NY: Erlbaum/Taylor & Francis.

Duff, P., & Abdi, K. (2016). Negotiating ethical research engagements in multilingual ethnographic studies in education: A narrative from the field. In P. De Costa (Ed.), *Ethics in applied linguistics research: Language researcher narratives* (pp. 121–141). New York, NY: Routledge.

Early, M., Kendrick, M., & Potts, D. (2015). Multimodality: Out from the margins of English language teaching. *TESOL Quarterly, 49*(3), 447–460.

Farrell, T. S. C. (2008). Critical incidents in ELT initial teacher training. *English Language Teaching Journal, 62*(1), 3–10.

Gardner, S., & Nesi, H. (2013). A classification of genre families in university student writing. *Applied Linguistics, 34*(1), 25–52.

Lightbown, P. (2014). *Focus on content-based language teaching*. Oxford, England: Oxford University Press.

Llinares, A., & Dalton-Puffer, C. (2015). The role of different tasks in CLIL students' use of evaluative language. *System, 54*, 69–79.

Lo, Y. Y. (2015). How much L1 is too much? Teachers' language use in response to students' abilities and classroom interaction in content and language integrated learning. *International Journal of Bilingual Education and Bilingualism, 18*(3), 270–288.

Lo, Y. Y., & Lin, A. M. Y. (2015). Special issue: Designing multilingual and multimodal CLIL frameworks for EFL students. *International Journal of Bilingual Education and Bilingualism, 18*(3), 261–269.

Lynch, B. (1996). *Language program evaluation: Theory and practice*. Cambridge, England: Cambridge University Press.

Mackey, A., & Gass, S. M. (2016). *Second language research: Methodology and design* (2nd ed.). New York, NY: Routledge.

McKay, S. L. (2006). *Researching second language classrooms*. Mahwah, NJ: Erlbaum.

Moate, J. M. (2011). The impact of foreign language mediated teaching on teachers' sense of professional integrity in the CLIL classroom. *European Journal of Teacher Education, 34*(3), 333–346.

Nikula, T. (2015). Hands-on tasks in CLIL science classrooms as sites for subject-specific language use and learning. *System, 54*, 14–27.

Nunan, D., & Bailey, K. M. (2009). *Exploring second language classroom research: A comprehensive guide*. Boston, MA: Heinle & Heinle.

Ortega, L., & Byrnes, H. (Eds.). (2008). *Longitudinal study of advanced L2 capacities*. New York, NY: Routledge.

Schleppegrell, M. J. (2002). Linguistic features of the language of schooling. *Linguistics and Education, 12*(4), 431–459.

Schleppegrell, M. J., Achugar, M., & Oteíza, T. (2004). The grammar of history: Enhancing content-based instruction through a functional focus on language. *TESOL Quarterly, 38*(1), 67–93.

Snow, M. A., & Kamhi-Stein, L. D. (2002). Teaching and learning academic literacy through Project LEAP. In J. Crandall & D. Kaufman (Eds.), *Content-based instruction in higher education settings* (pp. 169–181). Alexandria, VA: TESOL.

Talmy, S. (2010). Qualitative interviews in applied linguistics: From research instrument to social practice. *Annual Review of Applied Linguistics, 30*, 128–148.

Urmeneta, C. E. (2013). Learning to become a CLIL teacher: Teaching, reflection and professional development. *International Journal of Bilingual Education and Bilingualism, 16*(3), 334–353. doi:10.10 80/13670050.2013.777389

Part VI

Ongoing Challenges in Content-Based Instruction

Chapter 24

In Trust, We Collaborate: ESL and Content-Area Teachers Working Together in Content-Based Instruction

Faridah Pawan & Michelle C. S. Greene

> *When there is trust, no proof is necessary,*
> *when there is none, no proof is possible.*
> —Chinese proverb

||| A Glimpse into the Content-Based Classroom

In East Central Indiana, the district superintendent of a public school reinforces the central role that trust plays as an enabling factor in ESL and content-area teacher collaboration by describing the content teachers' trust in their ESL colleague Rosemund (a pseudonym). In the quote, he stresses how her efforts to facilitate with good intentions is essential in navigating the difficult but familiar terrain of CBI to those who aim to provide effective instruction to English learners (ELs) in their community:

> There are two communities in this district of ours in the southern part of our state. There is that good old community where they feel like they're being invaded and they're not real comfortable with the increase of who they would see as someone who is not typically who you would see around here. The other end, I think you see people who are committed and are trying to go out of their way to, to do just the opposite . . . very friendly and reaching out. Teachers are people in this community and they come from both camps . . . . And that is when our Rosemund [ESL teacher] being proactive is changing things, she is making this bridge. She sends out information to everybody— on what to know and what we do not know, when she is available to help, what she has we can use. She also comes right out to say that we should not give ELs a grade just because of language. If the students have the ability but they're not doing great because they're not doing the homework, then that's not okay. But if there's a legitimate language issue, then we need to look at some other alternative and what is fair and whatever. Teachers have learned to respect Rose but more and more I would say that

bit by bit, they trust Rose. She's always there with us, with me when I need little bit more teeth or a little bit stronger fist to come in to talk about our EL population, with teachers in helping to teach their content areas to ELs, and like I said before, to push us to make difficult decisions about what to test, to take out points for, to penalize, to accommodate, and more. It is not easy, it is often tense because you do not always agree but, at the end of the day, we trust Rose . . . .

Trust, as Sztompka (1999) asserts, is an indispensable element of all human interactions, which includes collaboration between individuals. Collaboration enabled by trust is essential in CBI when two groups of teachers must work together: for language teachers to understand the knowledge base and the intellectual foundations within a content area so that they can target and incorporate them into their language instruction; and for content-area teachers to understand that language is the basis of knowledge, in addition to being a means to express it, so that they can develop their instructional language to make content accessible to ELs.

There are many models in existence that describe how ESL and content-area teachers can collaborate, including those suggested by Benesch (1988), Crandall (1994), DelliCarpini (2008), Dove and Honigsfeld (2010), Kaufman and Brooks (1996), and Pawan's own work in collaboration with colleagues (see Pawan & Craig, 2011; Pawan & Ortloff, 2011; Pawan & Sietman, 2007; Pawan & Ward, 2007). In all these studies, ESL and content-area teachers working in tandem and using integrated and interdisciplinary curricula are a prerequisite to overcoming the disposition that EL instruction involves remediation instead of teaching for achievement. The models range from pre-service teachers working across disciplines to construct an inquiry-based curriculum; ESL and content-area teachers using joint preparation times to develop a year-long curriculum to support each other and to incorporate each other's expertise in teaching their subjects; peer-coaching and mentoring models where ESL and content-area teachers take turns teaching the same subject, with one teacher taking the lead in certain areas; and/or ESL and content-area teachers teaching jointly in class. In other work in this area, Davison (2006) developed a useful framework for the evaluation of the effectiveness of ESL and content collaboration, which often is difficult to sustain and is frequently limited to a few activities such as information exchange (Pawan & Ortloff, 2011).

One of the central reasons for limited collaboration is the lack of trust or the lack of opportunities for teachers to build trust with one another. The situation often leads to "turfism" (Pawan & Ortloff, 2011; Roegge, Galloway, & Welge, 1991), distrust in the other party's ability to have sufficient subject-area knowledge or knowledge about ELs to undertake effective instruction effectively. Some common misconceptions when distrust is present are that content- area teachers feel ESL teachers are "dumbing down" the curriculum when they incorporate content into instruction, that ESL teachers feel subject-area teachers do not have empathy for ELs, and that ESL teachers fall into the "service category" of being merely personal assistants/translators to connect with ELs and their families (Johnston, 1999). Also, the lack of time due to scheduling or an overload of responsibilities has been shown to be insurmountable for many teachers to overcome these sentiments build the trust needed for collaboration (Samuelson, Pawan, & Hung, 2012).

In the state of Indiana in the U.S., the focus on ESL and content-area collaboration in CBI is at a crucial juncture. Nearly 50 percent of all the ELs in Indiana are not able to progress beyond the near proficient level/advanced level (Level 4 out of 5) (Indiana Department of Education, 2014b). There is, thus, much consternation that ELs struggle to move to the Fluent English Proficient (FEP) level (Level 5), which is necessary for them to be successful participants in mainstream classrooms. ESL and content-area teacher collaboration is critical in bringing about the students' progression, namely the simultaneous achievement of language and academic skills, and the assumption of shared responsibility of ESL and content-area teachers to teach EL students. These elements underlie the WIDA standards, adopted by the state in 2015 in an effort to prioritize the standards as instructional goals and as an achievable commonplace school practice (World Class Instructional Design and Assessment Consortium, 2012). (See also K. Reynolds, this volume.)

Hence, we write this chapter with a focus on trust because we now see it as the foundation that has to be laid if any collaborative endeavors in CBI are to be undertaken effectively. We illustrate several teacher trust-building efforts toward CBI teacher collaboration based on our experiences. Faridah Pawan led several grant-funded projects within the Tandem Certification for Indiana Teachers (TACIT) Institute involving teachers from across 25 school districts. Central to the Institute was a joint professional development program for ESL and content-area teachers over an extended period of nine months, during which the teachers pursued online courses together, attended regularly organized face-to-face workshops in their school districts, and participated in a training institute in the summer months. Michelle Greene, for her part, has nearly ten years of U.S. public school teaching experience as an ESL teacher and practitioner researcher and is currently leading professional development seminars and teaching university courses for practicing and pre-service teachers who want to develop their skills to best serve ELs.

Trust and Collaboration Frameworks Applied to CBI |||

As the primary researchers, we used D'Amour's Interprofessional Collaboration (1997) framework to aid our explanations and descriptions of our observations, a model we see aligned with Sztompka's (1999) trust theorization. Pawan first adopted D'Amour's Model of Structuring Interprofessional Collaboration (1997) with health care professionals in Canada to describe ESL and content-area teacher collaboration. The linkage between the D'Amour and Sztompka models was made in Ortloff's (2011) dissertation describing the continuum of trust and distrust in teacher collaboration. In this chapter, both models are utilized to describe the efforts undertaken to enhance trust at the structural-organizational (macro) as well as interpersonal (micro) levels in ESL and content-area teacher collaboration.

D'Amour's (1997) model focuses on two main factors of collaboration: (1) processes that involve stakeholders' interactions, negotiations, and social exchanges with each other; and (2) the structural and organizational contexts in which the collaboration takes place. In the model, the two sets of factors are identified as *interactional* and *organizational* factors (see Table 24.1). The interactional factors and the organizational context complement and modify each other.

Table 24.1: D'Amour's (1997) Model of Structuring Interprofessional Collaboration

Interactional Factors (in interpersonal relationships)	
Finalization	Shared goals and vision
Interiorization	Sense of dependency, mutual trust and respect, and mutual knowledge
Organizational Factors (in mechanisms that regulate work)	
Governance	Central, local, expert leadership
Formalization	Explicit norms and formalization of structures (protocols, procedures, description of tasks, etc.)

The first two dimensions (*finalization* and *interiorization*) of the model provide insight into collaboration via interactional factors, and the remaining two (*governance* and *formalization*) provide a perspective on organizational mechanisms impacting collaboration. D'Amour (1997) describes finalization as the degree to which professionals share common goals and vision, while interiorization refers to the professionals' development of a sense of mutual trust and respect for each other as well as mutual knowledge of each other's contributions. Governance and formalization constitute structural and organizational factors that define the context in which collaboration takes place. Governance is defined by leadership coming from within or outside of the organization or institution; leadership can be either individual or collective. Formalization, on the other hand, is the presence of norms of conduct that are explicitly articulated by leaders, administrators, and institutions for the purpose of regulating and stabilizing collaborative actions. This is achieved through formal structures like protocols, procedures, and descriptions of tasks in bulletin boards, handbooks, and manuals. The D'Amour model demonstrates the utility of macro factors of leadership and formalized structures to support and reinforce collaboration. Interactional factors involving interpersonal relationships, on the other hand, can sustain the collaboration.

The relevance of Sztompka's argument to the D'Amour model lies in his linking personality/interpersonal factors with social/macro political factors as the bases of trust in human interactions. In that regard, Sztompka (1999) brings together D'Amour's interactional and organizational factors and considers them necessary to enact these three types of trust:

1. **Anticipatory trust,** that is, trust in others (e.g., leaders) who can direct their efforts in ways that they feel are favorable to their interests.
2. **Evocative trust,** whereby individuals (e.g., teachers) expect their trust in each other will be reciprocated.
3. **Responsive trust,** whereby individuals (e.g., ESL teachers) trust other individuals (e.g., content-area teachers) and expect valued action (appropriate instruction) to be undertaken regarding their highly valued entities (e.g., EL students).

Sztompka argues that trust becomes central amid rapid changes and uncertain times, situations that define the development of ESL/EFL teaching in the U.S and globally.

Perspectives and Challenges in Collaborative Practices |||

Organizational and Leadership Efforts

Collaboration for CBI requires anticipatory trust in leadership to bring people to the table to work together. One reason is that CBI requires a shared vision of the mission in order for the key stakeholders to work toward supporting individuals who experience marginalization. Leaders, in their role as individuals who communicate the core values of a school, are important in formalizing and uniting teachers in this mission. Furthermore, research demonstrates that leadership is essential in pulling stakeholders together to take on issues that are difficult to articulate on a one-to-one basis (see Peterson & Deal, 1998; Singleton & Linton, 2007; and Stone, Patton & Heen, 2010). This is particularly crucial for ELs, as conversations in the CBI classroom often involve highly charged topics of race and immigration. A second reason is that central leadership can be effective at the macro level in formalizing, implementing, or reinforcing the steps toward collaboration that have been articulated and agreed upon by teachers working together at the ground level (see Pawan & Craig, 2011).

Michelle Greene's Central School District

In this regard, the actions demonstrated by the centralized administration for Greene's school district in central Indiana represent the strengths of governance and formalization, as defined by D'Amour, to provide context and structure for trust-based collegial conversations. The district adopted "Cultural Competency and Responsiveness" as a district-wide goal for school improvement, work spurred by the annual state standardized test results that reflected a considerable drop in test scores across all subjects in the district, including great disparity in achievement scores between racial and linguistic minorities and their White classmates.

Pacific Educational Group (PEG), an educational consulting group, was hired by the Central School District to implement district-wide programming aimed at supporting teachers and administrators. Equity Teams were developed that intentionally included White, Black, Latino/Hispanic, and Asian teacher leaders as participants. Each member of the Equity Team was expected to fulfill three main responsibilities, as outlined in *Courageous Conversations About Race* (Singleton & Linton, 2007):

1. Engage in a process of investigation to discover how race impacts one's personal and professional attitudes and behaviors
2. Lead the school or central office staff in the examination of individual and institutional culture as it relates to equity and anti-racism
3. Establish a professional learning community in which adults can effectively develop skills and knowledge necessary to improve student performance and eliminate racial achievement disparities.

When Greene first began teaching at her school, the ESL program was new and she was the only ESL teacher in the building. School-level leadership made two significant decisions that aided in effective collaboration: (1) the ESL program was assigned to a classroom in a mainstream hallway, and (2) Greene was assigned to a mentor teacher who was an English/language arts (ELA) teacher leader. These strategic decisions proved fruitful for a number of reasons. The close geographic proximity of the ESL classroom in relation to students' other content-area classrooms provided accessibility for ESL students and all their teachers, allowing them to communicate fluidly. Likewise, ESL students had access to all of their teachers in one hallway, which helped formalize the sense of a unified teaching and learning team. The paired mentoring between Greene and the ELA teacher helped support curricular sensibilities, as the ESL academic standards are based on the Indiana English/Language Arts Standards (Indiana Department of Education, 2014a). Additionally, the two teachers had classrooms adjacent to one another, shared a team of students, and quickly discovered a mutually beneficial and reciprocal relationship with respect to professional growth.

Concurrently, all teachers in the building were assigned to a professional learning community (PLC), which met once weekly and was organized according to content area. Building-level leadership supported Greene, the sole ESL teacher, in selecting an optimal PLC team for the purposes of professional development and collaboration. For example, while it was initially suggested that Greene join the World/Foreign Languages PLC, leadership listened to Greene's suggestion, pairing her instead with ELA in an effort to better support collaborative efforts in serving ESL students and their academic language goals.

Pawan's TACIT Program

As mentioned earlier, in the program, the macro structures put into place that enabled the ESL and content-area teachers to work together also began with leadership. First, with the help of superintendents and principals of districts with the lowest performance and highest number of limited English proficient students, TACIT led the recruitment of teams of ESL and content-area teachers to pursue joint professional development in interdisciplinary collaboration to support ELs. Administrators were invited along with the teachers to participate and to put together a joint proposal. Upon acceptance, contracts were signed by both administrators and teachers to work together to pursue TACIT coursework and professional development activities over nine months, the completion of which led to state certification in ESL. From TACIT's perspective, the action to include administrators was aimed at sustaining accountability for teachers to pursue work together. It was also an enactment of evocative trust based on the expectation that administrators and teachers would develop a reciprocal relationship through the collaboration, based not only on common understandings but, more important, on essential mutual support as evidenced by this teacher quote:

> *We can get training until we are blue in the face but when we get home and there is nobody to support us, little will come out of it.*
>
> —High school mathematics teacher
> TACIT participant

In addition, TACIT's recruitment efforts, aided by principals and superintendents, were focused on teachers who were considered natural leaders by their colleagues. TACIT found that when teachers returned to the schools, it was clear that trust in colleagues, particularly in those they considered as capable of providing leadership, was one of the more significant outcomes of their experience in the professional development program. For example, in a school in north central Indiana, it was observed that even though TACIT-trained teachers were introduced to many experts who provided guidance on how to collaborate to integrate language and content in their instruction, they frequently sought out colleagues and relied more upon their expertise as guidance. Miriam, a high school social studies teacher, had the following to say about Dina, her ESL counterpart:

> *Dina has all those great ideas to help and I know they work because she knows my students . . . she knows what I have struggled with too.*
> —High school social studies teacher
> TACIT participant

In their school, the two teachers regularly led formally scheduled meetings on targeted topics of relevance to CBI as well as short informal meetings and email-sharing throughout the year that helped shape a community of practice.

As part of its services, TACIT also supported the work of teacher leaders and ESL teachers, such as Dina. In CBI collaboration, more often than not, it is the ESL teachers who initiate and lead the collaboration (see Pawan & Craig, 2011). TACIT staff supported the teachers through several means, including providing them with resources during the in-service trainings they conducted for content-area colleagues, using them as guest experts in workshops, and holding them up as exemplars of practice. The support was provided to these teachers so that they had visibility, thereby allowing their expertise to be acknowledged and trusted. TACIT offered an extended period of nine months of professional development for teachers to build and reinforce knowledge of CBI, which provided time for teachers to develop trust through familiarity with each other and served as a basis for collaboration. This framework was supported by TACIT's instructional format, which combined online and face-to-face platforms, enabling TACIT to provide assistance without having teachers leave their schools. This, in turn, allowed the teachers to continue to work together in their own settings.

Interactional Factors and Interpersonal Trust Efforts

The previous section described how macro structures enabled anticipatory and evocative trusts. In this section, we focus also on interpersonal interactions that illustrate Sztompka's third trust type, responsive trust.

Protocols in conversations are essential in interpersonal engagements as they provide opportunity, permission, and a transparent and organized process for sharing views, no matter how contentious the views may be. The protocols provide a transparent means to share and challenge views in a reciprocal, systematic, rational, and de-personalized manner.

Greene's Central School District

In Greene's school, PEG used Singleton and Linton's (2007) "Courageous Conversation" protocol: Participants must agree to: (1) stay engaged; (2) experience discomfort; (3) speak the truth; and, (4) expect and accept non-closure. One of the activities to spur discussions about race, which included using the protocol, was *The Color Line*, a reference to W. E. B. Du Bois' frequent use of the phrase. Participants began by individually completing an inventory based on McIntosh (2016) before they undertook conversations about it. In the article, McIntosh outlines 26 conditions that are descriptive of hidden privileges to which she has access as a result of her racial Whiteness. At the end of the activity, it became clear to participants why the exercise is called *The Color Line*, as the chronological inventory scores created a comprehensive privilege spectrum of light-skinned to dark-skinned participants. This thought-provoking exercise provided fertile ground for deep and personally relevant conversations among the teachers while they engaged in collaborative work. This quote is illustrative:

> . . . *In hind-sight, I wonder if my own anxieties about teaching non-native English speakers created a barrier—both for me in thinking about instruction, but also for the EL students, who probably sensed [the anxiety] in me and were perhaps afraid to approach me for help.*
>
> —Science teacher

Pawan's TACIT Program

TACIT also used conversation protocols during regularly scheduled collaborative workshop sessions. An example is the protocol used by Levine and Bunch (2007) at Bethune-Chavez Academy, a new school in a major urban area in California. The protocol was developed by teachers learning to work together as a community where two-fifths of the student body consists of ELs. Teachers were given release time to collaborate three times each week. In one of the times, the protocol was a guided discussion and conversational tool, laying out the phases of a conversation and providing clearly defined expectations regarding who says what, and for how long (see Appendix 24A). The protocol sought to give teachers "permission" as a means to trust the enterprise and, most of all, each other to share their vulnerabilities and the challenging aspects of teaching their content to non-native speakers of English. This quote reveals that the steps taken yielded such information:

> *This is my dilemma! I am a History teacher. I have no language education; I do not know Spanish, so it is very difficult for me to communicate.*
>
> —High school history teacher

TACIT also promoted trust through interpersonal teacher engagement to generate a knowledge base showing the utility and respect for each other's expertise while, at the same time, acknowledging concerns and differences. For example, in two key TACIT courses, the concept of "living syllabi" was implemented. Both ESL and content-area teachers were able to shape the syllabi through their participation in prioritizing and identifying the central questions they had under each topic. Those questions became central features of course discussions and collaborative projects, which included CBI instruction and assessment approaches, interdisciplinary collaboration, roles and responsibilities of all teachers of ELs, and advocacy (see Appendix 24B). In addition, TACIT prioritized teacher insider knowledge generated through discussions as part of the curriculum to reinforce the importance of teachers continuing to work together. For example, CBI strategies that were developed by Isabel (a high school algebra teacher) and Sophie (an ESL teacher) were used as part of the material in Collaborative Teaching Institute coursework (see Appendix 24C).

Another example is TACIT's 360-reflective (comprehensive reflections with multiple stakeholders) teaching project, which involved ESL and content-area teachers recording and reflecting upon their EL instruction. After the recordings, the teachers viewed and reflected upon several sessions sequentially, first on their own, followed by reflections with peers, administrators, and, finally, with TACIT staff. One outcome was that the joint reflections increased the teacher knowledge base; however, more important, they contributed to an environment whereby the teachers were able to see and understand colleagues' efforts to undertake informed and responsible EL instruction (responsive trust).

Underlying Principles |||

Table 24.2 summarizes the activities we described in the previous sections and their alignment with D'Amour's Interprofessional Collaboration (1997) and Sztompka's (1999) trust types.

Research Agenda |||

There are areas of trust and collaboration that continue to require research and exploration. First, further studies need to be undertaken so as to understand how collaboration could be taught purposefully to attain a specific goal and how trust building could be researched so that it can be a part of that instruction.

The examples we provided here indicate that existing pathways provide a means for teachers not only to envision ESL and content-area teacher collaboration in undertaking CBI but also to put it into practice. Collaboration, however, needs to be directed specifically to curricular development. Precedents are in existence, including Snow, Met, and Genesee's (1989) oft-cited CBI framework that offers a practical pathway for ESL and content-area teachers to collaborate in achieving content and language learning objectives in a classroom. Through the framework, ESL teachers and content-area teachers can see that their collaboration could involve identifying, planning, and teaching language that is essential for understanding and discussion of a particular topic or concept ("Content obligatory language"). "Content-compatible language" objectives can be attained when the two collaborate by focusing on language that is not content specific but rather supports student communication and engagement in the content classroom. The Sheltered Instruction Observation Protocol (SIOP) (Echevarriá, Vogt, & Short, 2017) model, on the other hand, is effective in making transparent the major elements involved in scaffolding the teaching of ELs. These models can provide a systematic guide as to how ESL and content-area teachers can seek help from each other, for example, in building students' background knowledge, in providing com-

Table 24.2: Alignment of Activities with D'Amour's Interprofessional Collaboration (1997) and Sztompka's (1999) Trust Types

District Program Activities	Underlying Principles

1. Organizational and leadership factors and macro-level efforts.
   a. Greene's Central School District:
     i. By adopting the common goal of cultural responsiveness to be achieved collaboratively by all teachers, district leaders spearheaded the collaboration by giving it a defined mission.
     ii. They also led by establishing the requirement for the teachers to serve as Equity Team members representing ethnic groups within the district.
     iii. District leaders supported the collaboration by delegating school-level leaders to make situated decisions that are practical and doable for teachers, including assigning ESL teachers to classrooms in the main hallways and adjacent to the content-area teachers they collaborate with, in mentoring content area teachers, and in requiring ESL and content area teachers to attend joint weekly PLC meetings.
   b. Pawan's TACIT Program:
     i. The program enlisted school-level leaders not only in recruiting and contractually sponsoring pairs of influential ESL and content area teachers to participate in the program but also in becoming participants themselves as teacher collaborators.
     ii. Program activities supported the collaboration by creating time and structured activities (e.g., joint curriculum development) and in providing resources as well as using the collaborators as guest experts in workshops in their schools and beyond.
     iii. The program's blended infrastructure (online and face-to-face) enabled the teachers to remain in their schools to continue collaboration while pursuing TACIT's professional development.
	Collaboration for CBI requires Sztompka's (1999) anticipatory and evocative trusts in others (leadership) to bring people to work together and to expect that their trust will be reciprocated. In this regard, CBI requires the implementation of D'Amour's (1997) governance and formalization principles where there is clear leadership and clear/formal articulation, respectively, of procedures and structures in place to make collaboration possible.

Table 24.2 (*continued*)

District Program Activities	Underlying Principles

2. Interactional/Interpersonal factors and efforts: These micro-level efforts are exemplified by the use of protocols to facilitate conversations on contentious topics that could inhibit collaboration.
  a. Greene's Central School District:
    i. The district used the "Courageous Conversation" protocol to engage collaborating teachers in discussions about race where they must agree to stay engaged, to experience discomfort, to speak the truth, and to expect non-disclosure.
  b. Pawan's TACIT program:
    i. The program used Levine and Bunch's (2007) trust-building conversational protocol to show respect for each other's expertise, to give permission to each other to share insecurities, and to acknowledge concerns and differences.
    ii. The program also used the 360-reflective teaching project in which ESL and content-area teachers, through joint reflections of recorded teaching sessions, were able to see and understand colleagues' teaching efforts and developed insight into their teacher insider knowledge.
	In addition to evocative trust, collaboration for CBI requires Sztompka's responsive trust, wherein teachers are willing to entrust their students to each other to undertake a valuable action (i.e., instruction). In this regard, CBI requires the implementation of D'Amour's principle of finalization or a joint sense of mission as well as interiorization or an uncompromised sense of trust and dependency on each other.

prehensible input, and in sustaining content and language teaching objectives in EL instruction. A central contribution of models such as the sheltered instruction model is that they can be non-threatening in nature. Rather than replacing teaching methods and strategies already in place, SIOP seeks to complement them while, at the same, time providing new approaches to add to teachers' existing instructional repertoires. Nevertheless, although more need to be developed, the next step of any model development must be to address the current internationalization of English as well as use of collaborative approaches already in existence in teachers' own local contexts. There is some urgency in this regard as English as a second/foreign language is increasingly taught overseas through content in major cities around the world, for example, in countries such as China and South Korea (Park & Pawan, 2016). In those countries, the interest lies in teachers working together to teach students to use the language not just to communicate but, more important, to use it also to learn. (See also Stillwell, this volume.)

Trust is difficult to research as it is embedded in relationships. Furthermore, current conceptualizations of trust such as that of Sztompka (1999) are only able to capture a static outcome where trust is in place or not in place instead of elucidating the processes of trust development. The latter is important for professional development programs such as TACIT so that interventions can be developed along the way as teachers collaborate. To address the situation, Ortloff (2011) developed an approach called *shadowflection*, where he identified and shadowed a central player in a network of teachers involved in the provision of ESL services in a school as the person interacted with individuals in daily work. Ortloff recorded the interactions, paying close attention to the content and mode of communication (including non-verbal communication) while also engaging the central player to reflect upon the interactions using open-ended questions. These questions were meant to help the central player reflect on the interaction itself and connect it to the ongoing school relationships of which the interaction was a part. Then the process was repeated as the next interaction was introduced. There are key limitations in the shadowflection approach, most critically that this method leads to the study being based on the opinions and activities of the key players. It is also limited by scope, as it can only be done on a relatively small scale since it is intensive for both participant and researcher. But the approach has allowed trust to come to the surface in ways that suggest that it is a key factor in ESL and content-area teacher collaboration. Shadowflection, of course, is in development and continues to require refinement and modification.

APPLYING WHAT YOU LEARNED
Questions and Tasks

1. What can we learn from the models of collaboration described in the chapter? What struck you about the importance of collaboration from the experiences of teachers and administrators illustrated in the various quotations? How might this learning need to be adapted to fit your current or future teaching/learning context?

2. What types of organizational leadership (formalization and governance) described in the chapter are already in place or might be possible or in your current/future teaching/learning context?

3. What specific examples of interpersonal factors (finalization and interiorization) might be already in place or might be possible within your current/future teaching/learning context?

4. Identify some potential key collaborators (administrators, content teachers, EL teachers, etc.) in your teaching situation. What do you think is needed from each of these parties in order to create the conditions/incentives for trust in collaboration? Make a chart with the key collaborators you have specified, and fill in the conditions and incentives you have identified.

REFERENCES

Benesch, S. (1988). *Ending remediation: Linking ESL and content in higher education.* Washington, DC: TESOL.

Crandall, J. A. (1994). Strategic integration: Preparing language and content teachers for linguistically and culturally diverse classrooms. In J. E. Alatis (Ed.), *Georgetown University Roundtable on Languages and Linguistics: Strategic interaction and language acquisition—Theory, practice and research* (pp. 255–274). Washington, DC: Georgetown University Press.

D'Amour, D. (1997). *Structuration de la collaboration interprofessionnelle dans les services de santé de première ligne au Québec* (Unpublished doctoral dissertation). University of Montreal, Quebec, Canada.

Davison, C. (2006). Collaboration between ESL and content teachers: How do we know when we are doing it right? *International Journal of Bilingual Education and Bilingualism, 9*(4), 454–475. doi: 10.2167/beb339.0

DelliCarpini, M. (2008). Teacher collaboration for ESL/EFL academic success. *The Internet TESL Journal, 14*(8). Retrieved from http://iteslj.org/Techniques/DelliCarpini-TeacherCollaboration.html

Dove, M., & Honigsfeld, A. (2010). ESL coteaching and collaboration: Opportunities to develop teacher leadership and enhance student learning. *TESOL Journal, 1*(1). doi: 10.5054/tj.2010.214879

Echevarría, J., Vogt, M. E., & Short, D. J. (2017). *Making content comprehensible for English learners: The SIOP model* (5th ed.). Boston, MA: Pearson

Indiana Department of Education. (2014a). *English/Language Arts Standards.* Indianapolis, IN: Author.

Indiana Department of Education. (2014b). *Indiana's WIDA implementation guide for English learners.* Indianapolis, IN: Office of English Learning and Migrant Education.

Johnston, B. (1999). The expatriate teacher as postmodern paladin. *Research in the Teaching of English, 34*, 255–280.

Kaufman, D., & Brooks, J. (1996). Interdisciplinary collaboration in teacher education: A constructivist approach. *TESOL Quarterly, 30*(2), 231–251.

Levine, T., & Bunch, G. (2007). Community. In F. Pawan & G. B. Sietman (Eds.), *Collaborative partnerships between ESL and classroom teachers: Helping English language learners succeed in middle and high school* (pp. 117–140). Alexandria, VA: TESOL.

McIntosh, P. (2016). White privilege: Unpacking the invisible knapsack. In P. S. Rothenberg (Ed.), *Race, class, and gender in the United States* (10th ed., pp. 176–180). New York: Worth Publishers.

Ortloff, J. (2011). *Toward a grounded theory of trust: Collaboration, trust, and cooperation between ESL and content-area teachers in a secondary school* (Unpublished doctoral dissertation). Indiana University, Bloomington, IN.

Park, J., & Pawan, F. (2016). Korean professors' pedagogical efforts and professional development needs in English-medium instruction. In J. Crandall & M. Christison (Eds.), *Teacher education and professional development in TESOL: Global perspectives* (pp. 193–204). New York, NY: Routledge.

Pawan, F., & Craig, D. (2011). ESL and content area teacher responses to discussions on English language learner instruction. *TESOL Journal, 2*(3), 293–311. doi: 10.5054/tj.2011.259956

Pawan, F., & Ortloff, J. (2011). Sustaining collaboration: English-as-a-second-language and content-area teachers. *Teaching and Teacher Education, 27*(2), 463–471. doi: 10.1016/j.tate.2010.09.016

Pawan, F., & Sietman, G. B. (2007). *Helping English language learners succeed in middle and high schools.* Alexandria, VA: TESOL.

Pawan, F., & Ward, B. (2007). Integrated curriculum development through interdisciplinary collaboration between ESL and content area teachers. In F. Pawan & G. B. Sietmann (Eds.), *Helping English language learners succeed in middle and high schools* (pp. 5–30). Alexandria, VA: TESOL.

Peterson, K., & Deal, T. (1998). How leaders influence the culture of schools. *Educational Leadership, 56*(1), 28–30.

Roegge, C., Galloway, J., & Welge, J. (1991). *Setting the stage: A practitioner's guide to integrating vocational and academic education.* Springfield: IL: State Board of Education.

Samuelson, B., Pawan, F., & Hung, Y. (2012). Barriers to collaboration between English-as-a-second-language and content area teachers. In A. Honigsfeld & M. Dove (Eds.), *Co-teaching and other collaborative practices in the EFL/ESL classroom: Rationale, research, reflections, and recommendations* (pp. 183–193). Charlotte, NC: Information Age Publishing.

Singleton, G. E., & Linton, C. (2007). *Facilitators' guide, Courageous conversations about race: A field guide for achieving equity in schools.* Thousand Oaks, CA: Corwin Press.

Snow, M. A., Met, M., & Genesee, F. (1989). A conceptual framework for the integration of language and content in second/foreign language instruction. *TESOL Quarterly, 23*(2), 201–217.

Stone, D., Patton, B., & Heen, S. (1999). *Difficult conversations: How to discuss what matters most.* New York, NY: Viking.

Sztompka, P. (1999). *Trust: A sociological theory.* Cambridge, England: Cambridge University Press.

World Class Instructional Design and Assessment Consortium. (2012). *2012 amplification of the ELD standards: Kindergarten–Grade 12.* Madison, WI: Author.

APPENDIX 24A
Bethune-Chavez Conversational Protocol (Levine & Bunch, 2007)

Who Does What?	For How Long?
Participants volunteer for key roles: presenter, facilitator, timekeeper, process-checker	to be determined
Presenter shares a teaching dilemma with descriptive detail	7 minutes
Colleagues ask clarifying questions	2 minutes
Colleagues discuss dilemma in ways that might help presenter rethink, reframe, or consider alternative courses of action	13 minutes
Presenter reflects aloud on what she heard, learned, or will try	5 minutes
Process-checker leads group reflection on the process	5 minutes

Used with permission.

APPENDIX 24B
Topical Areas, Description, and Frequently Asked Questions (Pawan & Craig, 2011)

Topical Areas	Description	Percentage of Most Frequently Asked Questions by ESL and Content-Area Teachers Regarding CBI Teacher Collaboration
1. CBI teaching approaches	Various instructional approaches for ELs that are known, utilized, read, and/or heard about respectively in the literature and meetings	Are student-centered approaches viable in CBI? (41.6%)
2. CBI assessment	Various assessment identified and to be modified for ELs	What are the uses of alternative assessment in CBI? (40.5%)
3. Conceptions of EL literacies	Types of literacies to be acquired or needed by ELLs	Is there an Academic/Standard English? (58.3%)
4. Interdisciplinary collaboration	Current practices, outcomes, and potentials of interdisciplinary collaboration between ESL teachers and content-area teachers	How receptive are teachers to collaboration? (49.3%)
5. Roles and responsibilities as teachers of ELs	The scope, nature, and extent of teacher responsibilities toward ELs	What is the nature of teacher responsibilities to ELs in the classroom? (58.1%)
6. Advocacy for ELs	The people and means to assist ELs	What should be teachers' investment and engagement outside the classroom? (57.4%)

APPENDIX 24C
Isabel and Sophie's Joint Strategies (Pawan & Ward, 2007)

Scaffolding Strategies for Content Classes	Content Incorporation Strategies for ESL Classes
Isabel (high school algebra teacher)	Sophie (ESL teacher)
<ul><li>Drawing pictures</li><li>Using gestures</li><li>Using Spanish as support</li><li>Speaking clearly</li><li>Writing everything down—and saying it too</li><li>Acting things out when possible</li><li>Connecting to prior knowledge</li><li>Grouping bilingual students with Level 1 (beginning) students</li><li>Daily manipulatives</li><li>Demonstration</li><li>Kinesthetic activities</li><li>Frontloading</li><li>Lower-level readings</li><li>Word banks for tests</li><li>Whole to part instruction knowledge (deconstructing & reorganizing information into smaller, meaningful segments)</li><li>Building background</li><li>Constructivist and problem-based activities</li><li>Teaching backwards<ul><li>Extension activities</li><li>Discuss</li><li>Answer questions</li><li>Read the text</li></ul></li></ul>	<ul><li>Comparison of academic and informal discourse</li><li>A priori introduction of content themes</li><li>Use of content textbooks</li><li>Use of content-specific vocabulary</li><li>Identifying and linking concepts that are similar across content</li><li>Conceptual mapping of difficult ideas</li><li>Discussion of background or personal knowledge related to academic topics</li><li>Identification and practice of content-area study skills</li><li>Identification and practice of personal study skills that would be useful in learning content</li><li>Identification and practice of common study skills across content areas</li><li>Working in groups with native speakers of English</li><li>Identification of content resources in students' L1</li></ul>

Used with permission.

Chapter 25

Looking Back and Looking Forward at the Adjunct Model: Are We Still Smiling through the Turbulence?

Lynn M. Goldstein

||| A Glimpse into the Adjunct/Paired Courses Classroom

Scenario 1: International graduate students at the Monterey Institute of International Studies (MIIS) (now known as the Middlebury Institute of International Studies) enrolled in a credit-bearing introductory policy course required for their MA degree were also enrolled in an adjunct writing class taught by a second language writing teacher who focused on the writing assignments assigned in the policy class. All sections of the policy class and the writing class were taught by full-time faculty, all with doctoral degrees. The writing teachers had release time to attend all class sessions of the policy course and also completed all of the readings and some of the writing assignments, while the policy teachers did not attend any of the writing class sessions. The writing and policy courses were not planned in tandem, collaboration among the writing teachers and the policy teachers was minimal, and the writing course was largely seen by the policy professors and students as "service" to the policy course (Goldstein, Campbell, & Cummings, 1997).

Scenario 2: ESL undergraduates at Kingsborough Community College were enrolled in a learning community, in which they took an ESL course linked with a credit-bearing content course. The content teacher was carefully chosen for a willingness to collaborate and to meet the needs of ESL students. Key administrators were enthusiastic supporters of the program and provided administrative, financial, and time support for course development, teacher and tutor professional development, and ongoing collaboration, allowing for frequent and sustained collaboration among the ESL teacher, content teacher, and tutors regarding course planning, materials, projects, pedagogy, student needs, and assessment (Babbitt & Mlynarczyk, 2000; Mlynarczyk & Babbitt, 2002).

The Adjunct Model |||

Adjunct language courses arose to meet the needs of underprepared and multilingual students enrolled in higher education. In the adjunct model, the primary aim of the language course is to provide support so students can succeed in their credit-bearing content courses (Brinton, Snow, & Wesche, 2003). The adjunct model has largely operated at the tertiary level, and in its typical configuration pairs a content course focused on the language needs of the targeted students, including reading, writing, public speaking, integrated skills, and / or academic study skills and strategies (see, e.g., Goldstein, Campbell, & Cummings, 1997; Iancu, 1997; Johns, 2001; Zhang, 2004) with a for-credit content course that these multilingual students take along with mainstream students. However, adjunct models have been employed in varied contexts and, as a result, curricular pairings are also varied, including, for example, non-matriculated students enrolled in an English language institute who may take a credit-bearing course within the academic institution (Adamson, 1993; Beckett, Gonzalez, & Schwartz, 2004) and matriculated students who take a for-credit language course paired with a for-credit sheltered[1] content course (Goldstein, 1993). Students may also participate as an intact cohort in a learning community and take a block schedule of classes, including credit-bearing content classes, paired with one or several language courses, along with other courses that may provide further support (Mlynarczyk & Babbitt, 2002). This configuration may be multidisciplinary, with different students enrolled in different content classes (Johns, 2001).

In its original conceptualization, the adjunct model was predicated on the language teacher and the content teacher working together (Snow & Brinton, 1988). As Davison (2006) points out, "An ideal collaboration between ESL and content-area teachers requires the integration of content-based ESL teaching and ESL-conscious content teaching" (p. 457). In reality, however, the connections between the paired content class and the language course(s) vary from closely aligned—that is, where the content and language teachers work in tandem to plan the syllabi, tasks, and assignments and collaborate throughout the semester (e.g., Gee, 1997; Mlynarczyk & Babbitt, 2002)—to very loosely or not aligned (e.g., Goldstein, Campbell, & Cummings, 1997)—that is, where the language teacher and content teacher work independently, but the language teacher provides support for the language needs the students experience in participating in and completing the work of the content class.

Adjunct model programs have also been modified to best fit the particular needs, advantages, and constraints of individual contexts, recognizing that a "pure" adjunct model may not work in all settings. For example, rather than pairing a language course with a content course, some programs employ a "simulated adjunct model" (Brinton & Jensen, 2002), because of certain constraints that mitigate against offering a true adjunct model. In the setting that Brinton and Jensen report on, authentic content, including videotaped lectures from carefully selected professors along with the accompanying readings, provide the content for the simulated adjunct course. In turn, the language teachers use this content to focus on all four language skills in supporting students to understand and use the content while developing their academic language skills. Brinton and Jensen (2002) note several advantages of the simulated adjunct model: It retains the strengths of the adjunct model (i.e., especially working with sustained authentic content and the linguistic demands of this content through authentic tasks) while avoiding some of the model's constraints, such as the need to coordinate with content faculty and the difficulty of both identifying content courses that might be relevant to the student population and scheduling these courses at times that are convenient for ESL students.

Another adaptation to the adjunct model is one where instead of pairing the content class with a language class, the students are enrolled in a content class and a tutorial class. Van Wyk (this volume) reports on her context in South Africa where the tutorial class is taught by non-language specialists who have been trained by a language specialist and who attend ongoing training sessions. The tutors, language specialist, and content teachers work collaboratively in identifying what content and language foci will be addressed and the pedagogical approaches for doing so. Consistent with all adjunct model configurations, students work with authentic content to both learn and understand that content and, in turn, to focus on the language skills they need to work effectively with this content and that they will need for future courses. Like the simulated adjunct model, this adaptation has grown out of the exigencies of the context, namely, in Van Wyk's setting, the dearth of trained language teachers.

There has also been a recent movement, especially in elementary and secondary school settings, where language teachers and content teachers are working collaboratively to support their shared students' content and language learning (Arkoudis, 2000, 2006; Creese, 2002; Davison, 2006; Kong, 2014). These collaborations range from the content and language teacher co-designing and co-teaching a set of activities over the course of a semester (Kong, 2014) to push-in models (Reynolds, Jiao, Nolin-Smith, & O'Brien, n.d.) where language teachers and content teachers work collaboratively and co-teach in the same elementary or secondary classroom (Arkoudis, 2000, 2006; Creese, 2002; Davison, 2006), to a collaborative model, "collaborative interdisciplinary team teaching," where the language and content teachers team teach within a university classroom (Stewart, Sagliano, & Sagliano, 2000).

The literature enumerates multiple benefits for multilingual students enrolled in adjunct model programs, including affective advantages such as increased student motivation (Pally, 2000) and self-confidence (Snow & Brinton, 1988) and interpersonal advantages such as the opportunities to integrate socially and academically with domestic classmates (Andrade & Makaafi, 2001; Harklau, 1994). Students also experience academic advantages, including learning how "to do" college (Johns, 2001), being able to simultaneously learn content and develop language skills (Brinton, Snow, & Wesche, 2003; Pally, 2000), learning strategies and skills applicable to the current and future content courses (Beckett, Gonzalez, & Schwartz, 2004; Chen, 2008), and learning academic English more quickly and succeeding in credit-bearing courses from the beginning of their academic studies (Mlynarczyk & Babbitt, 2002). In addition, program evaluation research has shown that students who participate in adjunct classes tend to do better than their counterparts who are not in adjunct classes (Guyer & Peterson, 1988; Kasper, 1994), achieve higher grade-point averages (Kasper, 1997; Tinto, 1998) and better grades in subsequent courses (Kasper, 1997), and perform as well as their domestic classmates in their content courses (Andrade & Makaafi, 2001; Snow & Kamhi-Stein, 2002).

Issues for the Language Teacher in Paired Courses |||

Despite the benefits for students, there is a growing conversation focused on the difficulties language teachers may face. In some cases, the content class and the status of the content teacher has been privileged over the language class and the status of the language teacher (Arkoudis, 2000, 2006; Creese, 2002; Goldstein, Campbell, & Cummings, 1997; Lo, 2014). As Benesch (1992) cautioned, the adjunct class is normally expected to "adapt to the demands of the content course" while the content course "retains its traditional format and curriculum" (p. 1). In certain instances, the adjunct teacher assumes the lion's share of the work to make the pairing pedagogically effective (Goldstein, Campbell, & Cummings, 1997). In addition, there can be variations in administrative support for this work despite Babbitt and Mlynarczyk's (2000) admonition that "the program functions best if driven by the college administration, which tends to lend stronger support to a program to which it has committed itself financially" (p. 38) and that "it is also essential for administrators to recognize the need to provide compensation to faculty participating in content-based linked programs for the time required to plan curriculum and coordinate coursework " (p. 38).

Returning to the two scenarios at the beginning of this chapter, we can see stark differences regarding collaboration, status, and workload; we can also see some of the issues for the language teacher noted in the literature. In Scenario 1, the L2 writing teachers and their content and expertise were marginalized, and the L2 writing teachers assumed the responsibility, both psychological and actual, to ensure that students were receiving the instruction and support they needed. The content teachers were absent from this process and work, except to attend a few meetings requested by the L2 writing teachers. In contrast, in Scenario 2, the ESL teachers and the content teachers were on equal footing, working together to meet the students' needs, recognizing that the responsibility to meet their students' academic needs was a shared one.

Returning to Scenario 1, we notice key difficulties that my colleagues (the writing teachers) and I (the writing program director) experienced (for a full discussion of this scenario, see Goldstein, Campbell, & Cummings, 1997). The beginnings of our work were auspicious: I was able to successfully argue for the strengths of the adjunct model and the administration agreed to provide a course release for the L2 writing teachers, enabling them to attend the policy class to understand the content and the nature of the content-area writing assignments. However, what the two writing teachers and I did not anticipate were the relations of power and the territorialism we encountered that served to marginalize both them and their students. These relations came into play even though the policy teachers had agreed to participate and initially seemed to support the adjunct model. It became increasingly apparent as the semester progressed that the policy teachers had agreed to participate solely because they wanted the writing teachers to address the issues of their multilingual students that they themselves did not know how to "solve," thus absolving them from this responsibility and allowing them to conduct business as usual. Our joint meetings made it clear that the policy teachers saw their L2 writers as "less than" and that the policy teachers believed it was solely the responsibility of the L2 writing teachers to "fix" the students' writing by attending to their language needs, especially at the sentence level.

In the face of mounting frustration, the writing teachers attempted to change the nature of their relationship with the content faculty by focusing on the issue of their shared responsibility for the students and by stressing how both parties could coordinate and learn from each other to best help the students. We invited the policy teachers to sit in on writing class sessions of their choice, just as the writing teachers were attending the policy classes, recognizing that both the policy teachers and the L2 writing teachers had expertise that would benefit each other as they worked with their shared students. We also asked the policy teachers to share with us their understandings of the genres of the papers they were assigning, and their expectations and descriptions of good writing; we also offered to assist with this process by using our expertise with genre analysis, to help the policy teachers analyze the purposes for which the students were expected to write, the intended audiences and their expectations, the content to be addressed, and the expected structure and style of these texts. Last, we offered to share our expertise and observations with the policy teachers regarding: (1) ways of responding to student writing that would help multilingual students strengthen their writing; (2) the challenges that students were encountering in understanding the policy course readings; and (3) difficulties students were having understanding the expectations for each writing assignment. These attempts were met with resistance and, ultimately, failure. In addition, the writing teachers were also warned off of invading the "policy territory"—that is, the content being covered in the policy classes.

Ultimately, the writing teachers and I were marginalized as having no content and no status, which undermined the writing teachers' sense of agency and confidence and also increased their workload. Meanwhile, the policy teachers maintained their workload "as is." This marginalization also undermined some of their students' trust in the writing teachers' expertise since they absorbed their policy teachers' implicit messages that the writing teachers were language "fixer uppers" who had no real understanding of the policy content. Martha Cummings, one of the teachers, aptly titled our account of our experience "Smiling through the turbulence: The flight attendant syndrome and writing instructor status in the adjunct model," capturing the "big boys" (the policy professors, all male) piloting while the flight attendants (us, all women) "served" them.

Looking Forward: Surveying Language Teachers within Paired Courses |||

Reading accounts such as the one described in Scenario 2, however, suggests that not all adjunct language teachers have experienced the issues we did in enacting paired courses. In fact, ten years after my experiences with the adjunct model, another EAP professor at MIIS and a different policy studies professor from those my colleagues and I had worked with, voluntarily decided to collaborate, without release time or remuneration, to meet the writing needs of matriculated policy students enrolled in the same paired EAP writing course and introductory policy course as the ones our students had taken. In stark contrast to our experience, these two teachers collaborated on the guidelines for the writing assignments and reading assignments; jointly collected and annotated sample papers to be shared with the students and designed classroom tasks around these papers; and, when feasible, audited each other's classes (see Leopold, 2010 for a full account).

Given that other language teachers have had more positive and more collaborative experiences, I decided to revisit the issues my colleagues and I had experienced by asking those who have been involved in teaching L2 writing courses within adjunct/paired course models to share their experiences through a survey administered through Google Docs. I solicited participation by posting my request and the link to the Google Doc on professional e-lists, on the Facebook pages of professional groups whose members work with L2 writers, and by emailing it to faculty whom I knew to be involved with teaching paired courses for L2 writers. I also shared it with administrators of programs with paired courses for L2 writers, asking them to distribute it to their faculty.

In response, 22 teachers in ESL and EFL settings completed the survey. Nine are currently teaching paired courses and 13 have taught these courses in the past but are no longer doing so. Twelve of the 22 participants reported considerable experience with teaching paired courses, ranging from ten with more than 25 years, and five reported 2–5 years of experience with paired courses. The participants have taught paired courses for non-matriculated undergraduates, as well as matriculated undergraduate, graduate, and law school students in the U.S., Australia, Finland, Israel, Mexico, Ukraine, and Taiwan.

In the discussions that follow, I have synthesized: (1) the participants' responses to the questions that elicited their description and evaluations of the administrative support they and their disciplinary colleagues received; (2) their descriptions of and reactions to their working and interpersonal relationships with the disciplinary content teacher; and (3) their answers as to what they saw as the overall benefits and strengths of paired courses along with the underlying issues and difficulties of offering paired courses.

Do Language Teachers in Paired Courses Receive Institutional Support?

Despite the extra work entailed in teaching a language course paired with a content course (such as learning the content and/or the genres from the content class, sitting in on the content class, and/or coordinating with the content teacher), many of the participants did not receive additional pay or release time support for teaching their paired language course. Likewise, only four participants reported that their counterpart disciplinary content teacher received release time and/or extra pay to prepare the content course and/or coordinate with the language teacher. Among the language teachers who had some form of institutional support, most commonly they received release time and/or extra pay to prepare their language course and to coordinate with their counterpart content teacher, and some also received pay or release time to attend the disciplinary content course with their students.

Those who did not receive institutional support had varied reactions. One participant felt support was not needed because she was hired as a competent language specialist; several others had altruistic reasons for participating in paired courses despite receiving no support, ranging from wanting to learn and collaborate across disciplines to being willing to create one's own support system. Other reasons given included wanting to be a better teacher (on the part of the content teacher) and wanting students to succeed (on the part of the language teacher). However, a number of the participants found a lack of institutional support to be personally problematic for them as teachers, citing the amount of work they did without such support. They noted how much easier it would have been to make the course work more effectively with release time or financial support, how a lack of support was "wearying" or created additional pressure, and how paired courses in the absence of support depended on motivated individual teachers. Some even expressed an unwillingness to participate in the future because of a lack of financial incentives or because they were part-time adjunct teachers.

The teachers who received some type of support credited this support with enhancing their students' learning, enhancing their pedagogical effectiveness and the pedagogical effectiveness of their counterpart content teacher, and enhancing their relationship with the disciplinary content teacher. One participant commented that with institutional support, she and her counterpart had "come to know and appreciate each other's expertise and... are successfully operating at the interface where both practices meet."

What Was the Nature of the Working and Power Relationship between the Adjunct Teacher and the Disciplinary Content Teacher?

The participants were divided between those who worked with the disciplinary content teacher to plan and integrate the paired courses and those who planned their respective courses separately. During the term, regardless of whether or not the two teachers had worked together to plan their courses before they began, some pairs met regularly, some met sporadically, some never met, and some of the language teachers indicated experiencing all three meeting conditions.[2]

Responses were mixed regarding the language and content teachers sharing their respective expertise with each other, from no sharing of expertise, one-directional sharing (i.e., with the language teacher sharing with the content teacher or the content teacher sharing with the language teacher), or bidirectional (i.e., with both teachers sharing their expertise with each other). Likewise, responses were mixed regarding sharing criteria for the assessment of student writing and sharing methods of feedback, from no joint discussions about assessment or feedback at all to working together to establish assessment criteria and share methods of giving students feedback on their writing assignments.

In characterizing the balance of power in their relationship with the content teacher, half of the participants reported being equal partners with the content teacher, with most also stating that the language teacher and content teacher gave equal weight to their respective content areas. Most often, where there was an equal balance of power, the language teacher and the disciplinary content teacher had equal academic status or the language teacher had higher status. However, almost half of the participants indicated having experienced a power imbalance in their relationship with the content teacher, and in all but one of these instances where the teacher said she had more power than the content teacher, participants reported that the content teacher had more power and/or that the content teacher's content was privileged over their L2 content knowledge and expertise. In all but one of these cases, the disciplinary teacher had higher academic status than the writing teacher.

When discussing the nature of their relationship with the content teachers, several of the participants commented that they had experienced a range of relationships and that these relationships were influenced by the individual content teacher with whom they were paired, the content teacher's attitudes, and the nature of and availability of administrative support. A third of the participants described an equal relationship, with mutual respect and with both teachers learning from each other. For some, this positive relationship enhanced their students' trust in them and in their adjunct language course. Some mentioned that they worked closely with the content teacher. Specifically, they reported sharing their respective content materials, co-designing the courses and assignments (and in some cases co-teaching some class sessions), and checking in weekly to reevaluate and re-plan. Several also remarked that they played an essential role in helping the content teacher to understand L2 development, language issues, genres, and L2 pedagogy; differentiate between students' content knowledge versus their language proficiency; and prepare assignments. Some described their relationships as evolving over time, from less than optimal initially to a positive relationship where their contributions and content were valued and where students built trust in their expertise.

Others, however, described less optimal experiences, ranging from the content teacher having poor pedagogy; the language teacher having to work independently from the content course teacher and the content course because the pairing was not working; the two teachers having limited discussion of L2 writing or the content of the writing classes; the language teacher experiencing a lack of administrative support; and the content teachers' unfair expectation that the writing teachers should "fix" the students. Some commented on relationships of unequal status or power, but perceived this as acceptable for different reasons—in one case, because the adjunct teacher felt the content teacher was doing the writing teacher a favor by working with the writing teacher without extra pay or support, even though the writing teacher did not have any support either. In another case, where the content class was privileged over the adjunct language course, the language teacher was not troubled by this as "the students and I were studying their classes as 'microcosms of the university'."

Benefits and Issues

The participants indicated numerous benefits for multilingual students enrolled in paired courses. Affective benefits included multilingual students not being separated from domestic students in content courses, the disciplinary teachers not treating multilingual students as deficient, and the disciplinary teachers being more inclusive of multilingual students in their classes. They also felt that their students' motivation in the adjunct language courses was enhanced because the language course was paired with a credit-bearing course, because the language course focused on the content and genres the students needed for their academic courses, and because the students completed real writing tasks with real content. In addition, they felt that their students' learning benefited because the students enjoyed the support of two teachers, they learned how to "do" college, they developed their vocabulary, had more opportunities to learn disciplinary content, had earlier (rather than delayed) opportunities to develop content area knowledge, had more opportunities to write, developed familiarity with academic genres, completed real tasks with real content and were writing for real academic purposes, and wrote more in-depth texts because they had numerous readings and discussions that informed their writing. In contrast, only a few participants mentioned drawbacks for students enrolled in adjunct writing courses: One felt that paired courses were sometimes confusing and messy; one felt that the content course teachers might position multilingual writers as deficient; and one felt that, in some cases, paired courses might increase the students' workloads.

In contrast to the benefits enumerated for the students, the participants detailed numerous drawbacks and few advantages for teachers of the adjunct language courses.[3] Advantages all focused on the pedagogical benefits, including not having to address everything in the writing class because the content was also covered outside the writing classes. Other benefits mentioned included that the content class provided meaningful content for the writing class, the format allowed the adjunct writing teacher to bridge content and writing, and the content class reinforced the importance of the adjunct language class.

The difficulties reported centered around issues for the teachers and their personal and professional well-being, including administrative support for the adjunct writing teachers and the status of the adjunct writing teacher and his/her content and expertise. A number of the adjunct writing teachers reported that either funding was not available or that the administration was short-sighted and did not make funds available for release time, additional pay to develop paired courses, time or pay for coordination with the content teacher, and/or stipends to attend the content course with which the writing course was paired. Some felt this reflected the administration's and the institution's marginalization of adjunct writing teachers, their content, and their students. One of the participants described the amount of work and time the paired course involved as a "labor of love," and this concern for their students echoed in many responses: A number of the writing teachers felt that while they were putting in an inordinate amount of uncompensated, undervalued time in designing and teaching the paired language course, they did so because they cared about their students and their learning. They also expressed concerns about their working relationships with the content teachers. These concerns were multiple and included feeling: isolated and left out due to a general lack of communication with the content teachers; frustrated about not having the expectations of the content teachers clearly communicated; discouraged by the content teachers' unwillingness to coordinate; upset about not being accorded equal status with the content teachers; and finally, resentful of the unreasonable expectations that content teachers had of them because of the content teachers' lack of understanding of the writing process, language development, or the writing genres that were assigned. One participant captured the views of a number of the adjunct language teachers, stating that there were no problems for the students, no problems for the content teachers, and all the problems for the adjunct language teacher.

Practices and Underlying Principles ||

Many of the adjunct writing teachers in this study have experienced similar issues as described in Scenario 1 and are still "flying through the turbulence," without fair compensation for their time, without opportunities to systematically coordinate with content teachers, and without the administration's and/or content teachers' respect for and/or understanding of the adjunct language teacher's content and expertise. While a number of the participants expressed a commitment to the adjunct model because of the benefits that accrue to multilingual students, language teachers should have fair working conditions and respect for the work they do and for their expertise. In addition, the efficacy of the adjunct model would be enhanced with bi-directional planning and sharing of expertise between the language teacher and the content teacher. Table 25.1 focuses on what practices should be in place to ameliorate less-than-desirable working conditions for the teachers and to enhance the efficacy of the adjunct model.

Future Research ||

Suggestions for future research are prompted by the experiences of those who participated in this study, one of whom commented that there is a need for "continuing to raise awareness around the interconnectedness of content, language and learning by publicly sharing experiences of successful collaborations" and for "continuing efforts to work against the marginalization of language in education by joint research/networking."

There is an urgent need to highlight the effects of marginalization on language teachers as a result of negative working conditions, including extra work without release time or extra pay or support systems, and including deleterious attitudes and relationships that position language teachers in adjunct models as having no real content and lower status (i.e., as being subservient to the content course and the content course teacher). It is important to document how pervasive these conditions are and how these working conditions affect language teachers' professional and job satisfaction, pedagogical confidence, and self-perceptions of their teaching effectiveness. Some of the participants in this study expressed support for the adjunct model because of the benefits for the students even when they did not have fair working conditions. We need to understand why some ESL or EFL teachers persist in teaching in programs where such negative work conditions exist, and we also need to examine situations where, because of adverse working conditions, the language teachers have decided against continued participation or the program as a whole has ceased to operate.

Largely missing from the research are the content teachers' voices. We need to understand the content teachers' perspectives on the adjunct model and whether and how it benefits students and teachers, their perceptions of the comparative importance for student learning and academic success of their content and expertise versus that of the language teacher, and their views about how/if the content and language teacher should coordinate (Lo, 2014; Snow, 1997; Srole, 1997; Trent, 2010). In addition, we need more qualitative research, such as

Table 25.1: Practices and Underlying Principles for Teacher Support and Coordination in the Adjunct Model

Practices for Teacher Support and Coordination	Underlying Principles
1. The administration supports the language and content teachers' coordination through various mechanisms (e.g., release time, paid time for coordination, in-service workshops, and so forth).	Language teachers are compensated for the work they do, instead of being expected to do so for "free" and thus avoid exploitation; the administration also signals to the content teachers the value of coordination by providing pay and/or release time to do so.
2. The administration provides in-service training for both the language teachers and the content teachers.	Doing so recognizes that the adjunct model is a unique pedagogical approach for which neither the language teacher nor the content teacher may have had prior training/preparation and also communicates the administration's support for this pedagogical approach.
3. The language teacher and the content teacher share their respective areas of expertise with each other; the administration treats this as the norm by communicating this as expected and valued and by providing sufficient, appropriate support.	To be pedagogically effective, both teachers need to value what each brings to their shared student learning; sharing that is materially supported (e.g., release time) and considered by all to be the norm avoids privileging one content/expertise over another and provides equal status and respect for both teachers. Further, they need to develop appropriate expectations regarding what each class "accomplishes" in terms of students' learning. Content teachers need to develop an understanding of multilingual students' needs, respect for the abilities of multilingual students within their classes, and respect for language teachers and how they meet their students' needs; conversely, language teachers need to develop an understanding of the linguistic demands of the content class.
4. The language teachers and content teachers identify where they can coordinate and/or complement each other's assignments, assessments, and feedback to students. The language and content teachers check in regularly about students' progress, difficulties, and needs.	It is crucial that all parties recognize that both teachers' areas of expertise are key for their shared students' learning; equally important are avoiding assessment and feedback practices that may be less than optimal or at odds with each other and both teachers sharing responsibility for their students' learning.
5. Administrators and teachers conduct a needs assessment to ascertain whether the working conditions exist to enact a paired course model. If such conditions do not exist, they either do not offer adjunct model courses or they work to ameliorate these conditions to make them suitable.	Institutions need to be sensitive to and avoid exploiting teachers through unfair practices.

that of Arkoudis (2006), which examines the discourse when language and content teachers collaborate to understand how these interactions themselves reify, negotiate, or change views about each others' contents, expertises, pedagogies, statuses, and responsibilities. It is difficult to advocate for equity between language teachers and content teachers without knowing the underlying ideologies of the content teachers and the roles of these ideologies in shaping content teachers' attitudes toward forms of participation in paired courses, and without understanding how the language and content teachers' ideologies shape their interactions.

Lastly, while there is literature regarding what factors should be in place for successful adjunct programs (e.g., Babbitt & Mlynarczyk, 2000), we know little about the administrative ideologies and material institutional conditions that have led to the experiences that the teachers in this study reported, both negative and positive. Case studies of adjunct programs would allow us to determine and compare the conditions that have led to fair and equitable working conditions for the language teacher versus those that have led to exploitation of language teachers and imbalances in power and work contributions between language and content teachers. Such studies would be informative for administrators and for teachers when making decisions regarding whether an adjunct program should be implemented or when making decisions about how to ameliorate detrimental conditions for language teachers in adjunct programs.

APPLYING WHAT YOU LEARNED
Questions and Tasks

1. What are the benefits and drawbacks of the adjunct model for language teachers?

2. What is your reaction to the teacher who is willing to teach adjunct classes without support (additional pay or release time) because she wants what is best for her students?

3. What are possible arguments you could use with administrators to encourage them to provide support for the language teacher and the content teacher (course release and/or additional pay) for course preparation and coordination and attending each other's classes?

4. Administrators and teachers need to avoid implementing an adjunct model when fair working conditions for the teachers cannot be put into place. Do you agree or disagree with this statement? Why?

ENDNOTES

1. Sheltered content courses are content courses that are designed specifically for and, typically, only enroll multilingual students (see Brinton & Snow, this volume).
2. Many of the participants had had multiple experiences with teaching adjunct courses.
3. Interestingly, the participants did not mention advantages or difficulties for the content teachers.

REFERENCES

Adamson, H. D. (1993). *Academic competence: Theory and classroom practice—Preparing ESL students for content courses*. White Plains, NY: Longman.

Andrade, M. S., & Makaafi, J. H. (2001). Guidelines for establishing adjunct courses at the university level. *TESOL Journal, 10*(2/3), 33–39.

Arkoudis, S. (2000). "I have linguistic aims and linguistic content": ESL and science teachers planning together. *Prospect, 15*, 61–71.

Arkoudis, S. (2006). Negotiating the rough ground between ESL and mainstream teachers. *International Journal of Bilingual Education & Bilingualism, 9*, 415–433.

Babbitt, M., & Mlynarczyk, R. (2000). Keys to successful content-based programs: Administrative perspectives. In L. F. Kasper (Ed.), *Content-based college ESL instruction* (pp. 26–47). Mahwah, NJ: Erlbaum.

Beckett, G., Gonzalez, V., & Schwartz, H. (2004). Content based ESL writing curriculum: A language socialization model. *NABE Journal of Research and Practice, 2*, 161–175.

Benesch, S. (1992). Sharing responsibilities: An alternative to the adjunct model. *College ESL, 2*, 1–10.

Brinton, D. M., & Jensen, L. (2002). Appropriating the adjunct model: English for academic purposes at the university level. In J. Crandall & D. Kaufman (Eds.), *Content-based instruction in higher education settings* (pp. 125–137). Alexandria, VA: TESOL.

Brinton, D. M., Snow, M. A., & Wesche, M. (2003). *Content-based second language instruction* (Classics ed.). Ann Arbor, MI: University of Michigan Press.

Chen, Q. (2008, April). *Creating significant learning experiences for ESL students*. Paper presented at the 42nd Annual TESOL Convention, New York, NY.

Creese, A. (2002). The discursive construction of power in teacher partnerships: Language and subject specialists in mainstream schools. *TESOL Quarterly, 36*, 597–616.

Davison, C. (2006). Collaboration between ESL and content teachers: How do we know when we are doing it right? *International Journal of Bilingual Education and Bilingualism, 9*, 454–475.

Gee, Y. (1997). ESL and content teachers: Working effectively in adjunct courses. In M. A. Snow & D. M. Brinton (Eds.), *The content-based classroom: Perspectives on integrating language and content* (pp. 324–330). White Plains, NY: Longman.

Goldstein, L. (1993). Becoming a member of the "Teaching Foreign Languages Community": Integrating reading and writing through an adjunct/content course. In J. Carson & I. Leki (Eds.), *Reading in the composition classroom: Second language perspectives* (pp. 290–298). Boston, MA: Heinle and Heinle.

Goldstein, L., Campbell, C., & Cummings, M. C. (1997). Smiling through the turbulence: The flight attendant syndrome and writing instructor status in the adjunct model. In M. A. Snow & D. M. Brinton (Eds.), *The content-based classroom: Perspectives on integrating language and content* (pp. 331–339). White Plains, NY: Longman.

Guyer, E. P., & Peterson, P. W. (1988). Language and/or content? Principles and procedures for materials development in an adjunct course. In S. Benesch (Ed.), *Ending remediation: Linking ESL and content in higher education* (pp. 91–111). Washington, DC: TESOL.

Harklau, L. (1994). ESL versus mainstream classes: Contrasting L2 learning environments. *TESOL Quarterly, 28,* 241–272.

Iancu, M. (1997). Adapting the adjunct model: A case study. In M. A. Snow & D. M. Brinton (Eds.), *The content-based classroom: Perspectives on integrating language and content* (pp. 149–157). White Plains, NY: Longman.

Johns, A. (2001). An interdisciplinary, interinstitutional, learning communities program: Student involvement and student success. In I. Leki (Ed.), *Academic writing programs* (pp. 61–72). Alexandria, VA: TESOL.

Kasper, L. F. (1994). Improved reading performance for ESL students through academic course pairing. *Journal of Reading, 37,* 376–384.

Kasper, L. F. (1997). The impact of content-based instructional programs on the academic progress of ESL students. *English for Specific Purposes, 16*(4), 309–320.

Kong, S. (2014). Collaboration between content and language specialists in late immersion. *The Canadian Modern Language Review, 70,* 102–122.

Leopold, L. (2010). Teaching writing within the disciplines: A viable approach for English for academic purposes (EAP) instructors. *The CATESOL Journal, 22,* 167–188.

Lo, Y. Y. (2014). Collaboration between L2 and content subject teachers in CBI: Contrasting beliefs and attitudes. *RELC Journal, 45,*181–196.

Mlynarczyk, R., & Babbitt, M. (2002). The power of academic learning communities. *Journal of Basic Writing, 21,* 71–89.

Pally, M. (2000). Sustaining interest/advancing learning: Sustained content-based instruction in ESL/EFL—theoretical background and rationale. In M. Pally (Ed.), *Sustained content teaching in academic ESL/EFL: A practical approach* (pp. 1–18). Boston, MA: Houghton Mifflin.

Reynolds, K. M., Jiao, J., Nolin-Smith, K., & O'Brien, E. (n.d.). *Teachers' perceptions of push-in or pull-out model effectiveness and learning outcomes.* Retrieved from https://www.academia.edu/3566441/Teachers_Perceptions_of_Push-In_or_Pull-Out_Model_Effectiveness_and_Learning_Outcomes

Snow, M. A. (1997). Teaching academic literacy: Discipline faculty take responsibility. In M. A. Snow & D. M. Brinton (Eds.), *The content-based classroom: Perspectives on integrating language and content* (pp. 290–310*).* White Plains, NY: Longman.

Snow, M. A., & Brinton, D. M. (1988). The adjunct model of language instruction: An ideal EAP framework. In S. Benesch (Ed.), *Ending remediation: Linking ESL and content in higher education* (pp. 33–52). Washington, DC: TESOL.

Snow, M. A., & Kamhi-Stein, L. D. (2002). Teaching and learning academic literacy through Project LEAP. In J. Crandall & D. Kaufman (Eds.), *Content-based instruction in higher education settings* (pp. 169–181). Alexandria, VA: TESOL.

Srole, C. (1997). Pedagogical responses from content faculty: Teaching content and language in history. In M. A. Snow & D. M. Brinton (Eds.), *The content-based classroom: Perspectives on integrating language and content* (pp. 104–116)*.* White Plains, NY: Longman.

Stewart, T., Sagliano, M., & Sagliano, J. (2000). An alternative team teaching model for content-based instruction. *Asia Pacific Journal of Teacher Education & Development, 3*(1), 211–243.

Tinto, V. (1998, January). *Learning communities and the reconstruction of remedial education.* Paper presented at the Conference on Replacing Remediation in Higher Education, Stanford, CA.

Trent, J. (2010). Teacher identity construction across the curriculum: Promoting cross-curriculum collaboration in English-medium schools. *Asia Pacific Journal of Education, 30(2),* 167–83.

Zhang, X. (2004). Teaching generation 1.5 students in content-based reading courses in a college adjunct model: An ethnographic case study. *The Reading Matrix, 4,* 118–133.

Contributors ||||||||||||||||||||||||||||||||||||||||||||

Maureen Snow Andrade is Associate Vice President for Academic Programs at Utah Valley University. She is a former editor of the *TESL Reporter*, a former member of the TESOL Book Publications Committee, and currently serves on the *TESOL Journal* editorial board and as associate editor for *Higher Education Pedagogi*es. Her interests include distance language learning, curriculum development, CBI, self-regulation, student transitions, and global higher education.

Laura Baecher is Associate Professor of TESOL and coordinator of the P–12 programs at Hunter College of the City University of New York. Her interests include the connection between teacher preparation and teacher practice including teacher language awareness, the use of video in teacher development, clinical supervision, and collaborative teaching for English learners. Laura is active in the TESOL International Association and is involved with the New York City public schools.

Donna M. Brinton currently works as a private educational consultant, having retired from her position of more than 30 years at the University of California, Los Angeles. Donna remains active in the field of international teacher education, having worked in more than 30 countries. Her areas of interest and expertise include CBI, TESOL methodology, the teaching of pronunciation, heritage language education, and the professional development of novice teachers.

Anne Burns is Professor of TESOL at the University of New South Wales, in Sydney, Australia and Professor Emerita at Aston University, Birmingham, England. At Macquarie University, she worked for more than 20 years in the National Centre for English Language Teaching and Research, the Australian government's key research center for the Adult Migrant English Program. Her interests include teaching speaking, curriculum development, teacher education, and action research.

Lisa Chou is an Online Language Support instructor at the Academy of Art University, San Francisco, where she also coordinates the Online Writing Lab. Lisa has overseas experience studying abroad in Beijing, China, and teaching English in China. She has also served in AmeriCorps National Service to improve literacy for at-risk youths. Lisa's interests involve integrating technology and language teaching for onsite and online ESL courses.

Viviana Cortes is Associate Professor in the Department of Applied Linguistics and English as a Second Language at Georgia State University in Atlanta, Georgia. Before moving to the United States, she worked as an EFL teacher in Buenos Aires, Argentina. Her areas of research and interest include corpus-based discourse analysis, ESP, and different applications of corpora and corpus tools to second and foreign language teaching.

Christiane Dalton-Puffer is Professor of English Linguistics at the University of Vienna, Austria, where she teaches in the TEFL BEd and MEd programs. She is a member of the editorial boards of *The Journal of Immersion and Content-based Education* (Benjamins), *Language Teaching* (Cambridge) and *Classroom Discourse* (Routledge). Her interests include classroom discourse, academic language, pronunciation teaching, language teacher education, as well as English historical linguistics.

Anne M. Ediger is Professor of TESOL and Applied Linguistics at Hunter College of the City University of New York, where she teaches in the M.A. TESOL program. She serves on the editorial review board of the *JALT Journal*. Her areas of interest include CBI, pedagogical grammar, novice teachers' development of grammatical and lexical knowledge, and the role of language in L2 literacy development.

Timothy Farnsworth is Associate Professor of Education at Hunter College of the City University of New York, where he teaches in the M.A. TESOL program. He conducts research in language assessment and teacher education and works with both public school teachers and with teachers of adults. In addition to his work at Hunter College, he has trained teachers in Vietnam and for the Peace Corps.

Shannon Fitzsimmons-Doolan is an Assistant Professor in the Department of English at Texas A&M University, Corpus Christi. She previously worked at the Center for Applied Linguistics (Washington, DC) as a research assistant and as an independent consultant, conducting professional development in the content-based SIOP Model for educators in the U.S. and Canada. Her areas of research inquiry include CBI, language ideologies, language policy, and corpus-based linguistics.

Jan Frodesen is Director of English for Multilingual Students and Senior Lecturer at the University of California, Santa Barbara. She has been teaching English for academic purposes for more than 30 years. Her primary research interests involve L2 writing and pedagogical grammar. Jan is involved with California higher education articulation issues related to English learners and serves on the Editorial Board of *The CATESOL Journal*.

Patricia (Patsy) Duff is Professor of Language and Literacy Education at the University of British Columbia. Patsy's interests are related to language; qualitative research methods in applied linguistics; the teaching, learning, and use of English, Mandarin, and other international languages in transnational contexts; CBI; the integration of L2 learners in schools, universities, and society; multilingualism and work; and sociocultural, sociolinguistic, and sociopolitical aspects of language(s) in education.

Pauline Gibbons is an Adjunct Professor at the University of New South Wales. Her work with teachers in remote indigenous communities in Australia, with English Language and subject/mainstream teachers across Australia, and in International Schools in Southeast Asia involves ways that teachers can provide challenging curricula for their English learners, while also providing them with the language scaffolding essential to the development of academic language and literacy.

Lynn Goldstein is Professor and Program Chair of TESOL, TFL, and Applied Linguistics at The Middlebury Institute of International Studies in Monterey, California and serves on the editorial boards of *The Journal of Second Language Writing* and *The Journal of Response to Writing*. Her interests involve interactions between sociolinguistics and intercultural competence; intercultural communicative competence; mis/problem communication in intercultural interactions; and teacher written feedback and student revision in L2 writing classes.

William Grabe is Regents' Professor of Applied Linguistics and Vice President for Research at Northern Arizona University. He is interested in reading, writing, literacy, written discourse analysis, and CBI. He has lectured and given teacher training workshops in more than 30 countries around the world. He is a past President of the American Association for Applied Linguistics (AAAL) and received the 2005 AAAL Distinguished Scholarship and Service Award.

Brent A. Green is Associate Dean of ESL, College Academic Readiness, and Testing at Salt Lake Community College. He has served as a Lecturer and Assistant Professor at Brigham Young University–Hawaii and Associate Professor at Salt Lake Community College. His areas of expertise include language testing, pronunciation, TESOL methodology, discourse analysis, and corpus-based language learning. Brent also teaches TESOL endorsement courses for preservice and in-service K–12 teachers.

Michelle C. S. Greene is an educational consultant focusing on SLA, cultural and racial identity development, and effective strategies for instruction and assessment of English learners. Her interest in building intercultural understanding has taken her to several regions of China and Hong Kong, Western Europe, and Central America. Michelle was a Fulbright Scholar and currently serves as a Teacher Educator for Indiana University–Purdue University at Indianapolis.

Tetsuo Harada is Professor of Applied Linguistics in the Faculty of Education and Integrated Arts and Sciences at Waseda University, Japan. He also served as Assistant Professor of Japanese Linguistics and Japanese Applied Linguistics in the Department of East Asian Languages and Literatures at the University of Oregon. His research interests include second language learning in such classroom settings as immersion programs, CBI, and bilingual education.

Joyce Kling is a postdoctoral fellow at the Centre for Internationalisation and Parallel Language Use at the University of Copenhagen, Denmark. Her research interests include English-medium instruction, teacher cognition research, language assessment, ESP, and higher education language policy. She was the founding director of The Language Centre at Copenhagen Business School and has been an active member of the Board of Directors of TESOL.

Sherise Lee is the Associate Director of the English for Art Purposes Department at the Academy of Art University, San Francisco. She graduated from the University of California at Davis with degrees in Art History and Sociology and completed her M.A. TESOL at Biola University. Her interests include teacher education, CBI, curriculum development, program administration, and technology in education. Sherise has also taught English to elementary school students in China.

Roy Lyster is Professor of Second Language Education in the Department of Integrated Studies Education at McGill University in Montreal, Canada. Along with a focus on professional development and collaboration among teachers, his research examines content-based second language instruction and instructional interventions designed to counterbalance form-focused and content-based approaches. Roy was president of the Canadian Association of Applied Linguistics and is on the editorial boards of several professional journals.

Mary Lou McCloskey, former President of the TESOL International Association, is Director of Teacher Education and Curriculum Development for Educo in Atlanta and serves as English Language Specialist for the Global Village Project in Atlanta. As a consultant and author in the field of English language education, she has worked with teachers, teacher educators, and departments and ministries of education on five continents and in 35 of the 50 United States.

Jennifer McCormick is an Associate Professor in the Division of Curriculum and Instruction at California State University, Los Angeles. Her current research centers on *Mendez v. Westminster*, legislation that ended the legal segregation of Latinos in the schools of California and laid the groundwork for *Brown v. Board of Education of Topeka*. Jennifer has worked to develop school-university-community partnerships around parent advocacy and student research.

David Nunan is President Emeritus and Distinguished Professor, Anaheim University, California and Professor Emeritus of Applied Linguistics at the University of Hong Kong. His publications concern the ELT curriculum; teacher education and development; research methods in language learning; technology and language teaching; and teaching English to young learners. Current research projects include a comparative evaluation of blended learning in elementary classrooms. David is a former President of the TESOL International Association.

Susan Ollerhead is a lecturer in literacies and TESOL in the School of Education at the University of New South Wales, Australia. She has worked in ESL and literacy training in Africa, Europe, and Australia, focusing extensively on the development of English-language development materials for schools in Sub-Saharan Africa. Her main interests are learner and teacher identity in language education and critical ESL and literacy pedagogies.

Anna V. Osipova is Assistant Professor at California State University, Los Angeles, where she teaches courses in atypical language development, literacy support, curriculum design, and effective teaching practices. Her research focuses on academic language development, professional development for special education teachers, and the impact of teacher training on the quality of the oral and written language of early adolescent English learners at risk for academic failure.

Faridah Pawan is Professor of Education in the Department of Literacy, Culture and Language Education at Indiana University, Bloomington. Her areas of specialization are second/foreign language teacher preparation and professional development and hybrid and online ESL/EFL teacher education. Although she has led projects in Macedonia and Mongolia, Faridah's primary research and teacher training/evaluation projects are in Indiana, U.S.; Beijing, China; and Istanbul, Turkey.

Dudley Reynolds, the 2016–17 President of the TESOL International Association, is a Teaching Professor of English at Carnegie Mellon University in Qatar. Dudley's research focuses on the development, assessment, and teaching of L2 reading and writing. He was the lead principal investigator for a Qatar National Research Fund grant on "Improving Reading Skills in the Middle School Science Classroom" and is currently working on a second QNRF project.

Kate Mastruserio Reynolds has held TESOL teacher education and leadership positions at the University of Wisconsin–Eau Claire and Qatar University and has taught ESL/EFL courses from kindergarten to university levels as well as ESL teacher preparation courses. Kate also served as a Fulbright scholar in Ukraine and as the 2013 TESOL International Association Convention Planning Chair.

Marguerite Ann Snow is Professor of Education at California State University, Los Angeles, where she teaches in the TESOL M.A. program. She was a Fulbright scholar in Hong Kong (1985) and Cyprus (2009). Her interests include immersion education, CBI, pedagogical grammar, standards, and EAP. In addition to working with public school teachers in the U.S., she has trained EFL teachers in many countries in North Africa, the Middle East, Asia, and South America.

Christopher Stillwell has worked at universities in Japan as a lecturer, research coordinator, and assistant director, and as a teacher educator in Laos. He is currently pursuing his PhD at the University of California, Irvine. In addition to working as an ESL/EFL educator, his work at Teachers College, Columbia University, included: teaching the MA practicum in TESOL, mentoring Peace Corps Fellows in public schools, and supervising master teachers in the Community English Program.

Fredricka L. Stoller is Professor of English at Northern Arizona University, where she teaches in the MA-TESL and PhD in Applied Linguistics programs. Her professional areas of interest include L2 reading, CBI project-based learning, disciplinary writing, language teaching methodology, and curriculum design. She has trained EFL teachers, teacher trainers, and language program administrators in more than 30 countries around the world.

Arlys L. van Wyk is Adjunct Professor of Applied Linguistics at the University of the Free State, Bloemfontein, South Africa, and head of the Unit for Language Development in the Centre for Teaching and Learning. She serves on the Pan South African Language Board of the Free State region. Her areas of interest include second-language reading and writing development, CBI, TESOL methodology, and the pedagogy of multilingualism.

Sandra Zappa-Hollman is an Assistant Professor in the Department of Language and Literacy Education at the University of British Columbia. Her research interests include EAP, integrated language and content, collaborations between EAP and disciplinary instructors, academic discourse socialization of international students, intercultural competence development, EAP curriculum and materials development, program research and evaluation, text-based literacy pedagogy, Systemic Functional Linguistics, and genre-based pedagogies.

Index ||||||||||||||||||||||||||||||||||||||||||||||

NOTE: Pages in **bold** refer to figures/tables.